IN DEFENSE OF INTERNMENT

The Case for "Racial Profiling"
in World War II and the War on Terror

Michelle Malkin

Since 1947
REGNERY
PUBLISHING, INC.
An Eagle Publishing Company • Washington, DC

Malkin, Michelle.
 In defense of internment : the case for "racial profiling" in World
War II and the war on terror / Michelle Malkin.
      p. cm.
 Includes bibliographical references and index.
 ISBN 0-89526-051-4 (acid-free paper)
 1. Racial profiling in law enforcement—United States—Case studies.
 2. Law enforcement—United States—Case studies. 3. Japanese
Americans—Evacuation and relocation, 1942-1945 4. War on Terrorism,
2001- I. Title.
 HV8141.M245 2004
 940.53'1773--dc22
                                        2004013396

Published in the United States by
Regnery Publishing, Inc.
An Eagle Publishing Company
One Massachusetts Avenue, NW
Washington, DC 20001

Visit us at www.regnery.com

Distributed to the trade by
National Book Network
4720-A Boston Way
Lanham, MD 20706

Printed on acid-free paper

Manufactured in the United States of America

10 9 8 7 6 5 4 3 2 1
Books are available in quantity for promotional or premium use. Write to Director of Special Sales, Regnery Publishing, Inc., One Massachusetts Avenue, NW, Washington, DC 20001, for information on discounts and terms or call (202) 216-0600.

In memory of John McCloy and David Lowman
who defended America's honor to the end

Contents

A Note to the Reader   xi

Introduction
A Time to Discriminate   xiii

Chapter 1
The Turncoats on Niihau Island   1

Chapter 2
The Threat of the Rising Sun   7

Chapter 3
Sympathizers and Subversives   17

Chapter 4
Spies Like Us   27

Chapter 5
The MAGIC Revelations   37

Chapter 6
The Internment of Enemy Aliens   53

Chapter 7
The Rationale for Evacuation   65

Chapter 8
Executive Order 9066   81

Chapter 9
The Myth of the American "Concentration Camp"   95

Chapter 10
Reparations, Revisionism, and the Race Card   113

Chapter 11
The "Puffery" Defense   129

Chapter 12
Damning America   143

Conclusion
12/7, 9/11, and Beyond   149

Appendix A
Richard Kotoshirodo   167

Appendix B
MAGIC Cables   175

Appendix C
Intelligence Memos   209

Appendix D
The Kenji Ito Case   271

Appendix E
The *Coram Nobis* Cases   273

Appendix F
The Camps and Centers   281

Photos   287

Notes   313

Acknowledgments   357

Index   359

And if all others accepted the lie which the Party imposed—
if all records told the same tale—then the lie passed into history
and became truth. "Who controls the past" ran the Party slogan,
"controls the future: who controls the present controls the past."
—George Orwell, *1984*

A Note to the Reader

In defense of *internment*? The Japanese American internment? Is she really going to defend *that*?

Well, yes and no. Now that I've gotten your attention, let me address the first of many historical distortions surrounding the so-called "Japanese American internment." When modern critics attack the "internment" episode in American history, they are usually referring to a series of steps taken during World War II to move an estimated 112,000 ethnic Japanese from the West Coast of the United States to the interior of the country. These evacuation and relocation measures were made possible by Executive Order 9066, signed by President Franklin D. Roosevelt on February 19, 1942. The order affected both first-generation Japanese resident aliens (who will be referred to throughout the book as *Issei*) and second-generation Japanese Americans (who will be referred to throughout the book as *Nisei*), as well as a relatively small but significant number of non-Japanese residents (noncitizens and citizens alike) across the country.

"Internment" is actually a precise legal term for the centuries-old, worldwide practice of detaining nonnaturalized immigrants during wartime. Under the Alien Enemies Act of 1798 (which remains in place today), "whenever there shall be a declared war between the United States and any foreign nation or government, or any invasion or predatory incursion shall be perpetrated, attempted, or threatened against the territory of the United States, by any foreign nation or government," all males aged fourteen and older who are not naturalized are "liable to be apprehended, restrained, secured and removed, as alien enemies."[1] During World War I, some six thousand three hundred European enemy aliens in America were interned by the War Department in prison barracks at Fort Oglethorpe, Georgia, Fort McPherson, Georgia, and Fort Douglas, Utah.[2] During World War II, more than thirty-one thousand enemy aliens from Axis nations—nearly half of whom were of European ancestry—were interned at Department of Justice camps.[3]

This book defends both the evacuation and relocation of ethnic Japanese from the West Coast (the so-called "Japanese American internment"), as well as the internment of enemy aliens, Japanese and non-Japanese alike, during World War II. My work is by no means all-encompassing; my aim is to provoke a debate on a sacrosanct subject that has remained undebatable for far too long. Unlike most who have written standard critiques of these measures, I am neither a historian nor a lawyer nor an affected party. Unlike most others who have published on this subject, I have no vested interests: I am not an evacuee, internee, or family member thereof. I am not an attorney who has represented evacuees or internees demanding redress for their long-held grievances. I am not a professor whose tenure relies on regurgitating academic orthodoxy about this episode in American history. I have received no grant money from the government or ethnic groups looking to justify their existence.

So what are my credentials for writing a book debunking the great myth of the "Japanese American internment" as "racist" and "unjustified"? The same credentials that you have displayed in picking this book up: an open mind, a willingness to reject political correctness as a substitute for thought, and the ability to view the writing of history as something other than a therapeutic indulgence.

A Time to Discriminate

I f you want to read a book decrying the loss of personal freedom in wartime America, this is the wrong book. If you want to read a book about the history of institutional discrimination against minorities in America, you're out of luck again. Bookstores, library shelves, and classrooms are already filled with pedantic tomes, legal analyses, and educational propaganda along these conventional lines.[1]

When most scholars, legal analysts, and political commentators speak of the need to "balance civil liberties and national security," they don't mean that at all. What they really mean is: civil liberties always and at all times outweigh national security, and anybody who doesn't think so is a free speech–hating, Bill of Rights–trampling, immigrant–bashing tyrant.

In Defense of Internment provides a radical departure from the predominant literature of civil liberties absolutism. It offers a defense of the most reviled wartime policies in American history: the evacuation, relocation, and internment of people of Japanese descent during World War II (three separate actions which are commonly lumped under the umbrella term "internment"). My book is also a defense of racial, ethnic, religious, and nationality profiling policies (widely differing measures that are commonly lumped under the umbrella term "racial profiling"), which are now being taken or contemplated during today's War on Terror.

I start from a politically incorrect premise: In a time of war, the survival of the nation comes first. Civil liberties are *not* sacrosanct. The "unalienable rights" that our Founding Fathers articulated in the Declaration of Independence do not appear in random order: Liberty and the pursuit of happiness cannot be secured and protected without securing and protecting life first.

No one was exempt from the hardships of World War II, which demanded a wide range of civil liberties sacrifices on the part of citizen and noncitizen, majority and minority alike. Ethnic Japanese forced to leave the West Coast of the United States and relocate outside of prescribed military zones after the Pearl Harbor attack endured a heavy burden, but they were not the only ones who suffered and sacrificed. Enemy aliens from all Axis nations—not just Japan—were subjected to curfews, registration, censorship, and exclusion from sensitive areas.[2] Thousands of foreign nationals from Germany, Italy, Hungary, Romania, Bulgaria, and elsewhere were deemed dangerous, interned, and eventually deported.[3] Hundreds of Italian and German naturalized citizens received exclusion orders banning them from military zones on the West, East, and Southern coasts of the U.S.[4] Every resident of Hawaii—not just those of Japanese descent—was subject to martial law.[5] And beginning in September 1940, more than a year before Pearl Harbor, more than 10 million young American men of all backgrounds were conscripted into our nation's armed forces. Approximately two-thirds of the 292,000 Americans killed and 671,000 wounded in the war were forced to serve.[6]

Mike Masaoka, the national secretary of the Japanese American Citizens League (JACL), the preeminent Japanese American organization, at the time understood and embraced the wartime imperative to put national security first. Explaining why his organization supported the West Coast evacuation of people of Japanese descent and other related military regulations, Masaoka announced in an April 1942 JACL bulletin: "Our primary consideration as good Americans is the total war effort...We may be temporarily suspending or sacrificing some of our privileges and rights of citizenship in the greater aim of protecting them for all time to come and to defeat those powers which seek to destroy them."[7]

Such unequivocal patriotism has been rejected ever since by ethnic activists of all stripes in America (including Masaoka himself, who later in life reversed his position on the evacuation). They are far too busy these days crying racism, demanding apologies, pursuing reparations, suing the government, and obstructing the current war effort in the name of preventing another "Japanese American internment."

CORRECTING THE RECORD

The phrase "Japanese American internment" belongs in scare quotes because it is historically and legally inaccurate. Hours after the Pearl Harbor attack, potentially dangerous enemy aliens—not American citizens—from Japan, Germany, and Italy were apprehended, detained, individually screened by review boards composed of prominent citizens, and released, paroled, or sent to internment camps run by the Department of Justice under authority of the Alien Enemies Act of 1798 (which remains in place today). These immediate apprehensions may have played an instrumental role in preventing further havoc on American soil (just as the detention of Middle Eastern illegal aliens following the September 11 attacks may have done six decades later). Two months after Pearl Harbor, President Roosevelt signed Executive Order 9066, which led to the mass evacuation and relocation of ethnic Japanese (including both first-generation, permanent resident noncitizen immigrants known as *Issei* and their American-born children known as *Nisei*[8]) from the West Coast.

This latter decision is the one most commonly and erroneously referred to as "internment," "incarceration," or "imprisonment" in America's "concentration camps." In fact, ethnic Japanese living outside of prescribed military zones were not affected by the order. Those who could not or would not leave the West Coast in the spring of 1942 were sent to temporary assembly centers (some of which were later used to house American GIs) and then on to relocation centers run by the War Relocation Authority (WRA) and the Department of Interior. Tens of thousands of evacuees who met national security requirements left the relocation centers for school or work. More than 200 people actually volunteered to enter the camps. When the WRA announced the camps' impending closure in late 1944, many residents protested, demanding that the camps remain open until war's end—or longer.[9]

This book challenges the religiously held belief that internment of enemy aliens and the West Coast evacuation and relocation of ethnic Japanese were primarily the result of "wartime hysteria" and "race prejudice." That was the conclusion of a national panel, the Commission on Wartime Relocation and Internment of Civilians, in 1981, which stated, "We firmly believe that it should be common knowledge that the detention of Americans of Japanese ancestry during World War II was not an act of military necessity but an act of racial discrimination." [10] This finding was the basis for a federal reparations bill granting nearly $2 billion to ethnic Japanese evacuees and internees. And it is the premise of virtually every high school and college history lesson on national security measures taken during World War II.

Leading critics of the World War II evacuation and relocation don't just argue that the military rationale for Roosevelt's actions was insufficient. They make the extremely radical and historically dishonest argument that there was no military justification whatsoever for evacuation, relocation, or internment—and that America's top political and military leaders knew this at the time. Roosevelt's decisions, according to this conventional view, were adopted to mollify West Coast politicians who were pandering to racism, hysteria, and economic opportunism among their nativist constituents. According to the JACL curriculum guide used by public school teachers nationwide, the West Coast evacuation was the result not of a sincere desire to protect the West Coast but of "prejudice," "legal discrimination," and the "culmination of the movement to eliminate Asians. . . that began nearly 100 years earlier."[11] In arguing for a congressional resolution in March 2004 to establish a "National Day of Remembrance for the restriction, exclusion and internment of individuals and families during World War II," Representative Mike Honda (a Democrat from California), an evacuee who had resided in the Granada, Colorado, relocation center as a child, asserted that the West Coast evacuation "was based on neither reason nor evidence but on

fear and panic."[12] This version of history has been perpetuated by hundreds
of books, videos, plays, and websites, many of them subsidized with public
funds.

Why write this book now? Because the prevailing view of World War II
homeland defense measures has become the warped yardstick by which all
War on Terror measures today are judged. In truth, the U.S. government's
national security concerns during World War II, particularly the threat of
espionage in support of the Japanese emperor, were real and urgent.

When former Attorney General Janet Reno declared in 2003 that there
was absolutely "no record"[13] that any Japanese Americans posed a security
threat during World War II, she demonstrated a common, utter ignorance
of the matter. American intelligence teams had decoded top-secret Japanese
diplomatic cables, dubbed MAGIC, revealing an aggressive effort to recruit
West Coast spies, including both Japanese aliens (*Issei*) and U.S.-born citizens of Japanese descent (*Nisei*). Just as the VENONA decrypts of Soviet
diplomatic communications revealed the long-hidden truth about Russia's
extensive espionage attempts to infiltrate the United States during the Cold
War,[14] the MAGIC decrypts exposed in startling detail how Japan had succeeded in establishing a formidable West Coast espionage network by mid-
1941. After Pearl Harbor, U.S. intelligence agencies believed that this
network remained in place.[15] With Pearl Harbor in ruins and the Japanese
Navy in nearly complete control of the Pacific—its submarines looming off
our coastline[16]—it would have been irresponsible to dismiss the possibility
of attacks on the mainland assisted by West Coast fifth columnists of Japanese ancestry.

In the face of rabid ethnic activism, historical revisionism, and political
capitulation, few have defended the wartime measures undertaken to protect the West Coast—or even acknowledged that the decision to implement
them was a close call. The national security concerns so clearly delineated
in the intelligence memos of the time are ignored. The War Department officials who pored over MAGIC messages every night are said to have had only
crass political motives. Even the venerable U.S. Supreme Court Chief Justice William Rehnquist, who provides a partial defense of the West Coast

evacuation in *All the Laws But One*, gives only a superficial treatment of the role of intelligence in Roosevelt's decision-making.[17] As the late David Lowman, a former National Security Agency official who participated in the declassification of MAGIC and wrote a groundbreaking book on the subject, noted, "Seldom has any major event in U.S. history been as misrepresented as has U.S. intelligence related to the evacuation. It has been twisted, distorted, misquoted, misunderstood, ignored, and deliberately falsified by otherwise honorable people... The United States did not act shamefully, dishonorably, and without cause or reason as charged."[18]

Roosevelt's defenders have been (and will continue to be) vilified and viciously smeared as morally equivalent to Holocaust deniers. Consider the reaction to Representative Howard Coble (a Republican from North Carolina) in February 2003 after he asserted that the West Coast evacuation and relocation were justified. "For many of these Japanese Americans, it wasn't safe for them to be on the street," Coble said. "Some probably were intent on doing harm to us, just as some of these Arab-Americans are probably intent on doing harm to us."[19] Coble, who serves as chairman of the House Judiciary Subcommittee on Crime, Terrorism and Homeland Security, made clear that he did not support such drastic measures in the current War on Terror, but argued that Roosevelt's decision was justified in its time. His remarks prompted protests by the AFL-CIO, the NAACP, and the Democratic National Committee chairman, who said Coble was "not fit to lead our country on security and constitutional matters and must resign from the chairmanship."[20] JACL also called for Coble's head, ignoring the fact that its own leaders[21] made some of the same arguments in support of evacuation and relocation during the war. It is "a sad day in our country's tradition when an elected official... openly agrees with an unconstitutional [sic] and racist policy," the American-Arab Anti-Discrimination Committee huffed.[22] The California State Assembly condemned Coble; Hawaii legislators called on the House Judiciary Committee to "educate and sensitize"[23] members about Japanese Americans during World War II. Coble kept his job, but was forced to apologize, "We all know now that this was in fact the wrong decision and an action that should never be repeated."[24]

U.S. Civil Rights Commissioner Peter Kirsanow received similar treatment from Japanese American and Arab American activists in the summer of 2002. During a panel hearing on racial profiling in Detroit, Noel John Saleh, an attorney and a member of the Detroit chapter of the American-Arab Anti-Discrimination Committee, stated, "[The current situation] does lead and could well lead to situations as embarrassing as the Japanese internment camps in the Second World War. . . if there is in fact another terrorist attack on the United States, then such things can be revisited."[25] Commissioner Kirsanow, a conservative Bush appointee, responded "that homeland security may be one of the best ways of protecting civil rights because as you alluded to, I believe no matter how many laws we have, how many agencies we have, how many police officers we have monitoring civil rights, that if there's another terrorist attack and if it's from a certain ethnic community or certain ethnicities that the terrorists are from, you can forget civil rights in this country. I think we will have a return to *Korematsu* [the 1944 Supreme Court decision that affirmed the constitutionality of the West Coast exclusion orders during World War II] and I think the best way we can thwart that is to make sure that there is a balance between protecting civil rights, but also protecting safety at the same time."[26]

Kirsanow wasn't endorsing a roundup of Arab Muslims. He was merely observing that adopting lesser measures that the ethnic grievance industry vehemently protests as civil rights atrocities—such things as airport profiling, targeted illegal alien sweeps, monitoring of mosques, and tighter visa screening procedures—can prevent acts of terrorism, which in turn can prevent larger infringements on civil liberties down the road. Some may disagree with Kirsanow's assertion,[27] but it is hardly a radical view. Nevertheless, the "Japanese American internment" has become such a sacred cow that even the mildest of considered comments related to it invites blind and vicious retribution. An apoplectic team of Japanese American lawyers who had worked unsuccessfully to get the Supreme Court to overturn *Korematsu* demanded that the Bush administration fire him. They railed that Kirsanow's "inflammatory rhetoric. . . now threatens to victimize innocent Arab Americans." Lawyer Dale Minami added, "What he has done

is raise the level of hysteria in this country."[28] Devon Alisa Abdallah penned
an opinion piece headlined, "Arab Community Pack Your Bags: Civil Rights
Commissioner doesn't believe in civil rights."[29] The Leadership Conference
on Civil Rights wrote that Kirsanow's remarks were "shocking, irresponsible, outrageous, and should be unacceptable."[30] Imad Hamad of the American-Arab Anti-Discrimination Committee fumed, "For someone in
[Kirsanow's] position to even entertain the idea of detention camps, it is like
he is making it an acceptable debate."[31]

Even those who simply profess lack of knowledge about the topic are
subjected to scathing criticism. When Middle East scholar Daniel Pipes,
whom the Bush administration nominated to serve on the U.S. Institute of
Peace, stated in an interview that he didn't know enough about the World
War II evacuation and relocation of ethnic Japanese to comment on whether
he supported it, ethnic activists launched an immediate attack. "Bush nominee refuses to condemn Japanese internment," the Council on American-
Islamic Relations (CAIR) proclaimed. "It is outrageous that someone with
undergraduate and doctoral degrees from Harvard University, both in history, would fail to condemn the unjust internment of Japanese Americans
by disingenuously claiming he is ill-informed," CAIR executive director
Nihad Awad bellowed.[32]

The real outrage lies in the smug orthodoxy of the civil liberties absolutists, to whom intellectual honesty poses a dire threat. The politically correct myth of American "concentration camps" has become enshrined as
incontrovertible wisdom in the gullible press, postmodern academia, the
cash-hungry grievance industry, and liberal Hollywood. This hijacking of
history is endangering us today.

CONNECTING THE DOTS

Civil liberties absolutists have invoked the World War II evacuation and
relocation of ethnic Japanese to attack virtually every homeland security initiative aimed at protecting America from murderous Islamic extremists.
Within weeks of the September 11 attacks, Japanese American activists

rushed to comfort Arab and Muslim Americans who felt unfairly targeted. "War on Terrorism Stirs Memory of Internment," the *New York Times* decried.[33] "Japanese Americans Recall 40s Bias, Understand Arab Counterparts' Fear," read a *Washington Post* headline.[34] "Japanese Americans Know How It Feels to Be 'The Enemy,'" the *Seattle Times* reported.[35] "Reaction Reopens Wound of WWII for Japanese Americans," the *Los Angeles Times* noted.[36]

Irene Hirano, executive director and president of the Japanese American National Museum, lamented, "Now, as in 1942 when America came under attack, the resulting emotions are: anger, hate, vengeance, and patriotism."[37] The National Asian Pacific American Legal Consortium (NAPALC) said that "solidarity between communities identified as 'the enemy' has in some cases forged a new alliance between Japanese Americans and Arab Americans and Muslims." NAPALC President Karen Narasaki proclaimed: "No one should be presumed to be any less loyal to our country just because of the color of their skin, their national origin, their immigration status or the religion that they follow."[38]

Soon after September 11, the Justice Department began interviewing Arab and Muslim foreigners for investigative leads. Although participation was strictly voluntary, commentator Julianne Malveaux complained, "It's beginning to look like the Japanese internment."[39] When two men were removed from a Continental Airlines flight in December 2001 based on the plane crew's security concerns, the ejected passengers (a Guyanese American and a Filipino immigrant) promptly filed racial discrimination lawsuits. Their American Civil Liberties Union lawyer, Reginald Shuford, didn't miss a beat: "The Japanese internment issue is the model for this type of thing. We look back in embarrassment upon that period in our history, as we will upon this."[40] When Attorney General John Ashcroft so much as sneezed, he triggered flashbacks of "internment" and howls of protest about "racial profiling"—including from a fellow cabinet member of the Bush administration.

Department of Transportation Secretary Norm Mineta, who was evacuated as a young boy from San Jose, California, to a relocation center in Heart Mountain, Wyoming, declared that any profiling taking into account race, ethnicity, religion, or nationality would be forbidden in airport security. He complained, "I think we are seeing shades of what we experienced in 1942."[41] When asked by CBS's *60 Minutes* correspondent Steve Croft whether he could envision any circumstance where it would make sense to use racial and ethnic profiling, Mineta responded, "Absolutely not." Croft persisted, "Are you saying at the security screening desks, that a 70-year-old white woman from Vero Beach, Florida, would receive the same level of scrutiny as a Muslim young man from Jersey City?" Mineta replied, "Basically, I would hope so." Croft followed up, "If you saw three young Arab men sitting, kneeling, praying, before they boarded a flight, getting on, talking to each other in Arabic, getting on the plane, no reason to stop and ask them any questions? "No reason," Mineta stubbornly declared.[42]

And what if he had seen the names Khalid Al-Midhar, Majed Moqed, Nawaf Alhamzi, Salem Alhamzi, and Hani Hanjour on a passenger manifest? Or Satam Al Suqami, Waleed M. Alshehri, Mohammed Atta, Wail Alsheri, and Abdulaziz Alomari? Or Marwan Al-Shehhi, Fayez Ahmed, Ahmed Alghamdi, Hamza Alghamdi, and Mohald Alshehri? Or Saeed Alghamdi, Ahmed Alhaznawi, Ahmed Alnami, and Ziad Jarrah? What if those four groups of September 11 hijackers were resurrected from hell and attempted to board airplanes today? Would their observable characteristics—young men of Arab appearance with Arab-sounding names and Arabic accents[43]— be reason enough to search them and their luggage, perhaps revealing clues, such as box cutters or Mohammed Atta's suicide note, that would have set off alarm bells? In Mineta's mind, so fixed on his childhood past as to blind him to the present threats to our nation, absolutely not.

Fellow evacuee Robert Matsui, a Democratic congressman from California who moved with his family from Sacramento to the Tule Lake, California, relocation center, also spoke out immediately after the September 11 attacks in opposition to profiling. Asked whether tracking Arab students with temporary visas studying physics would be an acceptable homeland security measure, Matsui attempted to connect the dots between World War II and the War on Terror in an emotion-choked (and barely comprehensible) monologue:

I think that [foreign student tracking] would be something that I would find to be somewhat intolerable. That's somewhat what happened to Japanese Americans. So there was a belief—you know, there was no espionage, there was no case of disloyalty among Japanese Americans, but there was a belief that Japanese Americans would be loyal to Japan, and so basically they profile all 120,000 Japanese Americans that happened to live in the United States. My mother and father, they were in their early 20s, and I was six months old, and there is no way that I was a security risk, nor were my parents. I mean, they were both born in Sacramento, California, actually. And there is—they lost everything. And the real fear I have is that when you are attacked like this in a time of international crisis, when your country is being threatened, there is an issue of questioning one's loyalty. And when one is branded a potential enemy to one's country, I think that has some deep implications. It's a scar that really never heals. When I hear Pearl Harbor, as some were relating the last few days to Pearl Harbor, it made me shudder somewhat, even though I had nothing to do with Pearl Harbor, I was six months old—three months old—when Pearl Harbor happened.[44]

Note that Matsui incorrectly refers to the profiling of "120,000 Japanese Americans." In fact, of the approximately 112,000 West Coast residents who were evacuated along with Matsui, more than one-third were *Issei* (Japanese permanent resident aliens) and less than two-thirds were *Nisei* (American-born children of Japanese immigrants).[45] Matsui also falsely asserts that "there was no espionage, there was no case of disloyalty among Japanese Americans," but much more on that later.

Matsui draws a patently absurd and offensive parallel between the post–Pearl Harbor evacuation of the West Coast ethnic Japanese and the post–September 11 monitoring of Arab and Muslim foreign students on temporary visas. In the former case, the government cast a wide emergency net that encompassed immigrants and citizens alike. In the latter case, the government trained a focused eye on a narrow subgroup of short-term foreign visitors with absolutely no right to be here and whose academic studies posed a clear and obvious danger to national security. Matsui would have the government turn a blind eye to Saudi Arabian students studying aviation and North Korean students studying nuclear science and Palestinian students studying explosives technology because doing so would cause intangible "scars that really never heal"—never mind the physical and economic destruction that might ensue.

HURT FEELINGS AND HOMELAND SECURITY

Americans today might be forgiven for not fully appreciating the wartime exigencies of early 1942. The bloodied waters off Oahu, the violent romp of Imperial forces across Southeast Asia and the South Pacific, the alarming submarine shellings along the California coastline, the shrieking air raid sirens and constant blackouts are historical abstractions to most citizens today. But how shockingly soon we seem to have forgotten the horror that prevailed in the immediate hours, days, weeks, and months after September 11, 2001: the ghastly sight of human beings falling en masse from the sky; the chilling sound of their bodies, one after another after another, crashing through glass; the deafening collapse of two of the mightiest symbols of American industry and innovation; the pungent smell of burnt flesh at the Pentagon; and the scarred earth on the outskirts of Shanksville, Pennsylvania.

If ever there were a time for our government to set aside cultural sensitivities and provide for the common defense, including through "racial profiling" (by which its opponents usually mean any and all attempts by law enforcement, immigration, or military authorities to take into account race, ethnicity, religion, nationality, or national origin[46]), this was it.

The embers of Ground Zero were still aglow, however, when the caviling about wartime threat profiling commenced. Barely three weeks after the attacks, *Oregonian* columnist David Reinhard marveled at the antiprofilers' refusal to deal with the clear and present danger to the nation, "Some of us still seem more interested in holding onto old abstractions than facing hard—and deadly—realities. Some of us are still more worried about hurt feelings than clear thinking designed to protect the larger public."[47]

Internment alarmists make no distinction between restrictions affecting foreign visitors, screening measures that subject individuals of certain nationalities to heightened scrutiny, and preventive detention of known illegal aliens, suspected terrorists, or enemy combatants. Many critics of both the World War II evacuation and the War on Terror blur the fundamental distinction between foreigners and U.S. citizens. And some argue that the full panoply of constitutional rights should be extended to noncitizens suspected of belonging to terrorist groups, including those captured on battlefields abroad.

Both Japanese American and Arab American leaders objected to the Justice Department's special registration program requiring young men from twenty-five high-risk countries (mostly in the Middle East) to check in with immigration authorities during their temporary stays on tourist, business, and student visas. Some eighty-three thousand individuals registered; at least thirteen thousand were referred for deportation proceedings.[48] Decrying "Ashcroft's roundup," antidetention protesters in Los Angeles chanted, "What's Next? Concentration Camps?"[49] *San Francisco Chronicle* writer Annie Nakao lamented the registration program's "haunting echoes of Japanese internment.[50] John Tateishi of JACL told Nakao, "It echoes something from our own experience in 1942. It is really about racial identity, racial profiling."[51]

Actually, no, it wasn't really about "racial profiling." The registration program was a narrowly-tailored exercise in age, gender, and *nationality* profiling, which simply means increased, commonsense scrutiny of young, male, temporary visitors from the kinds of countries that produced the September 11 hijackers. Those who followed the rules and were abiding by their visa restrictions had nothing to worry about. If anything, the special registration program did not go far enough. It would have been perfectly reasonable, given the circumstances, to place a moratorium on temporary visas to countries with large al Qaeda presences—and to ask temporary visitors from those countries who were already here to return home. Temporary visa-holding aliens are here by privilege. Their visas can and should be revoked whenever necessary to protect our national security.

The post–September 11 arrest and detention of 762 individuals being investigated by the FBI for ties to terrorism—nearly all of them Middle Easterners in the United States illegally[52]—came under fire. So did an initiative targeting six thousand Middle Eastern illegal aliens who were fugitives from deportation orders and the passage of provisions under the USA Patriot Act that gave the attorney general broad authority to detain until deportation any foreign national he certifies to be a terrorist or "engaged in any other activity that endangers the national security of the United States."[53] "While we do not support anyone breaking the laws of our country, the authorities should not target individuals based on their race, religion or ethnicity," said Ra'id Faraj, CAIR spokesman. "To do so," Faraj declared, would be "un-American."[54] In other words, if a Mexican illegal alien and an Arab Muslim illegal alien both carrying box cutters and flight manuals were stopped at the southern border on September 12, 2001, the "American" thing to do would be to treat them equally and release them both. Antiprofilers even objected to the questioning and arrest of Iraqi illegal aliens after Operation Iraqi Freedom began. "We think it is racial profiling because it targets people based on their ethnicity and not because they have done anything wrong," said Jayashri Srikantiah of the Northern California ACLU.[55]

Predictably, the selective enforcement of immigration laws against illegal aliens from high-risk countries prompted the usual hysterical comparisons to the World War II experience of ethnic Japanese. Legal scholars Susan M. Akram and Kevin R. Johnson wrote that "the September 11 dragnet carried out by the federal government resembles the Japanese internment during World War II."[56] Georgetown University Law School professor David Cole lamented that the post–September 11 response involved "the same kind of ethnic stereotyping that characterized the fundamental error of the Japanese internment."[57] The *Palm Beach Post* editorialized that the illegal alien roundup was "the worst example of indiscriminate abuse since the Japanese internment during World War II."[58]

Ideally, as I argued extensively in my first book, *Invasion*,[59] full, consistent, and vigorous immigration enforcement would be part of any meaningful homeland security plan. Political and economic forces have conspired against this vision. In the meantime, targeting the most obvious and most likely security risks through our immigration laws is a reasonable stopgap measure. Just because the nation lacks the will to remove *all* eight to thirteen million illegal aliens currently in the United States, it does not follow that the homeland security officials should be precluded from removing *some* of them. It is entirely appropriate[60] to take into account nationality when deciding which foreigners present the highest risks. And there is nothing wrong with using immigration laws to detain and deport foreigners considered potential terrorists. The government, after all, often brings lesser charges against individuals suspected of greater crimes that it has insufficient evidence to prove in court. Robert F. Kennedy's Justice Department vowed to arrest suspected mobsters for so much as spitting on the sidewalk. Prosecutors nabbed gangland boss Al Capone, suspected of dozens of murders, on tax evasion charges. Why shouldn't the same approach be applied to suspected fanatical terrorists?

HYPOCRISY OF THE ANTIPROFILERS

Fear of a political backlash has caused President Bush, Attorney General John Ashcroft, Homeland Security chief Tom Ridge, and the Pentagon to publicly disavow threat profiling. Consider the reaction of Sarah Eltantawi, communications director of the Muslim Public Affairs Council, to the idea that the twelve Muslim chaplains currently serving in the armed forces should be vetted more carefully than military rabbis or priests. When asked about this in a Fox News interview, Eltantawi brought up—you guessed it—Japanese internment.[61] Never mind that the Muslim chaplains were trained by a radical Wahhabi school and certified by a Muslim group founded by Abdurahman Alamoudi, charged in September 2003 with accepting hundreds of thousands of dollars from Libya, a U.S.-designated sponsor of terrorism.[62] Bowing to Eltantawi and her allies, the Pentagon pressed forward with a review of all two thousand eight hundred military chaplains, rather than focusing exclusively on the twelve Muslim chaplains. The refusal to be discriminating was, as Senator Jon Kyl (a Republican from Arizona) acknowledged, the "height of politically correct stupidity."[63]

The same fear of a PC backlash has hampered effective Federal Bureau of Investigation (FBI) counterterrorism efforts. When the FBI announced plans to tally the number of mosques in the country—a basic intelligence-gathering building block—Muslim civil rights groups and their supporters balked. It is an act of "political repression" by the U.S. government, said the American Muslim Council.[64] "It is religious profiling of the worst kind and must be rescinded if America is to maintain respect for religious freedom and for equal justice under the law," complained CAIR Executive Director Nihad Awad.[65]

It is indeed religious profiling, and it is an essential tool in a war where the enemies are religious extremists carrying out a religious crusade to kill Americans. If a Catholic, Protestant, Jewish, or Hindu sect declared the equivalent of jihad on America and killed thousands of Americans, the FBI would be thoroughly justified—indeed, obligated—to gather basic intelligence data on churches, congregations, or temples. Manhattan Institute scholar Heather Mac Donald, who has written cogently on racial profiling and national security before and after the September 11 attacks, observed, "Looking for Muslims for participation in Muslim jihad is not playing the odds, it is following an ironclad tautology. Nevertheless, anti-police and Arab advocates have co-opted the discourse about racial profiling to tar all rational law-enforcement efforts against Islamic terrorism as an outgrowth of blind prejudice."[66]

The hypocritical opponents of FBI profiling damn agents as bigots when they attempt the most modest of surveillance measures based on race, religion, or other politically incorrect criteria—then damn them as bumblers when they fail to act on information gathered through those means. In the summer of 2001, Phoenix FBI agent Kenneth Williams urged his superiors to investigate militant Muslim men whom he suspected of training in U.S. flight schools as part of al Qaeda missions. He had become suspicious of Arab students enrolled at an Arizona aviation academy. Williams's recommendation to canvass flight schools was rejected, FBI director Robert

Mueller later admitted, partly because at least one agency official raised concerns that the plan could be viewed as discriminatory racial profiling.[67] "If
we went out and started canvassing, we'd get in trouble for targeting Arab
Americans," one FBI official told the *Los Angeles Times*. Several law enforcement officials told the paper that "a culture of fear" had pervaded FBI
counter-terrorism agents."[68] Mueller acknowledged that if Williams's
Phoenix profiling memo had been shared with the agency's Minneapolis
office, which had unsuccessfully sought a special intelligence warrant to
search suspected twentieth hijacker Zacarias Moussaoui's laptop computer,
the warrant might have been granted.[69] And 9/11 might still be nothing
more than a phone number.

The *New York Times* characterized the FBI's failure to take Williams's
advice as "one indicator of the paralytic fear of risk-taking" at the bureau.[70]
But is there any doubt that the *Times* would have been the first to whip out
its broad brush and pot of racist-smearing tar if it had caught wind of
Williams's memo *before* September 11? Maureen Dowd, the *Times's* resident
chaise lounge general, jumped all over Mueller's admission, "Now we know
the truth: The 9/11 terrorists could have been stopped if . . . the law enforcement agencies had not been so inept, obstructionist, arrogant, antiquated,
bloated and turf-conscious—and timid about racial profiling."[71]

Where exactly does Dowd think such timidity stems from? Her colleague
Nicholas Kristof was honest enough to acknowledge the mau-mauing
media's role in a piece titled "Liberal Reality Check":

> As we gather around FBI headquarters sharpening our machetes and
> watching the buzzards circle overhead, let's be frank: There's a whiff of
> hypocrisy in the air. One reason aggressive agents were restrained as they
> tried to go after Zacarias Moussaoui is that liberals like myself—and the
> news media caldron in which I toil and trouble—have regularly excori-
> ated law enforcement authorities for taking shortcuts and engaging in
> racial profiling. As long as we're pointing fingers, we should peer into the
> mirror. The timidity of bureau headquarters is indefensible. But it
> reflected not just myopic careerism but also an environment (that we who

care about civil liberties helped create) in which officials were afraid of being assailed as insensitive storm troopers.[72]

In war, desperate times sometimes call for disparate measures. Make no mistake: I am not advocating rounding up all Arabs or Muslims and tossing them into camps, but when we are under attack, "racial profiling"—or more precisely, threat profiling—is justified. It is unfortunate that well-intentioned Arabs and Muslims might be burdened because of terrorists who share their race, nationality, or religion. But any inconvenience, no matter how bothersome or offensive, is preferable to being incinerated at your office desk by a flaming hijacked plane.

Some might argue that profiling is so offensive to fundamental American values that it ought not be done even if it jeopardizes the nation's security. Yet many of the ethnic activists and civil liberties groups who object most strenuously to the use of racial, ethnic, religious, and nationality classifications during war strongly support the use of similar classifications in peacetime—to ensure "diversity" on college campuses, to guarantee business contracts for minorities, and to achieve socially engineered "parity" in police departments and public works projects. Federal appeals court judge and legal scholar Richard Posner made the point nicely in observing that modern liberals consider the decision to uphold the constitutionality of the West Coast evacuation an outrage, "yet they believe that the prohibition against racial discrimination can be bent, without violation of the Constitution, if the race discriminated against, under the rubric of affirmative action, is white rather than yellow."[73] Encouraging public universities to assign "plus" factors to individuals according to their skin color is praiseworthy, in their view.[74] But allowing an airport screener or consular official or deportation officer or FBI agent to assign "negative" factors on the same basis is a human rights abuse.

The civil rights hypocrites have never met a "compelling government interest" for using racial, ethnicity, or nationality classifications they didn't like—except when that compelling interest happens to be the nation's very survival.

Korematsu and Combatants

When they haven't been attacking profiling, the civil liberties absolutists have been lobbying for the rights of detainees designated "enemy combatants" or "unlawful combatants" by the Bush administration. The imprisonment of American citizens Jose Padilla (aka Abdullah al-Muhajir) and Yaser Esam Hamdi, and the confinement of hundreds of Muslim foreigners at Guantanamo Bay, have evoked the usual contemptuous comparisons to the World War II evacuation and relocation. "The similarities are painfully obvious," a *Boston Globe* reporter noted.[75] "One of the darkest and most painful chapters of American history is repeating itself," proclaimed law professor Jonathan Turley.[76] A group called the Nikkei for Civil Rights and Redress warned, "We must not allow what happened to us to happen again."[77]

One of those who filed petitions on behalf of Hamdi and the Guantanamo Bay prisoners was Fred Korematsu, who was the subject of the 1944 Supreme Court case that upheld the exclusion of ethnic Japanese from the West Coast. "History teaches that we tend too quickly to sacrifice these liberties in the face of overbroad claims of military necessity," Korematsu's brief in support of Hamdi and the Guantanamo Bay enemy combatants says. "To avoid repeating the mistakes of the past, this court should make clear that the United States respects fundamental constitutional and human rights— even in time of war."[78]

Korematsu's comparison of ethnic Japanese evacuees during World War II with the Guantanamo Bay detainees is the most embarrassing use of the internment card yet. After arguing for nearly a quarter-century that the government committed a grave "personal injustice" because it took innocent American citizens' rights for granted, Korematsu and his fellow travelers now turn around and advocate that the fundamental distinction between citizens and noncitizens be completely obliterated. Even more flabbergasting, they argue that al Qaeda and Taliban fighters captured on foreign soil while in combat against American soldiers are on the same moral and legal plane as loyal Japanese Americans during World War II. The AK-47-toting jihadists of 2002 and the American flag–waving *Nisei* children of 1942, are deserving of the same "fundamental constitutional and human rights" in the clouded eyes of Korematsu and company.

In any case, the approach now being pursued by the Bush administration is fundamentally different from that pursued by Roosevelt. The Bush administration has not detained all individuals of a particular race or ethnicity—only suspected al Qaeda agents, regardless of their race or nationality. Rather than bypass criminal prosecutions, as the Roosevelt administration did for the most part, the Bush administration has pursued numerous criminal prosecutions of individuals suspected of aiding terrorists,[79] limiting "enemy combatant" status to just three[80] people. Nor has the Bush administration imposed martial law, as was done in Hawaii during World War II.

Contrary to popular impression, the Bush administration's approach actually echoes that advocated by *opponents*—not supporters—of the World War II evacuation and relocation. Two of the most oft–cited opponents of evacuation—FBI Director J. Edgar Hoover and Office of Naval Intelligence (ONI) analyst Kenneth Ringle—both supported the detention of U.S. citizens who, like Padilla, were suspected of working for our enemies but for various reasons could not be convicted of a crime in a civilian court. Hoover supported suspension of the writ of habeas corpus, as occurred during the Civil War, so that the government could lock up suspected subversives without trial. Ringle supported the establishment of a military tribunal to distinguish loyal citizens from disloyal citizens. He proposed that those deemed disloyal be confined without access to civilian courts. Ringle also supported racial profiling of Japanese Americans who worked in the defense industry, discouraged the use of Japanese Americans as teachers for any Japanese descended detainees, and recommended that the Shinto religion be banned because it was "not a true religion but a form of patriotism toward Japan"[81]—positions that today would put him to the right of every official in the current administration, including U.S. Attorney General John Ashcroft.

Some of the Bush administration's actions in this arena raise difficult constitutional questions. In particular, the president's decision to designate certain Americans "enemy combatants"—and to detain them indefinitely without access to legal counsel—can and should be debated. But drawing overwrought analogies to World War II confuses rather than clarifies the issues at hand.

POLICYMAKING WITH A REARVIEW MIRROR

The central thesis of this book is that the national security measures taken during World War II were justifiable, *given what was known and not known at the time.* It is unfair to judge the decision-makers of the time as though they had all the knowledge that we do today. To truly appreciate the decisions made by military and political leaders in early 1942, we must, in the wise words of historian Lord Macaulay, "place ourselves in their situation . . . put out of our minds, for a time, all that knowledge which they could not have and we could not help having."[82]

We know now that Japan would not invade or launch a major attack on the West Coast. We know now that the Battle of Midway of June 1942 would be a decisive victory for the United States, and a turning point in the war. We know now that "voluntary evacuation" (under which ethnic Japanese would move out of excluded zones on their own, rather than be sent to relocation centers) would be unworkable. We know now that thousands of *Nisei* would serve in the armed forces with honor and dedication. We know now that Allied forces would defeat Hitler's forces in Europe. We know now that we would develop the atomic bomb before our enemies. None of this was known at the time.

Middle school and high school teachers often teach their students about the World War II evacuation and relocation by asking them to imagine the experiences that evacuees and internees underwent.[83] Students are directed to make lists of the items they will carry with them to camp and to fold paper "peace cranes" to increase their multicultural sensitivity.[84] They are instructed "to empathize with what some Japanese Americans went through" [85] and to digest reading material "highlight[ing] the difficulties of having to relocate."[86] But never do these lesson plans assign students to walk in the shoes of the leaders who made these difficult wartime decisions. Most American schoolchildren are not even asked to consider the possibility that Roosevelt and his top advisers relied on the best available intelligence, military, and legal assessments of the time.

Among those whom Roosevelt trusted and sided with on the West Coast evacuation were two key Republican officials in his administration, Secretary of War Henry Stimson and his assistant John McCloy, as well as the provost marshal general's office, West Coast naval commanders, and the Western Defense Command. On the opposite side of the ideological spectrum, a trio of liberal New Deal lawyers affirmed the constitutionality of the decision in a letter to Roosevelt, "In time of national peril any reasonable doubt must be resolved in favor of action to preserve the national safety, not for the purpose of punishing those whose liberty may be temporarily affected by such action, but for the purpose of protecting the freedom of the nation which may be long impaired, if not permanently lost, by non-action . . ."[87]

These were all serious men, aware of the gravity of both their actions and inaction. They were men who did not have the luxury of a rearview mirror. Yet forty years later, with an intellectual arrogance that only 20/20 hindsight can instill, civil rights absolutists and ethnic lobbyists waged an intimidating campaign for reparations and redress on behalf of ethnic Japanese evacuees. In 1988, relying on the biased conclusion of a stacked federal panel that the World War II evacuation and relocation were based on "race prejudice, war hysteria, and a failure of political leadership," President Reagan issued a formal apology from the government and approved a law granting $1.65 billion in restitution to 82,219 individuals of Japanese ancestry—including not only those who had been subjected to the evacuation, relocation, and internment process but also those who had been arrested as suspect enemy aliens in the immediate post–Pearl Harbor aftermath.

The most damaging legacy of this apologia and compensation package has been its impact on national security efforts. The ethnic grievance industry and civil liberties Chicken Littles wield the reparations law like a bludgeon over the War on Terror debate. No defensive wartime measure that takes into account race, ethnicity, or nationality can be contemplated, let alone implemented, without government officials being likened to the "racist" overseers of America's World War II "concentration camps." This book seeks to rectify the grossly distorted history of the past before it further undermines the nation's ability to protect its borders and its people from harm.

What was true sixty years ago is now truer than ever: A nation paralyzed in wartime by political correctness is a nation in peril.

Chapter One

The Turncoats on Niihau Island

"Are you a Japanese?"

Those were the first English words spoken by downed Japanese fighter pilot Shigenori Nishikaichi on tiny Niihau Island, located about one hundred miles northwest of Honolulu.[1] It was December 7, 1941. Nishikaichi had had a busy, bloody morning at Pearl Harbor. Now, with the aid and comfort of a Japanese American couple, Nishikaichi was about to make the lives of the Niihau residents a living hell.

Around 7:00 a.m., Nishikaichi boarded his Zero single-seat fighter plane and took off from the carrier *Hiryu* in the Pacific. The plane bore the rising sun insignia on each wingtip, top and bottom. Nishikaichi's squadron, escorting nine level bombers, was part of the second wave of Japanese planes headed for the surprise attack on Oahu. An hour and a half later, the twenty-two-year-old Japanese pilot strafed planes, trucks, and personnel at Kanehoe Bay and Bellows Field. Headed for a rendezvous with his group, Nishikaichi and some fellow pilots encountered a group of American P36 fighter planes.

The Japanese quickly staved off the formation. During the air battle, Nishikaichi shot down one enemy plane, but his aircraft took several hits. One punctured the Zero's gas tank. Nishikaichi steered the crippled plane toward the westernmost Hawaiian island: Niihau. The 19-mile-long tract was privately owned by the Robinsons, a Scottish ranching family. Fewer

1

than two hundred residents, mostly native Hawaiians plus three laborers of
Japanese descent and their families, called Niihau home. Nishikaichi's superiors had mistakenly informed him that the land was uninhabited. In case
of emergency, the Japanese planned to use the island as a submarine pickup
point for stranded pilots.

Nishikaichi crash-landed the plane in a field near one of the ranch
homes. The first to reach him was Hawila "Howard" Kaleohano, a burly
native Hawaiian employed by the Robinson family. The island had no telephones. On that tranquil, late Sunday morning, with church services just
letting out, none of the inhabitants was yet aware of the death and destruction that had just rained down on Pearl Harbor.

Nonetheless, Kaleohano wisely confiscated the dazed Nishikaichi's gun
and papers. Kaleohano, perhaps the most educated native Hawaiian on
Niihau, had been keeping tabs on world affairs through newspapers supplied by ranch owner Aylmer Robinson (who paid weekly visits to the island
and lived twenty miles away on Kauai). Wary but warm, Kaleohano brought
the enemy pilot to his home. Along the way, Nishikaichi asked Kaleohano
if he was "a Japanese." The answer was an emphatic, "No."

"The question was a gambit in what was to become a search for a con-
federate," wrote Allan Beekman, a Hawaii-based historian who published
the definitive account of the Niihau incident. Nishikaichi would find a yes-
man soon enough.

After sharing a meal and cigarettes, Nishikaichi demanded that Kaleohano return his papers, which included maps, radio codes, and Pearl Harbor attack plans. Kaleohano refused. To make their communication easier,
Kaleohano asked his neighbors to summon one of the island's three residents of Japanese descent to translate for Nishikaichi. They first brought a
Japanese-born resident and laborer, Ishimatsu Shintani, to the house. He
reluctantly exchanged a few words with the pilot in Japanese, but the
spooked Shintani left in a hurry—apparently sensing trouble and wanting
nothing to do with his compatriot in name only.

The islanders then turned to Yoshio Harada and his wife Irene, both U.S.
citizens, born in Hawaii to Japanese immigrants. Harada had moved from

Kauai to California as a young man and lived there for seven years before relocating to Niihau with his wife in 1939. The hardworking and unassuming parents of three ran the Robinson ranch's company store. Nishikaichi was cheered by the Haradas' presence. "Oh, you're a Japanese!" the enemy fighter pilot exclaimed when Yoshio Harada addressed him in their native tongue. Instantly at ease with the *Nisei* couple, Nishikaichi dropped the bombshell news about the attack on Pearl Harbor. The Haradas did not inform their neighbors.

That night, the hospitable Niihau residents—still in the dark about the atrocity at Oahu—treated Nishikaichi to a festive luau. They roasted a pig and swapped songs. Silently, Nishikaichi despaired. He had lost hope that he would be rescued.

Later that night, the islanders apparently learned about the Pearl Harbor attack on the radio. They decided to confine the pilot in the Haradas' home until help arrived.

Exploiting their common ethnic ties and urging loyalty to the emperor, Nishikaichi won over the Haradas. They enlisted the other resident of Japanese descent—the skittish Shintani—in a conspiracy to retrieve Nishikaichi's papers from Kaleohano. On the afternoon of December 12, a reluctant Shintani visited Kaleohano and asked for the enemy pilot's papers. He offered his neighbor a wad of cash. Kaleohano refused. Shintani desperately told him to burn the papers. It was a matter of life and death, Shintani pleaded with Kaleohano. Japan made him do this, Shintani insisted. Kaleohano again refused.

An hour later, Nishikaichi and the Haradas launched a campaign of terror against the islanders. They overtook the guard on duty and locked him in a warehouse. Mrs. Harada cranked up a phonograph to drown out the commotion. Yoshio Harada and Nishikaichi retrieved a shotgun from the warehouse and headed to Kaleohano's home. Kaleohano, who was in the outhouse, saw them coming and hid while Nishikaichi and his collaborators unsuccessfully searched for the pilot's papers. They recovered Nishikaichi's pistol and headed toward his grounded plane. Harada watched as the enemy pilot tried in vain to call for help on his radio.

Meanwhile, Kaleohano fled from the outhouse and ran to the main village to warn his neighbors of Nishikaichi's escape. He returned to his house to retrieve the papers, hid them in a relative's home, and set out with a strong team of islanders in a lifeboat toward Kauai to get help. They rowed for fourteen hours before reaching shore, where they informed their boss, Aylmer Robinson, and military officials of the intruder Nishikaichi and the treachery of the Haradas. That night, Harada and Nishikaichi set both the plane and Kaleohano's home on fire. They fired off their guns in a lunatic rage and threatened to kill every man, woman, and child in the village. After gathering for a prayer meeting, many residents escaped to a mountaintop with kerosene lamps and reflectors in an attempt to signal Kauai. Others weren't so fortunate.

On the morning of December 13, Harada and Nishikaichi captured islander Ben Kanahele and his wife. It was a fateful choice that Harada and Nishikaichi would live to regret. Kanahele was ordered to find Kaleohano. In their own "Let's Roll" moment of heroism, the gutsy Kanaheles refused to cooperate. When Nishikaichi threatened to shoot Kanahele's wife, fifty-one-year-old Ben lunged for the enemy's shotgun. The young Japanese fighter pilot pulled his pistol from his boot and shot Kanahele three times in the chest, hip, and groin. Mrs. Kanahele pounced at Nishikaichi; her once-peaceful neighbor Harada tore her away.

Angered, the wounded Kanahele summoned the strength to pick up Nishikaichi and hurl him against a stone wall, knocking him unconscious. Quick-thinking Mrs. Kanahele grabbed a rock and pummeled the pilot's head. For good measure, Ben Kanahele took out a hunting knife and slit Nishikaichi's throat, ensuring his death. A desperate Harada turned the shotgun on himself and committed suicide.

The Kanaheles' harrowing battle against a Japanese invader and his surprising collaborator was over.

On Sunday afternoon, an army expedition party arrived with Kaleohano at the village and took Shintani and Mrs. Harada into custody. The next evening, the rest of Hawaii finally got wind of the nightmare on Niihau. Radio station KTOH in Kauai broadcast a news bulletin on the ordeal. The

Honolulu Star Bulletin published a follow-up account the next day.[2] Shintani was sent to an internment camp and later returned to Niihau; he became a U.S. citizen in 1960.[3] Irene Harada was imprisoned for nearly three years in Honouliuli. In 1945, after she was released, she asked for permission to bring the bodies of both Harada *and* Nishikaichi to Kauai for a funeral. Mrs. Harada was never charged with treason or any other crime.

Forgotten in today's history books, the bravery of Howard Kaleohano and Ben Kanahele was justly rewarded at the time. Kanahele received the Purple Heart and Medal of Merit; Kaleohano received the Medal of Freedom and an $800 award from the army to pay for belongings that had been damaged or destroyed in the fire set to his home by Nishikaichi and Harada.

The significance of the Haradas' stunning act of disloyalty and Shintani's meek complicity in collaboration with Nishikaichi was not lost on the Roosevelt administration. "The fact that the two [sic] Niihau [ethnic] Japanese who had previously shown no anti-American tendencies went to the aid of the pilot when Japan domination of the island seemed possible, indicates likelihood that Japanese residents previously believed loyal to the United States may aid Japan if further Japanese attacks appear successful," noted Captain Irving Mayfield, then district intelligence officer for the Fourteenth Naval District, after a naval intelligence investigation on the Niihau takeover in January 1942.[4] Lieutenant C. B. Baldwin was more emphatic. The facts of the case "indicate a strong possibility that other Japanese residents of the Territory of Hawaii, and Americans of Japanese descent . . . may give valuable aid to Japanese invaders in cases where the tide of battle is in favor of Japan and where it appears to residents that control of the district may shift from the United States to Japan," he said.[5]

Unbeknownst to Mayfield and Baldwin, at least one high-ranking Japanese naval intelligence officer apparently concurred. In November 1941, less than one month before the Pearl Harbor attack, Lieutenant Commander Suguru Suzuki met with Admiral Isoroku Yamamoto's chief of staff, Matome Ugaki, to discuss conditions in Hawaii. If Japan were to invade Hawaii, Suzuki informed Ugaki, local ethnic Japanese probably would cooperate with the occupying forces.[6]

The Haradas were neither radical nationalists nor professional spies. They were ordinary Japanese Americans who betrayed America by putting their ethnic roots first. How many other ethnic Japanese—especially on the vulnerable West Coast—might be swayed by enemy appeals such as Nishikaichi's? How many more might be torn between allegiance for their country of birth and kinship with Imperial invaders? These were the daunting questions that faced the nation's top military and political leaders as enemy forces loomed on our shores.

Chapter 2

The Threat of the Rising Sun

s President Franklin D. Roosevelt sat down to deliver his White House fireside chat on the night of February 23, 1942, a Japanese submarine rose up from the Pacific Ocean. The 384-foot vessel emerged off the coast of Goleta, California, not far from Santa Barbara. Unaware of the enemy lurking in their midst, diners at the Wheeler's Inn in neighboring Ellwood gathered around the radio to hear FDR's update on progress in the war against the Axis powers. "We know now that if we lose this war it will be generations or even centuries before our conception of democracy can live again," Roosevelt warned from the Oval Office.[1] On the opposite side of the country, Imperial Navy Commander Kozo Nishino ordered five of his sailors to train their *I-17* submarine's deck gun on the Ellwood oil fields. Above the mundane din of silverware clinking, food sizzling, and diners murmuring, FDR's message crackled over the airwaves, "The broad oceans which have been heralded in the past as our protection from attack have become endless battlefields on which we are constantly being challenged by our enemies."[2]

About fifteen minutes into the speech, the diners in Ellwood—many of them workers at the local oil refinery—felt two violent blasts that unwittingly punctuated the president's distant words. Witnesses saw bright flashes light up the oil fields. J. J. Hollister III, a boy of ten at the time who lived in

a nearby canyon home, heard "a whistling noise and a thump as a projec-
tile hit" the grounds bordering his house. Following the flashes came "an
eerie whistling and caterwauling," Hollister recounted. "It was a sickening
sound."[3]

And so began the first foreign attack on the U.S. mainland since the War
of 1812.

Commander Nishino's men fired up to two dozen shells on the coast.
They scored a direct hit on an oil derrick and damaged a pier. "My God, all
the sirens went off and the blackout happened and there were searchlights
all over the skies," remembered Santa Barbara resident Joan Martin, who
was twenty-two-years-old at the time of the shelling.[4] A besieged refinery
worker, answering a phone call from the town police inquiring about damage, retorted, "I don't know. I'm too busy dodging shells."[5]

"War for a moment seemed very real for the first time and indeed closer
than we ever thought it could be," observed sixth-grader Joan Churchill,
who wrote an eyewitness report of the shelling for her schoolmates.[6]

This little-known attack on the tranquil California coast lasted less than
half an hour; the *I-17* snuck away untouched. Army captain Bernard Hagen,
an artilleryman, was wounded while deactivating the fuse of what he
thought was a dud shell. It exploded and shrapnel embedded itself permanently in Hagen's thigh. He later received the Purple Heart for his wounds.[7]
While no one else was injured or killed and property damage was minimal,
the Imperial Navy claimed yet another psychological victory against fearful
Americans still reeling from the Pearl Harbor attack two months earlier. In
Japan, Radio Tokyo boasted, "Sensible Americans know that the submarine
shelling of the Pacific Coast was a warning to the nation that the Paradise
created by George Washington is on the verge of destruction."[8]

THE WEST COAST UNDER SIEGE

Critics of the WWII evacuation and relocation contemptuously dismiss the
Roosevelt administration's homeland defense measures as the result of
unequivocal "wartime hysteria." It is true that there were many phony

rumors of sabotage and erroneous reports of attacks. The most infamous pieces of misinformation were the tall tales of Hawaiian farmers of Japanese descent aiding Imperial bombers by cutting arrows in their sugarcane fields in advance of the Pearl Harbor attack[9] and the so-called "Battle of Los Angeles" two days after the Ellwood oil field shelling. Panicky American antiaircraft gunners stationed at Fort MacArthur fired more than fourteen hundred shells into the southern California skies during what they mistakenly thought was a Japanese air raid.[10]

But for every false alarm, there were many more real and unsettling forays along our shores that, when added to Japan's shocking military triumphs abroad, rightfully heightened America's anxiety.

In and around Hawaiian waters, Japanese submarines roamed free. At almost the same moment as the Pearl Harbor blitz, a Japanese submarine, the *I-26*, torpedoed and sank the SS *Cynthia Olson*, an unarmed U.S. army-chartered steam schooner, about one thousand miles northwest of Honolulu. All thirty-three members of the crew, plus two army passengers, died.[11] On December 11, another Japanese sub, the *I-9*, sank the freighter SS *Lahaina* off Honolulu. Four crewmembers died. Thirty survivors were stranded at sea for more than a week before washing ashore on the island of Maui.[12] Six days later, the *I-76* sank the SS *Manini*, a merchant marine ship, in Hawaiian waters—killing two more sailors. The rest of the crew was stranded for weeks before a navy patrol ship rescued them.[13] On December 18, the *I-72*, sank the SS *Prusa*, another merchant marine ship, near the Big Island as the freighter headed to Manila. Nine crewmen were killed immediately. Radio operator Lawrence Gianella rushed to rig up an emergency radio set and refused to abandon ship until he completed an SOS call. Nine minutes later, he went down with the vessel; twenty-four others survived.[14]

Under orders from the Imperial High Command, two submarine groups were dispatched to the West Coast to wreak havoc on shipping, shell coastal cities, and destroy communications. The oil field shelling at Ellwood and Goleta was just one of many long forgotten (or deliberately ignored) attacks that exacerbated America's feelings of vulnerability to Japanese invasion. On the day the SS *Prusa* went down, the Japanese sub *I-17* (the same vessel that later shelled Ellwood) attacked the SS *Samoa*, an American freighter, fifteen miles from Cape Mendocino, California. During the next week, Japanese subs attacked the lumber schooner SS *Barbara Olson* and the oil tankers LP *St. Clair,* SS *Agwiworld,* SS *H. M. Storey*, and SS *Larry Doheny* within twenty miles of the California and Oregon coastlines.[15] On December 20, the ubiquitous *I-17* attacked the SS *Emidio*, an oil tanker, blowing away the ship's radio mast and killing five crew members—three of whom were murdered while lowering a lifeboat.[16] Three days later, the *I-21* sank a second oil tanker, the SS *Montebello*. Dodging shell fragments that rained down on their four lifeboats, the crew of thirty-six survived. On Christmas Eve, the *I-23* fired on and hit the steamship SS *Dorothy Philips*, which ran aground near Monterey Bay. The next day, Christmas, an *I-19* torpedo attack damaged the SS *Absaroka*, a lumber carrier, whose crew was forced to abandon ship. One sailor died. Two days later, the *I-25* chased the oil tanker SS *Connecticut* near the Columbia River. The tanker sustained one torpedo hit and ran aground.[17]

By the end of the month, the Japanese submarines harassing West Coast ships were low on fuel and provisions, and were ordered back to their bases in the Marshall Islands to re-supply and refuel.[18] They would return in 1942 to shell the Goleta oil fields, sink a freighter in the North Pacific, sink the previously targeted *Larry Doheny* and *H. M. Storey*, and launch seaplanes that would drop incendiary firebombs over southwest Oregon forests.

The Japanese submarine attacks along the West Coast caused far less damage and claimed far fewer lives than German U-boat attacks along the East Coast, but were more psychologically damaging because they highlighted the vulnerability of the West Coast to Japan's powerful naval forces. There was no analogous threat on the East Coast, since neither Germany nor Italy had any aircraft carriers. But whereas the German U-boat attacks have received considerable attention in the popular media,[19] the little-known Japanese submarine attacks are disregarded, downplayed, or denied altogether in the oversimplified, comic-book version of history plied by critics of the West Coast evacuation.[20]

JAPAN'S ASCENDANCE

Military context is critical in assessing the mindset of those responsible for World War II relocation, evacuation, and internment policies. Bear in mind: the December 7, 1941, attack on Pearl Harbor sent shock waves that reverberated across the islands and shook the nation's psyche. Oahu, after all, had been touted as "Our Gibraltar in the Pacific." Military officials, politicians, and the press had repeatedly assured the American public that Pearl Harbor was "the strongest fortress in the world" (Army Chief of Staff General George C. Marshall); that the navy was "not going to be caught napping" (Secretary of the Navy Frank Knox); that "it would be impossible for hostile planes to come over the island" (Honolulu magazine *Paradise of the Pacific*); and that "a Japanese attack on Hawaii is regarded as the most unlikely thing in the world" (*Honolulu Star Bulletin*).[21]

So unexpected was the attack that most Honolulu residents watching it being carried out initially believed it was an elaborate training exercise staged by the U.S. Navy. As Thurston Clarke, author of *Pearl Harbor Ghosts*, reports:

> Explosions woke correspondent Joseph C. Harsch in his room at the Royal Hawaiian Hotel. He told his wife they were "a good imitation" of what a European air raid sounded like. They then took their morning swim, assuming, like the other guests, it was another practice maneuver by the Navy.
>
> After seeing bursts of antiaircraft shells from his Waikiki apartment, Admiral Pye told his wife, "It seems funny that the Army would be having target practice on Sunday morning." At Wheeler Field, General Davidson believed he was hearing "those damn Navy pilots jazzing the base," and continued shaving.[22]

The humiliating raid on Oahu claimed the lives of twenty-four hundred U.S. soldiers and civilians. Another twelve hundred Americans were wounded. Japanese forces sank or damaged a total of twenty-one vessels of the Pacific

Fleet, along with three-quarters of the planes on the airfields surrounding
Pearl Harbor. On this same day of unimaginable infamy, the Japanese also
landed forces at Singora and Patani in Thailand and at Kota Bahru, Malaya.
The next day, they attacked Hong Kong and destroyed one hundred aircraft
in the Philippines.

The invading rays of the Rising Sun seemed nearly indomitable at the
time. America was poorly armed. Troops and equipment were scarce. The
December 7 attack left the United States with a seriously shocked and damaged military presence in the Pacific. Meanwhile, the Japanese were win-
ning victory after victory. On December 10, the Japanese landed in the
northern Philippines and captured the American island of Guam. They also
took the British islands of Tarawa and Makin, and sank both the British battleship HMS *Prince of Wales* and the British cruiser HMS *Repulse* off the
Malay Peninsula. Wake Island surrendered to Japanese forces on December
23, the same day the Imperial Army forced Fil-American troops to retreat
from Manila to Bataan. On Christmas Day, Hong Kong surrendered. By January 2, 1942, Manila was occupied; the loss of the Philippines was a foregone conclusion; Rabaul, New Guinea, fell on January 23. On February 4,
the Japanese launched attacks on British, Dutch, and American squadrons
in the Battle of the Java Sea. The Dutch East Indies were doomed. Singapore,
the British Empire's "Gibraltar of the Pacific," fell on February 15.

Among both military and civilian leaders there was widespread agreement that the West Coast of the continental United States was vulnerable.
While a full-scale Japanese invasion of the U.S. mainland was considered
unlikely, hit-and-run raids were, in the view of Secretary of War Henry Stimson, "not only possible, but probable in the first months of the war, and it
was quite impossible to be sure that the raiders would not receive important help from individuals of Japanese origin."[23]

At least one high-ranking Japanese military official—Admiral Tamon
Yamaguchi, commander of the Imperial Navy's Second Carrier Division—
was eager to carry the war to the U.S. mainland, according to historian John
Stephan. Yamaguchi advocated taking over Hawaii then "hitting the enemy
in its homeland and denying it access to overseas supplies. Carrier task

forces based at Pearl Harbor would stalk everything that floated between Anchorage and San Diego. The Panama Canal would be rendered unusable. California oilfields were to be seized."[24] Such ideas also surfaced in the Japanese mainstream media.[25]

By February 19, when President Roosevelt signed Executive Order 9066 authorizing the secretary of war to exclude "any and all persons" from pre-scribed military zones, reports of Japanese wartime atrocities in many of its conquered lands were circulating worldwide. Before Pearl Harbor and even before the Rape of Nanking in China, American civilians had been targets of this savagery. In the mid 1930s, Japanese forces attacked schools and hos-pitals of American missionaries. Japanese planes strafed five Americans on an outing in Shanghai. An American church in Chungking was bombed eight times before it was finally destroyed in the ninth bombing. And one day before Nanking fell, Japan deliberately attacked an American gunboat, the USS *Panay*, in the Yangtze River without warning. Aboard were West-ern journalists, diplomats, and crewmembers. The vessel was escorting two Standard Oil tankers filled with refugees from Nanking. Japanese motor-boats machine-gunned survivors in the water and mowed down the wounded who had reached the banks of the river and were trying to escape by crawling into the thicket.[26]

Despite persistent efforts to whitewash this history, Japan's unbridled ambition and ruthlessness—and its hostility to America—were indisputable historical facts known well and widely before Pearl Harbor. *After* December 7, 1941, it would have been unforgivably irresponsible of American officials to ignore the possibility of attacks on the mainland—and the horrific threat Imperial forces might pose to our soldiers and civilians alike.

The Advance of the Fifth Column

With much of the Pacific in the Imperial Navy's control and Japan achieving military triumphs once thought unimaginable, West Coast military base com-manders from Seattle to Los Angeles felt justifiably more vulnerable to espi-onage, sabotage, and raids than they ever had felt before. Their sentiments

were reflected in a famous op-ed piece penned on February 13, 1942, by the
most influential columnist and preeminent liberal intellectual of the day, Walter Lippmann:

> The enemy alien problem on the Pacific Coast, or much more accurately,
> the fifth column problem, is very serious and it is very special... The
> peculiar danger of the Pacific Coast is in a Japanese raid accompanied by
> enemy action inside American territory... It is the fact that the Japanese
> navy has been reconnoitering the Pacific Coast more or less continually
> and for a considerable period of time, testing and feeling out the Ameri-
> can defenses... From what we know about Hawaii and about the fifth col-
> umn in Europe, this is not, as some have liked to think, a sign that there
> is nothing to be feared. It is a sign that the blow is well organized and that
> it is held back until it can be struck with maximum effect.... The Pacific
> Coast is officially a combat zone; some part of it may at any moment be a
> battlefield. Nobody's constitutional rights include the right to reside and
> do business on a battlefield.[27]

The term "fifth column" first appeared during the Spanish Civil War, in reference to the hidden sympathizers of rebel General Francisco Franco. Propagandists spoke of four army columns marching on Madrid, with a fifth
column of clandestine supporters stationed inside the city and ready to
assist in the attack. "By the spring of 1939 Europe was in turmoil," historian Arnold Krammer wrote, "and the American public grew increasingly
anxious about the presence of a possible internal Fifth Column of enemies."
Hitler's use of such internal agents was critical to Germany's successes in
Poland, Belgium, Holland, and France.[28]

Krammer described "German citizens and Nazi sympathizers, living qui-
etly among the population, [who] cast off their sheepskins when Hitler sig-
naled, revealing themselves as enemy wolves. As Germany attacked each
nation in turn, a hidden force donned armbands and arose to aid incoming
troops, help parachutists, draw huge arrows on the ground to point the
Luftwaffe toward strategic targets, and sabotage home defenses. Fifth

columnists were disguised as workmen and priests, farmers, tourists, teachers, students, and train engineers."[29] In Norway, fifth columnist Vidkun Quisling—the nation's defense minister!—collaborated with Hitler and paved the way for German occupation forces.

Similar activities occurred throughout the Pacific theater, where Japanese invaders received aid and comfort from countless compatriots committed to the ultranationalist tradition of *doho* (unbending loyalty to the Emperor regardless of residence or citizenship status). In Hong Kong, according to Oxford University scholar Philip Snow, Japanese forces "were able to call on the services of local Japanese who had been in the colony so long as to become part of the landscape."[30] The fifth columnists included a barber at the Hong Kong Hotel who cut the hair of leading British officials; bar girls at Nagasaki Joe's, a popular hangout in the Wanchai district; and officials employed by local Japanese companies.[31] In addition, the Imperial Army's Special Service Organization, the Tokumu Kikan, dispatched hundreds of undercover agents to Hong Kong. "Within two or three years the industry of this legion of spooks was producing all the data Japan could desire," Snow wrote in his account of the fall of Hong Kong.[32]

In the Philippines, Pulitzer Prize-winning author and statesman Carlos Romulo described massive Japanese espionage activity in the country prior to the war. Bars and military bases were primary targets. "Japanese establishments were beside every important bridge, electrical plant, and public utility," Romulo reported.[33] The Japanese owners of huts built around Camp Murphy near Manila were prosecuted and jailed before the war for illegal possession of explosives—"enough dynamite to blow up the city." Japanese-owned and operated eateries sprang up outside the gates of American military bases and communications stations. The Balintawak Beer Brewery in Manila, Romulo reported, had concealed a radio station that ultimately guided in Japanese warplanes.[34] Throughout 1940 and 1941, Japanese Consul Katsumi Nihro and his staff of trained agents informed Tokyo of warship movements, airport construction, the size of Philippine armed forces and reserves, and the number of American troops and aircraft stationed on the islands.[35]

In the Dutch East Indies, the Japanese Foreign Office enlisted throngs of Japanese fishermen who pulled nets and took notes and pictures for the Empire. They were joined by Japanese timber company owners, farmers, mining engineers, industrialists, merchants, and prostitutes who had settled in areas designated as part of Japan's "Greater East Asia Co-Prosperity Sphere."[36] In Macassar, Japanese residents helped occupying Imperial Navy units as guides and interpreters.[37]

In Malaya, an espionage network of two hundred agents gathered information on military strengths, dispositions of troops, and landing sites. Tsugunori Kadomatsu, a colonel working for Japanese Naval Intelligence, posed as a steward and infiltrated the officers' club at the Singapore naval base. Cooperative *doho* in Malaya included Tatsuki Fuji, editor of the *Singapore Herald*, diplomat Mamoru Shinozaki (convicted of espionage), and an array of Japanese plantation owners.[38] The largest iron mine in Malaya was run by a subsidiary of the Nissan group, which supported Japanese militarists. Other important mines were under the control of Koichiro Ishihara, a Japanese ultranationalist who supported southward expansion. There is evidence that his company, Ishihara Sangyo Koshi (I.S.K.), was involved in intelligence activities, according to historian Eric Robertson.[39]

Although most ethnic Japanese in Southeast Asia were not involved in espionage, sabotage, or fifth columnist activities, the conquering Japanese troops treated all resident ethnic Japanese as reunited comrades. Historian John Stephan notes that resident Japanese in Davao, Philippines, gave Japanese forces "a tempestuous welcome."[40] An American living in the Philippines, Natalie Crouter, recalled that one of the first invasion sounds she and her husband heard was the roar of *"Banzai!"* as Japanese soldiers released their interned fellow nationals.[41]

Some of these details didn't emerge until after the war ended, but the presence of fifth columnists in both Europe and the Pacific was known to U.S. intelligence officials and military leaders at the time.[42] It would have been foolish to dismiss the possibility that a similar organized network of Japanese operatives was operating within the United States.

Chapter 3

Sympathizers and Subversives

Long before the Pearl Harbor attack, Japanese imperialists had been planting the seeds of ethnic ultranationalism throughout the mainland U.S. and Hawaii. In the late 1930s, a network of innocuous-sounding Japanese patriotic associations called *kais*, Japanese-language newspapers, Japanese schools, religious institutions, cultural exchange programs, and businesses supported Japan's campaign of military aggression in China and elsewhere. The organizations infused members with the martial spirit of Yamato Damashii, linking soul and country.

General George S. Patton, Jr., stationed in Oahu in 1937 serving as a senior army intelligence officer, was so troubled by potential fifth column activity on the island that he drew up a plan to take 128 ethnic Japanese community leaders hostage in case of an outbreak of war. "Clearly, Patton considered Hawaii's Japanese to be of questionable loyalty to the United States," wrote USS *Arizona* memorial historian Michael Slackman, who uncovered the plan. "He apparently believed that only the threat of strong retaliation would prevent the emergence of a fifth column in the event of war or crisis between the United States and Japan."[1]

Although most Americans today remain in the dark about the large number of pro-Japanese propagandists and sympathizers embedded in Hawaii and along the West Coast, American intelligence officials at the time were well aware of their existence and activities.

LONG LIVE JAPAN!

In the summer of 1937, a group of fifty ethnic Japanese living in and around San Francisco established the headquarters of the Japanese Military Servicemen's League (also known as the Heimusha Kai). By 1940, the league had grown to more than ten thousand members, according to intelligence officials.[2] Members included both *Issei* and *Nisei*. They paid dues to support the Japanese Army and Navy War Relief Fund and to defray the costs of the ongoing Sino-Japanese War.

The league and its companion organization, the Imperial Comradeship Society, had engaged in intelligence activities and had pledged to carry out sabotage against railroads and harbors in times of emergency, according to U.S. intelligence officials.[3] The Heimusha Kai's prospectus declared, "whenever the Japanese government begins a military campaign, we Japanese must be united and everyone must do his part." Furthermore, "We are proud to say that our daily happy life in America is dependent upon the protective power of Great Japan."[4]

League chapters hosted warmongering Japanese speakers and showed propaganda films to raise funds. Meetings began with the singing of the Japanese national anthem and ended with exclamations of loyalty to the emperor. Near San Francisco, members pledged support "for our emperor, our country, our race, and our posterity."[5] A San Diego meeting ended with three rousing cheers of "Long Live Japan!"[6] In Gardena Valley, California, League members heard heated exhortations "to encourage the proudest Japanese national spirit which has ever existed, to fulfill the fundamental principle behind the wholesome mobilization of the Japanese people, to strengthen the powers of resistance against the many hindrances which are to be faced in the future," and to "assist in financing the war with the utmost effort on the part of both the first and second generation Japanese and whoever is a descendant of the Japanese race. Now is the time to awaken the Japanese national spirit in each and everyone who has the blood of the Japanese race in him. We now appeal to the Japanese in Gardena Valley to rise up at this time."[7]

Related organizations included the Hokubei Butoku Kai (Military Virtue Society of North America), which was organized in 1931 to spread the ideals of *bushido,* the moral code of Japanese samurai; the Kanjo Kai (Society for Defending the Country by Swords, or Sword Society), whose leadership came from former Japanese officers and whose members were former Japanese soldiers; the Sakura Kai (Patriotic Society); the Nippon Kaigun Kyokai (Japanese Naval Association); the Suiko Sha (Reserve Officers' Club);[8] and the Togo Kai to raise money for the Japanese Navy. Women could join the Aikoku Fujin Kai (Patriotic Women's Society). Teachers could join the Zaibei Ikuei Jai (Society of Educating the Second Generation in America).[9]

Such organizations were regarded by intelligence officials as "intensely nationalistic" and subversive.[10] Members of many *kais* were believed to be veterans or reservists of the Japanese armed forces who were cooperating closely with the Japanese government, especially Japanese consular officials. A December 4, 1941, Office of Naval Intelligence (ONI) memo stated that "In the event of war between the United States and Japan, Japanese organizations of this general type are certain to be delegated important espionage and sabotage functions in the area where they now operate."[11]

Similar groups operated in Hawaii. The Society for the Promotion of Japanese Culture (Nihon Bunka Shinkokai) showed its members newsreels and war propaganda promising "excitement inspiring 100 million *doho.*"[12] According to historian John Stephan, Hawaiian residents of Japanese descent purchased 3 million yen ($900,000) worth of Imperial war bonds and contributed 1.2 million yen ($350,000) to the Japanese National Defense and Soldiers' Relief Fund between 1937 and 1939 alone. (In current dollars, this is equivalent to about $12 million in war bonds and $4 million in donations.) The transactions were handled through Hawaii-based branches of Yokohama and Sumitomo banks or through consular officials stationed throughout the islands.[13] Takashi Isobe, a Shinto priest, called Hawaii's Japanese residents "emigrant warriors."[14] Ethnic Japanese in Hawaii (and on the West Coast) sent Imperial soldiers generous care packages that included warm blankets, canned pineapples, oranges, raisins, and chocolate Hershey Kisses. Donors dutifully scraped together tinfoil, Kodak film wrappers, and scrap metal from various household products to supply the land of the Rising Sun with war matériel.[15]

Many Japanese-language newspaper editors reinforced the theme of racial solidarity and provided unquestioning support of their homeland's campaign of military aggression. The *New World Sun Daily News* and the *Japanese American News* based in San Francisco were staunchly pro-Japanese.[16] Breathlessly reporting on a celebration of the Japanese empire in Lindsay, California, in January 1941 attended by some three hundred ethnic Japanese, the *New World Sun* editorialized that the attendees were "ready to respond to the call of the mother country with one mind. . . . Our fellow Japanese countrymen must be of one spirit and should endeavor to unite our Japanese societies in this country."[17]

Japanese-language newspapers were in close contact with Japanese consular officials and other Japanese government officials. In 1941, prior to Pearl Harbor, representatives from many publications, including the *New World Sun Daily News* and the *Japanese American News*, traveled to Tokyo, where they were urged to function as intelligence-gatherers for Japan. As the ONI observed, "many Japanese newspapers in the U.S. are being pressed into service by the [Japanese] embassy, the [Japanese] consulates and officials in Tokyo to assume intelligence duties previously carried on by regular military and naval agents."[18]

In Hawaii, the Japanese-language papers referred to "*our* army" and "*our* angry eagles"—meaning the Imperial Army and military aviators, not American forces.[19] The newspaper *Jitsugyo no Hawaii* rallied ethnic Japanese on the islands, "What's wrong with serving your ancestral land? Are not those who vacillate about contributing money at this time of national emergency being unpatriotic?"[20] Criticism of the Japanese military, according to Hawaii-based newsman Tado Tamaru, was "unthinkable."[21]

Some Japanese-language newspapers contained both English-language and Japanese-language sections. These sections often reported the same news events quite differently. As John Stephan notes, "Treatment of Japan in the English sections was comparatively detached. However, the sections written in Japanese reverberated with patriotic [pro-Japan] rhetoric."[22]

When Japanese naval ships docked at Pearl Harbor, they were greeted warmly by well-wishers of Japanese ancestry. John Stephan recounts:

> Many *Issei* saw the Rising Sun on an Imperial Naval vessel as gratifying reassurance that the mother country still cared about its overseas subjects. Nor were the *Nisei* unaffected. One of them recalled: "A naval ship, being an extension of the suzerainty of the homeland, is a tonic of the first magnitude . . . and the reception is therefore both elaborate and sincere. We were brought up in such an atmosphere, and so the sailors and officers of the training ships were welcomed with both affection and respect.[23]

The visiting Japanese delegation reciprocated by providing lectures, movies, and other events proclaiming the greatness of Japan.[24] Japanese Admiral Koichi Shiozawa declared, "an unseverable relationship binds overseas compatriots and the Imperial Navy. We are thankful for your warm hospitality whenever our training squadrons enter your ports."[25] As early as 1936, President Roosevelt expressed concern about fraternization between Japanese sailors and ethnic Japanese residing in Hawaii. "One obvious thought occurs to me," he commented, "every Japanese citizen or non-citizen on the island of Oahu who meets these Japanese ships or has any connection with their officers or men should be secretly but definitely identified and his or her name placed on a special list of those who would be the first to be placed in a concentration camp in the event of trouble."[26]

Japanese religious leaders carried the banner of the Rising Sun as well. Above the altar of Buddhist temples was the inscription, "Now let us worship the Emperor every morning." Shinto temples were no less restrained in promoting Japanese propaganda.[27] The ONI noted with alarm that not only were many Buddhist and Shinto priests embedded in Japanese-language schools, they also served as Japanese consular officials (that is, official agents of the Japanese government) and held leadership positions in subversive *kais*:

Inasmuch as strict supervision of religion has for centuries been a characteristic of Japanese governmental policy, it follows that both priests and
teachers are to a considerable extent subject to orders from Tokyo or, what
amounts to the same thing, from their religious superiors in Japan. . . .
Affiliated with Buddhist and Shinto temples are Japanese Language
Schools, welfare societies, young people's Buddhist societies, and Buddhist
women's organizations. They provide excellent resources for intelligence
operations, have proved to be very receptive to Japanese propaganda, and
in many cases have contributed considerable sums to the Japanese war
effort.[28]

Japanese-language schools, too, served as a powerful source of Japanese propaganda. Japanese consular agents, former Japanese army officers, and Buddhist priests often served as principals or teachers.[29] Ostensibly, the purpose
of these schools was to instruct young Japanese Americans about Japanese
language, culture, and traditions, such as sushi, origami, and sumo
wrestling. But the schools also disseminated ultra-nationalist cant, with a
strong emphasis on Japanese solidarity and emperor-worship. The schools
were "in practical fact agencies of Japanese nationalism," historian Page
Smith notes.[30] Teachers usually began instruction by having students "line
up in ranks at stiff attention like miniature soldiers. The teacher would then
hold up a picture of the emperor or a famous Japanese general or admiral
and the students would raise their hands in a salute and shout *Banzai.*"[31]
Daniel Inouye, a U.S. Senator from Hawaii, recalled his experience with his
Japanese-language school:

Day after day, the [Buddhist] priest who taught us ethics and Japanese history hammered away at the divine prerogatives of the Emperor. . . He
would tilt his menacing crew-cut skull at us and solemnly proclaim, "You
must remember that only a trick of fate has brought you so far from your
homeland, but there must be no question of your loyalty. When Japan
calls, you must know that it is Japanese blood that flows in your veins.[32]

On the eve of Pearl Harbor, thirty-nine thousand *Nisei* youths attended
Japanese-language schools in Hawaii.[33] Tens of thousands more attended the
schools on the mainland, including nearly eighteen thousand pupils in California alone.[34] A smaller contingent of *Nisei*—about one in five over the age
of fifteen[35]—had received schooling in Japan. These Japanese Americans,
known as *Kibei*, often returned to the United States as fanatical Japanese
nationalists. Some could barely speak English. Even opponents of the World
War II evacuation believed firmly that a substantial number of *Kibei* were
agents of Japan who had been sent back to the United States just prior to
Pearl Harbor to carry out espionage, sabotage, and other pro-Japan activities during the war.[36]

Another connection between most of America's ethnic Japanese and
Japan was Japanese citizenship. With the exception of a small handful of
World War I veterans who were granted citizenship through special legis-
lation, all of the *Issei* were Japanese citizens because they were precluded by
U.S. law from becoming U.S. citizens. For many *Issei*, the connection to
Japan was naturally much stronger than the connection to the United States.
After Pearl Harbor, most Hawaiian *Issei* remained loyal to Japan, according
to two Japanese postwar historians cited by John Stephan.[37] Stephan writes
that Japan's surrender in 1945 came as a traumatic blow to many Hawaiian
Issei: "Confronted with the emperor's 15 August broadcast, *Issei* women
wept. The men heard the news, eyes downcast, in stony silence.... A sizeable proportion of the *Issei* in Hawaii psychologically refused to accept the
events of August 1945 as reality. Rumors gave their delusions sustenance.
Japan, it was said, had actually won the war."[38]

The overwhelming majority of *Nisei* adults were citizens of both Japan
and the United States (that is, dual citizens). Children born to Japanese
fathers before 1924 were automatically given Japanese citizenship, no matter where they were born. Beginning in 1924, under the Japanese Nationality Law, children born in the United States retained Japanese citizenship
only if their parents registered them at the Japanese consulate within two
weeks of birth. This same law also made it easier for dual citizens to

renounce their Japanese citizenship. By December 1941, few had done so, according to the ONI.[39]

Japan's Department of Education supplied Japanese-language schools with textbooks reminding ethnic Japanese youngsters of their citizenship ties to Japan. "The objective of Japanese education, no matter in what country it may be, is to teach the people never to be ashamed of their Japanese citizenship," said one junior high school textbook. "We must never forget— not even for a moment—that we are Japanese."[40] A 1941 ONI memo reports that Japan placed considerable pressure on *Nisei* dual citizens to serve in the Japanese military. According to the memo, Kazuichi Hashimoto of Terminal Island, California, took a group of forty young ethnic Japanese (presumably *Nisei* dual citizens) to Japan, supposedly to teach them fencing. "However," the memo states, "it is suspected that these young people were taken to Japan for military duty."[41]

Though critics of the West Coast evacuation and relocation say dual citizenship was of no consequence, the presence of *Nisei* in Japan's military suggests otherwise. Estimates of how many *Nisei* ended up joining the Imperial Army and Navy forces range from 1,648 (the official figure given by the Japanese government) to as high as 7,000—not including those who assisted the Japanese military in other capacities.[42] Perhaps the most notorious was Tomoya Kawakita, a translator for the Japanese Army who tortured scores of American POWs held in a Japanese prison camp. After the war, Kawakita returned to the United States, where he enrolled at the University of Southern California. He was identified by a POW at a Sears department store in Boyle Heights, California.[43] Kawakita was convicted of treason after the war. Later, President Eisenhower commuted Kawakita's sentence to life in prison, and in 1963 President John F. Kennedy freed him on the condition that he spend the rest of his life in Japan.

Kawakita's dual citizenship was the central issue in his legal case. He stated that he had registered as a Japanese citizen while in Japan, and that this act—coupled with his obvious loyalty to Japan during the war—effectively ended his United States citizenship. Thus, he argued, he could not be found guilty of engaging in treason against the U.S. But at the end of the war, Kawakita swore allegiance to the United States, claiming he had been a United States citizen all along. By a 4–3 margin (two justices recused themselves), the Supreme Court rejected this ploy of fair-weather citizenship and ruled against Kawakita. Justice William O. Douglas, writing for the majority, stated, "An American citizen owes allegiance to the United States wherever he may reside." At the same time, Douglas acknowledged the obvious fact that "one who has a dual nationality will be subject to claims from both nations, claims which at times may be competing or conflicting."[44] Kawakita was an extreme example, but he was hardly alone in demonstrating the dangers of dual loyalty overseas—and on American soil.

Chapter 4

Spies Like Us

The single most deeply entrenched myth about the WWII evacuation and relocation—repeated endlessly in the popular press and in the classroom—is that ethnic Japanese residing in the U.S. posed no threat whatsoever to U.S. security. As the final report of the Commission on Wartime Relocation and Internment of Civilians put it, "careful review of the facts . . . has not revealed *any* security or military threat from the West Coast Japanese in 1942" (emphasis added).[1] An honest look at the historical record, however, shows that Japan in fact had established an extensive espionage network within the United States. According to U.S. intelligence officials, Japan's meticulously orchestrated espionage effort to undermine our national security utilized both *Issei* and *Nisei*, in Hawaii and on the West Coast, before and after the Pearl Harbor attack. Within the intelligence community, there was no dispute with regard to these assessments, although there were disagreements about what should be done about it.

To understand how the presence of Japanese espionage cells compromised U.S. security, consider the network's Honolulu ring. According to Pacific Fleet intelligence officer Edward T. Layton, the Honolulu office was "home base for more than two hundred subconsular agents scattered throughout the territory of Hawaii"—at least forty of whom were being monitored for espionage activity.[2] Among them was Richard Masayuki

Kotoshirodo, a twenty-five-year-old Hawaiian-born *Kibei* (*Nisei* who were sent to Japan to study and then returned to the United States) who assisted three Japanese officials based at the Honolulu consulate. Kotoshirodo possessed a valuable trait: He had a photographic memory that allowed him to mentally catalogue and instantly recall the names and locations of U.S. Navy warships. Like most adult *Nisei*, Kotoshirodo was a dual citizen of the United States and Japan. He was made an "honorary spy" by the Japanese consulate. "In the city he posed as a patriotic American," wrote historian Ladislas Farago. "In the consulate he was a Japanese patriot. His sympathies were fiercely with the land of his ancestors."[3]

Japanese naval spy Takeo Yoshikawa (who went by the alias Tadasi or Tadashi Morimura) personally coached Kotoshirodo on surveillance techniques. Yoshikawa had studied with the U.S. Navy and had extensive expertise on America's Pacific Fleet. He was recruited by the Japanese naval general staff's intelligence division and trained for four years as an undercover agent for American operations.[4] Yoshikawa arrived in Honolulu harbor aboard the passenger liner *Nitta Maru* in late March 1941. Assigned a desk in the vice consul's office, Yoshikawa aroused the curiosity of his fellow employees—but no suspicions—by often arriving late and leaving early on mysterious excursions. He blended easily among the ethnic Japanese on Oahu. For the next eight months, Kotoshirodo and Yoshikawa roamed the islands on "sightseeing" tours in Kotoshirodo's 1937 Ford. On occasion, Yoshikawa would dress as a day laborer and hide out in sugarcane fields to spy on American naval positions[5] or pose as a Filipino worker at American officers' clubs.[6] Yoshikawa monitored Battleship Row, took geishas from local teahouses on tourist planes to conduct aerial surveillance, and cruised in glass-bottomed boats to check out harbor conditions. Meanwhile, Kotoshirodo scoped out Kauai on his own, toured Maui to observe the port at Lahaina, and conducted reconnaissance on the Big Island.

Along with Kohichi Seki, treasurer of the Japanese consulate, Vice Consul Otojiru Okuda, and Consul General Nagao Kita, the Honolulu espionage cell monitored ship movements, water currents, and available support sys-

tems, and made note of military routines on installations and at airfields.[7] As
historian Gordon Prange put it, they constituted "a highly efficient central
team [that] carried out the consulate's espionage mission."[8] Among the spy
ring's observations: that no American warships were stationed off the west
coast of Maui, so that attacking planes could concentrate exclusively on
Oahu;[9] that the American battleships moored in pairs, so that the inshore
ship could not be struck by a torpedo; that a large number of ships were
always in the port on Saturdays and Sundays; and that the Americans conducted hardly any patrols at all north of Oahu. This information was "essential to the last-minute planning and timing of the attack," author Thurston
Clarke points out.[10] The Honolulu cell also provided Japan with detailed
maps, copies of which were found in the cockpits of downed Japanese fighter
planes following the attack.[11] To maintain the secrecy of the Pearl Harbor
attack plan, the cell members were not told of the urgent importance of their
reports. Others who aided the Japanese effort included John Yoshige Mikami,
an *Issei* taxi driver who chauffeured Yoshikawa when Kotoshirodo was
unavailable, and Bernard Julius Otto Kuehn, a German spy whose daughter,
Ruth, was the mistress of Nazi Propaganda Minister Josef Goebbels.

Senior intelligence officials knew of the men's activities—the Fourteenth
Naval District Intelligence Office even wiretapped Yoshikawa's telephone at
the consulate—but since it was not illegal to observe strategic operations
from public locations, nothing could be done to stop them.

Not until after the war broke out did interrogations reveal how extensive
the help from Kotoshirodo and Mikami was to Japan's espionage efforts in
advance of the Pearl Harbor attack. Kotoshirodo admitted to the FBI, "I
understood that I was gathering naval information for the Japanese government when I made these trips, but I gave no thought as to what my superiors in the consulate were going to do with it."[12] At an October 14, 1942,
hearing before an Internee Hearing Board in Honolulu, Kotoshirodo stated
that at the time he was engaged in his consulate work—work he himself
described as "espionage activity"[13]—his loyalties lay with Japan, not the
United States:

Q: Well, what I am trying to get at is this: how did you feel in your own mind up to the war? Did you class yourself as being 100 percent for Japan, or did you class yourself as being an American?

A: As I recall, I was 100 percent Japanese.[14]

Kotoshirodo denied advance knowledge of the surprise attack at Pearl Harbor, but admitted that even if he had known of the impending war, he could not be certain he would have ceased his surveillance activities:

Q: Would you have left the Consul if you had thought there was going to be a war, or would you have stayed there?

A: I do not know. I really do not know. I really did not know what the real meaning of war was.[15]

Despite the conclusion of a hearing board in Hawaii that Kotoshirodo was a willing collaborator (see Appendix A), despite the determination by FBI head J. Edgar Hoover that he should be charged with espionage, and despite Kotoshirodo's own confession of his involvement with the Honolulu spy ring, the U.S. attorney in Hawaii blocked prosecution. Kotoshirodo and his wife were instead interned briefly in Hawaii, then were sent to relocation centers in Topaz, Utah, and Tule Lake, California.[16]

Mikami, the taxi driver, remained a staunch defender of Japan; according to the FBI, he "was intensely pro-Japanese and claimed that the Japanese Navy was in every way superior to the United States Navy... He stated that if the American ships went near Japan, Japan would take all of the ships."[17] Mikami was interned at Sand Point, Hawaii, then sent to a detention station at Santa Fe, New Mexico. Even during his internment at Sand Point, Mikami continued to monitor ship movements in and out of Pearl Harbor.[18]

Ringleader Yoshikawa left the United States undetected and continued working for the Japanese government after the war as a diplomat, but revealed his covert activities in a Japanese newspaper interview in 1953.[19] "I look back on my single top-secret assignment," he reflected, "as the *raison d' être* of the long years of training in my youth and early manhood. In truth, if only for a moment in time, I held history in the palm of my hand."[20]

Japan's espionage activities were by no means limited to Hawaii. As Admiral Layton, who was responsible for keeping the commander in chief of the Pacific Fleet informed about Japan's strategic objectives, capabilities, and intended operations—wrote in his memoirs, hundreds of suspected Japanese agents were believed to have engaged in espionage directed from the Japanese embassy in Washington and Japan's main consulates in New York, Los Angeles, and San Francisco. Outposts of large Japanese corporations in San Francisco "such as the Yokohama Specie Bank, Mitsubishi Shoji Kaisha, and Nippon Yusen Kaisha, provided protection and a channel of communications for the Imperial Navy's undercover agents," Layton noted. "The Los Angeles headquarters of the North American branch of the Nippon Kaigun Kyokai (Japanese Naval Association) collaborated with the language officers to obtain information about naval bases and defense plants."[21]

THE ITARU TACHIBANA SPY RING

Itaru Tachibana, a Japanese Navy lieutenant commander, was a key member of a large espionage ring that encompassed the entire West Coast. He was one of dozens of Japanese agents sent to the United States in the 1930s posing as language students and technical experts. Upon arrival, these agents reported to the Japanese embassy in Washington for briefings by Second Secretary Hidenari Terasaki, the Brown University–educated diplomat purported to be the mastermind of Japan's entire espionage network in the western hemisphere. Tachibana ran a chain of brothels for cover and supplemental income. His immediate supervisor in Los Angeles was Japan's local representative of the naval attaché.[22]

In early 1941, Tachibana came to the attention of U.S. authorities after he had attempted to recruit a former U.S. Navy sailor, Al Blake. Blake initially agreed to cooperate with the Japanese spy, but changed his mind and notified the FBI. After the navy was notified, Pearl Harbor Fleet Intelligence Officer Edward Layton coordinated a sting operation in Hawaii using Blake. The FBI arrested Tachibana in the summer of 1941 for violations of federal espionage statutes. Documents seized from Tachibana included names of espionage agents; locations of military installations, power stations, and dams; data on defense factories and harbors; and correspondence between Tachibana and officials of the *kais* in California. Among Tachibana's possessions were $4,300 in cash (equivalent to more than $50,000 in current dollars), two loaded handguns, ammunition, cameras, and photo-developing equipment. The haul "was so voluminous that the Navy had to send three of its best translators to go through the documents," wrote espionage scholar Pedro Loureiro. "A truck was required to remove everything; the FBI list of the items found in Tachibana's room totaled 107 pages."[23]

A suitcase belonging to Lieutenant Commander Sadatomo Okada, a fellow language officer and suspected spy, was found in Tachibana's trove. It contained details of naval ships under construction, data on antiaircraft defenses for the Boeing plant in Seattle, aerial photographs of naval and army bases, and test data on naval aircraft.[24] Others furnishing information to Tachibana were identified by first names or initials only. The large amount of cash seized by the FBI "was undoubtedly to be used as payment to agents," according to Loureiro.[25]

The names of agents mentioned in Tachibana's documents—Fukuchi, Maki, and Kurokawa—suggest that most of Tachibana's spies were ethnic Japanese. Peter Irons, a prominent anti-evacuation activist/historian, has acknowledged that "there was no question that Tachibana headed an espionage ring on the West Coast that enlisted a number of Japanese Americans [*sic*[26]], both aliens and citizens."[27]

Prominent *Issei* associated with Tachibana included Shunten Kumamoto, president of the Los Angeles Japanese Association; Gongoro Nakamura, president of the Central Japanese Association of California; and Los Angeles doctor Takashi Furusawa.[28] All were members of the Sakura Kai (mentioned earlier), which was considered a subversive organization by the ONI and FBI. The ONI reported after Tachibana's arrest that both the Sakura

Kai and the Suiko Sha "were supplying [Tachibana] with intelligence information to be sent to Tokyo."[29] Another of Tachibana's colorful associates, Toraichi Kono, an *Issei*, served as Charlie Chaplin's valet and personal assistant in Los Angeles before being recruited to work for the Imperial intelligence organization. It was through Kono that Tachibana connected with former sailor Al Blake. Alarmed that Kono might dish to federal prosecutors, Japanese diplomats recommended that Kono be bribed with a twenty-five thousand dollar payoff (equivalent to nearly three hundred thousand current dollars).[30]

Though navy intelligence agents and FBI Director J. Edgar Hoover felt they had accumulated more than enough evidence to prosecute Tachibana and other members of his ring, the Department of Justice acquiesced to the State Department—which opposed prosecution because it was more concerned with appeasement of Japan than with bringing spies to justice.[31] Tachibana was released on a fifty thousand dollar bond; he and other undercover Japanese naval officers involved in his spy network left the country in June 1941. Kono was also allowed to depart for Tokyo.

Tachibana associate Dr. Furusawa had been an active spymaster in southern California since 1930. A graduate of Stanford University, Furusawa set up a medical clinic in Los Angeles that served as a front for espionage activities. His "patients" were known Japanese and German agents monitoring West Coast naval operations.[32] He was the head of the Nippon Kaigun Kyokai (Japanese Navy Association) and served on the board of directors of the Suiko Sha (Reserve Officers Club).[33] Furusawa's wife, Sachiko, eagerly aided her husband. She founded the Los Angeles branch of the Women's Patriotic Society of Japan, known to the FBI as an espionage front, and would often escort Japanese officers off ships when they reached Los Angeles harbor. Furusawa was exposed in a strange twist of fate in 1932, when one of his contacts, Japanese naval officer Takuya Torii, was killed in a Gardena, California, car accident. Torii was carrying a leather briefcase containing classified documents. Local police received a call from an agitated man seeking the briefcase. The cops notified the FBI, which traced the call to Furusawa's "clinic." Once again, although the Justice Department was able to gather useful information on the West Coast operation, the State Department blocked any espionage prosecutions. The Furusawas continued their espionage activities throughout the 1930s and early 1940s, then sailed back to Japan unmolested a few weeks before the Pearl Harbor attack.

The Tachibana ring may have been only the tip of the iceberg. A December 24, 1941, classified ONI memo named dozens of West Coast residents considered potential agents of Japan, almost all of them ethnic Japanese.[34] The description of Charles Theodore (Takeo) Takahashi is illustrative:

> TAKAHASHI, Charles Theodore (Takeo)—American-born, Class "A" suspect. Wealthy head of C.T. TAKASHASHI COMPANY, an export-import firm dealing mostly in lumber and scrap metal and formerly known as the ORIENTAL TRADING COMPANY. (Same firm is sometimes called the CHINA IMPORT AND EXPORT COMPANY, probably with the intention of hiding its Japanese ownership.) Also head of RESILIENT HAMMER INC., and C.T. CONTRACTORS, INC., the latter supplying labor to fisheries, lumber camps, and railroads. All of these firms are reported to be fronts for widespread and diversified activity of a subversive nature; contacts and affiliations with known Japanese and Occidental pro-Nazi elements in the U.S. and Mexico have been both consistent and long standing
>
> TAKAHASHI himself does considerable travel, frequently to Japan, and acts as a go-between in arranging for so-called "inspection trips" to important plants, airports, strategic areas, etc., by visiting Japanese military-naval officers and business men. Over a long period he was in intimate contact with such key men as Colonel Usaburo OKA, Inspector of the Imperial Japanese Army Ordinance Inspector's Office in New York City, Commanders Shigeru FUJII and Taro ISOBE, IJN, and Majors Otoji NISHIMURA and [illegible] TOMANI (now Lt. Col.).[35]

Those named were not isolated loners but in many cases prominent civic leaders within the ethnic Japanese community. Many, like Takahashi, had close ties to Japanese military officials, consular officials, or both. At least one person listed, *Nisei* Hiroshi ("Paul") Hoshi, had a shortwave radio license—a matter of no small concern given worries about illicit ship-to-shore and shore-to-ship communications.[36] As Admiral Layton reported, "Many of the suspects were *Nisei* on the West Coast who belonged to one of the patriotic societies with close links to Tokyo."[37]

Stating the obvious, Admiral Layton asserted in his postwar autobiography, "*And I Was There*," that "the evidence of extensive espionage discovered in these and similar operations on the West Coast probably influenced Roosevelt" when he issued Executive Order 9066, which led to the evacuation and relocation of ethnic Japanese on the West Coast. This was but a fraction of the alarming knowledge that prompted the president to act.

Chapter 5

The MAGIC Revelations

Through much diligent sleuthing and sometimes just sheer luck, military and FBI investigators gained valuable information on Japan's systematic targeting and recruitment of ethnic Japanese into U.S.-based information-gathering networks. Wiretaps and informants supplemented their knowledge. But more than any other source of intelligence, it was the so-called MAGIC messages—Japan's diplomatic communications that were intercepted and decoded by American signal intelligence officers—that revealed in message after message the alarming extent of Japan's ongoing espionage operations on the West Coast, in Hawaii, and along America's southern border. (Key cables discussed below are reprinted in Appendix B.)

Virtually every popular account of the ethnic Japanese experience during World War II has ignored MAGIC and its vital importance in shaping FDR's national security policies abroad and at home. Leading high school textbooks condemn evacuation, relocation, and internment as shameful injustices—without informing students of the vast amount of communications intelligence that informed FDR's decisions. "The rising current of fear on the West Coast *and the evidence from the Magic intercepts* (emphasis added) were important factors in the President's decision to sign Executive Order 9066," concluded acclaimed military historian John Costello.[1] Yet even government-sponsored educational programs, such as the Smithsonian Institution exhibition, "A More Perfect Union: Japanese Americans and the U.S. Constitution," fail to mention any of the details of Japanese espionage operations along the West Coast revealed in MAGIC cables, which were declassified and published in an eight-volume set by the Department of Defense in 1977. This stunning omission amounts to educational malpractice. By maligning the Roosevelt administration as hysterical and irresponsible, the strident opponents of evacuation, relocation, and internment perpetuate ignorance, discourage honest intellectual debate, and undercut the legacy of the amazing military code breakers who revealed Japan's nefarious designs and protracted deception.

With little support or funding, a small and eclectic clique of brilliant American cryptanalysts labored for years on Japan's highest-security codes. On the army side, the father of modern U.S. cryptology, William Friedman, established the Signal Intelligence Service (SIS). In 1936, Friedman supervised a team led by Franklin B. Rowlett that cracked a top-level diplomatic code dubbed RED by the United States. The naval intelligence counterpart, known as OP-20-G, focused mainly on breaking Japan's naval codes.

In 1937, Japan introduced a new machine cipher used for all Foreign Office communications classified as "state secret." This included almost all the diplomatic traffic between Tokyo and its key embassies and consulates in the United States and around the world. Our cryptanalysts dubbed the new code PURPLE. Friedman's code wizards worked day and night to solve the system. The enormity of the task is said to have driven Friedman to a nervous breakdown. By August 1940, the SIS had completed its first paper-and-pencil solution of the PURPLE code. The next month, team member Genevieve Grotjan made a major cryptanalytic breakthrough that led to production of the blueprint for an analog machine. Built from scratch, sight unseen, the American analog duplicated the complex wiring and stepping switches of Japan's machine cipher. Two navy-built analogs based on the army team's blueprint cost taxpayers $684.65—an investment that paid lifesaving dividends throughout the war.[2] Reproducing the Japanese device allowed American code breakers to crack the enemy's diplomatic messages as quickly as the Japanese code clerks themselves. It was a landmark feat in American intelligence, so miraculous, in fact, that the code-breaking team's superior, Major General Joseph Mauborgne, started referring to its members as "magicians." The term MAGIC was chosen as the cover name for the entire code-breaking operation involving Japan's highest-level diplomatic systems.

The MAGIC messages provided astonishing information about Japan's activities and intentions. Roberta Wohlstetter noted in her landmark book, *Pearl Harbor: Warning and Decision*:

> The ability to read these codes gave the United States a remarkable advantage over the enemy—an advantage not likely to be repeated. America's military and government leaders had the privilege of seeing every day the most private communications between the Japanese government and its ambassadors in Washington, Berlin, Rome, Berne, Ankara, and other major Japanese embassies throughout the world. They saw the reports of Japanese military attachés and secret agents in Honolulu, Panama, the Philippines, and the major ports of the Americas. They knew in advance the diplomatic moves that Japan was contemplating and the sorts of information that her agents were collecting on American defense preparedness.[3]

MAGIC was at least as important to the European theater as the Pacific. The Japanese ambassador to Germany, Hiroshi Oshima, was well connected to Adolf Hitler and other high-ranking officials in Germany's government. Oshima's messages to Tokyo provided considerable detail on German wartime secrets, sometimes in Hitler's own words. As MAGIC cryptanalyst Frank Rowlett later explained, "the information provided by Oshima was of incalculable importance in leading the Allies to victory in World War II. . . I consider that our timely access to his messages is one of the greatest intelligence achievements of all time."[4]

Knowledge of what the Magicians had accomplished was a closely held secret. Obviously, it had to be. If the Japanese had found out about MAGIC they would have quickly changed their codes. Consequently, knowledge of and access to MAGIC information was initially limited to only a dozen or so people outside the code-breaking unit, including the secretary of war, the army chief of staff, the assistant secretary of war, the director of military intelligence, the secretary of the navy, the chief of naval operations, the chief of the war plans division, the director of naval intelligence, the secretary of state, the president's top military aide, and the president himself.[5] At the urgent behest of General George C. Marshall, translated message briefs were placed in locked, brown leather pouches and delivered personally to each recipient, who owned his own pouch key. General Marshall was so adamant about protecting MAGIC that he did not even allow one of his closest assistants, Colonel Walter Bedell Smith, secretary to the general staff, to have access to a key to his MAGIC briefcase.[6] Field commanders of the major military and naval forces were excluded from the list of eligible MAGIC recipients, though they received some intelligence extracted from it that was attributed to "highly reliable sources."[7]

Roosevelt, an intense and active consumer of intelligence throughout the war, kept the top-secret decrypts in what he called The Magic Book, tucked away in the tightly guarded Map Room of the White House.[8] David Kahn, author of the seminal book *The Codebreakers*, noted that tight-lipped Navy Secretary Frank Knox did not explain to his wife what he was receiving when MAGIC was delivered to his apartment. Before delivering the decrypts, Lieutenant Commander Alvin D. Kramer would notify recipients with a vague phone message that he had "something important that you should see."[9] With the exception of MAGIC decrypts delivered[10] to the president, the messages were not retained by recipients. It was common practice never to mention MAGIC on the phone, in conversation, or in written memos.

There were, inevitably, a few sloppy security breaches (Roosevelt's aide "Pa" Watson carelessly left one MAGIC decrypt in the trash; Secretary of State Cordell Hull allowed a few of his blabbermouth subordinates to mimeograph messages). But despite these gaffes, Japan, arrogantly confident that its diplomatic traffic was impenetrable, never caught on to the

Magicians. In fact, Japanese diplomats continued to use the PURPLE code to transmit classified information to Tokyo even after the war ended.

The three highest-ranking government officials who approved the decision to evacuate ethnic Japanese from the West Coast—President Roosevelt, Secretary of War Henry Stimson, and Assistant Secretary of War John McCloy—all had full access to MAGIC. McCloy later stated that he reviewed the MAGIC messages every day and night.

By contrast, none of the prominent government figures who opposed the evacuation knew about MAGIC. Not FBI Director J. Edgar Hoover. Not Attorney General Francis Biddle. Not Office of Naval Intelligence officer Kenneth Ringle. Not special State Department representative Curtis Munson. That didn't mean all these individuals were totally ignorant of all of the information contained in the MAGIC messages. Hoover, for example, occasionally received MAGIC-derived information about Japan's espionage networks attributed to "highly reliable sources," which he then passed along to his top agents and to Biddle. But those outside the MAGIC loop could never fully appreciate just how reliable the information was since they didn't know it came straight from high-ranking Japanese diplomats.

The decision to evacuate ethnic Japanese from the West Coast cannot be placed in proper perspective without a full understanding of the MAGIC messages. Beginning in December 1940, with the possibility of war looming, a series of MAGIC messages revealed Japan's intent to establish an espionage network in the United States. Two MAGIC cables sent from Tokyo on January 30, 1941, ordered the Japanese embassy and its North American consulates to begin establishing espionage nets designed to function in a wartime environment. The first announced, "We have decided to de-emphasize our propaganda work and strengthen our intelligence work in the United States." Cable copies of the message were sent, as "Minister's orders," to Mexico City, San Francisco, Honolulu, Los Angeles, Portland, Seattle, Vancouver, New York, New Orleans, and Chicago. Detailed intelligence requirements followed, with directions to recruit agents from "our 'Second Generations' and our resident nationals"—as well as "U.S. citizens of foreign extraction (other than Japanese), aliens (other than Japanese),

communists, Negroes, labor union members, and anti-Semites with access
to governmental establishments, governmental organizations of various
characters, factories, and transportation facilities." These cables also discussed cooperation "with the German and Italian intelligence organs in the
U.S.," as already agreed to among the Axis powers."[11]

The messages were translated on February 7, 1941, and less than one
week later, on February 12, officials at both the army Military Intelligence
Division (MID) and the Office of Naval Intelligence (ONI) wrote up classified memos summarizing almost verbatim the salient points of the
decrypts[12] (see Appendix C). The MID distributed the MAGIC-derived
information with a rating that both the source and information were "reliable" to army units in its nine corps areas, including Lieutenant General
John DeWitt's, as well as Puerto Rico, the Canal Zone, the Philippines, and
Hawaii.[13] About one month later, J. Edgar Hoover sent a confidential memo
to twenty-two of his top senior FBI officials stating that "highly confidential and reliable sources" had revealed that Japanese diplomats and consular
officials had "been instructed to reorganize and strengthen their intelligence
networks in this country" (see Appendix C). Hoover attributed this information to "naval authorities."[14] The source was MAGIC, though Hoover did
not know it.

On February 5, a message from Tokyo to Mexico City focusing on the
need to "investigate the general national strength of the United States"
directed intelligence-gatherers to "organize Japanese residents, including
newspaper men and business firms for the purpose of gathering information." The message, relayed to eight Latin American consular offices,
warned that "care should be taken not to give cause for suspicion of espionage activities."[15]

Tokyo sent another MAGIC cable to Washington on February 15 with
more detailed instructions:

The information we particularly desire with regard to intelligence involving U.S. and Canada, are [sic] the following:

1. Strengthening or supplementing of military preparations on the Pacific Coast and the Hawaii area; amount and type of stores and supplies; alterations to air ports (also carefully note the clipper traffic).

2. Ship and plane movements (particularly of the large bombers and sea planes).

3. Whether or not merchant vessels are being requisitioned by the government (also note any deviations from regular schedules), and whether any remodelling [sic] is being done to them.

4. Calling up of army and navy personnel, their training, (outlook on maneuvers) and movements.

5. Words and acts of minor army and navy personnel.

6. Outlook of drafting men from the view-point of race. Particularly, whether Negroes are being drafted, and if so, under what conditions.

7. Personnel being graduated and enrolled in the army, navy and aviation service schools.

8. Whether or not any troops are being dispatched to the South Pacific by transports; if there are such instances, give description.

9. Outlook of the developments in the expansion of arms and the production set-up; the capacity of airplane production; increase in the ranks of labor.

10. General outlooks on Alaska and the Aleutian Islands, with particular stress on items involving plane movements and shipment of military supplies to those localities.

11. Outlook of U.S. defense set-ups.

12. Contacts (including plane connections) with Central and South America and the South Pacific area. Also outlook on shipment of military supplies to those areas.

Please forward copies of this message as a "Minister's Instruction" to New York, San Francisco, Los Angeles, Seattle, Portland, (Chicago or New Orleans?) Vancouver, Ottawa, and Honolulu. Also to Mexico City and Panama as reference material.[16]

In March, Tokyo ordered Washington to put Secretary Hidenari Terasaki "in full charge of directing information and propaganda in the United States." The message noted that "cooperation of Jap bank and business officials in U.S. will be sought in connection with propaganda and intelligence work in U.S."[17] On April 19, Tokyo demanded and received detailed accounting figures of *Issei*, *Nisei*, and dual citizens from New York, Portland, Chicago, and Vancouver. Within the next two weeks, the consulates supplied statistics for first- and second-generation ethnic Japanese men and women, including counts of those *Nisei* with dual citizenship and those with American citizenship only.[18] New York provided further breakdowns, noting that of the ethnic Japanese in its area, "1595 are independent financially. 1057 are dependent."[19]

Continuing to use the PURPLE code, the Los Angeles and Seattle consulates reported to Tokyo in May 1941 on their progress in setting up the spy network's surveillance of military posts and bases, shipyards, airfields, and ports. "We have already established contacts with absolutely reliable Japanese in the San Pedro and San Diego area, who will keep a close watch on all shipments of airplanes and other war materials, and report the amounts and destinations of such shipments. The same steps have been taken with regard to traffic across the U.S.-Mexican border," a May 9, 1941, cable from the Los Angeles consulate reported.[20] The message also stated that the network had *Nisei* spies in the U.S. Army, and that it was maintaining close connections with the Japanese Association, the Chamber of Commerce, and the Japanese-language newspapers. The message was translated on May 19, 1941. Just two days later, on May 21, the chief of the MID's intelligence branch completed a classified memo paraphrasing the contents of the May 9 decrypt[21] (see Appendix C). The memo specifically mentioned "second generation Japanese at present in the U.S. Army or working in aircraft factories." A confidential FBI memo by Hoover covering similar ground was sent to Attorney General Francis Biddle the very next day[22] (see Appendix C). The information was also distributed to the Japanese Counter Intelligence Section of the ONI; Naval Districts 1 to 15; FBI field offices in

Los Angeles and San Diego; and the Army G-2 of the 9th Corps Area with a rating from the MID of "reliable" for both the source and information."[23] On June 27, Hoover sent a similar memo to President Roosevelt's secretary along with a cover letter stating that the report was "of possible interest to the President."[24] The State Department and attorney general received copies of the FBI memo as well.

A May 11, 1941, message from the Seattle consulate to Tokyo was divided into five parts. The first part outlined the consulate's efforts to collect "intelligences revolving around political questions."[25] The next part, headlined "Economic Contacts," described efforts to procure intelligence regarding war-related production:

> We are using foreign company employees, as well as employees in our own companies here, for the collection of intelligences having to do with economics along the lines of construction of ships, the number of planes produced for their various types, the production of copper, zinc and aluminum, the yield of tin for cans, and lumber.[26]

The next portion of the message, entitled "Military Contacts," stated:

> We are securing intelligences concerning the concentration of warships within the Bremerton Naval Yard, information with regard to mercantile shipping and airplane manufacturer, movements of military forces, as well as that which concerns troop maneuvers.
>
> With this as a basis, men are being sent out into the field who will contact Lt. Comdr. OKADA, and such intelligences will be wired to you in accordance with past practice. KANEKO is in charge of this. Recently we have on two occasions made investigations on the spot of various military establishments and concentration points in various areas. For the future we have made arrangements to collect intelligences from second generation Japanese draftees on matters dealing with the troops, as well as troop speech and behavior. - - - - - - - -.[27]

(A series of hyphens where words should appear means that a portion of the original encrypted text was not intercepted, was garbled, or could not be decrypted.)

The fourth section of the memo, entitled "Contacts With Labor Unions" stated:

> The local labor unions A.F. of L. and C.I.O. have considerable influence. The (Socialist?) Party maintains an office here (its political sphere of influence extends over twelve zones.) The C.I.O., especially, has been very active here. We have had a first generation Japanese, who is a member of the labor movement and a committee chairman, contact the organizer, and we have received a report, though it is but a resume, on the use of American members of the (Socialist?) Party. - - - OKAMARU is in charge of this.[28]

"OKAMARU" is apparently "Welly" or "Welley" Shoji Okamaru, a Seattle labor union member identified by the ONI as a *Nisei* and a "Class 'A' espionage suspect."[29]

The final part of the message stated that "we are making use of a second generation Japanese lawyer" to collect intelligence on "anti-participation" organizations and the anti-Jewish movement.[30] Though the name of the lawyer was not mentioned, a classified MID memo written the same day the decrypt was translated—June 9—referred to "a second-generation Japanese lawyer named Ito" who "collects information on anti-war-participation organizations."[31] This appears to be a reference to Kenji Ito, a *Nisei* lawyer who was later identified by the ONI as a "Class 'A' suspect."[32] After Pearl Harbor, Ito was unsuccessfully prosecuted for failing to register as a Japanese agent (see Appendix D).

By the summer of 1941, MAGIC messages sent by Japan's Seattle, San Francisco, and Los Angeles consulates made it clear that Japan's espionage network was up and running. Throughout the summer and fall, these three consulates sent dozens of cables providing detailed information on ship movements, aircraft production, and military-related construction activities.

The Seattle consulate seems to have been especially productive. A June 23, 1941, message to Tokyo read as follows:

FROM: Seattle (Sato)   June 23, 1941
TO: Tokyo (Gaimudaijin)   #056
(1) Ships at anchor on the 22nd/23rd (?):
(Observations having been made from a distance, ship types could not be determined in most cases.)
1. Port of Bremerton:
    1 battleship (Maryland type)
    2 aircraft tenders (one ship completed and has letter "E" on its funnel).
2. Port of - - - :
    1 destroyer
    11 coast guard cutters
    (ships under repair)
    1 destroyer
    11 (appear to be) minesweepers
3. Sand Point:
    2 newly constructed hangars
4. Boeing: New construction work on newly built factory building #2. Expansion work on all factory buildings.[33]

On August 16, the Seattle consulate informed Tokyo that, "according to a spy report, the English warship *Warspite* entered Bremerton two or three days ago."[34] An August 18 message reported on the whereabouts of military airplanes, and their likely destinations.[35] A September 4 message described the movements of "the 39th Bombardment Group (44 planes), the 89th Observation Squadron (15 planes), and the 310th Signal Company," all of Spokane.[36] This message also stated that the "*steering apparatus* (?) (*diameter 8 inches, double cylinders* (?), *gear ratio 410 to 1* (?) for the 312 10,000 ton freighters to be leased to England are to be manufactured in two factories, one in Everett and one in New York (?)"[37]—information potentially of

interest to would-be saboteurs. A September 20 message listed the ships at
the Port of Bremerton and noted the departure of a New Mexico class ship.[38]

The San Francisco and Los Angeles consulates sent similar messages
describing ship movements and cargo loads. A June 2, 1941 message from
Los Angeles stated, "On the 20th, the Saratoga, and on the 24th, the Chester
(?), Louisville, the 12th Destroyer Squadron and Destroyers # 364, 405, 411,
412, and 412 entered San Diego, and all of them left on the 31st."[39] A September 18 message from San Francisco stated, "According to a spy report,
the English warship *Warspite* arrived here from Bremerton on the - - - and
is at present moored near the (naval arsenal at Mare Island?). It has been
determined that it requires two more months for repairs at Liverpool."[40]
Messages sent from San Francisco in October described the arrival of an
Oklahoma class battleship and a Russian freighter, and described the cargo
of another ship, the *Nantes*.[41]

After Germany attacked the Soviet Union in June 1941, MAGIC traffic
revealed a keen interest by Tokyo in U.S.-Soviet relations.[42] Accordingly,
many West Coast intelligence reports concerned the movement of ships
between the United States and Russia. An August 16 message from Los
Angeles stated that "the St. Claire took on a cargo of 95,000 barrels of aviation gasoline and left port for Vladivostok on the afternoon of (date). The
Fitzsimmons is in the process of taking on a similar cargo of 75,000 barrles
[*sic*] at Erusegundo."[43] The same message stated that all these ships were
planning to rendezvous at some point in the Pacific: "It is understood that
a number of United States destroyers are on maneuvers at the present time.
Rumor has it that they are bound for Vladivostok."[44] An August 21 message,
also from Los Angeles, stated that "the Russian ship *Vladimar Mayskovsky*
arrived one or two days ago and entered dry dock for repairs which will
require a week or more. The present movements of the ship are - - -, but as
soon as it is repaired, it is going to California to load on freight for Vladivostok."[45] This message also described the whereabouts of the *Minsk* and
the *Patrovsuky*, both Russian ships.[46] An August 26 message from San Francisco described the movements and cargo of a Russian freighter, the *Yakut*,
and the movements of two other Russian ships.[47] A September 8 message,

also from San Francisco, stated that "the *Minsk*, having completed its repairs, left here on the 6th loaded with 8,000 drums of aviation oil, airplane engines, machine guns, ammunition, snow plows, etc."[48] A September 18 message stated that a Russian freighter had entered port in San Francisco from Vladivostok, and that the American tanker LP *St. Clair* was expected to arrive on the 19th.[49] An October 12 message from Los Angeles described movements of the Russian ship the *Kiev*.[50]

A message sent on September 4 from Washington asked the Seattle, San Francisco, and Los Angeles consulates to provide intelligence on the Russian Military Commission, which had just arrived in the United States.[51] In response, a September 6 message from Los Angeles to Tokyo stated that "the Russian Air Mission inspected the B-19 heavy bomber at March Field on the 2nd, and on the 3rd came to Los Angeles where they are inspecting various airplane facilities."[52] A September 20 message from Seattle to Tokyo stated that two Soviet planes had left Sand Point the day before, "Of the forty-seven members of the mission, ten of them returned with the hydroplanes (five on each ship). The remaining thirty-seven members are staying in the United States to study the production of airplanes."[53] A September 22 message from Seattle to Tokyo stated that nineteen of the thirty-seven Russians who were left behind were "receiving training in bomber operation (?) at Spokane."[54]

Some of this intelligence was relayed to Japan's Berlin consulate. An August 21 message from Tokyo to Berlin stated that "America appears to have begun the transportation of oil to Russia using American, Russian and neutral ships. There are also reports that perhaps several hundred airplanes have been transported."[55] Given the close relationship between Oshima Hiroshi, the Japanese ambassdor to the Third Reich, and top-ranking German officials, it would not be surprising if this information was passed on to Hitler himself.

Much of the intelligence regarding the entrance and exit of ships and airplanes presumably was based on surveillance or espionage by Japan's agents. A few of the messages, however, contained information from open sources. A September 4 message from Seattle to Tokyo, for example, described a statement of a Boeing official to a U.S. Senate committee.[56] The same message described a public announcement made by Lieutenant General John DeWitt (who would later play a key role in the West Coast evacuation of ethnic Japanese).[57] A September 16 message from Los Angeles to Tokyo furnishing detailed information about several defense contractors[58] apparently was obtained from an article published in the *Los Angeles Times*.

It must be borne in mind that the MAGIC messages were only a small portion of Japan's communications. Only a fraction of Japan's diplomatic radio traffic was successfully intercepted. Japan was also sending vital information through diplomatic pouches out of U.S. cryptanalysts' reach and via naval and military codes, some of which were only partially cracked or not cracked at all until after the war.

The value of MAGIC was underscored by the fatal neglect of the coded diplomatic traffic between Tokyo and Honolulu in the weeks prior to the Pearl Harbor attack. The messages had a different character from those sent to and from other consulates—they were more detailed and more urgent in tone, with Tokyo demanding a steady stream of information on fleet exercises, barrage balloons, anti-torpedo nets, and naval air reconnaissance.[59] A September 24, 1941, message requested that information on ship locations be divided into five parts:

FROM: Tokyo (Toyoda)   September 24, 1941
TO: Honolulu   # 83
Strictly Secret.

 Henceforth, we would like to have you make reports concerning vessels along the following lines insofar as possible:

1. The waters (of Pearl Harbor) are to be divided roughly into five subareas. (We have no objections to your abbreviating as much as you like.)

 Area A. Waters between Ford Island and the Arsenal.

 Area B. Waters adjacent to the Island south and west of Ford Island. (This area is on the opposite side of the Island from Area A.)

 Area C. East Loch.

Area D. Middle Loch.

Area E. West Loch and the communicating water routes.

2. With regard to warships and aircraft carriers, we would like to have you report on those at anchor, (these are not so important) tied up at wharves, buoys and in docks. (Designate types and classes briefly. If possible we would like to have you make mention of the fact when there are two or more vessels along side the same wharf.)[60]

A November 15, 1941, message from Tokyo to Honolulu stated, "As relations between Japan and the United States are most critical, make your 'ships in harbor report' irregular, but at a rate of twice a week. Although you already are no doubt aware, please take extra care to maintain secrecy."[61] A series of messages sent from Honolulu to Tokyo in the latter half of November and the first days of December provided painstakingly detailed reports on the ship moorings and movements within each of the five subareas in Pearl Harbor[62] (see Appendix B).

Coupled with other information, including messages from Tokyo ordering its diplomats to immediately destroy their cipher machines and codebooks,[63] the Tokyo–Honolulu messages were, as author James Gannon put it, "a smoking gun" signaling impending war—but because of decryption backlogs, courier delays, petty rivalries, and bureaucratic bungling, not a single one of them reached Hawaii before December 7.[64] It was a monumental mistake—one that Roosevelt and his top advisers were determined not to make twice.

Chapter 6

The Internment
of Enemy Aliens

T he date that would live in infamy had barely begun. Battleship
Row still smoldered. Immediately following the Pearl Harbor
attack, local and federal authorities launched their counteroffensive
by rounding up foreign nationals from Axis nations who had been deemed
"dangerous enemy aliens" by the Department of Justice. Within one week
of the air raid, a total of 2,451 Axis nationals in the United States and Hawaii
considered dangerous—including 1,002 Germans, 169 Italians, and 1,370
Japanese—had been apprehended by FBI agents. Under the direction of
Department of Justice official Edward J. Ennis, a network of screening
boards would review each alien detainee's case and recommend release,
parole, or internment for the duration of the war.

In all, more than 31,275 citizens of Axis countries and abettor nations
were interned during the course of the war.[1] This included the following:

25,655 enemy aliens
- 11,229 Japanese
  - 8,004 from the continental U.S.
  - 910 from Hawaii
  - 95 from Alaska
  - 2,220 from Latin America (mostly Peru)

- 10,905 Germans
- 3,278 Italians
- 52 Hungarians
- 25 Romanians
- 5 Bulgarians
- 161 others

5,620 *Nisei* who renounced their U.S. citizenship, becoming deportable Japanese enemy aliens

Enemy aliens of European ancestry made up nearly half of the total internee population. The statistics make clear that FDR's internment measures were based not on anti-Japanese racism, as so many Asian-American activists now claim, but on common-sense *nationality* distinctions in time of war.

A Tradition of Wartime Profiling

America's wartime internment of enemy aliens is deplored by modern ethnic activists, but it was the norm around the world during both world wars. During World War I, Canada interned some eighty-five hundred enemy aliens from Germany, Ukraine, and other Austro-Hungarian states;[2] Australia interned sailors arrested on ships and German enemy aliens from British possessions in Asia;[3] Britain interned thousands of its resident enemy aliens at camps on the Isle of Man;[4] New Zealand interned enemy aliens at Somes Island.[5] During World War II, virtually every major country—from Japan to Germany, from China to Egypt, from Holland to New Zealand—interned its enemy aliens. (Japanese Americans who resided in Japan, however, generally were not interned, presumably because they were dual citizens and hence were not considered enemy aliens. Indeed, many Japanese Americans served in Japan's military.)

As mentioned at the outset of this book, the U.S. government's well-established authority to detain and deport enemy aliens from hostile nations comes from Title 50 of the U.S. Code, based on the Alien Enemies Act of 1798, which remains on the books today.[6] During the War of 1812, the

United States removed British citizens from East Coast cities and interned them in nearby towns. During World War I, the United States interned some six thousand three hundred German, Austrian, Greek, Dutch, French, Belgian, and other European-born civilians.[7] Approximately one-third of those interned by the U.S. during World War I were repatriated to Europe. Under authority granted by the Alien Enemies Act, President Woodrow Wilson required those enemy aliens who were not interned to register at post offices and carry a government registration card at all times. They were also forbidden to own guns, radios, or explosives, or live within a half-mile of munitions factories, aircraft stations, forts, arsenals, or naval vessels.[8] Additional restrictions required enemy aliens at large to register at U.S. post offices and report any change of residence or employment to the government.

As World War II loomed, America began taking necessary steps to track potential national security threats within its alien population. After Britain and France declared war against Germany and Italy in September 1939, President Roosevelt ordered the FBI, MID, and Office of Naval Intelligence (ONI) to control all espionage, counter-espionage, and sabotage investigations. In December of that year, FBI Director J. Edgar Hoover notified his special agents that he was preparing a list of individuals, both aliens and citizens, who were considered potentially dangerous in the event of war. The list came to be known as the Custodial Detention Index.

The Special Defense Unit of the DOJ compiled its own list, modeled after a British national security program, which classified aliens in three categories: (A) leaders of nonpolitical cultural organizations considered dangerous because they were influential in their ethnic communities or their work could facilitate espionage; (B) potentially dangerous members of such organizations; and (C) donors and non-dues-paying supporters of such organizations who merited close observation.[9] This became known as the ABC list. The organizations under watch included the Japanese military *kais*, the Federation of Italian War Veterans, and the pro-Nazi German-American Bund.

In addition, Congress passed the Alien Registration Act in 1940, requiring all aliens fourteen years old and up to register with the U.S. government and submit their fingerprints, address, date and place of birth, physical description, occupation, arrest record, number of relatives in the United States and membership in clubs, organizations, and societies among other data. A total of 4,921,452 foreign nationals complied with the registration requirements.[10] Similar enemy alien registrations occurred during the War of 1812 and World War I. In the spring of 1941, Roosevelt issued Proclamation 2487, which declared a state of "unlimited national emergency" as a result of the outbreak of war in Europe and established defense measures to "repel the threat of predatory incursion by foreign agents into our territory and society." (Recall that enforcement of the Alien Enemies Act required either the declaration of war or a public proclamation of a perpetrated, attempted, or threatened invasion or predatory incursion by foreign enemies.) In the summer of 1941, the secretary of war and attorney general forged an agreement on general procedures for the apprehension, exclusion, detention, and internment of enemy aliens in the event of war.[11]

Following the Pearl Harbor attack and pursuant to the Alien Enemies Act, Roosevelt issued Presidential Proclamations 2525, 2526, and 2527, designating Japanese, German, and Italian nationals respectively as enemy aliens. A blanket presidential warrant authorized U.S. Attorney General Francis Biddle to have the FBI arrest enemy aliens identified on the Custodial Detention Index and ABC lists, as well as all other enemy aliens deemed dangerous to the public peace and safety of the country. The West Coast— with its vast number of military installations, airplane production plants, agricultural resources, and other strategic facilities and industries—was declared a theater of war. The Western Defense Command was established with Lieutenant General John L. DeWitt as commander. The enemy alien proclamations authorized not only internment, but also property ownership restrictions and travel bans in these sensitive areas. As in World War I, enemy aliens were prohibited from owning guns and radios; they could not fly without permission; and their presence was barred from railroads, waterways, and utilities.

Despite advance planning as the administration braced for war, those involved in the enemy alien program experienced many procedural hurdles and bureaucratic snafus in the post–Pearl Harbor chaos. Hoover scrupulously warned his agents not to arrest any American citizens under the authority of the enemy alien proclamations, but some districts received faulty lists that mistakenly included citizens; some arrests "had to be held up for several hours while we checked our files in order that we might be sure we were not arresting American citizens," Hoover noted on the morning of December 9.[12] Meanwhile, the Western Defense Command believed Attorney General Francis Biddle was engaged in foot-dragging over the full implementation of the proclamations, particularly enforcement of the regulations prohibiting aliens from possessing contraband items.

After Hoover's urging, the federal government ratcheted up registration requirements in January 1942 and ordered all noncitizens to return to their local post offices to apply for certificates of identification. A copy of each alien's photo ID card was sent to a local FBI office. During the next month, the military and DOJ established strategic zones surrounding vital West Coast installations off-limits to all enemy aliens. Strict curfew laws were enacted. The entire coastline of California extending from thirty to one hundred fifty miles inland was declared a restricted area for all enemy aliens. Spot searches for contraband were conducted in the homes of enemy aliens.

Military authorities were especially worried about illicit radio transmissions. This was not the result of "wartime hysteria" but of concern well grounded in MAGIC decrypts and other intelligence. As early as 1940, the FBI had seized a shortwave radio set from an ethnic Japanese family near a Bremerton, Washington, naval facility.[13] The search of Itaru Tachibana's files revealed a message from a spy named Fukuchi who suggested setting up a small mining company in the mountains of southwest Arizona as cover for transmitting radio signals to Japanese submarines.[14] A July 7, 1941, MAGIC cable from Tokyo to Washington revealed Japan's desire to send intelligence dispatches with wireless sets "under the guise of 'amateur use.'"[15] A month later, Japan's Washington consulate replied that interference would make it difficult to use such a radio set in the embassy compound.[16] Three days before Pearl Harbor, an ONI memo noted the following:

There is strong evidence that the Naval Attache's Office in Washington operates short-wave sending and receiving set disguised as an "Amateur Station," and that it is linked to the numerous "Ham" stations known to be operated by Japanese on the West Coast and in Hawaii. This fact has yet to be proved, but the interest shown by the Naval Inspector for Radio in New York City seems to be a bit out of the ordinary. In addition, leads from a radio transmitting antenna enter the building of the Japanese Embassy in Washington, and one of the Embassy clerks recently made an unsuccessful attempt to secure an amateur radio operator's license.[17]

More than a month after the Pearl Harbor attack and the initial enemy alien roundup, concerns had not been allayed. A January 16, 1942, letter from FBI director J. Edgar Hoover to Federal Communications Chairman James L. Fly sounded the alarm over continuing transmissions of illicit radio stations in the Hawaiian Islands. It "is apparent that illicit short-wave radio transmissions are being sent from clandestine stations operating in the islands themselves, in communication with mobile units of the Japanese Navy, through which intelligence information is being reported to the enemy," Hoover wrote. "It is extremely important that clandestine stations be located and eliminated from operation and that the individuals concerned with their operation be dealt with appropriately as rapidly as possible."[18] Two weeks later, in a confidential February 1, 1942, memo, Hoover stated that the army had neglected to deal with intercepted radio transmissions at Point Reyes, California.[19] (Much of this alleged traffic was later debunked, but this was not known when the evacuation decision was made.)

FBI raids a week later turned up numerous illegal short-wave radio sets and equipment in Portland, Seattle, and the Palos Verdes Hills area of Los Angeles adjoining Fort MacArthur.[20] One search turned up "seven radio sets capable of receiving shortwave, one radio oscillator, four boxes of assorted radio equipment, two cameras, twenty-three flashlights, four large searchlights, three telegraphers' keys, one small radio transmitting set, one microphone, one .38 caliber revolver, fifty cartridges, one .22 caliber rifle, four blasting caps, three pounds of black powder, three feet of fuse, and two reels of 8 millimeter film containing photographs of battleships and fortifications."[21] All of this equipment was prohibited under the president's enemy alien proclamations. There were innocent explanations and legitimate uses for some of these items. But post-Pearl Harbor, the concern of intelligence officials over such illegal contraband was certainly warranted.

The Justice Department made clear that enemy alien detainees in America would be treated according to international human rights standards. Federal detention rules—based on the Geneva Convention of 1929—outlined requirements for food, religious services, visitors, clothing, and sleeping provisions.[22] "Physical coercions must not be resorted to....No measures calculated to humiliate or degrade shall be undertaken," the instructions read.[23] Unlike many other countries, the United States allowed many family members—including American-born children and spouses—upon their request, to join internees in the camps. (Chapter 9 will cover camp conditions in greater detail.) These measures were taken not merely out of compassion but also because it was hoped that treating enemy aliens humanely would prompt reciprocal humane treatment of U.S. civilians and soldiers captured by the Axis powers. "Nothing must be done or permitted to be done... [which would provide] an excuse under the guise of retaliation for harsh treatment and cruel abuse of nationals of this country in the hands of our enemies," wrote a DOJ official.[24]

Unfortunately, such consideration for the well-being of enemy aliens in the United States did not prevent the brutal wartime atrocities committed by the Axis powers—especially Japan—against our civilians and prisoners of war abroad. Snubbing international conventions followed by its Western counterparts, Japan put more than five thousand American civilian men, women, and children living in the Philippines into harsh internment camps plagued by malnutrition, disease, torture, and executions.[25] From China to Java, from the Bataan Death March to the Thai-Burma Death Railway, from the transport of thousands of American POWs on unmarked Japanese "hell ships" to the kidnapping and forced services in brothels of over one hundred thousand civilian "comfort women" across Asia,[26] Imperial Japanese forces perpetrated atrocities on an unprecedented scale against civilians and prisoners of war alike in occupied countries.

The German and Italian Seamen

In the spring of 1941, the United States rounded up German and Italian merchant seamen whose ships had been stranded at American ports. The British had refused to assure safe transatlantic passage to ships carrying crewmembers from Axis countries. Some 775 Italian and 69 German seamen were served warrants for having overstayed the 60-day limit allowed to alien merchant seamen in any U.S. territory.[27] They were sent to internment camps at Fort Lincoln in North Dakota, Fort Stanton in New Mexico, and Fort Missoula in Montana.[28] Also interned at Fort Missoula in May were 125 Italian civilians who had worked in the United States as World's Fair employees, as well as the crew and entertainment staff of *Il Conte Biancamano*, an Italian luxury liner seized in the Panama Canal.[29] More Italian seamen continued to stream in, and by October 1942 there were 1,133 in captivity at Fort Missoula.[30]

The Latin American Internees

In January 1942, the United States convened an Emergency Advisory Committee for Political Defense in Rio de Janeiro. Foreign ministers in South America and Central America agreed with American counterparts on a plan to deport Axis enemy aliens to America. Those deported included approximately 4,100 ethnic Germans, 2,300 ethnic Japanese, and 300 ethnic Italians. They were brought to the United States on ships under military guard, deemed illegal enemy aliens upon landing, and then sent to internment camps at Crystal City, Seagoville, and Kenedy—all in Texas.

Critics have characterized the agreement as a racist "kidnapping" plot[31] or a "cunning" imperialist plan[32] driven by nativist resentment of Axis residents in Latin America. But both U.S. and Latin American leaders had legitimate national security concerns. Before the outbreak of war, the U.S. State

Department had raised alarm over Nazi penetration in Brazil, Argentina, Paraguay, Guatemala, and Bolivia.[33] Pro-Nazi Falangists flooded Latin America after General Franco's victory in Spain. The Nazi Party had created a special unit for the recruitment of German expatriates, the Auslandsorganisation (Foreign Organization), to unite the German communities of Latin America solidly behind Hitler.[34] Both American and Latin American intelligence agencies also worried about long-established Japanese espionage rings from Baja California to Brazil.[35] The security of the Panama Canal was of particular concern.

These concerns were supported by dozens of MAGIC messages sent to and from Japan's Latin American consulates in 1941. A February 5, 1941, message from Tokyo to Mexico City asked Latin American consular offices to organize Japanese residents in Central and South America for espionage activities. A June 2, 1941, message from Tokyo to Mexico revealed that in the event of war with the United States, Japan's headquarters for U.S. espionage would be moved to Mexico City, Rio de Janeiro, Buenos Aires, and Santiago.[36] More than a dozen messages sent from Panama to Tokyo and Washington, D.C., throughout the summer and fall provided detailed descriptions of ships passing through the strategically crucial Canal. Axis espionage and sabotage in Latin America, in short, were bona fide threats.

Another motivation for the roundup was to enable the United States to trade Axis nationals for American civilian nationals interned by Axis powers abroad. The United States sent eight hundred Japanese Latin American internees to Japan in exchange for U.S. civilians who had been interned by Japan. At least two thousand German Latin American internees and their family members were traded for Americans and Latin Americans held by the Third Reich in Germany.[37]

THE TERMINAL ISLAND INTERNEES

Terminal Island is located in a strategic area within Los Angeles Harbor. At the time of the Pearl Harbor attack, the tiny tract sandwiched between San Pedro to the west and Long Beach to the east was shared by one of the nation's six naval operating bases, one hundred fifty oil-producing wells, and an isolated Japanese community of several thousand ethnic Japanese—most of them involved in the fishing and canning industries. Following the Oahu air raid, federal authorities immediately removed a number of Terminal Island enemy aliens considered dangerous and sent them to internment camps in Montana and North Dakota. In late January 1942, the island was designated a strategic area from which enemy aliens would be barred. In early February, hundreds of Japanese enemy aliens with commercial fishing licenses who were considered potentially dangerous were taken into custody by the Justice Department. A total of about 375 Terminal Island *Issei* were interned during the course of the war.

Based on years of intelligence abroad and at home, intelligence officials had considerable cause for concern about the potential for sabotage by Japanese fishermen. In Malaya, for example, the British had long suspected that Japanese fishing boats—many of which were outfitted with expensive equipment and detailed maps unnecessary for fishing—were gathering intelligence for the Japanese Navy.[38] Intelligence officers were similarly worried about the Japanese on Terminal Island. One intelligence report noted that the island was "a stretch of open beach ideally suited for landing purposes, extending for fifteen or twenty-one miles, on which almost the only inhabitants were ethnic Japanese. Such a distribution of the Japanese population appeared to manifest something more than coincidence."[39]

A MAGIC message intercepted from Japan's Los Angeles consulate to Tokyo in May 1941 reported that espionage agents had "already established contacts with absolutely reliable Japanese in the San Pedro and San Diego area[s], who will keep a close watch on all shipments of airplanes and other war materials, and report the amounts and destinations of such shipments."[40]

A SOUND LEGAL AND LOGICAL BASIS

The constitutionality of enemy alien internment was reaffirmed by the U.S. Supreme Court after the end of World War II.[41] In *Johnson v. Eisentrager*, the high court concluded:

Executive power over enemy aliens, undelayed and unhampered by litigation, has been deemed, throughout our history, essential to war-time security. This is in keeping with the practice of the most enlightened of nations and has resulted in treatment of alien enemies more considerate than that which has prevailed among any of our enemies and some of our allies. This statute was enacted or suffered to continue by men who helped found the Republic and formulate the Bill of Rights, and although it obviously denies enemy aliens the constitutional immunities of citizens, it seems not then to have been supposed that a nation's obligations to its foes could ever be put on a parity with those of its defenders. The resident enemy alien is constitutionally subject to summary arrest, internment and deportation whenever a 'declared war' exists.[42]

In short, internment in an enemy country during wartime is par for the course. Americans caught in Axis countries or Axis-occupied territories were fortunate if getting locked up was all that happened to them.

Some opponents of the World War II internment of enemy aliens argue against making distinctions between enemy aliens and U.S. citizens. Georgetown University law professor David Cole complains that the Alien Enemies Act "substitutes a group-based presumption of potential threat for individualized determinations of actual culpability and equates nationality with dangerousness.[43] Of course it does. It would be idiotic—and suicidal— to presume that foreign nationals from hostile countries *with which we are at war* are as loyal or friendly to the United States as native-born Americans or naturalized citizens who have sworn sole allegiance to their adopted homeland.

Chapter 7

The Rationale for Evacuation

Despite the internment of thousands of enemy aliens in the weeks following the Pearl Harbor attack and the implementation of alien registration requirements, curfew laws, and travel limitations, America's wartime leaders remained concerned about the threat from within. Now that suspicious enemy aliens had been rounded up, to what extent might disloyal American citizens pose a threat?

The problem was especially vexing on the West Coast, home to many strategic army and naval installations, aircraft factories, shipyards, and other war plants and vital defense resources and utilities. Indeed, it contained one-fourth of the nation's aircraft production and one-third of its shipbuilding capacity. Through the three major ports of Seattle, San Francisco, and Los Angeles, vast quantities of men and matériel were being shipped to the war zones of the Pacific. Immediately after the Pearl Harbor attack, General George Marshall and his staff "worked feverishly to strengthen the west coast defenses as rapidly as they could," according to army historian Stetson Conn.[1]

Was the alien enemy control program run by the Justice Department sufficient to combat possible espionage, sabotage, and fifth column activity in this vulnerable zone? Roosevelt relied on a variety of sources to cast light on this question—not only official intelligence agents at the ONI, the MID, and the FBI, but his own confidential network of civilian informants which he had established in early 1941 using a secret slush fund.

In the fall of 1941, after MAGIC messages had revealed Japan's creation of espionage networks in the United States, Roosevelt commissioned this coterie of confidants to prepare a secret study of the "Japanese situation" on the West Coast and in Hawaii. The main objective of the study was to determine whether ethnic Japanese, both *Issei* and *Nisei*, were engaged in espionage or other disloyal activities, and whether they would side with Japan in the event of a war. Roosevelt confidant John Franklin Carter meted out this particular assignment to Curtis Munson, a wealthy civilian businessman from Chicago with no previous intelligence experience and no access to the MAGIC messages. Somewhat of a blowhard, Munson filed his first (admittedly hurried) report to Carter, who then passed it to the president in November 1941 after spending three weeks studying the issue on the West Coast. After kibbitzing with locals and chatting with a few district-level intelligence officers, Munson proclaimed that *Nisei* were "universally estimated from 90 to 98 percent loyal to the United States if the Japanese educated element of the *Kibei* is excluded."[2] He also indicated that a very small number of ethnic Japanese, either paid agents of the Japanese government or fanatical worshipers of the emperor, would engage in suicide bombing attacks against key U.S. targets. In Munson's view, then, the *Kibei* (who numbered more than 9,000 on the West Coast) along with 2 percent to 10 percent of non-*Kibei Nisei*, had questionable loyalties, and an unknown number of these were willing to give their lives in support of the Japanese war effort. While attempting to put a positive spin on the situation, Munson was troubled that key West Coast installations were appallingly vulnerable to sabotage:

> Your reporter. . . is horrified to note that dams, bridges, harbors, power stations, etc. are wholly unguarded everywhere, The harbor at San Pedro could be razed by fire completely by four men with grenades and a little study in one night. Dams could be blown and half of lower California might actually die of thirst. One railway bridge at the exit from the

mountains in some cases could tie up three or four main railroads . . . his
is the second greatest port in the United States! This is the home base of
at least the South Pacific Fleet! This is the greatest collection of inflam-
mable [sic] material we have ever seen in our lifetime concentrated in a
small vulnerable area![3]

Munson concluded that while the Japanese "are loyal on the whole . . . we
are wide open to sabotage on this Coast and as far inland as the mountains,
and while this one fact goes unrectified I cannot unqualifiedly state that
there is no danger from the Japanese living in the United States which otherwise I would be willing to state."[4] Roosevelt was sufficiently alarmed by
Munson's observations on sabotage that he dashed off a personal note
directing Secretary of War Henry Stimson to look into it.[5] After a nine-day
visit to Honolulu, Munson came to similar conclusions regarding the ethnic Japanese in Hawaii, where he guessed that while *Nisei* were "approximately ninety-eight percent loyal . . . it would mean that fifteen hundred
were disloyal."[6]

The Munson reports have been immortalized by critics of the West Coast
evacuation as "definitive loyalty findings" and "certification of Japanese
American loyalty"[7] that "conclusively repudiated the existence of Japanese
fifth column forces in America and should have laid to rest any fears about
the internal security of the West Coast."[8] But the FBI didn't think much of
Munson or his reports. The agency's internal analyses of his work noted that
he admitted "no knowledge . . . of investigative work"; his November 1941
report contained "no specific factual information of importance to the
Bureau"; and his pronunciations about ethnic Japanese loyalties were
"purely theoretical and conjectural." One agent reported that "Munson did
considerable talking and probably gave people more information than he
got out of them."[9]

After Pearl Harbor, Munson erroneously stated that espionage in Honolulu had been carried out entirely "by Caucasians and by paid infiltrators
brought from Japan."[10] Nonetheless, he urged law enforcement officials to
take aggressive action against suspect *Nisei*. In a December 10, 1941, FBI

memo from Special Agent in Charge R. B. Hood to Director J. Edgar Hoover (see Appendix C), Hood recounts a conversation with Munson in which Munson upbraided the FBI agent for not taking more aggressive measures to round up suspect *Nisei* on the West Coast. Hood explained that the FBI was authorized to apprehend suspicious *Issei* only—not *Nisei*—"and, therefore, we cannot take any action against any other group at this time." According to Hood, Munson responded that:

> Only half of the persons who should be picked up have to date been apprehended because we have not gone into the citizens group; and it is his impression from what he has learned on the Coast that the citizens who are disloyal constitute a large group of possible troublemakers in the emergency. He feels that the apprehension of the aliens is only half of the job, and the citizens constitute the other half of it.[11]

In addition, Munson supported racial profiling. A plan he promoted to President Roosevelt in late December 1941 would have subjected *Nisei* working in defense plants to heightened scrutiny.[12]

OMINOUS SIGNS OF INTELLIGENCE

A number of post–Pearl Harbor intelligence reports warned that threats from ethnic Japanese persisted within the U.S. mainland. A December 24, 1941, ONI memo reported, "Although handicapped by the detention of many of its key individuals, the Japanese Intelligence Network in this hemisphere continues in operation."[13] Another ONI report the same day noted:

> It must constantly be kept in mind in this connection that Japan strove to put into operation in the United States and its territories a highly integrated and specialized intelligence network which could 'take over' from regular established agencies in wartime.

Under such circumstances, Japanese nationals and pro-Japanese *Nisei* who are well settled in normal and yet strategic occupations are likely to be the mainstay of Japanese espionage-sabotage operations in this country.[14]

A January 3, 1942, army MID memo echoed the ONI's findings, stating that "there can be no doubt that" most of the leaders within the Japanese espionage network of Japanese clubs, business groups, and labor organizations "continue to function as key operatives for the Japanese government along the West Coast."[15] The commanders of the Twelfth and Thirteenth Naval Districts called for all American-born ethnic Japanese who could not show "actual severance of all allegiance to the Japanese Government" to be excluded from the coast.[16] The army braced itself for "raiding parties" of Japanese consisting of "small groups of men sent for the purpose of disturbing the morale of the citizenry" on the West Coast.[17]

In short, the U.S. intelligence community was clear, consistent, and unequivocal in warning of ongoing espionage on the West Coast, just as it had been before Pearl Harbor, when these warnings were underpinned by the MAGIC messages. The "experts" who now flatly assert that the intelligence community "saw only a very limited security risk from the ethnic Japanese"[18] are either unaware of these warnings or are deliberately ignoring them because they do not fit their preconceived notions regarding the reasons for the evacuation and relocation decisions.

As the Roosevelt administration contemplated its options, officials in other countries moved forward with evacuation programs to ensure the safety of coastal areas vulnerable to invasion and raids. With Japan posing the most immediate threat—it was the only Axis country capable of launching an invasion—these evacuation programs focused exclusively on ethnic Japanese. In late December 1941, the commander of the Canadian Army's Pacific forces recommended that all ethnic Japanese, three-quarters of whom were Canadian citizens,[19] be immediately evacuated from Canada's west coast.[20] This recommendation was quickly implemented, and by March

1942, all ethnic Japanese living on Vancouver Island and in coastal regions had been evacuated; soon after, twenty-one thousand more ethnic Japanese were moved away from the "Defence Zone"—a one hundred-mile-wide coastal area of British Columbia.[21] Earlier, a MAGIC message had revealed Tokyo's order to Japan's Vancouver consulate to devote particular attention in intelligence-gathering to "General outlooks on Alaska and the Aleutian Islands, which particular stress on items involving plane movements and shipment of military supplies to those localities."[22]

On January 2, 1942, Mexico ordered ethnic Japanese, including Mexican citizens, to relocate away from both the West Coast and a sixty-two-mile long strip along the U.S.-Mexico border.[23] Earlier, a number of MAGIC messages had revealed Tokyo's plan to move espionage operations to Mexico in the event of war with the United States. A July 4, 1941, message from Mexico City to Tokyo stated:

> It is clear that one of the most urgent requirements of the present time is the establishment of an (international ?) route for the communication of intelligences between the United States and Mexico. In my opinion, this route which is to be established should be used by our embassy, the consular offices, and semi-official offices in the United States, as well as in espionage net connections with Mexico City.
>
> In the case of war, the method under consideration involves the direct linking of all our espionage agents in the United States directly with this city. The various observations and opinions gathered from our espionage net in the United States should, in my opinion, be carried out here.[24]

A July 19, 1941, message—also from Mexico City to Tokyo—revealed that Japan's consular officials had met with representatives of ethnic Japanese in Mexico, and that these representatives had pledged that they would "do everything in their power to adhere to our [consular officials'] decisions."[25]

Did intelligence derived from MAGIC influence Canada and Mexico's decision to undertake evacuations? It is worth noting that the United States had delivered components to construct a copy of the PURPLE-encoding machine to the British in February 1941 in exchange for some Allied code-breaking secrets, and that Roosevelt was in regular contact with Canadian Premier Mackenzie King.[26] Whether the U.S. or Britain shared MAGIC intelligence with Canada or Mexico, possibly influencing their decisions to evacuate ethnic Japanese from their coasts, has not been explored in the extensive literature I have reviewed.

On January 25, the "Roberts Report" was publicly released. The report, which confirmed the existence of the Honolulu-based espionage ring discussed in Chapter 3, was issued by a commission chaired by Supreme Court Justice Owen Roberts. The report stated that "There were, prior to December 7, 1941, Japanese spies on the island of Oahu. Some were Japanese consular agents and other persons having no relations with the Japanese foreign service. These spies collected, and through various channels, transmitted, information to the Japanese Empire respecting the military and naval establishments and dispositions on the island."[27] (The Roberts report is derided as "exceedingly vague"[28] by modern critics such as scholar Greg Robinson. But as Army Chief of Staff George C. Marshall pointed out in 1944 in a private letter to Republican presidential candidate Thomas Dewey, the Roberts report "had to have withdrawn from it all reference to" top-secret MAGIC to protect the code-breaking operation from being compromised and "therefore in portions it necessarily appeared incomplete."[29]) Although Navy Secretary Frank Knox had made somewhat similar allegations a month earlier,[30] public acknowledgment of the spy network's existence by a prominent jurist received considerable attention and heightened legitimate anxieties among elected officials and the nation at large regarding ethnic Japanese on the West Coast, who—coincidence or not[31]—were concentrated in and around strategic military areas from Seattle down to San Diego.[32]

Just prior to the release of the report, Roberts met with Roosevelt twice—on January 18 and January 24—and with Secretary of War Henry Stimson once, on January 20. While there is no contemporaneous record of the conversations between Roberts and the president, Roberts told Stimson that a substantial number of ethnic Japanese in Hawaii were loyal to Japan. According to Stimson's diary, "The tremendous Japanese population in the Islands he regarded as a great menace particularly as a large portion of them are now armed under the draft. He did not think that the FBI had succeeded in getting under the crust of their secret thoughts at all and he believed that this great mass of Japanese, both aliens and Americanized, existed as a great potential danger in the Islands in case a pinch came in our fortunes."[33]

On January 26, the day after Roberts' report was released, Naval Lieutenant C. B. Baldwin issued a second intelligence report summarizing the shockingly disloyal behavior of Yoshio and Irene Harada on Niihau Island—reinforcing Roberts's assertions and, presumably, further exacerbating concerns among military leaders about the so-called "Japanese situation."

The same day the report on the Haradas was issued, January 26, 1942, Kenneth D. Ringle, a district-level ONI official who did not have clearance for MAGIC, sent a classified memo to the Chief of Naval Operations stating that "the large majority" of Japanese aliens were "at least passively loyal to the United States" and that the "Japanese problem" was no more serious than problems presented by ethnic Germans or Italians (see Appendix C). He recommended that Japanese agents be rooted out one at a time rather than through a race- or nationality-based mass evacuation. The memo, which was solicited by the chief of naval operations at the behest of Curtis Munson (who had befriended Ringle while in Los Angeles), was passed along to FBI director J. Edgar Hoover, who relayed Ringle's findings to Attorney General Francis Biddle.

The Ringle memo, which was leaked in October 1942 to *Harper's* magazine and published anonymously,[34] is heavily cited by modern anti-evacuation activists as evidence that the risks posed by ethnic Japanese were considered minor and that no intelligence officials believed the mass evacuation of West Coast ethnic Japanese was warranted. Yet while Ringle opposed mass evacuation, he stated that a substantial minority of ethnic Japanese, particularly *Kibei*, posed a very serious threat. Moreover, he estimated that as many as 25 percent of *Issei* were potentially disloyal and would pass along intelligence to Japan if given a convenient opportunity to do so. More ominously, he stated that up to 3,500 ethnic Japanese (including both *Issei* and *Nisei*) were active supporters of the Japanese war effort and could be expected to engage in sabotage or espionage (or both). Ringle went on to describe *Kibei* as "essentially and inherently Japanese in nature" despite their U.S. citizenship and suggested they "may have been deliberately sent back to the United States by the Japanese government to act as agents." He recommended that at least 1,200 *Kibei* living in Southern California be immediately placed in custodial detention—"in spite of their legal citizenship and the protection afforded to them by the Bill of Rights." In an expanded version of his memo written for the War Relocation Authority, he stated unequivocally that *all Kibei*, of which he estimated there were 8,000-9,000, should be guarded in detention camps, stripped of citizenship, and deported to Japan "at the first opportunity." He emphatically recommended that they be "considered guilty until proven innocent."[35] Finally, he endorsed racial profiling of *Nisei* involved in defense production activities, urging that they be subjected to more rigorous background investigations than Caucasian Americans;[36] discouraged the use of Japanese Americans as teachers for any ethnic Japanese detainees; and urged that Shintoism be banned because it was "not a true religion but a form of patriotism toward Japan."[37]

Ringle, in short, was no civil liberties purist. If he were alive today, he might well be perfectly comfortable with many of the measures being taken or contemplated by the Bush administration in the War on Terror. Indeed, his support for racial profiling would put him to the right of Attorney General John Ashcroft, who has publicly disavowed the practice.

Hoover—also cited favorably by modern critics of the World War II evacuation and relocation—held views similar to Ringle's. Though not persuaded that mass evacuation of the entire West Coast was necessary, he strongly supported actions to neutralize the threat posed by U.S. citizens who were believed to be subversive. Hoover urged that he be given the authority to confine such individuals without trial, and believed this authority could be granted through either a suspension of habeas corpus or an Act of Congress. In a December 17, 1941, memo to Assistant Attorney General

Francis Shea, he opined that "there should be some specific authority per-
mitting the apprehension of any citizen or alien as to whom there may be
reasonable cause to believe that such person has been or is engaging in giving aid or comfort to the enemies of the United States."[38] As a model,
Hoover mentioned Britain's Defense of the Realm Act, which gave that
nation's homeland security officials the authority to detain without charges
both aliens and citizens deemed pro-Axis sympathizers and subversives.
Later, Hoover gathered information in support of mass evacuation of ethnic
Japanese from specific areas, including San Diego (where local ethnic Japanese, many of whom were *Kibei*, had received military training in Japan, and
lived near strategic locations) and Seattle (where, according to Hoover's
memo, between ten thousand and twelve thousand dual citizens of questionable loyalties, plus five thousand *Issei* and their families, resided in critical areas near army and naval installations, the Boeing factory, and other
industrial plants).[39]

Hoover's opposition to mass evacuation of the entire West Coast may
have stemmed in part from his own sense of bureaucratic rivalry with the
Western Defense Command and his desire to receive credit and avoid
blame. Just weeks after the Pearl Harbor attack, Hoover and his agents
griped about the need to "get the credit" for picking up undesirable individuals on the West Coast and the need to "be careful that we don't get
caught holding the bag if these people start hollering and the Army comes
back by saying that they moved the people because the FBI said they were
bad."[40]

Western Defense Commander John DeWitt, who is often mistakenly por-
trayed by modern ethnic historians as the primary instigator of the West
Coast evacuation, at first opposed any measure that encompassed American
citizens. In a telephone conversation with Provost Marshal General Allen
Gullion on December 26, DeWitt observed:

> I'm very doubtful that it would be common sense procedure to try and
> intern or to intern 117,000 [ethnic] Japanese in this theater. . . . I told the
> governors of all the states that those people should be watched better if

they were watched by the police and people of the community in which they live and have been living for years... and then inform the F.B.I. or the military authorities of any suspicious action so we could take necessary steps to handle it... rather than try to intern all those people, men, women and children, and hold them under military control and under guard. I don't think it's a sensible thing to do... I'd rather go along the way we are now... rather than attempt any such wholesale internment.... An American citizen, after all, is an American citizen. And while they all may not be loyal, I think we can weed the disloyal out of the loyal and lock them up if necessary.[41]

DeWitt's preferred course at the end of 1941 was to rely on the Justice Department to vigorously enforce the enemy alien proclamations issued by President Roosevelt immediately after the Pearl Harbor attack. Smeared unfairly as a single-mindedly anti-Japanese racist by modern ethnic activists,[42] DeWitt had initially insisted that enemy aliens of every extraction on the West Coast be evacuated aggressively from a list of 88 vital defense areas, mostly around ports, bases, and factories. And he was adamantly opposed "to any preferential treatment to any alien irrespective of race."[43]

Derided today as a paper-pushing career bureaucrat, DeWitt was an able theater commander who took his mission—defending the coast—seriously. It appears that DeWitt did not have clearance to MAGIC in early 1942, but he did have access to intelligence reports that were derived from MAGIC— reports that warned of Japanese-controlled espionage cells up and down the West Coast. Notwithstanding the explanations DeWitt later gave in public as a possible cover story (for example, concerns about shore-to-ship signaling and vigilantism against ethnic Japanese, which were offered as justifications in his final report on the West Coast evacuation released publicly in January 1944), it was the MAGIC-derived intelligence that served as the principal basis for the recommendation to evacuate, according to War Department official Karl Bendetsen, assistant chief of staff of the 4th Army. At the time, the real reason for the evacuation could not be disclosed without revealing the fact that U.S. cryptanalysts had broken Japan's diplomatic codes.

The army's history of the evacuation, written by Stetson Conn long before the declassification of MAGIC, suggests that DeWitt was following the lead of military leaders and War Department officials in Washington, D.C.—not vice versa. On February 6, according to the army report, Provost Marshal General Gullion sent a memo to Assistant Secretary of War John McCloy advising that steps be taken immediately to eliminate what General Gullion described as "the great danger of Japanese-inspired sabotage on the West Coast." He advised that these steps should include the internment by the army of all alien Japanese east of the Sierra Nevada Mountains, together with as many citizen members of their families as would voluntarily accompany them, and the exclusion of all Americans of Japanese ancestry from restricted zones and their resettlement with the assistance of various federal agencies.[44] Gullion was dismayed that DeWitt had vacillated on the question of mass evacuation. When DeWitt apparently refused to rubber-stamp Gullion's recommendations, McCloy sent Bendetsen to the West Coast to confer with DeWitt personally—a mission "whose purpose was to produce new and detailed recommendations from the west coast commander." While drafting the plan, on February 11, General DeWitt referred to the recommendations collectively as "the plan that Mr. McCloy wanted me to submit."[45] McCloy's files contain an unsigned February 8 memo that reads in part as follows:

> Japanese Evacuation, West Coast, Prepare definite instructions for DeWitt on following basis: Select key points where danger is great and size not too large. Put them in order of importance. Evacuate everybody, aliens and citizens. Institute system of permits. Whole matter to be handled by Army authorities. Then, as matter progresses, we will soon find out how far we can go.[46]

Under normal operations in the military, the local commander—in this case DeWitt—would be the one to make the recommendation based on his evaluation, which he would then send to War Department officials in Washington, D.C., for approval. This has been the assumption of virtually every popular account of the West Coast evacuation, written by historians convinced that DeWitt's alleged racism and West Coast hysteria drove the decision. In truth, the push came from higher up, where knowledge of the MAGIC intelligence outlining Japan's alarming espionage operations rested. Army historian Stetson Conn's account makes this clear. On February 11, 1942, McCloy informed Bendetsen that Roosevelt "had specifically authorized the evacuation of citizens."[47] This was two days before DeWitt's final recommendations had been sent to Washington, dated February 13. DeWitt's recommendations arrived at Army General Headquarters (GHQ) on the evening of February 18. The next day, GHQ staff decided to recommend against adopting DeWitt's plan to evacuate citizens from sensitive military areas and to instead limit the evacuation to enemy aliens. But General Mark Clark, the army deputy chief of staff, "recognized the futility of a GHQ nonconcurrence" and instead sent an endorsement of mass evacuation "in view of the proposed action already decided upon by the War Department."[48] The decision from the top had already been made.

When McCloy testified before Congress in 1984, he affirmed that the MAGIC cables helped shape the decisions of those who ordered the evacuation. He stated that he read MAGIC messages on a daily basis, and that it was a "very important" factor in the development of the evacuation policy.[49]

McCloy's eminent background is worth mentioning here. Born on the wrong side of the tracks in Philadelphia, McCloy put himself through college and Harvard Law School by waiting tables. He interrupted his education to serve as a U.S. Army field artillery captain and fought at the front in France during World War I. While working as a Wall Street lawyer, he made a name for himself in the investigation of the "Black Tom" case for a corporate client, Bethlehem Steel. In July 1916, a munitions depot at Black Tom Island on the Jersey City, New Jersey, waterfront exploded. At least three were killed and hundreds injured. For more than a decade, McCloy chased down leads in Baltimore, Vienna, Warsaw and Dublin to prove that German agents had caused the explosion. The case was settled when an international com-

mission at the Hague found Germany responsible for the blast.[50] Mr.
McCloy's tenacity and expertise caught the attention of Secretary of War
Stimson. As Stimson described him in his memoirs, McCloy was "a man
whose record so distinguished him that Stimson's principal difficulty was to
retain his services for the War Department."[51] McCloy first served as a Stimson's counterintelligence adviser. In October 1940, he was appointed special
assistant, working on everything from the Lend-Lease Act to interdepart-
mental negotiations. The following spring, he became assistant secretary of
war. "His energy was enormous," Stimson wrote, and his opinion so highly
respected in Washington that Stimson "wondered whether anyone in the
administration ever acted without 'having a word with McCloy.'"[52]

ROOSEVELT MAKES A CHOICE

Even if Japan were operating espionage nets along the West Coast, the
forced evacuation and relocation of 112,000 ethnic Japanese might seem
unnecessarily draconian, since the proportion of ethnic Japanese involved
in espionage or other subversive activities presumably was small. But poli-
cymakers had no easy options. Mere monitoring of suspected subversives
seemed an inadequate response, given what was at stake and the scope of
the effort that would have been required. Bear in mind that close monitoring of ethnic Japanese agents in Honolulu had done nothing to prevent the
transmission of sensitive information to Tokyo. An alternative approach,
criminal prosecutions, would have proved largely fruitless because (a) many
of those suspected of serving Japan had not committed any crime (remember that the gathering and transmission of intelligence information from
open sources before the declaration of war, such as that performed by
Richard Kotoshirodo, probably was not criminal) and (b) where crimes
were suspected (for example, espionage or failure to register as a foreign
agent), classified intelligence could not be submitted as evidence. (See
Appendix D for a discussion of the administration's inability to secure a
criminal conviction of Kenji Ito, a Seattle-based *Nisei* who was apparently
referenced in one of the MAGIC messages.) A third option, imposition of

martial law, was never seriously considered outside of Hawaii. No one in the Roosevelt administration wanted to impose a *de facto* military dictatorship on millions of Americans living on the West Coast, as was done in Hawaii if other, less drastic actions would suffice. A fourth option, favored by ONI analyst Kenneth Ringle, was to set up some kind of quasi-judicial military tribunal to determine which *Nisei* could be locked up without a trial in a civilian court. This may have been unconstitutional—witness the current legal controversy regarding the detention of Jose Padilla and other enemy combatants—and had drawbacks from a military standpoint, both because of the time required to implement it and because it would not have resulted in the confinement of Japanese agents or sympathizers whose ties to Japan could not be unearthed by military authorities.

A fifth option—the one that ultimately was adopted—was exclusion and/or evacuation of ethnic Japanese from militarily sensitive areas. This approach, as noted above, was already being implemented by Canada and Mexico. By itself, evacuation would not eliminate the potential threat posed by ethnic Japanese, but it would severely disrupt established espionage cells and ensure that any subversive activities carried out by ethnic Japanese took place outside of the most vulnerable areas on the West Coast. It would also hinder surveillance of fleet movements at West Coast ports—an important component of the Japanese espionage network's activities.

No less important, it was the opinion of Biddle's legal advisers that evacuation was legal—an opinion later vindicated by the Supreme Court's decision in *Korematsu v. United States.*[53]

Once it was determined that evacuation was the preferred policy, several ancillary decisions had to be made. Should ethnic Japanese along the entire West Coast be evacuated or only those living in selected cities? Should all ethnic Japanese be evacuated or only those whom intelligence agencies considered high risks? Should low-risk groups—children, women, and the elderly—be evacuated, too? Certainly there was no legitimate military argument for evacuating, say, young children. On the other hand, most dependents could not be expected to survive on their own if the family breadwinner was forced to evacuate.

The War Department pressed for the establishment of military zones surrounding all vital national defense installations, from which all ethnic Japanese, alien and citizen alike, could be excluded.[54] Provost Marshal General Allen Gullion made the national security stakes clear:

> If our production for war is seriously delayed by sabotage in the West Coastal states, we very possibly shall lose the war... from reliable reports from military and other sources, the danger of Japanese-inspired espionage is great. That danger cannot be temporized with. No half-way measures based upon considerations of economic disturbance, humanitarianism, or fear of retaliation will suffice. Such measures may be 'too little and too late.'[55]

Biddle and several of his underlings at the Department of Justice continued to lobby against mass evacuation of *Nisei*, but McCloy and Stimson at the War Department ultimately prevailed. Clearly, these were difficult choices. Even with the benefit of hindsight (which War Department officials did not have), it is not at all clear that mass evacuation was unwarranted. At the very least, it should be obvious to any fair-minded person that the decisions made were not based primarily on racism and wartime hysteria. As Stimson noted in his diary on February 10, 1942:

> It is a terrific problem, particularly as I think it is quite within the bounds of possibility that if the Japanese should get naval dominance in the Pacific they would try an invasion of this country; and, if they did, we would have a tough job meeting them. The people of the United States have made an enormous mistake in underestimating the Japanese. They are now beginning to learn their mistake.[56]

Chapter 8

Executive Order 9066

uring the first two weeks of February 1942, FDR was preoccupied with a string of devastating losses being handed to the Allies by Japan in the Pacific and by its Axis partners in Europe. In the Dutch East Indies, Japanese forces had overcome Dutch and Australian forces on Amboina Island. Imperial attacks leveled Java, Srabaya, and other bases in the East Indies. The Brits were in disarray in North Africa, where German general Erwin Rommel's Afrika Korps romped from victory to victory. In the South China Sea, the British troop transport *Empress of Asia* was sunk by Japanese bombers off the coast of Singapore, which fell to Japan on February 15. In Malaya, the Allied counterattack against the Japanese invaders had failed miserably and forced a retreat.

So when Secretary of War Stimson requested a meeting with FDR on February 11 to discuss the details and logistics of a mass evacuation of aliens and citizens from the West Coast, it is not hard to understand why the president was too busy to discuss the matter in person. The president did what an effective leader does in wartime—he delegated authority and deferred to the judgment of his military experts. In a phone conversation with Stimson, FDR instructed his war secretary to do what he saw fit as dictated by military necessity. "He was very vigorous about it and told me to go ahead on the line that I had myself thought the best," Stimson noted in his diary.[1]

Stimson asked Assistant Secretary of War John McCloy to make a final update on the West Coast situation. McCloy in turn contacted General Mark Clark, the army deputy chief of staff, who provided McCloy with the latest army Military Intelligence Division (MID), assessment on Japanese espionage dated January 21, 1942.[2] This memo concluded that the "espionage net containing Japanese aliens, first- and second-generation Japanese, and other nationals is now thoroughly organized and working underground."[3] From his perch at the FBI, Hoover warned of the West Coast's continued vulnerability to attack. In a confidential February 1, 1942, memo, he outlined in scathing detail the army's failure to adequately defend the coastline, neglect of intercepted radio transmissions at Point Reyes, California, and inattention to unguarded strategic installations, including bridges, wharfs, dams, and (sounding a theme that has a familiar ring in the post-September 11 world) failure of various intelligence-gatherers to share information and coordinate efforts.[4] In a separate memo written the following day, Hoover noted that in Los Angeles, it was "impossible to keep any appreciable number [of ethnic Japanese] under surveillance so as to prevent espionage and sabotage" and that their location "near oil fields, ship yards, airplane factories and national defense factories" gave them "a splendid opportunity for 'fifth column' activity on their part if so inclined."[5] Around the same time, Hoover was also receiving pressure to evacuate—not from racists and political opportunists, but from Japanese Americans themselves. On February 9, Attorney General Francis Biddle sent to his assistant James Rowe a memo "from Mr. Hoover to the effect that the Japanese-American Citizens' League wants us to evacuate its members and alien parents." Biddle added, "I think we should begin exploring with Mr. McNutt the possibility of having some refugee camps for the Japs, which we will need."[6]

Meanwhile, the Roosevelt administration received the opinion of three liberal New Deal legal advisers on the constitutionality of evacuation. Benjamin Cohen, Oscar Cox, and Joseph Rauh[7] wrote:

> In time of national peril any reasonable doubt must be resolved in favor
> of action to preserve the national safety, not for the purpose of punishing

those whose liberty may be temporarily affected by such action, but for the purpose of protecting the freedom of the nation which may be long impaired, if not permanently lost, by non-action...

So long as a classification of persons or citizens is reasonably related to a genuine war need and does not under the guise of national defense discriminate against any class of citizens for a purpose unrelated to the national defense no constitutional guaranty is infringed. Such action as may be taken to meet the Japanese situation on the West Coast should be taken and considered not as a punitive measure against the Japanese, whether they be American citizens or aliens, but as a precautionary measure to protect the national safety.[8]

His plate full with wartime crises at home and around the world, Stimson met with McCloy, Gullion, Clark, and Bendetsen on February 17 to draft an order. Biddle signed off on it the next day. They did not take the job lightly. "It will involve the tremendous task of moving between fifty and one hundred thousand people from their homes and finding temporary support and sustenance for them in the meanwhile, and ultimately locating them in new places away from the coast," Stimson wrote in his diary.[9]

On February 19, 1942, Roosevelt signed Executive Order 9066 directing Stimson and his military commanders "to prescribe military areas in such places and of such extent as he or the appropriate Military Commanders may determine, from which any or all persons may be excluded, and with such respect to which, the right of any person to enter, remain in, or leave shall be subject to whatever restrictions the Secretary of War or the appropriate Military Commander may impose in his discretion." DeWitt appointed Bendetsen commanding officer of the Wartime Civil Control Administration, which was assigned to carry out the order. Four days after the order was signed, the Japanese shelled the Goleta, California, oil fields (see Chapter 2). "By the night of 24–25 February," when the panicked "Battle of Los Angeles" took place, "both the military defenders and the civilian population of the Los Angeles area were expecting the worst to happen at any time," reported army historian Stetson Conn.[10]

By a voice vote in both houses, Congress ratified E.O. 9066 on March 21 in the form of Public Law 503, making it a federal offense to violate any order issued by a designated military commander under authority of Executive Order No. 9066.

The order did not single out any race, but all of the key decision-makers understood that it was mainly ethnic Japanese who would be evacuated. Thousands of ethnic Germans and ethnic Italians, including hundreds of naturalized American citizens,[11] were excluded from military areas as well. In California, for example, over 10,000 Italian enemy aliens were evacuated from their homes and over 52,000 were subject to strict curfew regulations.[12] Additionally under the executive order, Eastern Defense Commander General Hugh Drum declared Maine, New Hampshire, Vermont, Massachusetts, Rhode Island, Connecticut, New York, New Jersey, Delaware, Pennsylvania, Maryland, Virginia, North and South Carolina, Georgia, parts of Florida, and the District of Columbia to be a military zone from which any and all persons could be excluded. The resulting exclusions on the East Coast, however, were few in number compared with the West Coast evacuation of ethnic Japanese.

The disparate treatment of ethnic Japanese versus ethnic Germans and ethnic Italians is often assumed to be based on anti-Japanese racism rather than military necessity. Japan, however, was the only Axis country with a proven capability of launching a major attack on the United States. Some ethnic Germans and ethnic Italians had divided loyalties, but there was no evidence that Germany or Italy had organized a large-scale espionage network akin to the one described by Japan's diplomats in the MAGIC messages. Moreover, any attempt to evacuate all ethnic Germans or ethnic Italians away from coastal areas would have done more harm than good to the war effort because so many Americans had German or Italian ancestry. An East Coast evacuation of ethnic Germans and Italians, as envisioned by General Drum, would have resulted in the relocation of some 52 million people.[13] By comparison, the total U.S. population at the time was 135 million.

On March 2, DeWitt issued the first of several public proclamations designating military areas from which groups of individuals might be excluded under Executive Order 9066. Military Area No. 1 was a "prohibited" zone along the Pacific, running through vulnerable coastal areas in Washington, Oregon, and California, as well as the southern half of Arizona. The reasons for including coastal areas in the exclusion zone are fairly obvious: the desire to prevent espionage at ports and other naval installations, worries about illicit ship-to-shore and shore-to-ship signaling, and concern about the risk of fifth column activities in the event of an invasion. As for those modern critics who discount the impact of MAGIC on the decision to evacuate, the designation of southern Arizona as a prescribed area is a clear rebuttal. MAGIC decrypts from January and June 1941[14] outlined Japan's plans to shift espionage operations to Mexico in case of war and to use Mexicali, a planned branch intelligence center, as an entry point into Mexico. (FBI intelligence also indicated that an Axis "underground railway" had been constructed between Mexico and either Phoenix or Tucson.[15]) Military Area No. 2 included the remaining areas of the Pacific Coast states. A second proclamation outlined four more military areas covering Idaho, Montana, Nevada, and Utah (though there was no subsequent exclusion from these states), plus more than 900 small prohibited zones.

There was no mass evacuation of ethnic Japanese in Hawaii, despite military officials having considered an invasion of Hawaii much more likely[16] than an invasion of the West Coast. Critics of the West Coast roundup often argue that the absence of an evacuation in Hawaii proves that the West Coast evacuation was unnecessary. As Joan Bernstein, chairwoman of the Civilian Wartime Relocation and Internment Commission, noted in congressional testimony, "The conduct of the Government in Hawaii, which had a very substantial Japanese-American population but no mass exclusion or detention, vividly underscores the fact that there were real and effective alternatives in keeping with the principles of American Government which could have been pursued on the West Coast."[17]

Navy Secretary Frank Knox initially urged Roosevelt to evacuate ethnic Japanese from Oahu (the largest Hawaiian island, which contains Pearl Harbor). Roosevelt concurred with Knox and directed him and Stimson to proceed.[18] In the end, however, mass evacuation was deemed impractical. Ships weren't available, and evacuation would have caused severe shortages of skilled workers. Instead, the entire territory of Hawaii was placed under martial law, giving military authorities unchecked power to root out suspected subversive citizens and confine them.

The territorial governor declared over 150 "defense act rules"; the territorial director of civilian defense and military governor issued hundreds of separate directives and regulations. Mail and newspapers were censored. Phone calls were monitored. Liquor sales were banned. Every civilian over the age of six was registered, fingerprinted, and required to carry identification at all times. Americans of German, Italian, or Japanese ancestry were prohibited from assembling in groups, and from owning firearms, cameras, and radio receivers.[19] The writ of habeas corpus was suspended, and hundreds of U.S. citizens considered potentially subversive, almost all of them *Nisei*, were confined without trial[20]—an option that was unavailable to military and law enforcement officials on the mainland, where civilian courts were still operative. These aggressive measures enabled Hawaii's military authorities to keep subversion in check without resorting to mass evacuation. It is ironic that those who are so critical of evacuation and relocation are so blasé about civil liberties infringements that took place in Hawaii— infringements that were arguably more sweeping than those adopted on the West Coast.

THE EVACUATION BEGINS

The World War II evacuation on the West Coast began with an earnest attempt at "voluntary" (that is, self-directed) evacuation. It was hoped that ethnic Japanese would leave prohibited zones on their own, finding suitable jobs on the East Coast or in the interior of the country. In fact, E.O. 9066 did not even mention relocation centers, because initially none were envisioned. Years later, Japanese American Citizens League leader Mike Masaoka conceded this point in congressional testimony: "Originally . . . the intent of the U.S. Government in issuing Executive Order 9066 was not to imprison us. It was simply to—I suppose they had the idea from the refugees in Europe. We would be kind of like war refugees and we would wander away and find someplace where we could reside."[21]

Bendetsen stressed a similar point in an oral history interview after the war:

> It was never intended by Executive Order 9066 and certainly not by the Army that the Japanese themselves be held in Relocation Centers. The sole objective was to bring relocation anywhere in the interior—east of the Cascades and Sierras Nevada and north of the southern halves of Arizona and New Mexico. Japanese were urged to relocate voluntarily on their own recognizance and extensive steps were taken to this end. The desire was to relocate them so that they could usefully and gainfully continue raising their families and educate their children while heads of families and young adults became gainfully employed. They were to be free to lease or buy land, raise and harvest crops, go into businesses. They were not to be restricted for the "duration" so long as they did not seek to remain or seek to return to the war "frontier" during hostilities.[22]

Thousands of ethnic Japanese did evacuate on their own.[23] But many families of Japanese ancestry on the West Coast were unwilling or unable to evacuate. Most had no relatives or friends in other parts of the country or lacked the resources to relocate outside the prohibited areas. Moreover, Mike Masaoka of JACL noted there was hostility in areas where evacuees were moving and feared retaliatory "mob violence."[24] (In some cases, hostility came not from white nativists but from other Japanese Americans who protested that an influx of evacuees in their area would "disturb and disrupt" their established reputation.[25]) In a February 25 memo updating the "Japanese situation," ONI officer Kenneth Ringle noted with alarm that California was "tending toward civil strife" because of animosity by Caucasians toward ethnic Japanese, the vast majority of whom had not yet left the state. He also blamed the "failure of the federal government to apprehend or control any of the *Kibei*... the most dangerous element of the Japanese population."[26] A little over a week later, Ringle reported that unless the federal government took positive steps, "there will be uprisings, riots, lynchings, and vigilante committees active in California in 30 days."[27] A telegram from the San Francisco representative of the Office of Government Reports on March 5 echoed that warning, noting that there was a "serious possibility of mob violence and vigilante committees."[28]

Initial planning of the evacuation was poor. Leaders in Washington underestimated the scope of the task. Secretary of War Stimson wrote in his diary: "There was general confusion around the table arising from the fact that nobody had realized how bad it was, nobody wanted to take care of the evacuees, and the general weight and complication of the project."[29] Critical historians looking back on this underestimation of the problems associated with evacuation could fairly accuse the planners of poor foresight. But to equate poor foresight with "racism" and "hysteria" is ridiculous. By mid-March it was becoming clear that "voluntary" evacuation was not working. On March 18, Executive Order No. 9012 established the War Relocation Authority "in order to provide for the removal from designated areas of persons whose removal is necessary in the interests of national security."[30] A week later, DeWitt issued Public Proclamation No. 3 establishing a dusk-to-dawn curfew for all enemy aliens and persons of Japanese ancestry in Military Area No. 1. On March 29, Public Proclamation No. 4 (the "freeze" order) forbade ethnic Japanese residents from leaving the area and required them to evacuate, assemble, and relocate under army supervision.

In the meantime, the White House continued to worry about Japanese attacks on the West Coast. After the daring Halsey-Doolittle raid in Tokyo in April, "eight Japanese carriers had returned from their operations around southeastern Asia and the Japanese could release at least three of the eight for a retaliatory attack on the west coast without jeopardizing successes already achieved," army historian Stetson Conn recounted. Secretary of War Stimson "called in General Marshall and had a few earnest words with him about the danger of a Jap attack on the West Coast." Stimson confessed that he was "very much impressed with the danger that the Japanese, having terribly lost face by this recent attack on them . . . will make a counterattack on us with carriers." [31] General DeWitt's superiors warned him to be on guard against a carrier attack at any time after May 10, and was informed that two more antiaircraft regiments were being sent to bolster the Los Angeles and San Francisco defenses.

Preceding the pivotal Battle of Midway, which the United States was alerted to thanks to another extraordinary communications intelligence operation that partially cracked JN-25, the Japanese navy's operational code,[32] the West Coast again prepared for the worst. General Marshall informed General DeWitt that a Japanese attack with a chemical weapon might be expected; in mid-May, 350,000 gas masks (the entire available supply), protective clothing, and decontamination supplies were hastily shipped to the West Coast. The MID concurred with the navy that a strong Japanese attack on American territory was in the offing before the end of the month, but it forecast that the "first priority" target of the attack would be "hit and run raids on West Coast cities of the continental United States supported by heavy naval forces."[33] Army intelligence held that such action was entirely within Japanese capabilities, considering the weakness of American naval power, and urged the concentration on the Pacific coast of all available continental air power to meet the threat.[34]

Even after America's triumphant but narrowly won victory at Midway, the army continued to be apprehensive of West Coast raids. The Japanese invasion and occupation of the Aleutian Islands in June 1942 did not help allay the public's concerns. Nor did the torpedoing of a Canadian lumber schooner off of Cape Flattery; the shelling of a Canadian radio compass station on Vancouver Island; the shelling of the Fort Stevens military reservation at the mouth of the Columbia River; and the attempted torpedoing of a tanker off the southern coast of Oregon in late June. In July, Assistant Chief of Staff G-2 (Intelligence) Colonel John Weckerling of the Western Defense Command advised General DeWitt that he still was concerned about "sabotage or attempted sabotage on a mass scale."[35] Two months later, Japan's *I-25* submarine—on orders from the imperial general's staff still smarting from the Halsey-Doolittle raid—carried a small plane with folded wings fitted for bombing out to the unprotected Oregon coast. On September 9, pilot Nobuo Fujita and his crew man Shoji Okuda catapulted from

the sub on the first of three incendiary bombing runs on a forested mountain slope near Brookings, Oregon. While the fires caused by the air raid
were quickly extinguished and no widespread panic ensued, they were a
reminder of Japan's continuing menace. In Tokyo, the air raid was touted as
heroic. A front-page headline run by the *Asahi* newspaper read, "Incendiary
Bomb Dropped on Oregon State. First Air Raid on Mainland America. Big
Shock to Americans."[36] The *I-25* returned in October to torpedo and sink
two tankers off the southern Oregon coast.

Back to Terminal Island

The first forced relocation of West Coast residents that included American
citizens occurred on Terminal Island in Los Angeles Harbor, which had been
singled out in MAGIC messages as a hotbed of Japanese espionage activity.
As Kenneth Ringle noted in a February 7, 1942, ONI memo (which, unlike
his earlier memo on the "Japanese question," was officially approved by his
superior, the Eleventh District intelligence officer, and circulated to the
director of Naval Intelligence, MID assistant chief of staff G-2, Aliens division of the War Department Office of Provost Marshall General, FBI headquarters, and FBI Los Angeles field office): "There are several hundred
[*Kibei*] presently residing on Terminal Island and engaged either in the taking or processing of fish. It is felt that these persons constitute the greatest
menace of the whole colony to the security of the United States."[37]

Even after the removal of some 375 enemy aliens on February 2, 1942,
Ringle concluded that "it is very evident that a hazard definitely [still] exists
due to the location of this large Japanese colony in the heart of the Los
Angeles harbor district." Ringle estimated the national security risks from
the remaining 2,000 or so Terminal Island *Nisei* as follows:

(a) Physical observation and espionage—75 percent

(b) Sabotage—20 percent

(c) Fifth column activity (preparation for and assistance to any attempted
    attack or invasion from outside sources)—5 percent. [38]

Further, Ringle stated that *Nisei* spies on Terminal Island would be in an excellent position to observe and report on such items as:

> ... arrival and departure of convoys, including size, strength of escort, and bulk of cargo; troop movements; arrival and departure of major units of the fleet; progress of shipbuilding, including launching and commissioning of men-of-war, as well as merchant marine; progress of construction of Naval Operating Base, including the new dry dock and the channel approaches thereto; delivery of new aircraft; the strength or lack of strength of the aerial defenses of the Naval Air Station and Naval Operating Base; and similar matters.
>
> As long as this colony, which contains known alien sympathizers even though of American citizenship, is allowed to exist in the heart of every activity in the Los Angeles Harbor, it must be assumed that items such as the above are known, observed, and transmitted to the enemy quickly and easily.

The only reason that sabotage was considered to be no more than 20 percent of the total hazard was that the safeguards that had been implemented during the previous six months. Nevertheless, Ringle warned that full protective measures remained inadequate:

> There still exists a great need for increased police and fire protection and the reduction of possible fire hazards due to the tremendous lumber yards, free-flowing oil wells, exposed water, gas, gasoline, oil and transmission lines, and installations, etc. These hazards are at the moment beyond the control of the naval and military authorities, but would serve as ideal objectives for saboteurs having as ready access to them as the Japanese colony on Terminal Island.

After the War Department declared Terminal Island a critical area, jurisdiction of the property was transferred to the navy. Military officials initially gave the Terminal Island *Nisei* thirty days to depart, but on February 25, in

the wake of the Goleta oil field shelling and the air raid scare over Los Angeles, the deadline was shortened to forty-eight hours. This caused considerable hardship for the evacuees, who scrambled to sell off household goods
(typically at rock-bottom prices) and pack for their move. Some relocated
to the interior; others eventually relocated to the Manzanar camp in eastern
California's Owens Valley, on the edge of the Mojave Desert.

THE BAINBRIDGE ISLAND EVACUATION

Bainbridge Island, located in Kitsap County, Washington, is home to Fort
Ward, which had been built at the turn of the century to guard the water
entrances to the Bremerton Naval Shipyard. At the outbreak of World War
II, it became the site of a navy radio school, training men to send and
receive Morse code. On the south end of the island, the navy built a top-
secret radio listening station, dubbed "Station S," where intelligence officers
intercepted Japanese radio communications.

Also on the island lived some fifty families of Japanese descent. MAGIC
traffic sent in the spring of 1941 indicated that Japan had spies in the Puget
Sound area observing warships in the Bremerton Naval Shipyard, and gathering information on "mercantile shipping and airplane manufacturers,
movements of military forces, as well as that which concerns troop maneuvers."[39] On March 24, 1942, the military ordered all residents of Japanese
descent to leave the island. Those who could arrange for employment and
shelter in approved areas outside of Military Area No. 1 were allowed to
leave on their own. For the rest, the army provided transportation and food
for the trip to temporary residence centers. Two hundred and twenty Bainbridge Islanders were sent to Manzanar, and then on to the Minidoka relocation center in Idaho.

On hand to assist the army in the evacuation were representatives from
Public Assistance, the Farm Security Agency, the Federal Reserve Bank, the
Office of Emergency Management, and United States Employment Service.
Government officials provided evacuees with storage for household items
such as iceboxes, washing machines, pianos, and other heavy furniture.

They also helped evacuees with the management, leasing, sale, and storage of farms, livestock and farm equipment, boats, and automobiles.[40]

After the residents' departure, field supervisor Tom Rathbone reported to General DeWitt that:

> The move was carried out with precision and orderliness, and there were no incidents of any description detrimental to the interests of the evacuees. The actual leave-taking between friends of long standing was a sad occasion, and everyone involved tried to cooperate understandingly in every way possible. The ferry left the Island at 11:20, and upon arrival in Seattle the Army cleared the immediate area around the train and the Japanese were escorted to the train immediately. The whole process was orderly and very well handled.... All of the evacuees expressed satisfaction and gratitude for the efforts of those persons who were operating in their behalf.[41]

Following the Bainbridge Island move, an additional 107 evacuation zones were created. By August 1942, some 112,000 individuals had been evacuated from their West Coast homes and moved into temporary assembly centers and relocation areas. The military order banning them from the western states was lifted in December 1944. Entrusted with a complex logistical assignment, the army on the whole did its best to carry out these difficult national security duties with professionalism and humanity.

Chapter 9

The Myth of the American "Concentration Camp"

C lose your eyes and envision a "Japanese American internment camp." What comes to mind?

Modern American history books and media portraits have seared universal images into our collective conscience: scared children and frail elderly grandparents trapped behind barbed wire, racist armed guards bullying captives in desolate barracks, prisoners suffering from malnutrition and mistreatment. The cover of *Last Witnesses: Reflections on the Wartime Internment of Japanese Americans* depicts two young girls peering through red bars, which double as the stripes of a vertically hung American flag. Two different books titled *Behind Barbed Wire*—one by Daniel S. Davis, the other by Lila Perl—share the same cover photo of a somber Japanese grandfather and two little boys wearing identification tags waiting to be evacuated.

The *Philadelphia Daily News* asserts that "the Japanese Americans were treated like convicts. And if they breached the compound walls, they were shot."[1] An academic pamphlet on Japanese Americans and World War II claims that camp residents were threatened with "isolation, exile, forced labor, public humiliation, and even torture and death."[2]

Many modern critics of the World War II evacuation and relocation refer to the centers and camps as "concentration camps," invoking the imagery of the Holocaust. One popular high school textbook describes 110,000

Japanese Americans "forcibly herded . . . together in concentration camps."[3] Author Roger Daniels, defending the comparison of American camps to Nazi concentration camps, sermonizes:

> The American camps were not death camps, but they were surrounded by barbed wire and by troops whose guns were pointed at the inmates. Almost all the 1,862 Japanese Americans who died in them died of natural causes, and they were outnumbered by the 5,918 American citizens who were born in the concentration camps. But the few Japanese Americans who were killed 'accidentally' by their American guards were just as dead as the millions of Jews and others were who killed deliberately by their German, Soviet, or Japanese guards.[4]

It is true that many politicians and public officials, including President Roosevelt himself, used the phrase "concentration camps" to describe the relocation centers. But it wasn't until the liberation of the Nazi death camps beginning in 1945 that the phrase took on the popular meaning that it retains today—that is, places of barbaric cruelty and torture on the order of what the Jews and others suffered under Hitler. In no way should the real suffering of ethnic Japanese evacuees and all Axis internees be minimized. But to compare American's internment and relocation centers to the Third Reich's extermination camps is to recklessly distort history and to trivialize the experience of Holocaust victims. Even the Commission on Wartime Relocation and Internment of Civilians, a panel stacked with critics of the relocation centers, noted, "To use the phrase 'concentration camps' summons up images and ideas which are inaccurate and unfair."[5] By exploiting the stigma attached in the public mind to the term "concentration camp," opponents of racial/ethnicity/nationality profiling seek to cut off the homeland security debate—rather than inform it.

The Distinction Between Internment and Relocation

As discussed in Chapter 6, internment camps were set up on the mainland[6] to detain designated enemy aliens from all Axis countries, not just Japan.

Dual citizens who renounced their American citizenship were also interned, under the authority of the 1798 Alien Enemies Act, as were Latin Americans of German, Japanese, and Italian descent (see Chapter 6) and some naturalized citizens born in Axis nations whose citizenship was stripped during the war because of associations deemed subversive. Adhering to the guidelines of the Geneva Convention, the Justice Department and army ran forty-six internment and detention camps for enemy aliens, renunciants, and their families (many of whose members were American-born and entered the camps voluntarily).[7] Enemy alien internees could not depart from the camps, although some were allowed to leave temporarily on work assignments.

By contrast, those of Japanese ancestry who were evacuated from the West Coast and could not find accommodations elsewhere were first sent to temporary assembly centers run by the U.S. military. They were then transferred to ten relocation centers managed by the civilian War Relocation Authority, operating under the Department of Interior after 1943. Many critics argue that the difference between enemy alien "internment" camps and evacuee "relocation" facilities is meaningless because both enemy alien internees and evacuees of Japanese descent suffered devastating hardships as a result of their confinement.

But blurring the distinction between internment and evacuation obscures some important facts about the evacuees who populated the relocation centers. In truth, they were:

- **Free to move elsewhere (initially).** Those excluded from the West Coast in early 1942 were initially allowed to move—and were encouraged to move—anywhere else among the forty-four states in the United States that were not in the prescribed military areas. (Remember: People of Japanese ancestry outside the West Coast were not required to move.) Several thousand West Coast residents did move on their own.[8] But limited resources and hostility toward evacuees by inland communities, including hostility from other Japanese Americans, prevented more from doing so.[9] The relocation centers supplied government-provided shelter, food, health care, and education to those evacuees of Japanese descent unable to make living arrange-

ments outside the exclusionary zones. In upholding the constitutionality of the exclusion orders, the U.S. Supreme Court in *Korematsu v.
United States* ruled that no one of Japanese ancestry was compelled
"either in fact or by law" to enter a relocation center.[10]

- **Free to leave,** provided they had a school or job to go to (outside the
  exclusion zones) and were not considered subversive. Many historians insist that relocation center residents "were not free to come and
  go as they wished"[11] and assert that residents of the camps were
  "incarcerated."[12] But beginning in July 1942,[13] approximately forty-
  three hundred students of Japanese ancestry did leave the relocation
  centers to attend colleges and universities outside the exclusion
  areas.[14] Among them was Michi Weglyn, author of *Years of Infamy: The
  Untold Story of America's Concentration Camps*, who left the Gila, Arizona, relocation center to attend Mount Holyoke College in Massachusetts on a full scholarship.[15] Kiyoaki Murata, a Japanese national
  who arrived in the United States on a student visa and was evacuated
  from California, departed from the Poston, Arizona, relocation center
  after nine months to seek educational opportunities in the Midwest.
  Murata recounted his experience in his World War II memoir, *An
  Enemy Among Friends:*

  > On May 10 [1943], I finished assembling the documents for
  > my application for an indefinite leave.... I submitted the doc-
  > uments to the block manager, bracing myself for a long
  > wait... To my surprise, my application for indefinite leave was
  > approved only two days later. The fact that my request was
  > granted so quickly was solid evidence of the policy of the
  > WRA of that time: to let the evacuees leave the camps with
  > the utmost alacrity as long as they had a prospect for employ-
  > ment outside... I decided to leave on May 17.[16]

  In addition, an estimated thirty thousand camp residents
  departed from the camps when offered work outside the
  exclusion zones.17 Jeanne Watatsuki noted in Farewell to
  Manzanar that her sister and her sister's husband left the

camp "to harvest sugar beets in Idaho. It was grueling work
up there, but when the call came through the camp for workers to alleviate the wartime labor shortage, it sounded better
than their life at Manzanar."[18]

- **Free to enter**. Some 219 persons actually volunteered to move *into*
the camps for their own comfort and safety.[19] One who did so, Ralph
Lazo, was a sixteen-year-old student of Mexican and Irish descent
from Los Angeles who entered because he wanted to show support for
his Japanese-American high school classmates. He stayed at the Manzanar relocation center for two and a half years.[20] In addition, a number of ethnic Japanese who had left the West Coast before the camps
were opened applied for admission to assembly centers where they
had family and friends.[21]

Historians who compare the American relocations camps to Dachau and
Bergen-Belsen will be hard-pressed to find a single European Jew who willingly entered—or was given permission to leave—a Nazi death camp. Yet
today's ethnic activists have successfully exploited the myth of the American concentration camp to assail any homeland security measure—from
registration of foreign visitors to detention of illegal aliens—that takes into
account nationality, ethnicity, or race. An honest debate about the World
War II evacuation and relocation requires an accurate and balanced view of
conditions in both the internment and relocation centers run by the Roosevelt administration. The record shows they were neither luxury resorts
nor barbaric prisons nor edifices of institutional racism, but spartan facilities that for the most part were administered humanely. The worst conditions were found in the hastily constructed assembly centers, most of which
were in operation for less than six months and some of which were subse-
quently used to house U.S. military personnel.

LIFE IN THE INTERNMENT CAMPS

The Justice Department detained enemy aliens from Japan, Germany, Italy,
and a small number of Eastern European countries in transit centers and

internment camps across the country. International Red Cross and Swiss embassy representatives conducted regular visits to check on the treatment of internees. Ellis Island was a temporary internment center for some three hundred fifty German enemy aliens and their families. They had access to religious services, a library, movies, athletic facilities, and a reading room.[22] At the Gloucester City, New Jersey, internee site, historian Arnold Krammer reported, "medical care was especially good... an average dinner might be lamb roast with gravy, potatoes, green beans, cooked onions, fresh pears, bread, and coffee." Internees received regular visitors and passed the time playing gin rummy and poker.[23]

The "permanent" internment camps did indeed feature armed guards, barbed wire, floodlights, and watchtowers. Some, such as Fort Stanton, New Mexico, and Fort Lincoln, North Dakota, were converted Civilian Conservation Corps camps. The Seagoville, Texas, internment camp was a converted women's reformatory. At the Santa Fe, New Mexico, site, Japanese enemy alien internees actually demanded that the barbed wire fence surrounding the compound be made at least a foot *taller* after the camp received threats from an outside mob angered by the spring 1942 Japanese victory in the Philippines. Antagonism was "so great," according to historian Richard Melzer, "that most internees believed they were much safer within their fenced-off compound."[24] Inside, Santa Fe internees built a small golf course, two tennis courts, and four baseball diamonds. The Santa Fe-shisha Tanka Poetry Club met regularly, and camp residents attended Kabuki performances held in an outdoor theater.[25]

Fort Missoula, Montana, was surrounded by twenty-four hundred feet of chain-link fence topped by barbed wire. Inside, the camp were barracks, a hospital, school, library, bakery, two-winged mess hall, and a recreation hall built of lodgepole pine that seated more than eight hundred. Italian internees, many of them seamen and entertainers from an Italian luxury liner seized in the Panama Canal, nicknamed the camp Bella Vista after the individual flower gardens they had planted on the grounds. Internee musicians held concerts that outside Missoula residents were permitted to attend for a small admission fee. Hundreds of internees received work paroles allowing them to take farming and forest-fighting jobs. Others found outside work at St. Patrick's Hospital, the Great Western Railroad and the Garden City Floral Company.[26]

According to author and scholar Jerre Mangione, who reported on the experience of Italian seamen at Fort Missoula, "none questioned the American government's right to intern them for the duration of the war.... Some were openly pro-American. One seaman told me he was grateful to the American government for interning him, for otherwise he would be risking his life in the war for a philosophy of government he despised. He and several others wanted to know what steps they could take to become permanent American residents after the war."[27]

Weather conditions were harsh in many camps; internees and their families often endured cramped, leaky living quarters and chronic lack of privacy. Tension and hatred between pro-Nazi militants and other enemy aliens (including Jewish refugees) often resulted in threats and violence.

Some troublemakers griped about more esoteric concerns. At Ellis Island, Japanese internees complained that they were not allowed enough outdoor exercise and were not being served Japanese-style meals.[28] At Crystal City, Japanese internees complained that too few Japanese were being transferred to the camp, and too many Germans.[29] At Seagoville, a pro-Nazi German enemy alien protested because the camp did not provide internees with "fresh figs, celery, and rhubarb."[30] The camp did, however, feature a library with three thousand books, open-air evening concerts and songfests, a weaving room, a dressmaking factory, and a trained dietitian on staff.[31] At Fort Lincoln, one enemy alien complained to visiting Attorney General Francis Biddle about not getting enough butter. Biddle noted that American citizens outside the camps were subject to strict rationing, and that internees were receiving more butter than that allotted to citizens.

"But that's not the point Mr. Attorney General," the internee argued. "Under the Geneva Convention we are entitled to as much butter as the American troops—and we are not getting it!"[32]

THE RELOCATION EXPERIENCE

The first stop for the vast majority of West Coast evacuees of Japanese descent who could not relocate outside the exclusion zones was an "assembly center." Among these emergency army-run facilities, nine were at fairgrounds, two were at horse racetracks (Santa Anita and Tanforan, California), two were at migrant workers' camps (Marysville and Sacramento, California), one was at a livestock exposition hall (Portland, Oregon), one was at a mill site (Pinedale, California), and one was at an abandoned Civilian Conservation Corps camp (Mayer, Arizona). In addition, staging areas under construction near Parker Dam in Arizona (Poston) and in the Owens Valley of eastern California (Manzanar), originally set up to expedite the voluntary evacuation, were also used as assembly centers. Both would later be designated relocation centers.[33]

Conditions at the government's seventeen assembly centers, which were erected in less than a month's time, were often unpleasant and sometimes miserable. The "use of facilities of this character is not highly desirable," the army readily acknowledged.[34] Barracks were hastily constructed; privacy was nil. And because of delays in constructing the relocation centers, evacuees stayed weeks and often months longer at the assembly centers than federal officials had planned. Families set up makeshift apartments in horse stalls and under grandstands. "In 1941," author David Fremon observed, many Japanese Americans "had gone to these places as customers. Now they were entering as prisoners." The evacuees slept on straw-filled mattresses and waited in long lines to use latrines. Diarrhea outbreaks were common. Most of the assembly centers were operative for only a few months; all were shut down by the end of October 1942.

Citizens of Japanese ancestry weren't the only ones who inhabited these sites. The Pinedale assembly center was taken over by the Fourth Air Force. The Sacramento assembly center was converted to a signal corps training school.[35] Members of the U.S. Army Ordnance Corps moved into the Santa Anita racetrack in November 1942 and stayed for two years. The racetrack had housed some thirteen thousand residents of Japanese ancestry for six months before they were sent to relocation centers. "Much has been written about Santa Anita being an assembly center for Japanese Americans immediately after Pearl Harbor and how they were billeted in 12x12-foot horse stalls during their six-month internment before going to permanent camps," *Los Angeles Times* sportswriter Shav Glick noted. "Rarely mentioned is that as soon as they left, those stalls were filled by GIs."[36]

The army's task in building and organizing the assembly sites was not an easy one. Some centers were overcrowded. Some guards were too harsh. Some mess halls weren't as clean as they could have been. But overall, the evacuation and assembly process went as smoothly as could be expected given wartime conditions—and even earned praise from relocation critic and civil liberties crusader Carey McWilliams, who wrote for *Harper's*:

> In effecting this vast movement of people in such a brief allotment of time, the conduct of the Army has been wholly admirable. Both officers and troops behaved, at all times, with the utmost tact, good judgment, and consideration. There were, to be sure, minor flaws in the planning, but as a whole the evacuation went through on schedule without a hitch . . . it must be credited as a major feat for the Army.[37]

The Red Cross concurred:

> Generally, the sites selected were satisfactory with the possible exception of Puyallup, where lack of adequate drainage and sewage disposal facilities created a serious problem. . . In studying the housing facilities in these centers, it is necessary to keep in mind that the job was without precedent, and that the sites were selected and buildings completed in record-breaking time in the face of such handicaps as material and labor shortages and transportation difficulties.[38]

So did Saburo Kido, national president of the Japanese American Citizens League:

> While many evacuees hold no great love for General DeWitt for his part
> in the evacuation, the great majority of us feel that he was doing his
> duty...The fact that evacuation was carried out in an orderly manner,
> without a single incident, speaks well of the military's efficiency as well
> as the cooperation of the evacuees.[39]

JACL leaders were, in fact, instrumental volunteers in the initial planning,
construction, and administration of the assembly centers—a role that they
considered a "civic responsibility" but that bred resentment and hostility
among other evacuees.[40]

By the fall of 1942, as war raged on, some 112,000 evacuees had been
moved from the assembly centers (as well as institutions and home communities) into ten relocation centers. "Each of the ten sites was relatively
isolated," reported University of California, Berkeley, researchers Dorothy
Swaine Thomas and Richard Nishimoto. "The six western projects were
wind and dust swept. Tule Lake, Mindoka, and Heart Mountain were subject to severe winters. Poston and Gila, both in the Arizona desert, had tem-
peratures well above 100 degrees for lengthy periods, and Rohwer and
Jerome experienced the excessive humidity and mosquito infestations of
swampy delta land."[41]

The camps were located in isolated areas for good reason. Army engineers were required to situate the camps away from strategic areas. They
needed large tracts of federal land to accommodate thousands of evacuees.
Desert outposts such as Poston and Gila were logical choices. Military planners and camp residents did the best they could to turn desolate areas into
decent, self-sustaining communities. Camp residents could enlist in the
Work Corps, serving in paid jobs related to agriculture, irrigation, manufacturing, small businesses, medicine, education, and camp administration.
They could continue to receive rents, profits, dividends, and royalties from
businesses or property owned outside the camps. They could also continue
to make investments and conduct outside business negotiations. The WRA
left it up to each camp community to establish local governments, whose
leaders met and negotiated with camp management.[42] Camp residents

served on agricultural crews to produce vegetables, poultry, eggs, and meat for their communities. They operated consumer enterprises, including stores, canteens, barbershops, and shoe-repair establishments on a consumer cooperative basis. Each camp published its own newspaper. And there were many opportunities for social and cultural activity.

Residents passed the time playing Go, attending flower-arrangement classes, competing in team sports, and watching Kabuki theater. Children attended both regular school classes and Japanese-language schools. Ministers and priests from the evacuee population were free to carry on their religious activities at the centers. Ordinary barracks were used for religious services by Protestants, Catholics, and Buddhists alike.

Under regulations adopted in September 1942, the War Relocation Authority (WRA) began working toward a steady depopulation of the relocation centers by encouraging all able-bodied residents with good records of behavior to reenter private employment in agriculture or industry (outside the prohibited zones). At a number of key cities throughout the interior of the country, the WRA employed relocation officers who worked with local volunteer committees of interested citizens and with the United States Employment Service to seek out employment opportunities for evacuees in their respective areas. The following requirements had to be met:[43]

1. A careful check is made of the evacuee's behavior record at the relocation center and of other information in the hands of WRA. In all questionable cases, any information in the possession of the federal investigative agencies is requested and studied. If there is any evidence from any source that the evacuee might endanger the security of the Nation, permission for indefinite leave is denied.

2. There must be reasonable assurance from responsible officials or citizens regarding local sentiment in the community where the evacuee plans to settle. If community sentiment appears so hostile to all persons of Japanese descent that the presence of the evacuee seems likely to cause trouble, the evacuee is so advised and is discouraged from relocating in that particular area.

3. Indefinite leave is granted only to evacuees who have a definite place to go and some means of support.

4. Each evacuee going out on indefinite leave must agree to keep WRA informed of any change of job or change of address.

WRA officials conducted background checks with help from military intelligence and the FBI. Students applying to leave the centers were subject to similar requirements. Those who had contributed to Japanese war funds, whose fathers held memberships in subversive *kais* (military societies), and who had made substantial foreign investments were subjected to heightened scrutiny. *Kibei* were generally ineligible for leave clearance.

In the winter of 1942–1943, WRA administrators stirred resentment and anger among many evacuees with the introduction of a registration process asking draft-age male evacuees to answer a loyalty questionnaire. The first peacetime draft had been introduced in the United States in September 1940. More than thirty-one hundred *Nisei* were inducted by November 1941. Amid doubts about the loyalty of ethnic Japanese following the Pearl Harbor attack, however, the War Department discharged about half of these *Nisei* draftees in the interest of national security. The remainder, including a *Nisei* Hawaiian National Guard unit designated the 100th Battalion, were reassigned to noncombat and nonsensitive duties. Soon after, the military stopped inducting Japanese Americans. In the fall of 1942, some Japanese American leaders lobbied the government to give *Nisei* the opportunity to demonstrate loyalty through voluntary military service. JACL leader Mike Masaoka claimed an instrumental role. Among government and military officials, World War II veteran and historian Ted Tsukiyama credited army Commander Delos C. Emmons, Colonel Moses Pettigrew, Assistant Secretary of War John McCloy, and Office of War Information Director Elmer Davis with bringing the idea of segregated combat units to fruition. The 100th Battalion served as a "test" unit before the creation of the famed 442nd Regimental Combat Team in February 1943. The call for army volunteers in the camps was accompanied by the institution of the registration process. The process also required other non–draft–eligible evacuees to fill out leave clearance forms to expedite work and education releases.

One survey question asked potential volunteer recruits, "Are you willing to serve in the armed forces of the United States on combat duty, wherever ordered?" Another asked all respondents whether they would "swear unqualified allegiance to the United States of America . . . and forswear any form of allegiance or obedience to the Japanese emperor, to any other foreign government, power or organization?" Many were offended by the commonsense wartime presumption that enemy aliens and dual citizens might possess divided loyalties. Others were understandably upset that renouncing their ties to Japan would render them citizens without a country (since the United States barred them from naturalizing). But as National Security Agency (NSA) official David Lowman noted, the controversial loyalty oath was not materially different from the loyalty oath required by the Japanese American Citizens League, which asked members to "renounce any other allegiances" which they "may have knowingly or unknowingly held in the past."[44] Moreover, the process to separate loyal from disloyal evacuees was vigorously supported at the time by prominent Japanese American leaders. Saburo Kido of JACL asserted, "Japanese Americans would be the first to deny that all of their number are 100 percent loyal. At the same time, we feel that with our help—which we have proffered without reluctance—the sheep can be separated from the goats."[45]

The process was hardly foolproof. Wouldn't subversives simply lie about their loyalty to the country? Maybe so. (If they did, and the government later discovered the deception, they could be prosecuted for lying.) Ultimately, among American citizen males of draft age, some 28 percent refused to swear allegiance to their country or forswear allegiance to the emperor of Japan.[46] However "improper, unfair, and utterly outrageous"[47] the administration of the program might appear, the fact of the matter is that it yielded useful information to help register volunteers for combat and to distinguish troublemakers from the rest of the evacuees. Along the spectrum of impositions the government was making on all citizens during wartime, answering a loyalty questionnaire was hardly the worst psychological trauma suffered.

One of the first *Nisei* to depart from the camps, Charles Kikuchi, a resident of the Gila, Arizona, relocation center, reflected that "on the whole the *Nisei* group didn't get too damaged" by relocation. "Generally, we probably gained as a result." He was not alone in this view. The editor of Kikuchi's diary, John Modell, noted that many students of the Japanese American experience "concur that the relocation helped effect a transfer of power from the *Issei* to the *Nisei* that otherwise had seemed difficult or impossible."[48]

Barbed Wire and Bullies

Much has been made of the presence of barbed wire and armed guards at the relocation centers. But the military forces were scant, and at most camps the fencing was erected more to mark property boundaries and keep out wildlife and range cattle than to corral camp residents. The army had responsibility for maintaining external protection, patrolling the perimeters, and controlling entry into and exit from the camps. Military police were allowed inside only at the request of camp administrators. Internal policing was maintained by the civilian War Relocation Authority and resident communities. Historian Page Smith reported:

> While barbed wire was eventually strung around all of the centers it was more for definition and to control access and egress to and from the center than to prevent escape. At most of the centers, hundreds and sometimes thousands of evacuees came and went freely, along with visitors, purveyors of food, evacuees with outside jobs, teenagers on shopping expeditions (where there were nearby towns), athletic teams going to play Caucasian teams "outside," church groups visiting congregations in neighboring communities, and so on.
>
> Although soldiers were a constant presence, they were few in number (except at times of major disturbances in the centers) and, like the barbed wire, more symbolic than practical.[49]

Evacuee Kiyoaki Murata, who stayed at Poston, Arizona, for nine months, independently confirmed Smith's impression (at least at one camp):

> The camp was not the prison I had expected it to be. I have since heard accounts of camps with high barbed-wire fences and rifle-bearing MPs threatening to shoot any evacuee attempting to escape. But for whatever reason, Poston Unit Three was not at all like this. At first there was a token stretch of barbed wire fence around the camp, but it was gone in a few months. And I did see one helmeted MP by a guard post. On one of the first days of my life in Poston, I chatted with a lone, black MP who appeared quite bored. I even sauntered out into the mesquite woods without his showing any signs of disapproval. Within a few days, he was no longer to be seen.[50]

Violence and unrest did occur at some relocation centers. Sociologist Wendy Ng recounted shootings of residents by armed guards at Manzanar, Gila River, Tule Lake, and Topaz.[51] Author Michi Weglyn labeled the shootings of two rioters at Manzanar by MPs as "atrocities."[52] Author Daniel S. Davis described military police as "trigger-happy" and asserted that "all evacuees were fearful that they too might someday be gunned down."[53]

In truth, evacuees often had more to fear from militant, pro-Japanese residents—especially the Japanese-educated *Kibei*—than from guards or administrators. Two major riots at Manzanar and Poston were instigated by *Kibei* who had beaten residents suspected of cooperating with camp authorities. At Manzanar, the *Kibei* had terrorized pro-American residents and drawn up a hit list of *Nisei* whom they vilified as traitors and labeled *inu* (dogs). Some evacuees believed the militants intended to turn the list over to the Japanese government. Manzanar subversives etched pro-Japanese graffiti at the camp and marked their territory on behalf of the Mafia-like Black Dragon Society. At Poston, militants harassed innocent families, including relatives of Lyle Kurisaki, who cooperated with the Office of Naval Intelligence. A memo from the District Intelligence Officer of the 11th Naval District noted that while Kurisaki was on leave from the camp, his family was "made to suffer serious mistreatment"—not from guards, but at the hands of fellow camp residents.[54] Ultra-nationalist hoodlums preyed on young girls and attacked elderly residents. In one case, three old men returning from a religious meeting—where they had condemned *Kibei* agitators—were beaten with sticks by a gang of a half dozen young men. One of the victims recalled:

> The three of us were coming home from a religious meeting at block 52. I heard noisy footsteps. One of my friends was at my side, the other was 15 feet ahead. The first man who was attacked yelled. I turned around and saw that big stick. I can still see the club like a frozen picture, but I didn't know anything after that.[55]

Many *Kibei* also harassed those who volunteered for the all-*Nisei* combat unit. Sadly, while progressive historians have exalted belligerent *Nisei* draft resisters,[56] they have derided as "accommodationists"[57] those who—at risk of great bodily harm—worked inside the camps to keep the peace and inform the government of potential subversives in their midst.[58]

In July 1943, the Tule Lake relocation center was converted into a "segregation camp" for those who refused to renounce fealty to the emperor and swear loyalty to the United States and for troublemakers from other relocation centers who were fanatically loyal to Japan. Many who were original residents of the Tule Lake center before it was converted to a segregation camp remained when the outside segregants moved in; segregants' families also moved in. The total population of the camp, now a volatile mix of loyal and disloyal, was roughly eighteen thousand.

The pro-Japan segregants leaned on all *Kibei*, as well as *Nisei* who had never been to Japan and spoke no Japanese, to adhere to rigid cultural ceremonies and language study. Americanized *Nisei* were harassed and threatened with beatings until they joined the program.[59] Leaders formed the Hokuku Seinen-Dan (Young Men's Organization to Serve Our Mother Country), openly pledged loyalty to the emperor, and vowed "to sacrifice life and property in order to serve our mother country in time of unparalleled emergency."[60] The group, shouting *"Banzai,"* led daily militaristic marches, drills, and ceremonies around the camp. The routine began at dawn with outdoor *taiso* (exercises) and goose-stepping drills punctuated by shouts of *"Wa-shoi! Wa-shoi!"* (Hut! Hut!). Each militant shaved his head and donned a sweatshirt emblazoned with the rising sun. Every month, to commemorate the Pearl Harbor attack, the men faced east and offered prayers for Japan's military victory.[61] One of the group's leaders preached that "to help the great cause, we have to kill those who stand in its way."[62] It was not an idle threat. Minoru Kiyota, a *Kibei* at Tule Lake, recounted that soon after the militant groups were formed there, the manager of the camp's consumer co-op, Yaozo Hitomi, was found with his throat cut. "This crime was never solved, but the fact that such a murder could take place and not be solved illustrates the psychological hold these violent gangs had on the general population of the segregation center," Kiyota noted.[63]

A total of eighty-three residents (all but four of them male *Nisei*) who caused the most trouble for camp administrators were sent to isolation centers in Moab, Utah, and Leupp, Arizona.[64] (Women were ineligible to join the Hokuku Seinen-Dan, but formed their own spin-off group called Hokoku Joshi Seinen-Dan [Young Women's Organization to Serve Our Mother Country].)

In July 1944, President Roosevelt signed a law enabling extremists to abandon their U.S. citizenship. A total of 5,620 *Nisei*, most of them the most militant of militants from Tule Lake, formally cut their ties to America and assumed enemy alien status. A total of 2,360 renunciants were sent to DOJ internment camps at Fort Lincoln and Santa Fe; 2,031 were deported to Japan.[65] It is not hard to imagine what these pro-Japanese loyalists, who were willing to attack and kill their fellow residents of Japanese descent, may have been capable of doing to the rest of the American citizenry had they been allowed to roam freely at the height of wartime hostilities. "If the Japanese had landed on U.S. soil, who knows?" mused Teruo Nobori, a *Nisei* who volunteered for the 442nd Regimental Combat Team and has been an outspoken critic of the radical draft resisters in the camps. America's pro-Japanese militants, Nobori concluded bluntly, "might've shot the other way." [66]

Chapter 10

Reparations, Revisionism, and the Race Card

On August 10, 1988, despite the objection of intelligence and military experts and his own Justice Department, President Ronald Reagan signed a law handing over taxpayer-subsidized payments of $20,000 each to American citizens and permanent residents of Japanese ancestry who had endured "significant human suffering" during World War II.[1]

The Civil Liberties Act of 1988 (Public Law 100-383) provided nearly $1.65 billion in restitution to 82,000 individuals of Japanese ancestry who had been subjected to the evacuation, relocation, and internment process. A new agency, the Office of Redress Administration, was created to determine eligibility and send out the checks. The federal government also delivered a presidential letter of apology to each reparations recipient. In addition, $5 million was authorized to fund education programs about the World War II evacuation and relocation "so that the causes and circumstances of this and similar events may be illuminated and understood."[2]

Ethnic activists recount this chapter in American history as a political and moral triumph over personal injustice. But the road to reparations itself was paved with injustice, irony, intellectual dishonesty, and incompetence. The federal panel created by Congress to assess whether the World War II evacuation and relocation were militarily necessary didn't include a single member with a military or intelligence background. In fact, the five hundred-page report of the Commission on Wartime Relocation and Internment of Civilians devoted just ten pages to intelligence.[3] Worse, the commission failed to acknowledge the existence of long-declassified MAGIC cables–which revealed Japan's extensive espionage activities along the West Coast–until *after* it had published its famous (or rather, infamous) indictment that wartime relocation and internment were the result of "race prejudice, war hysteria and a failure of political leadership."[4] The commission's legal counsel hastily and recklessly dismissed the importance of the MAGIC intelligence in Roosevelt's decision to approve Executive Order 9066 and the West Coast evacuation.

The travesty lies not merely in *what* the commission concluded, but *how* it did so. The panel's nationwide hearings were an untold embarrassment. Several commission members declared strident anti-evacuation and anti-relocation sentiments before and during the panel's twenty-day hearings process. Pro-reparations witnesses had been prepped in mock hearings to sharpen the "effectiveness of their presentations."[5] The few witnesses who were invited to testify in defense of the World War II evacuation and relocation were berated, ridiculed, and cut off by commission members. Other opponents of reparations were openly booed and hissed at by audience members. The dissenters' testimony was almost completely ignored in the commission's final report, *Personal Justice Denied*, which, despite its many omissions and misrepresentations, now represents the "official" history of the World War II internment and evacuation. Moreover, although intended to heal racial tensions, the reparations law exacerbated resentment by creating a special entitlement for evacuees and internees of Japanese ancestry (including American citizens, dual citizens, enemy aliens, and even renunciants who had returned to Japan), while evacuees and internees of German or Italian descent received no compensation and relatively little attention in the commission report.

Today's military and political leaders are besieged by ethnic activists exploiting distorted World War II history. In their efforts to fight terrorism, the current wartime administration is hampered by politically correct sensitivity to, and unwarranted guilt over, a false account of its predecessors' actions to protect the homeland six decades ago.

INITIAL ACTS OF COMPENSATION

During the rush to comply with the West Coast evacuation order, many ethnic Japanese families suffered terrible and debilitating property losses. The popular perception is that the majority of their assets, from household goods to vast commercial and agricultural holdings, were confiscated by the government. But in fact, the War Relocation Authority actively assisted evacuees in keeping such properties in productive use through lease or sale. The WRA established government warehouses for storage and acted as an intermediary in connection with real estate and commercial holdings. Still, many families fell victim to unscrupulous neighbors or partners outside the camps who stole their property or sold it off.

A shameful fact is that many *Issei* farmers and business leaders were conned by *Nisei* opportunists who exploited their distress. According to JACL official Togo Tanaka, there was "a considerable body of evidence, not all of it reliable, to indicate that it was not rare for *Nisei* individuals to take advantage of the *Issei* businessman's or farmer's weakened position and attempt literally to expropriate the latter's holdings."[6] Lyle Kurisaki, a JACL official in Brawley, California, a farming community in the Imperial Valley, told Tanaka in December 1944 that he "personally knew of 20–30 *Nisei* who cheated the poor wives of *Issei* internees. And I put the pressure on a lot of them and told them that the JACL wouldn't stand for any such monkey business. I wouldn't, anyway. Trouble was, some of the JACL members were crooked, too."[7] One racket documented by an officer of the Manzanar relocation center involved a sham business called the "Pacific Service Bureau," run by two *Nisei*, who charged older Japanese residents in California a $50 "fee" for travel permits that could be obtained free at federal government offices.[8]

In prompt recognition of the financial hardships a large number of evacuees suffered as a result of relocation, Congress passed the American-Japanese

Evacuation Claims Act in 1948. The law authorized payment of more than $37 million to individuals and families of Japanese descent who made any claim for damage to or loss of property because of evacuation or exclusion. A few years later, the compensation rules were loosened to expedite payments to elderly residents. The feds processed a total of 26,568 settlements, averaging $1,400 each (equal to more than $10,000 in current dollars).[9] The act specifically stated that payment was a full discharge of the United States and its agents with respect to all claims arising from evacuation.

Critics griped that the 1948 law was unfair because it only covered tangible losses and required documentation to back up claims. Scholar Tetsuden Kashima deemed the claims act "grossly inadequate."[10] Writer Michi Weglyn bemoaned the fact that the Justice Department was "rigidly unyielding" in ensuring that claims were legitimate.[11] She also complained that renunciants who had voluntarily returned to Japan were not eligible for compensation. She advocated a reparations scheme similar to one offered by the German government which allowed "a sizable number of former victims of Nazi-ism [to] continue to collect lifelong annuities" regardless of where they lived in the world.[12]

Congress passed eight more compensation-related laws between 1951 and 1978. These included benefits for federal employees of Japanese ancestry; a Social Security Act amendment deeming Japanese Americans over the age of eighteen to have earned and contributed to the government retirement system during their relocation; and amendments to the federal civil service retirement provisions giving Japanese Americans credit for the time spent in relocation centers after the age of eighteen. But it was not enough for an increasingly vocal group of young Japanese American activists.

THE REPARATIONS MOVEMENT IS BORN

In the late 1960s and the 1970s, antiwar agitation and ethnic identity politics became all the rage. Third- and fourth-generation Japanese Americans embraced the America-bashing, victim culture and launched a nationwide bid for blanket payments to evacuees and their families.[13] The Japanese

American Citizens League (whose leaders had supported evacuation and relocation during the war) passed a resolution in the summer of 1970 seeking reparations on a per diem, tax-free basis. Seattle activists, led by Boeing engineer Henry Miyatake, circulated a plan in 1973 proposing payments of $5,000 to each person of Japanese descent, plus $10 for each day spent in camps. A radical bill introduced in 1979 by Seattle-area Representative Mike Lowry, Democrat, upped the ante. The WWII Japanese American Human Rights Violations Act (H.R. 5977) proposed direct payments of $15,000 per victim plus an additional $15 per day spent in the camps.

A supposedly more moderate proposal by Senator Daniel Inouye to form a federal panel to study the matter and then formulate recommendations on wartime redress won congressional approval in the summer of 1981. The Commission on Wartime Relocation and Internment of Civilians convened twenty days of hearings across the country—ostensibly to research and debate the military justification for the evacuation and relocation, but mostly to provide a form of catharsis for the Japanese American community and build political support for redress.[14] Some seven hundred fifty witnesses testified, a majority of them evacuees who provided emotional testimony about the hardships they endured. In an op-ed piece entitled "Redressing Wrongs: A Never-Ending Hurt for Japanese Americans," Tetsuden Kashima praised the hearings for giving evacuees the chance "to express publicly, under the government's aegis, their collective grievances and to recover from the blight of being considered second-class citizens."[15]

The commission's findings, delivered in the February 1983 report *Personal Justice Denied*, categorically dismissed the military-necessity argument and documented the evacuees' suffering and property losses. The panel recommended that the government issue an apology and reparations. Few in the public arena dared to criticize the redress juggernaut. Among those willing to take the politically incorrect stance was iconoclastic Japanese-American U.S. Senator S. I. Hayakawa of California, who blasted the pro-reparations group as a "wolf-pack of dissident young Japanese Americans who weren't even born during World War II."[16] During House debate, Representative Bill Frenzel of Minnesota remarked: "What a funny way to ask

us to rub ashes on our heads! The bill asks us to purge ourselves of someone else's guilt with another generation's money."[17]

Thoughtful observers realized the danger of judging the wartime measures after the fact and out of historical context. As redress legislation
moved through Congress, journalist James J. Kilpatrick reflected:

> Only a heart of stone, it is said, could fail to be moved by the injustice vis-
> ited upon loyal American citizens 46 years ago. It is time to apologize, we
> are told; it is time to make amends. The trouble with that compassionate
> plea is that it comes to us through a rear-view mirror. It embodies the
> hindsight wisdom of the Monday morning quarterback. The bill carries a
> finding that "there was no military or security reason for the internment,"
> but that is the conclusion now. It assuredly was not the conclusion then.
> Two generations have grown up since the Japanese launched their attack
> on Pearl Harbor. Today we count the Japanese as friends and allies. In the
> winter of 1941–42 they were enemies. Today it seems absurd to imagine
> that the Japanese might have invaded California. This seemed not at all
> absurd at the time. In 1988 we scarcely can imagine risks of sabotage and
> espionage. Reasonable men vividly perceived them then.[18]

Justice Department Assistant Attorney General John R. Bolton, writing on
behalf of his agency, pointed out that the 1948 Evacuation Claims Act
already had provided a reasonable remedy to affected evacuees. "Congress
recognized long ago that many loyal Americans of Japanese descent were
injured by the wartime relocation and internment program.... There is no
good reason to question that settlement now three-and-one-half decades
later."[19] The claims act, he continued, "was in keeping with our nation's best
tradition of individual rather than collective response and was more contemporaneous with the injuries to the claimants than would be any payments at this late date."[20] Moreover, the Justice Department noted, no
further apology was necessary given President Gerald Ford's formal revoca-
tion of Executive Order 9066 in 1976, which called the evacuation "a set-

back to fundamental American principles" and declared to "resolve that this kind of action shall never again be repeated."[21]

Ignoring the advice of his top legal advisers, President Reagan signed the Civil Liberties Act of 1988. According to the *National Journal*, the heart-string lobbying of former New Jersey GOP governor Thomas Kean proved instrumental in persuading Reagan to support the law. Kean had been asked to intervene in the matter by a former book editor of his, JACL official Grant Ujifusa. "I used whatever persuasive powers I could," Kean recalled. [22] He reminded Reagan that in 1945, when Santa Ana, California, refused to allow a *Nisei* soldier killed in action to be buried in the local cemetery, Reagan had participated in a ceremony awarding the Distinguished Service Cross to the young man's family. This emotional plea, devoid of any fundamental discussion of the intelligence and military considerations that led to the World War II evacuation and relocation of ethnic Japanese, won over Reagan and key social conservatives outside the Justice Department (such as then-education secretary William J. Bennett and presidential assistant Gary L. Bauer). The timing of the legislation, during an election season (electoral-rich California being a state where most ethnic Japanese reside), also helped seal the victory for reparations activists.

"This is a great day for America," the president proclaimed upon signing the apology and compensation package into law.[23] The first $20,000-per-individual check was issued two years later along with an apology signed by President George H.W. Bush. Eligible recipients included Japanese enemy aliens arrested by the FBI immediately after Pearl Harbor, West Coast residents who evacuated on their own after Pearl Harbor but before Executive Order 9066 was signed, the 4,300 students who left relocation centers for college, tens of thousands of camp residents who left to live and work outside the West Coast, and the 5,918 babies born in the relocation centers during the war. (Later, eight Japanese Americans who were ineligible for reparations sued successfully to bend the eligibility requirements. Half were *Nisei* conceived during the evacuation and relocation period, but born after the reparations-eligibility cutoff date.)[24]

Also eligible were 450 Aleut residents evacuated from their home islands by the United States when the Japanese attacked and invaded the Aleutian Islands at Kiska and Attu in June 1942. They received $12,000 each despite the commission's acknowledgment that "the evacuation of the Aleuts was a rational wartime measure taken to safeguard them."[25]

Under the compensation scheme, an evacuee who refused to take a loyalty oath, an evacuee who renounced his American citizenship, an evacuee who resisted the draft, and an evacuee who volunteered to serve in the U.S. armed forces were all equally deserving of an apology and a check. A disloyal evacuee who terrorized other camp residents received the same payment as a patriotic evacuee who assisted military authorities in the relocation and war efforts. Those who returned to Japan during the war were barred from receiving payments, but renunciants who returned to Japan immediately after the war were eligible for reparations. Japanese who were interned at Justice Department camps—including those from Latin America—received compensation as well. The Clinton administration expanded eligibility for reparations to 155 family members of Japanese railroad and mine workers who were fired from their jobs as security risks during World War II, but were not evacuated, relocated, or interned.[26]

Japanese enemy aliens individually arrested by the FBI immediately after the Pearl Harbor attack received compensation. But their German and Italian counterparts did not. German and Italian internees and their families who lived side-by-side with their Japanese counterparts in Justice Department-run internment camps were also denied reparations. In October 1992, the U.S. Supreme Court refused without comment to hear an appeal by retired U.S. Air Force Major Arthur D. Jacobs, American-born son of a German internee, who lived with his family at the Crystal City, Texas, internment camp alongside Japanese internees who received reparations payments. Jacobs had argued pointedly that the reparations law unconstitutionally discriminated against non-Japanese internees in violation of the Equal Protection clause.[27] A lower court had dismissed his argument, blindly citing the Commission on Wartime Relocation and Internment of Civilians' conclusion that ethnic Japanese evacuees and internees were uniquely singled out exclusively because of their race without any military justification.

This race-based awarding of reparations seemed not to bother the law's supporters. "For the first time in history," *International Examiner* writer Chizu Omori noted approvingly, "the U.S. government actually apologized for something that it had done, and admitted . . . it had done so out of an act of racism."[28] Activist William Hohri, who led a separate Japanese American campaign to sue the government "for an unambiguously adversarial sum of twenty-seven billion dollars,"[29] crowed, "Though I intend to enjoy the money—it will be my way of dancing on the graves of John J. McCloy, Karl R. Bendetsen, and all the other bastards—I think something more than the transfer of funds has happened to us. It is something like renewal, rebirth, a reawakening. Like the Tao, it may be nameless, yet real and true."[30]

"HAUNT THE CONSCIENCE OF THIS NATION"

The case for reparations was based almost entirely on the eighteen-month-long study of the nine-member commission, which concluded in its final report that, "Executive Order 9066 was not justified by military necessity, and the decisions that followed from it—exclusion, detention, the ending of detention, and the ending of exclusion—were not founded upon military considerations. The broad historical causes that shaped these decisions were race prejudice, war hysteria, and a failure of political leadership."[31]

Panel members and staff seemed predisposed to arrive at that sweeping conclusion before the hearing process began. "We tried to get as many liberals as possible on the commission," Mike Masaoka, former JACL executive secretary, admitted to the *National Journal*.[32] Responding to a reporter's question about why the witness list was so light on former government officials with direct knowledge and expertise on the World War II evacuation and relocation, a panel spokesman glibly stated, "When you've got bad guys, they don't usually show up. For forty years we lived with what we knew and what scholars knew was wrong."[33] Before the panel launched its investigation, chairwoman Joan Bernstein, a Washington attorney, called the World War II evacuation and relocation "a blot upon the history of the United States"[34] and said her duty was to determine "how"—not *whether*—"it was that the nation's military and civilian leaders decided to evacuate and confine one hundred twenty thousand people for no reason other than their ancestry."[35] Sen. Daniel Inouye (Democrat from Hawaii) goaded unabashedly, "Make your report one that will haunt the conscience of this nation—haunt it so that we will never forget that we are capable of such an act."[36]

Two of the commission members, Philadelphia-area common-pleas judge William Marutani and Aleutian Island priest Ishmael Vincent Gromoff, were themselves evacuees. While Marutani renounced any monetary recompense, Gromoff stood to benefit directly from passage of a reparations law. Other commissioners had already gone on record condemning Executive Order 9066. Former Supreme Court Justice Arthur Goldberg said it was "very wrong" and that the "basic question before our commission is: what can we appropriately recommend to redress a constitutional violation of such magnitude?"[37] Commission member Father Robert Drinan, a former congressman, began with the question, "How much are we going to give them?" Among those who served as consultants and researchers for the commission were Roger Daniels, then a history professor at the University of Cincinnati who had already authored *Prisoners Without Trial: Japanese Americans in World War II* and a nine-volume history entitled *American Concentration Camps: A Documentary History of the Relocation and Incarceration of Japanese Americans, 1941–1945*; Jack Herzig, a prominent redress advocate; and Herzig's wife, Aiko Herzig-Yoshinaga, who was hired as a research associate and is cited three times[38] as an anecdotal source in the final commission report.

While working for the commission, Herzig-Yoshinaga parlayed her tax-subsidized archival research—which "formed the core" of the commission's primary documentation[39]—into evidence for private lawsuits challenging the Supreme Court's World War II rulings upholding the war powers of the executive branch.[40] She had met and befriended Peter Irons, an activist

attorney and legal historian, during her tenure on the commission and surreptitiously shared confidential documents with him. Irons later used the
documents to challenge the *Hirabayashi*, *Yasui*, and *Korematsu* rulings (see
Appendix E). Herzig-Yoshinaga also shared her research with the National
Council for Japanese American Redress, a group she belonged to that unsuccessfully pursued a $27 billion class-action lawsuit against the government
on behalf of evacuees.[41]

The agenda of a commission hearing held in Seattle during the fall of
1981 highlights how stacked the deck was.[42] In a seven-and-a-half-hour
marathon, forty-two witnesses testified. Thirty-nine supported redress and
reparations. They included Robert Sadamu Shimabukuro, who later
authored a cheerleading account of the reparations campaign called *Born in
Seattle*, and Tetsuden Kashima, who later wrote the forward to the panel's
final report and authored his own book, *Judgment Without Trial: Japanese
American Imprisonment during World War II*. Kashima was joined by four
other Japanese American professors for an hour-long "panel on social
impact." The invitees also included two members of the American Civil Liberties Union, a Japanese Peruvian internee, four witnesses who testified
about how Aleuts suffered during the evacuation of Alaska, a member of the
American Jewish Committee, and a representative of the "Cosmopolitan
Brotherhood Association." Not until the end of the day did three pro-
government witnesses, all military officials during World War II who had
knowledge of the relocation process, have a chance to testify. They were
allotted a total of fifteen minutes to speak.

Similar travesties took place at the San Francisco and Los Angeles hearings, the latter of which Chinese-American journalist Frank Chin referred
to as a "circus of freaks" dominated by the "mob-like reaction of spectators.
The audience, Chin noted, "came not to listen but to cheer their side at a
sporting event... The Japanese Americans at the L.A. hearing, in the audience and at the witness table, were indulging themselves."[43]

Tellingly, the commission was stacked with left-leaning lawyers, politicians, and civil rights activists—but not a single military officer or intelligence expert. Only at the tail end of the hearings were two high-ranking

officials from the Roosevelt administration—Assistant Secretary of War John McCloy and evacuation coordinator Karl Bendetsen—called to testify. The audience treated both rudely. Recounting his experience before the panel at a 1984 congressional hearing, McCloy noted, "Every time I tried to say anything in favor of the United States or in favor of the president of the United States, there were hisses and boos and stomping of feet, which was disgraceful."[44] Bendetsen had a similar experience, "The Commission didn't keep order in these hearings. Those who were the proponents of [reparations] booed and hissed. When I testified in the caucus room of the Russell Senate Office Building, many of the proponents were there and they booed and hissed me. It wasn't very well run."[45] Explaining why he didn't testify about MAGIC to the Commission, Bendetsen said, "I knew it would be fruitless. Every Commissioner had made up his mind before he was appointed—I know most of them—except the congressman from California [Dan Lungren]."[46]

LOYALTY AND INTELLIGENCE

The panel's final report is touted by ethnic Japanese activists as containing "mountains of evidence and detail."[47] Kashima's foreword boasts that "No other volume on the wartime incarceration experience has had the benefit of drawing from such as extensive array of materials, investigatory skill, and assistance from witnesses and other scholars."[48] Yet the report's section on intelligence is just ten pages long, much of it devoted to the work of Curtis Munson, the FDR confidant who was not a professional intelligence officer. The report's review of intelligence did not consider most of the ONI, MID, and FBI memos reproduced in Appendix C. One of the few reports cited, the January 26, 1942, memo by Kenneth Ringle, was quoted selectively; passages that did not support the commission's position were ignored. The report contains no mention of intelligence agencies' unequivocal assessments in late 1941 and early 1942 that Japan's West Coast espionage network continued to function after Pearl Harbor. The Niihau incident merits only a brief footnote.

The commission report, however, does contain an entire chapter on the military service of *Nisei* volunteers in the Military Intelligence Service language school, the 100th Battalion, and the 442nd Regimental Combat Team formed in early 1943.[49] "The question of loyalty had been most powerfully answered by a battlefield record of courage and sacrifice," the panel concluded. There is no question that the *Nisei* soldiers who fought and died for their country were unassailably patriotic, loyal, and brave. But the record of the brave *Nisei* who served in the U.S. military does not prove that all *Nisei* (including the thousands who refused to serve) were loyal to America any more than the thousands of *Nisei* who served in the Japanese military proved that all *Nisei* were loyal to Japan. Interestingly, the logic behind the commission's position is the obverse of the complaint that ethnic Japanese were grouped for evacuation not on individual conduct but on the perceived faults of a few. Why, if ethnically based generalizations are wrong, is it acceptable to make sweeping pronouncements about *Nisei* loyalty based on the good conduct of a few? In any case, at the time the decision to evacuate the West Coast was made, the impressive record of *Nisei* military service had not yet occurred and thus could not be taken into account by the White House, the military, or intelligence officials.

The commission's report claims that the ethnic organizations that many *Nisei* and *Issei* belonged to, such as *kais*, Buddhist temples, and language schools were "wrongly viewed as mechanisms through which the Japanese government could influence and control the *Issei* and *Nisei*."[50] But as intelligence analysts pointed out at the time, the Japanese language schools used nationalistic textbooks that had been selected by Japan's Department of Education. The schools were often run by Japanese consular agents who were under the direct control of the Japanese Foreign Ministry, or by Buddhist priests who were supervised from headquarters in Japan, or by many senior *kais* officials who had close connections to Japanese government officials (military officials, consular officials, or both).[51]

The commission's report claims that "the FBI and members of Naval Intelligence who had relevant intelligence responsibility were ignored when they stated that nothing more than careful watching of suspicious individuals or individual reviews of loyalty were called for by existing circumstances."[52] This is apparently a reference to Kenneth Ringle and J. Edgar Hoover—neither of whom believed that "nothing more than careful watching of suspicious individuals" was called for. Both men urged that the government be given the authority to lock up suspected subversives without proof of a crime.

The commission lambastes Western Defense Commander Lieutenant General John DeWitt for repeating "the prejudiced, unfounded themes of anti-Japanese factions and interest groups on the West Coast" in formulating his support for mass evacuation. In particular, the report includes many pages criticizing the explanations for evacuation given in DeWitt's document, *Final Report: Japanese Evacuation from the West Coast, 1942,* but fails to mention that because the report was distributed to the public at the time of its release in January 1944, when the war was still under way, DeWitt could not discuss the major evidence supporting the evacuation: MAGIC. Moreover, while the commission preferred to leave the impression that the supposedly bigoted DeWitt instigated the evacuation, it is clear that military and War Department leaders in Washington initiated the West Coast evacuation recommendation under the direction of President Roosevelt.

The commission report criticizes the Roosevelt administration for taking "no effective measures to disabuse public belief that disloyalty had contributed to massive American losses on December 7, 1941. Thus the country was unfairly led to believe that both American citizens of Japanese descent and resident Japanese aliens threatened American security."[53] Yet, while some false rumors were spread about the Pearl Harbor attack, the existence of the spy ring based at Honolulu's Japanese consulate—aided by at least one *Nisei* and at least one *Issei*—was real, and its vital role in gathering intelligence central to the air raid's implementation is indisputable.[54] As the MAGIC cables and other intelligence revealed, similar spy rings operated in Los Angeles, Seattle, and San Francisco.

The report blasts Attorney General Francis Biddle, who opposed evacuation, for not arguing to FDR that "the Constitution prohibited exclusion on the basis of ethnicity given the facts on the West Coast." But in fact, Biddle's legal advisers had concluded that the evacuation would pass constitutional muster—a judgment later proved correct when the U.S. Supreme Court upheld the evacuation in *Korematsu v. United States*.

The commission attacks Roosevelt for "not raising the question to the level of Cabinet discussion or requiring any thoughtful or thorough review of the situation."[55] But the evacuation issue was discussed in at least one cabinet meeting on January 30, 1942;[56] the War Department, Justice Department, and the Provost Marshal General's Office, among others, devoted countless hours to studying the situation; and the decision, far from being thoughtless, was based in large part on remarkable intelligence, MAGIC, that had been obtained by America's sharpest minds. Certainly our wartime leaders could have been even more thorough if they had pushed everything else aside and devoted eighteen months to study the issue, as the commission did. But with Japanese and German submarines looming off our coastlines and Axis forces advancing around the world, it is not hard to understand why FDR wanted decisions made quickly.

The commission report claims that from a military standpoint, the evacuation policy was "bizarre" and "utterly impractical," because it did not eliminate any alleged threat of subversive activities by ethnic Japanese but, rather, merely moved it inland.[57] But the same "bizarre" policy was already being implemented in Canada and Mexico, both of which viewed it as a reasonable precautionary measure designed to ensure that subversive activities by ethnic Japanese didn't occur in their most vulnerable coastal areas.

The report attacks Secretary of War Henry Stimson and Assistant Secretary of War John McCloy for "fail[ing] to insist on a clear military justification" for mass evacuation and relocation.[58] But in fact, the intelligence reports received by Stimson and McCloy described very clearly the threats posed by disloyal ethnic Japanese on the West Coast.[59] The report neglects to note that in late January both top cabinet officials were given copies of an army MID report warning of continued Japanese espionage,[60] that both men had access to MAGIC,[61] and that MAGIC significantly informed McCloy's recommendations (and most likely Stimson's, too).[62]

The commission failed to even acknowledge the existence of long-declassified MAGIC cables until months after it had published its report. Only when David Lowman garnered attention for a *New York Times* critique of the commission report in late May 1983—a piece that raised potent questions about the omission of MAGIC—did the panel finally, grudgingly, and flippantly address the MAGIC messages.[63] "Anyone reading this flow of messages during 1941 could easily conclude that thousands of resident Japanese were being organized into subversive organizations," Lowman, who helped oversee the declassification and public release of MAGIC in the 1970s, told the *Times*.[64]

How did the commission answer Lowman's arguments? As we shall see, those with vested financial and emotional interests in perpetuating their false history of events responded with an astonishing display of intellectual dishonesty.

Chapter 11

The "Puffery" Defense

When challenged by reporters about the glaring omission of the MAGIC cables from their final report, members of the Commission on Wartime Relocation and Internment of Civilians and its special counsel, Angus MacBeth, confessed that they had not been aware of MAGIC.[1] MacBeth explained that the commission hadn't located any references to the cables "in the extensive documents of the time which deal with exclusion and detention."[2] MAGIC was not mentioned explicitly in "documents *of the time*" (emphasis added) because it was, of course, top secret and limited to only a select number of FDR's closest advisers, all of whom took pains not to mention it in written documents that could fall into the wrong hands. Immediately after the war, however, the existence of MAGIC was revealed through lengthy congressional hearings on the Pearl Harbor attack. The joint congressional committee that investigated Pearl Harbor concluded that MAGIC "contributed enormously to the defeat of the enemy, greatly shortened the war, saved many thousands of American lives," and was "some of the finest intelligence in our history."[3] By 1970, three key historical accounts covered the story: Roberta Wohlestetter's *Pearl Harbor, Warning and Decision*, Ladislas Farago's *The Broken Seal*, and David Kahn's *The Codebreakers*. And the eight-volume MAGIC publication, which reproduced some five thousand-plus cables, was published by

the Department of Defense in 1977. MacBeth and his staff's failure to connect MAGIC with the West Coast evacuation underscores their disregard
for intelligence and their faulty investigative techniques. Their dishonest
use of the MAGIC cables underscores their bias and unreliability.

MacBeth produced a hasty, thin analysis—tacked on to the end of the
final report as a five-page addendum—pooh-poohing the decrypted messages that served as the principal basis for the evacuation decision. It was
"very difficult to distinguish puffery from truth in the 'Magic' documents,"
MacBeth sniffed.[4] MacBeth and his staff of civilian lawyers may have had
trouble comprehending Japan's designs, but the Roosevelt administration's
top military and intelligence officials seem to have understood them well.
The MAGIC messages stated in plain detail how enemy agents of the Japanese government were establishing elaborate espionage networks, recruiting
West Coast residents of Japanese ancestry to monitor U.S. military installations, and gathering information on ship, plane, and troop movements.
MAGIC revealed that Japanese American collaborators were planted in the
U.S. military and in strategic areas such as Bremerton, San Pedro, San Diego,
and along the Mexican border.[5]

America's leaders took this alarming information seriously and acted on
it. After the Pearl Harbor attack, which might have been foreseen if the
MAGIC messages had been read more closely and more quickly by the right
people, it would have been ridiculously reckless for military and intelligence
officials to have treated as "puffery" top-secret cables sent by Japan's highly
trained, professional diplomatic corps. Why on earth would our enemy's
embassy and consular officials have wasted so much time and energy trying
to keep their messages secret if all they were doing was sending harmless
bluster? While MacBeth suggested that these "minor" MAGIC cables had
no bearing on the decision to evacuate,[6] it is clear, as noted in Chapter 8,
that several actions taken by the Roosevelt administration were uniquely
influenced by MAGIC—including the evacuation of Bainbridge Island,
Washington, Terminal Island, California, and southern Arizona. Both of the
senior administration officials who testified before the commission—John

McCloy and Karl Bendetsen—later stated in congressional testimony that the MAGIC messages (or intelligence derived directly from them) played a major role in the development of the evacuation policy.

McCloy's detractors knocked him for neglecting to mention MAGIC in his testimony before the commission, and for giving conflicting answers on the role that espionage reports played in the decision to evacuate the West Coast. At the time of his appearance before the commission in the fall of 1981, he was eighty-six-years old. Advanced in age, his memory simply needed refreshing. Unlike so many Japanese-American activists and their sympathizers in academia, whose narrow obsession was (and continues to be) the perceived injustice of the West Coast evacuation, McCloy did not dedicate his life to this singular event and its ramifications. The wartime evacuation was just one of myriad policy areas he was involved in before, during, and after World War II. Contrary to the comic book portrayal of McCloy as a simpleminded bigot with a grudge against ethnic Japanese, he was a distinguished American with an impressive record of service to his country: Harvard Law School graduate, artillery officer during World War I, assistant secretary of war under Roosevelt, U.S. high commissioner in postwar Germany, World Bank president, arms adviser to President John F. Kennedy, member of the Warren Commission which investigated Kennedy's assassination, and foreign policy adviser to Presidents Lyndon Johnson, Richard Nixon, Jimmy Carter, and Ronald Reagan.

It is also important to recall the culture of secrecy surrounding MAGIC. The decrypts weren't mentioned by name in phone conversations or written memos. This habit was no doubt deeply engrained in McCloy. At the time he testified before the CWRIC, he might not have even known the decrypts had been declassified.

Given time to reflect and review the evidence leading to the signing of Executive Order 9066, however, McCloy testified before Congress two years after his commission appearance—without the unsettling rudeness, boos, and hisses that marred his earlier testimony—and was unequivocal that MAGIC had played an instrumental role in War Department decision-making.[7]

Despite imperiously dismissing MAGIC's veracity and importance, MacBeth selectively quoted from the cables to show that they somehow supported the commission's foregone conclusions that the World War II evacuation and relocation were motivated by "race prejudice, war hysteria, and a failure of political leadership." MacBeth notes, for example, that one MAGIC cable outlined plans to utilize non-Japanese (including "communists, Negroes, labor union members, and anti-Semites") as well as "our 'Second Generations' and our resident nationals."[8] This echoes similar assertions earlier in the commission report, such as that "the professionals largely agreed that the Japanese did not rely on *Issei* and *Nisei* for espionage,"[9] and "experience showed that [Japan] did not trust the *Nisei*, employing Occidentals for espionage."[10]

The MAGIC messages do indeed provide definitive evidence that Japan sought or used ethnic non-Japanese for espionage activities—a fact that was well known to U.S. intelligence agencies at the time. But MAGIC also showed diplomats discussing *Nisei* and *Issei* agents by name, asserting that "absolutely reliable" ethnic Japanese espionage agents were monitoring shipments of war matériel and airplanes in Southern California, and reporting that "our second generation draftees in the (U.S.) Army" were collecting intelligence on matters pertaining to the U.S. military.[11] There was no mention of "absolutely reliable" white or black agents; nor was there any mention of white or black agents in the U.S. military.

And consider the totality of the intelligence evidence available at the time: the ethnic Japanese fifth columnists who assisted invading Japanese forces throughout Southeast Asia; the ethnic Japanese (e.g., Richard Kotoshirodo, John Mikami, Toraichi Kono, Dr. Takashi Furusawa and his wife, Sachiko) in the Honolulu and Los Angeles spy rings; the names of the espionage agents uncovered in Itaru Tachibana's documents (Maki of San Francisco, Kurokawa of Honolulu, and Fukuchi of an unspecified location[12]); the dozens of ethnic Japanese Tokyo Club Syndicate members who were suspected by ONI of espionage or other subversive activities; the existence of large groups loyal to the emperor up and down the West Coast; the presence of thousands of *Nisei* in *Japan's* military; and the West Coast presence of thousands of *Kibei* whom intelligence officials considered extremely dangerous. In short, there is no question that Japan utilized spies of all races, but there is also no question that ethnic Japanese were routinely included in espionage activities and were much more likely to serve as Japanese agents than members of other races.

California Representative Dan Lungren later wrote a brief rebuttal to MacBeth's addendum buried at the back of the final report. Unlike the rest of the panelists, Lungren expressed incredulity at MacBeth's claim that MAGIC had no bearing on the West Coast evacuation:

> For us as a Commission to deny that the decoded Japanese cables compiled in the MAGIC volumes did not influence the decision made by America's leaders, tends to undercut the credibility of our historical pursuit. Although history now shows that the Japanese government was not successful in its efforts, the cables clearly indicate that there were verifiable and overt attempts made by the Japanese government to organize Japanese Americans into various categories and recruit them for espionage activities . . . it seems inconceivable that these classified cables did not play at least a limited role in the decisions that were made. This is especially true, since it seems certain that the Secretary of War, the Army Chief of Staff, the Director of Military Intelligence, the Secretary of the Navy, the Chief of Naval Operations, the Chief of the Navy's War Plans Division, the Director of Naval Intelligence, the Secretary of State, and the President all had knowledge of the contents of the cables dealing with Japanese espionage activities.[13]

Lungren was right to question the commission's dismissal of MAGIC, of course, but his statement that "history now shows that the Japanese government was not successful in its efforts" is inaccurate. Numerous MAGIC messages sent by Japan's West Coast and Hawaii consulates in the summer and fall of 1941 contained sensitive military information such as ship movements—information that in at least two instances was explicitly attributed to Japan's spies. These messages clearly supported the assessments of ONI and MID that by late 1941 Japan's West Coast espionage network was not just some figment of consular officials' imagination but had been in fact successfully established (see Appendix C).

(Lungren voted against reparations, and was later punished at the ballot box for daring to dissent; in 1988, Japanese American activists led a successful campaign to torpedo his confirmation to the California state treasurer's post. This was a preview of the attempt to strip Representative Howard Coble of a crucial subcommittee chairmanship in 2003 after he defended the West Coast evacuation.)

Aside from MacBeth, only two significant rebuttals dismissing the role of MAGIC in the West Coast evacuation have been attempted. One came from Jack Herzig, the aforementioned adviser to the commission and a retired army counterintelligence officer, who testified before Congress in 1984 in response to David Lowman's testimony. The other rebuttal came from the aforementioned activist lawyer Peter Irons, who submitted written testimony to Congress in 1984 and wrote briefly about the dispute in his book, *Justice Delayed: The Record of the Japanese Internment Cases.*

Herzig's rejoinder began inauspiciously by denying that the commission was ignorant of MAGIC. As noted, the chairwoman of the commission, Joan Bernstein, as well as commissioner Robert Drinan and counsel Angus MacBeth, had already stated unequivocally that they had not been aware of the decoded cables. Next, Herzig tried to discredit the MAGIC cables cited by Lowman. Downplaying the vital role played by MAGIC intelligence in both the Pacific and European theaters, Herzig pooh-poohed the value of the remarkable cables, claiming that they contained "unsubstantiated information, subject to many errors"[14]—as if any intelligence is foolproof. He made a great fuss over the fact that one of the messages[15] contained information that could have been derived from open sources such as newspaper articles—even though it is common for espionage agents to supplement classified information with information gathered from open sources. An ONI analysis of Los Angeles-based spymaster Itaru Tachibana's materials, for example, revealed that "about 70% of the national defense information was compiled from public reading material."[16]

Like MacBeth, Herzig flatly stated his belief that MAGIC did not play a key role in the decision to evacuate the West Coast:

I don't see any evidence that points to that. Had that been the case, I think the representatives of those agencies that I mentioned would have mentioned it. I think the official historian, Dr. David [sic] Conn, in the Army's series of volumes on actions that they took during the war and are still continuing to do—I don't see any reason that those cables, had they played a key part, would not have been mentioned in any documentation since that time.[17]

At the time army historian Stetson Conn wrote his report in 1964, the MAGIC material was still classified. While it is true that others (not government officials) were writing about MAGIC, Conn was bound by the official classification—a basic fact Herzig ignores repeatedly when questioning why Conn and other government officials did not mention MAGIC explicitly. This is a strange omission coming from someone who claims expertise in counterintelligence.

Peter Irons recycled Herzig's main arguments, emphasizing that Lowman "had found only six cables that mentioned Japanese Americans as possible intelligence sources."[18] Just how many cables were our military leaders supposed to see before being persuaded that infiltration of aircraft plants and the military by "absolutely reliable" ethnic Japanese agents posed a bona fide threat? Spy rings have been broken with less information than that contained in a single MAGIC message. In addition, it is worth noting that the eight volumes of MAGIC cables published by the Defense Department contain "a major part of the communications intelligence which the United States derived from intercepted Japanese communications during 1941"— but not all of it, only those messages that related to Pearl Harbor.[19]

In any case, voluminous pre-war intelligence, not just from MAGIC, raised serious concerns about ethnic Japanese espionage. As Irons himself concluded in earlier research, there was "no question" that the Los Angeles–based Tachibana spy ring enlisted "both aliens and citizens" of Japanese descent (see Chapter 3).

To counter the congressional testimony of Roosevelt officials John McCloy and Karl Bendetsen, who directly affirmed the role of MAGIC in the decision to evacuate the West Coast, Irons introduced Edward Ennis, a Justice Department lawyer under Roosevelt, who "bluntly denied" their claims. Unlike McCloy and Bendetsen, however, Ennis did not play a primary role in the West Coast evacuation decision. Moreover, he was not privy to MAGIC.

Unlike the modern-day detractors of America's World War II leaders, the Roosevelt administration's contemporaneous political opponents demonstrated extraordinary respect for the strategic value of our code-breaking operations and cooperated to protect them at all costs. When Republican presidential candidate Thomas Dewey vowed to make intelligence failures at Pearl Harbor a campaign issue in 1944, which raised the dire possibility that the cracking of Japanese codes might become a public issue, Army Chief of Staff General George Marshall appealed directly and confidentially to Dewey (without Roosevelt's knowledge) to desist. "The main basis for information regarding Hitler's intentions in Europe is obtained from Baron Oshima's messages from Berlin reporting his interviews with Hitler and other officials," Marshall explained. "These are still in the codes involved in the Pearl Harbor events." He continued:

> To explain further the critical nature of this set-up which would be wiped out almost in an instant if the least suspicion were aroused regarding it, the battle of the Coral Sea was based on deciphered messages and therefore our few ships were in the right place at the right time. Further, we were able to concentrate our limited forces to meet their naval advance on Midway when otherwise we almost certainly would have been some 3,000 miles out of place. We had full information on the strength of their forces in that advance and also of the smaller force directed against the Aleutians which finally landed troops on Atta and Kiska.

> Operations in the Pacific are largely guided by the information we obtain of Japanese deployments. We know their strength in various garrisons, the rations and other stores continuing available to them, and what is of vast importance, we check their fleet movements and the movements of their convoys. The heavy losses reported from time to time which they sustain by reason of our submarine action, largely result from the fact that we know the sailing dates and routes of their convoys and can notify our submarines to lie in wait at the proper points.

Marshall then asked Dewey to consider "the utterly tragic consequences if the present political debates regarding Pearl Harbor disclose to the enemy, German or Jap, any suspicion of the vital sources of information we possess." Putting the national interest above his political ambitions, Dewey heeded Marshall's advice.[20]

Then, as now, any fair-minded assessment of MAGIC could only conclude that it contained intelligence vital to U.S. security and integral to homeland defense policies. It was not, as the commission and its supporters have for so long maintained, mere "puffery" or "unsubstantiated information" to be shrugged off or cherry-picked to suit a political agenda geared toward disproving the military arguments for the West Coast evacuation and relocation. Nevertheless, respected scholars continue to publish accounts of the World War II evacuation and relocation that virtually ignore the role of MAGIC and other espionage-related intelligence in the Roosevelt administration's national security decision-making.

In 2001, Harvard University Press published Canadian history professor Greg Robinson's book, *By Order of the President: FDR and the Internment of Japanese Americans* [sic]. Praised by reviewers as a "a precise, sobering account of racism, misinformation, hysteria, and the violation of democratic rights and procedures in the name of national interest" and as a "careful, thorough, and scrupulously fair analysis," Robinson's work condemns Roosevelt's "prejudicial" and "racialist" approval of the "unprecedented mistreatment" of ethnic Japanese during World War II. Mention of MAGIC is relegated to two brief sentences related to prewar negotiations with Japan

and a single footnote that tersely asserts that "The MAGIC excerpts [sic²¹]
do not reveal conclusive evidence of any espionage activities by Japanese
Americans."²² What could be more conclusive than a simple declarative
statement from Japanese diplomats that they were utilizing ethnic Japanese
spies? In any case, the MAGIC messages did not reveal "conclusive" evidence of Germany's intent to attack Russia in June 1941, but the top-secret
messages sent to Tokyo by Japan's German ambassador indicating that an
attack was imminent proved stunningly correct. Decoded naval messages
did not provide "conclusive" evidence that Japan intended to attack Midway, but those messages turned out to be accurate as well. Few knowledgeable observers would dispute the conclusion of the Joint Congressional
Committee that investigated the Pearl Harbor attack:

> With extraordinary skill, zeal and watchfulness, the intelligence services
> of the Army Signal Corps and the Navy Office of Naval Communications
> broke Japanese codes and intercepted messages between the Japanese
> Government and its spies and agents and ambassadors in all parts of the
> world and supplied the high authorities in Washington with *reliable secret
> information respecting Japanese designs, decisions, and operations at home,
> in the United States, and other countries* (emphasis added).²³

In 2003, the University of Washington published Tetsuden Kashima's book
*Judgment Without Trial: Japanese American Imprisonment During World War
II*. In more than three hundred pages, MAGIC received a scant two paragraphs. Kashima recycled Herzig's anemic criticism that the messages didn't
matter much because some of them showed Japan using open sources to
gather information. Kashima also noted there was "no indication among all
the messages of any plan to organize sabotage activities"—a crafty argument
shift away from the MAGIC revelations of Japan's intricate and extensive
espionage operations in the United States and around the world. Finally,
Kashima observed that "of the nineteen suspects convicted of committing
acts of espionage in the United States in the years before and during World
War II, none had a recognizably Japanese name."²⁴

The latter argument was also made by Angus MacBeth and has often been used as a trump card in the debate over the West Coast evacuation and relocation. Critics of the roundup are quick to point out that no *Issei* or *Nisei* were tried for espionage during World War II, whereas a number of Caucasians were tried and convicted for espionage-related crimes. The implicit assumption is that if ethnic Japanese were engaged in espionage, prosecutions would have been pursued. This assumption, however, is not valid. In the case of the Los Angeles–based spy ring, as noted in Chapter 4, prosecutions of ethnic Japanese residents, including Charlie Chaplin's valet, an *Issei*, were not pursued because DOJ deferred to the State Department, which had hoped to reach a diplomatic solution to the troubled U.S.-Japan relationship.

Another reason that ethnic Japanese spies were not prosecuted is that they were more difficult to root out than Caucasian spies. There is not one documented case of an ethnic Japanese espionage agent or saboteur—*Issei* or *Nisei*—turning himself in to U.S. authorities. By contrast, a group of German saboteurs was apprehended after two of the ring's members turned themselves in. In addition, a German spy ring was broken up as a result of the efforts of a double agent—a German citizen—who infiltrated the ring on behalf of the United States. In hearings shortly after the Pearl Harbor attack, ONI Chief Irving Mayfield said, "It has been my experience [with] which I believe the other two investigative agencies [the FBI and Army] agree, that to investigate a Japanese is exceedingly difficult."[25]

FBI field agents certainly shared that view. In a February 2, 1942, memo, FBI Director J. Edgar Hoover reported that the FBI's Seattle office had found that "Japanese individuals either alien or American, do not volunteer information. It is believed that since December 7th, at best, there have been less than 20 [ethnic] Japanese individuals who called at the Seattle Field Office for the purpose of offering information."[26] The same memo passed along similar information from the FBI's San Francisco office:

> This office has since the declaration of war attempted to develop confidential informants, sources of information and contacts among the Japanese colony in San Francisco through mass contact; [for] example, by

contacting all professional Japanese such as doctors, dentists, lawyers, barbers, beauty salon operators, pool halls, et cetera. These individuals were contacted with a view of getting coverage on all places where Japanese might congregate or frequent and engage in gossip and general conversation. In this project there was no distinction made as to whether the individual was alien or citizen. The results of these contacts have been nil almost without exception. Out of approximately fifty contacts, only four or five appeared to be cooperative enough to consider as possible informants. None of these individuals has yet furnished any information of value.[27]

The memo goes on to identify specific ethnic Japanese who had repeatedly promised their full cooperation but never furnished any information that would warrant the opening of a case. One of these individuals, a *Nisei*, stated at a JACL meeting that he had been contacted by the FBI but "had no intention of becoming a 'stool pigeon,'" according to the memo.[28]

Some individuals working on behalf of Japan, it should be noted, provided Japan with information that was sensitive but unclassified. Though some advocated prosecution of Hawaiian *Nisei* Richard Kotoshirodo, for example, it was not clear that he violated any law. In other cases it seems likely that laws were broken, but it would have been impossible to win a conviction in a civilian court without revealing classified intelligence sources. As discussed in Appendix D, the failed prosecution of Kenji Ito for failing to register as a foreign agent probably would have been successful had the jury been able to view the MAGIC messages. Pursuing fruitless cases—in which prosecutors were unable to use smoking-gun evidence—would have required time, effort, and resources that would have been diverted from critical counterespionage operations.

The most important reason for the paucity of prosecutions against ethnic Japanese for espionage-related activity was the existence of viable alternatives—internment camps for enemy aliens, relocation centers for West Coast evacuees, and, in Hawaii, draconian controls on civilians' movements and activities and military tribunals—that made prosecution of ethnic

Japanese in civilian courts unnecessary. Such alternatives were generally unavailable on the mainland for U.S. citizens of non-Japanese descent.

The Roosevelt administration, in short, had good reasons for avoiding criminal prosecutions of ethnic Japanese. That doesn't change the fact that intelligence officials had assembled compelling evidence of a Japanese spy ring operating along the West Coast, that there was good reason to believe this espionage network routinely utilized ethnic Japanese, that intelligence officials firmly believed the network continued to operate after Pearl Harbor, and that intelligence officials regarded the presence of ethnic Japanese espionage agents on the West Coast as a serious security threat.

Unfortunately, the "Puffery Defense" has obscured the Roosevelt administration's solid rationale for evacuation—and it remains embedded in modern American history books, pop culture, and official government accounts.

Chapter 12

Damning America

Mass-market novels and movies such as *Farewell to Manzanar*, *Come See the Paradise*, and *Snow Falling on Cedars* have popularized the view of the West Coast evacuation as an unmitigated wrong, but the most worrisome propagandizing is that carried out by the U.S. government.

At the Manzanar relocation center in California, a government-endorsed plaque refers to the national historic site as the first of ten "concentration camps"—a phrase that, used today, is loaded with unmistakable connotations of evil and barbarity far beyond the dry dictionary definition. "May the injustices and humiliation suffered here as a result of hysteria, racism and economic exploitation never emerge again," the plaque concludes.[1] When the late *Dallas Morning News* editorial writer and esteemed syndicated columnist Richard Estrada politely challenged these fundamental distortions, angry letter writers compared him to "the misguided people who claim that the Holocaust never happened."[2] Estrada argued:

> The attempt to portray events as worse than they were is morally indefensible. And not only because it unfairly casts aspersions on good and decent people faced with enormous leadership responsibilities at a moment of national crisis. It sabotages our sense of national unity and purpose by

spawning distrust among the nation's ethnic groups. . . The citizenry also has a responsibility to challenge an injustice against the American people as a whole. And that is precisely what the racially aggrieved or the politically correct are perpetrating when they promote the slander that the United States ran concentration camps during World War II.[3]

In response, Japanese American activists cited (what else?) the commission report's conclusion that the evacuation was racist[4] and chastised Estrada for being (what else?) an ignorant bigot.[5] The National Park Service is planning a similar display at the Minidoka relocation center, which was designated a national monument in 2001; legislation is pending that would confer national monument status on Bainbridge Island.

In 1989, the California state legislature passed a resolution adopting the commission's mantra that the West Coast evacuation/relocation (incorrectly referred to as "internment") was "a violation of human rights rather than an act of military necessity." The resolution urged schools to incorporate this theme in teaching materials. When California state assemblyman Gil Ferguson, a Republican and retired marine from Newport Beach, objected to the characterization of World War II decision-makers as racist, he was accused of being anti-Japanese and whitewashing history. "You should be ashamed," Democratic assemblyman Phillip Isenberg said in remarks blasting his colleague. "I think it just demonstrates [Ferguson's] racist attitudes and ill will toward Japanese Americans," Audrey Yamagata-Noji, a Santa Ana Unified School District trustee, lashed out.[6] Ferguson's counterresolution proposing that children learn the full military context of the evacuation went down in flames.[7] Two of his colleagues who sided with him were castigated by Japanese American activists and accused of "creating problems in race relations."[8]

For more than a decade, the influence of the commission's final report on mainstream history books has been enormous, so much so that its conclusions have been adopted as gospel no longer worth countering (or even footnoting). One popular public high school textbook, *The American Pageant*, reads as follows:

There was virtually no government witch-hunting of minority groups, as had happened in World War I. A painful exception was the plight of some 110,000 Japanese Americans, concentrated on the Pacific Coast.... The Washington top command, fearing that they might act as saboteurs for Japan in case of invasion, forcibly herded them together in concentration camps, though about two-thirds of them were American-born U.S. citizens. This brutal precaution was both unnecessary and unfair, as the loyalty and combat record of Japanese Americans proved to be admirable. But a wave of post–Pearl Harbor hysteria, backed by the long historical swell of anti-Japanese prejudice on the West Coast, temporarily robbed many Americans of their good sense—and their sense of justice.[9]

Another leading high school textbook, *America: Pathways to the Present*, strikes a similar chord:

Japanese Americans suffered official discrimination during the war. In late 1941, they were a tiny minority in the United States, numbering only 127,000 (about 0.1 percent of the entire population). Most lived on the West Coast, where racial prejudice against them was strong. About two-thirds of Japanese Americans had been born in the United States. Although they were native-born citizens, they still often met hostility from their white neighbors.

Hostility grew into hatred and hysteria after Japan attacked Pearl Harbor. Rumors flew about sabotage on the West Coast. The press increased people's fears with inaccurate reports carrying headlines such as "Jap Boat Flashes Message Ashore" and "Japanese Here Sent Vital Data to Tokyo." Such reports left Americans feeling that Japanese spies were everywhere.[10]

And *The American Odyssey: The United States in the 20th Century* includes the following passage:

Spring 1942 brought events that are burned into the memories of Japanese Americans. Even though they showed no evidence of disloyalty, more

than 120,000 Japanese Americans were moved from their homes to relocation camps. One evacuee, Helen Murao, explained why. 'We looked like
them [the enemy]. That was our sin.'

Of the 120,000 Japanese Americans who lived on the West Coast and
in Hawaii, about one-third were *Issei*—foreign-born Japanese who had
entered the United States before the National Origns Act of 1924 had dra-
matically cut the number of immigrants allowed into the country. Two-
thirds were *Nisei*—mainly children of *Issei* who were citizens because they
had been born in the United States. In February 1942, the government
decided that all Japanese Americans, citizens as well as aliens, would be
relocated to internment camps located in Arkansas and the Western
states.[11]

All three texts refer to *Issei* enemy aliens as "Japanese Americans." None of
the three texts mentions Japanese espionage in Honolulu and Los Angeles
or MAGIC messages referring to espionage on the West Coast and in the
military or treasonous acts committed by a Japanese American on the
Hawaiian island of Niihau. Like the commission, two of the three texts
indulge in typical rearview mirror critiques of decision-makers who did not
know at the time that "the loyalty and combat record of Japanese Americans" would later prove to be admirable. And all three stress racial animus
as the primary motivating factor behind the evacuation decision.

This is just as Japanese American activists behind the commission and
the reparations law intended. The act signed by President Reagan set aside
five million dollars for "education" projects related to the World War II
evacuation and relocation of ethnic Japanese. The members of the Civil Liberties Public Education Fund openly declared their intention to make it
"common knowledge that the detention of Americans of Japanese ancestry
during World War II was not an act of military necessity but an act of racial
discrimination"—in other words, to perpetuate the myths created by the
Commission on Wartime Relocation and Internment of Civilians and publicize the erroneous conclusions of its final report.[12] As Claremont Institute
scholar Ken Masugi warned when the foundation dispensing the educa-

tional funds was first proposed, "Such a foundation, captured and manned by the constituency that created it, would damn America for its past in the most irresponsible way possible. The studies and so-called public educational activities of this foundation would be little more than ideological fulmination masquerading as scholarship."[13] Indeed, the Civil Liberties Public Education Fund and state-level programs in California[14] and Washington have perpetuated countless historical errors, myths, and distortions through government-sponsored exhibits, memorials, documentaries, books, and other tax-subsidized projects. These include the following:

- The Japanese American Memorial in Washington, D.C., where a brief historical narrative carved in stone erroneously refers to the "the removal of 120,000 Japanese American men, women, and children from their homes in the western United States and Hawaii" as a result of Executive Order 9066. Roughly one-third of those affected were Japanese citizens, not "Japanese Americans." Moreover, "120,000" is an estimate of the total number of individuals who ultimately moved into or were born in the camps, not the number (112,000) who were initially relocated from the West Coast. Much more important, the memorial repeats the ill-informed conclusion of the commission that "there had been no military necessity for the mass imprisonment [sic] of Japanese Americans [sic] and that a grave injustice had been done."[15]

- Documentaries, films, plays, paintings, slide presentations, graphic novels, books, concert performances, websites, CD ROMs, teacher training workshops, and curriculum material with such one-sided perspectives as "Ancestry is Not a Crime" and "How Could This Have Happened in a Democracy?" authored by special-interest groups such as the Japanese American Citizens League and the National Coalition for Redress and Reparations.[16] With a few minor exceptions, all these projects reinforce the findings of the Commission.

- The Smithsonian Institution's exhibit "A More Perfect Union: Japanese Americans and the U.S. Constitution," which fails to mention the

MAGIC messages and ignores the congressional testimony of John McCloy and Karl Bendetsen affirming that the intelligence was critical in the decision to evacuate the West Coast. In 2002, the Smithsonian also admitted using at least one fabricated quote and several faulty statistics to exaggerate the accomplishments of Japanese American soldiers. The exhibit inflated the number of Purple Hearts and Silver Stars awarded to those soldiers and used false casualty figures.[17] After the Institution agreed to fix the errors at the behest of Lieutenant Colonel Lee Allen (founder of the Utah-based Athena Press, which published David Lowman's book, *MAGIC: The Untold Story*) and his son, Sam, the younger Allen noted that Japanese American soldiers "served with great gallantry. Those who exaggerate and fabricate their achievements dishonor them. If an individual had made such outrageous claims it would be called fraud."[18] Colonel Allen concurred:

> This is just the tip of the iceberg in the effort to bring accuracy to the history of the Japanese Americans in World War II. Since the September 11th attacks it has become even more important that we understand what really happened because government policy is being made based on a false understanding of the event. The politically correct notion that race was the main motivation, which the Smithsonian with its poor scholarship buys into, results from denying, ignoring, exaggerating and fabricating important facts.[19]

Critics of the World War II evacuation and relocation are fond of quoting philosopher George Santayana, who warned that "Those who cannot remember the past are condemned to repeat it." Forgetting history is dangerous indeed. But falsifying it is a far worse sin.

12/7, 9/11, and Beyond

Always will we remember the character of the onslaught against us. No matter how long it may take us to overcome this premeditated invasion, the American people in their righteous might will win through to absolute victory. —*President Roosevelt, December 7, 1941*

America has stood down enemies before, and we will do so this time. None of us will ever forget this day. Yet, we go forward to defend freedom and all that is good and just in our world.
—*President Bush, September 11, 2001*

September 11, like December 7 "changed everything" in America.[1] But not enough. The entrenched myths of the "Japanese-American internment" persist. Millions of American schoolchildren have been taught that there was no evidence of ethnic Japanese disloyalty or espionage before, during, or after Pearl Harbor; that Roosevelt was hoodwinked by bigoted military leaders; that the absence of espionage convictions of ethnic Japanese "proved" that the West Coast evacuation and relocation were unnecessary; and that, ultimately, the decision to evacuate the West Coast and relocate ethnic Japanese was motivated primarily or exclusively by racism and wartime hysteria.

The telling and retelling of these legends have served as personal catharsis for some, and reaped financial rewards for many. Tax-subsidized reparations and the never-ending slogging in white guilt were the price the nation paid for the effort to protect the West Coast during World War II. But in a post–September 11 world, we can no longer afford the indulgent abuse of history as multicultural group therapy. Lies about the past continue to color and poison the current national security debate over how best to defend ourselves from terrorist invasion and infiltration in the future.

For far too long, it has been unacceptable to debate the subject of the "Japanese American internment." I was compelled to write this book after watching ethnic activists, historians, and politicians repeatedly play the World War II internment card after the September 11 attacks. Virtually without challenge,[2] the critics of the Bush administration have equated every reasonable measure to interrogate, track, detain, and deport potential terrorists with the "racist" and "unjustified" West Coast evacuation and relocation of ethnic Japanese. To make amends for this "shameful blot" on our history, the critics argue against any and all uses of race, ethnicity, nationality, and religion in shaping homeland security policies.

There are parallels between World War II and the War on Terror, but the antiprofilers don't make the proper comparisons. The Japanese espionage network and the Islamic terrorist network exploited many of the same immigration loopholes and relied on many of the same institutions to enter the country and insinuate themselves into the American mainstream. Members of both networks arrived here on student visas and religious visas. Both used spiritual centers—Buddhist churches for the Japanese, mosques for the Islamists—as central organizing points. Both used native-language newspapers to foment subversive tendencies. Both leaned on extensive ethnic- or religious-based fundraising groups for support—*kais* for the Japanese, Islamic charities for Middle Eastern terrorists. Both had operatives in the U.S. military. Both aggressively recruited American citizens as spies or saboteurs, especially (but not exclusively) inside their ethnic communities. Both were spearheaded by fanatics with an intense interest in biological and chemical weapons.

While some people who cannot remember the past are merely condemned to repeat it, the civil liberties absolutists want to force us to commit new mistakes that previous generations were wise enough to avoid. If these forces prevail, Americans cannot expect the high level of homeland security that their parents and grandparents benefited from during World War II.

If blanket opposition to internment and rejection of "racial profiling" are the wrong lessons from World War II, what are the right lessons? It is beyond the scope of this book to settle every question about the proper measures to take, and which to avoid, in the War on Terror. In part because of the geographical dispersion of the current threat of Islamofascism, it is hard to imagine parallel circumstances under which America would be compelled to replicate something on the scale of the West Coast evacuation and relocation during World War II. But there is much else we can learn from the past if it is viewed without a knee-jerk impulse to cry "racism" at every turn.

THREAT PROFILING

The Roosevelt administration supported many national security measures—not just the West Coast evacuation and relocation—that took race, ethnicity, and nationality into account. Before Pearl Harbor, according to author Greg Robinson, the secretary of war and the secretary of the navy informed the president "that they were instituting a program of employment discrimination on a racial basis whereby they would assure that future civil service vacancies in defense installations in Hawaii would be filled by 'selected citizens of unquestionable loyalty rather than by citizens generally of alien extraction whose loyalty may be questionable.'"[3] Ethnic Japanese were barred altogether from working within naval reservations.[4] Immediately following the Pearl Harbor attack, about half of the nation's *Nisei* draftees were discharged amid espionage and sabotage concerns, no doubt because MAGIC messages had revealed Japanese spies had infiltrated the military. The rest were reassigned to noncombat and nonsensitive duties. Soon after, the military stopped inducting *Nisei*. The creation of a segregated combat unit later permitted the demonstration of *Nisei* courage and loyalty to the world. That unit was barred from the Pacific Theater of operations. With few exceptions, *Nisei* volunteers were prevented from choosing the branch of service they preferred. The navy, marines, coast guard, merchant marine, and air force for the most part did not accept *Nisei* into their ranks except on temporary duty as Military Intelligence Service specialists. With virtually no exceptions, *Nisei* soldiers were barred from participating in any cryptographic operations.

It was prudent, while fighting a war against Japan, to apply heightened scrutiny to ethnic Japanese in the military. It is also prudent, while fighting a war against Muslim extremists, to apply special scrutiny to Muslims working in sensitive areas, including law enforcement, the prison system, and the armed forces.

The need for such measures was underscored in 2003 by the arrests of two Arab-American translators at Guantanamo Bay. One of the men, Senior Airman Ahmad I. al-Halabi, a naturalized U.S. citizen originally from Syria, is accused of sending secrets about the base, such as the names and cell numbers of prisoners and messages from the inmates, to a Middle East contact, possibly in Syria. The other man, Ahmed Mehalba, a civilian who worked for the military, is accused of making false statements to federal agents about whether he had classified documents in his possession at Logan Airport in Boston—marked "Secret" on a CD-ROM—after he returned from a trip to Egypt. Kevin Hendzel, a spokesman for the American Translators Association (which works closely with the military), told the *Washington Post* that officers often are so desperate for Arabic linguists they employ them despite fears they are al Qaeda plants, "Al Qaeda knows we're short of linguists, so it's a natural pipeline for infiltration by them."[5]

At least one Muslim, Ali A. Mohamed, joined al Qaeda after accessing classified documents while serving in the U.S. Army. He later admitted his role in the 1998 African embassy bombings that killed more than 200 people, including a dozen Americans.[6] Another Muslim, Semi Osman, served in a naval reserve fueling unit based in Tacoma, Washington, where he had access to fuel trucks similar to the type used by al Qaeda in the 1996 bombing of the Khobar Towers, which killed nineteen U.S. airmen and wounded nearly four hundred other Americans. Osman, tied to al Qaeda through his membership at a radical London mosque, was arrested as part of a federal investigation into the establishment of a terrorist training camp in Bly, Oregon. He pleaded guilty to a weapons violation as part of a deal with the feds. A third Muslim soldier, National Guardsman Ryan G. Anderson, also known as Amir Abdul Rashid, was charged in early 2004 with attempting to give intelligence to al Qaeda.

In addition, there have been a number of troubling incidents during the past several years in which Muslim soldiers engaged in or were accused of engaging in freelance acts of Islamic terrorism. In December 2003, Jeffrey Leon Battle, a former army reservist and black Muslim American convert, was sentenced to eighteen years in prison for conspiracy to levy war against the United States. He enlisted in the Reserves to receive military training to use against America, according to the Justice Department, and planned to wage war against American soldiers in Afghanistan. In another case, black Muslim American Asan Akbar stands accused of lobbing hand grenades and shooting his M-4 automatic rifle into three tents filled with his fellow sleeping commanding officers at the 101st Airborne Division's 1st Brigade operations center in Kuwait. The attack resulted in the deaths of two U.S. soldiers. Witnesses said Akbar ranted after the assault, "You guys are coming into our countries, and you're going to rape our women and kill our children."[7] And John Muhammad, the convicted Beltway sniper who became a Muslim convert in 1985, was allegedly involved in an eerily similar incident as a member of the Army's 84th Engineering Company six years later. He is suspected of throwing a thermite grenade into a tent housing sixteen of his fellow soldiers as they slept before the ground-attack phase of Gulf War I in 1991. Muhammad's superior, Sergeant Kip Berentson, told both *Newsweek* and the *Seattle Times* that he immediately suspected Muhammad, who was "trouble from day one," was responsible for the grenade attack.[8] Eight years later, he was arrested after his twenty-one-day Beltway shooting spree that left ten dead and three wounded. "It's bad enough we have to worry about enemy forces, but now we have to worry about our own guys," Specialist Autumn Simmer told the *Los Angeles Times* after the assault on the 101st Airborne.[9]

Penetration of our prisons by radical Muslim clerics is no less troubling. A February 2003 *Wall Street Journal* article revealed that radical imams sympathetic to al Qaeda are widely prevalent in New York's prisons.[10] On September 11, 2001, one New York prison's Muslim cleric informed inmates "that God had inflicted his punishment on the wicked and the victims deserved what they got, according to a labor arbitrator's subsequent ruling upholding his firing." [11] Another chaplain said that Osama bin Laden "is a soldier of Allah, a hero of Allah." [12]

The Islamist infiltration of key institutions is as perilous now as the infiltration of Japanese loyalists would have been sixty years ago. America's military and civilian commanders made no apologies for putting security over diversity during World War II. Yet, out of fear of being labeled as jackbooted racists, today's politically correct Pentagon and prison officials have rejected singling out Muslim soldiers and clerics[13] for extra scrutiny.

There are many ways that loyal Muslims in the armed forces can serve our country. But for the duration of this war—and it admittedly may not end in our lifetime—it is of questionable wisdom to continue allowing Muslims to serve the U.S. military in combat roles in the Middle East and to have access to classified information, except under extraordinary circumstances and after thorough background checks. Muslim chaplains in the military and prisons should be subjected to the strictest scrutiny. The government should not hesitate to bring charges against Muslims it suspects of disloyalty, even if those charges sometimes have to be dropped for lack of unclassified evidence, as in the highly publicized case of U.S. Army Muslim chaplain Captain James Yee.[14] Moreover, military, FBI, and other intelligence and security personnel, including airport security officials, should be allowed to take into account race, ethnicity, religion, and nationality in the course of identifying threats to U.S. interests. As Judge Robert H. Bork put it, "It is undeniable that ethnicity, national origin, nationality, and religion are correlated with terrorism. Given the stakes involved—the possible deaths of thousands or hundreds of thousands—it seems excessively politically correct to insist that no attention be paid to a factor we know to be relevant when present with other indicators."[15]

In the wake of September 11, savvy opponents of profiling have shifted away from arguing against it because it is "racist" and now claim that it endangers security because it "spreads our finite investigative resources too thin"[16] and "damages the faith minorities have in the American justice system," thereby hampering intelligence-gathering activities.[17] These assertions are cleverly fine-tuned to appeal to post–September 11 realities, but they are unfounded and disingenuous. University of Toledo professor David Harris, for example, makes the bizarre case that allowing profiling based on race, ethnicity, or religion would "enlarge the suspect pool," requiring "all of those in the suspect category . . . to be stopped, questioned, searched, and investigated, even when their behavior would not have pointed to any reason to do this."[18] But allowing airport security officials to take a passenger's ethnicity into account is not a mandate to stop every person of that ethnicity. Profiling is just one discretionary investigative tool among many to narrow the suspect pool, not to expand it. It is far from an infallible aid, but if law enforcement officials were permitted to use only foolproof techniques, they would be left with no tools to fight terrorism at all.

As for the claim that profiling alienates minorities, the argument conveniently ignores post–September 11 polling that showed broad support among minorities, including Arab-Americans, for heightened scrutiny of those who appear to be of Middle Eastern descent. A poll conducted in October 2001 found that more than half of Arab-Americans agreed that law enforcement officials are justified in asking extra questions or conducting extra inspections of people who appear to be Middle Eastern. According to the *Detroit Free Press,* "The reason Arab-Americans may support profiling is that they want to show they're patriotic and want to help out any way they can," said James Zogby, president of the Arab-American Institute, which conducted the poll with his brother, John, of Zogby International."[19] Separate polls showed strong support for racial profiling of Arab-Americans among blacks and other minority groups. Pollster John Zogby explained, "I think what they are saying is, 'We get profiled all the time and we survived. Maybe they ought to, too.' "[20]

On this issue, civil rights absolutists argue out of both sides of their mouths. They condemn homeland defense measures that use narrowly targeted criteria such as nationality (e.g., the special registration program, which required temporary visa holders from Muslim-dominated countries deemed to be of "elevated national security concern" to submit to fingerprinting, photographing, and stricter exit controls). Yet they complain just as bitterly when the government eschews narrow profiling policies in favor of broad security programs (such as the Computer-Assisted Passenger Prescreening System, for citizens and noncitizens alike, to be used at airports). They argue against racial profiling in favor of behavioral profiling. But when airport officials announced the adoption of behavioral profiling measures at Boston Logan (from which two of the September 11 terrorist flight crews departed), American Civil Liberties Union official Barry Steinhardt complained that it "likely will result in new forms of racial and ethnic profiling."[21]

The antiprofilers' ultimate solution, in other words, is to do nothing to defend the homeland. For most Americans, this is not a rational option.

DETENTION AND PROSECUTION

The World War II evacuation and relocation of *Nisei* were carried out in part because of the inability of law enforcement authorities to detain suspected subversives who were U.S. citizens. Countless West Coast *Nisei* were regarded by the U.S. intelligence community as potentially subversive, but the civilian legal system did not permit them to be detained in the absence of individualized evidence that they had committed crimes. Only one *Nisei* that we know of, Kenji Ito, was charged with an espionage-related crime. The jury, not privy to smoking-gun classified evidence against Ito, found him not guilty of failure to register as a foreign agent (see Appendix D). Had it not been for evacuation and relocation, Ito and untold numbers of other suspected subversive ethnic Japanese would have been allowed to remain in vulnerable, militarily sensitive areas while we were at war.

Some say that is as it should be. According to this argument, potential enemies—even suspected terrorists captured on battlefields *abroad*—should never be detained unless they are charged with a criminal offense and tried for that offense within the U.S. criminal justice system. Not only must suspected terrorists be charged with a crime, civil liberties purists argue, but the crime they are charged with must be related to terrorism. In the wake of September 11, when the Immigration and Naturalization Service detained hundreds of Middle Eastern illegal immigrants who had been referred to the FBI for possible terrorist ties, critics griped that the apprehensions amounted to racial profiling and selective law enforcement.

The idea of prosecuting suspected terrorists the way we would prosecute burglars or drug dealers seems to make sense in principle, but just as the Ito case showed the limitations of wartime jury trials during World War II, jury trials for War on Terror suspects are fraught with peril. "In ordinary civilian trials, there is no significant cost to sharing everything the government knows," notes Johns Hopkins international law professor Ruth Wedgwood. "But this does not hold against the background of al Qaeda's stated ambition of mounting new attacks."[22] Affording accused al Qaeda operatives the Sixth Amendment right to a public trial threatens to compromise classified information necessary to prosecute future terrorist trials. Other rights guaranteed by the Sixth Amendment—the right to subpoena witnesses and compel them to testify, the right to an attorney—can interfere with interrogations of captured suspected al Qaeda agents. These interrogations have yielded a tremendous amount of useful information, according to Defense Department officials. Moreover, in civilian courtrooms, prosecutors are severely restrained from closing off classified information under the existing federal Classified Information Procedure Act. Anonymous testimony and intelligence based on hearsay are often inadmissible in civilian courts. And while the lives of those immediately involved in, say, a mob trial might be endangered, the entire nation could be at risk when we allow suspected members of a terrorist network to partake in the discovery process.

The prosecution of the 1993 World Trade Center bombers in our civilian court system, though successful, demonstrated the pitfalls of prosecuting the War on Terror as if it were an episode of the TV show *Ally McBeal*—a courtroom comedy. The trials gave the bin Laden network a multi-million-dollar, tax-subsidized defense team, free translation services, personal dry-cleaning services, and access to information that was allegedly used by Islamists to evade surveillance. All the convicted World Trade Center bombers received life sentences. Two had faced the death penalty, but were spared by a minority-dominated jury that swallowed the race-baiting of defense witness Ramsey Clark (the former U.S. attorney general under Lyndon Johnson). Clark testified that no member of a racial minority group could expect a fair trial in the United States. He also blamed the Gulf War and U.S. sanctions on Iraq for creating the psychological "suffering" that led to the embassy attacks. On another front, convicted mastermind Sheik Omar Abdul Rahman may have exploited his right to counsel in order to establish a terrorist message center from behind bars. His lawyer, Lynne Stewart, was indicted in the fall of 2003 on charges of providing material support to terrorists and faced trial in May 2004; she is accused of aiding a plot to kidnap and kill people to help win the release of Rahman and making false statements regarding her efforts to pass messages between Rahman and third parties.

The Bush administration is now suffering from the *Ally McBeal*–ization of terror trials as a result of its fateful decision to allow accused al Qaeda operative Zacarias Moussaoui to be tried in an ordinary civilian court. In a bad miscalculation, the administration opted to bring a criminal case against Moussaoui rather than have him tried in a military tribunal or detained as an enemy combatant. Moussaoui, an avowed al Qaeda member deemed "mentally unstable" by several experts, has had a field day making fools of the prosecution. (Indeed, confiscated al Qaeda training manuals reveal that recruits are instructed in how to manipulate the Western legal system if they are captured.[23]) He asserted the right to see classified documents and the right to interrogate captured al Qaeda combatants, such as Ramzi Binalshibh, being detained abroad. Understandably, Justice Department lawyers refused to allow Moussaoui to speak to Binalshibh. The court may now hold the DOJ attorneys in contempt. If that happens, the Bush administration has hinted it will do what it should have done from the start: Declare Moussaoui an enemy combatant and throw him into a military brig.

Which brings us to the most controversial aspect of the Bush administration's process for detaining suspected terrorists: its claim that the president has the authority to detain indefinitely anyone it designates an "enemy combatant," including U.S. citizens. The Supreme Court is expected to rule on the constitutionality of the Bush administration's policy in June 2004. If the Court strikes down the policy, Padilla and other suspected al Qaeda agents are likely to be set free. More ominously, the ability of future Administrations to detain and interrogate suspected terrorists will be seriously compromised. The civil liberties of our suspected enemies will be preserved—but at what cost to national security?

In the long run, Congress should explore structural reforms that allow our country to better meet the potential threat posed by future Kenji Itos, Jose Padillas, and Zacarias Moussaouis but that also allow enemy combatant designations to be reviewed by an independent board or court. One approach that has been proposed (whose implementation may require a constitutional amendment) is to establish special courts specifically designed to deal with terrorist suspects. These courts would allow certain evidence that is not admissible in a conventional civilian court, and for national security reasons, the defendant and his or her lawyer would not be allowed to view certain evidence.

Civil rights absolutists who oppose all such wartime detention measures by invoking the internment card have distorted history and obscured a valuable lesson of the World War II experience. As this book has shown, even those who opposed mass evacuation of the entire West Coast understood and endorsed the need to provide some means other than the traditional criminal justice system, whereby "potentially dangerous United States citizens may be held in custodial detention as well as aliens."[24] The much-vilified Western Defense Command raised prescient concerns about the limitations of the common-law system in wartime:

> Ordinarily in peacetime, if a criminal, who has committed a theft or some crime of violence, has been acquitted, there is little likelihood that the public as a whole will be penalized for this inaccurate judgment of the court or jury, for such a criminal will only again commit a crime probably affecting one member of society; but in the case of one committing espionage or sabotage, the effect upon the population as a whole is quite different. The furnishing of a vital piece of information to the enemy may affect thousands of lives, rather than just one individual.[25]

All the more so now that the enemies we fight may soon have access to chemical, biological, or nuclear weapons that could wipe out tens of thousands, if not millions of lives, rather than just thousands.

Secrecy in an Age of Terror

The Roosevelt administration's internal security policies underscored the critical need for secrecy in certain wartime decision-making based on classified intelligence. Revealing the MAGIC code-breaking operation in open court, or in public reports from the Western Defense Command, or during a presidential fireside chat while war was raging would have killed the goose that laid the golden intelligence egg. Roosevelt and his closest military advisers kept a tight lid on what they knew through the MAGIC decrypts, of Japan's espionage operations and designs on the West Coast. Even the nation's top law enforcement official—the attorney general—was out of the loop.

There is still much that is unknown about the true scope of the espionage and sabotage threat from ethnic Japanese on the West Coast. Countless names of *Nisei* have been redacted from FBI and intelligence documents. Public disclosure requests take years to fill, if they ever are filled at all. On the other side of the ocean, Japan has destroyed or buried wartime records that could have answered questions that —contrary to the politically correct historians—have yet to be settled. And may never be.

Today, in our complacently open society, which has grown accustomed and entitled to knowing everything about anything—from the type of undergarments former President Bill Clinton wears to the location of pop star Britney Spears's tattoos—the notion of maintaining secrecy for national security reasons is alien and discomfiting to many. Even after the September 11 attacks, we remain an insatiable culture of blabbermouths.

When President Bush surprised U.S. troops in Baghdad on Thanksgiving Day 2003, it was necessary to provide a cover story to the press before take-off. Bush's parents were expecting to have their son join them for dinner at his Texas ranch and weren't told about the trip until after the president's plane had departed. For obvious safety reasons, reporters accompanying the president were forbidden from making cell phone calls to their families and prevented from filing stories until after Bush left the war zone.[26] Most military leaders in Iraq were left in the dark until the last minute.

Back at home, *Washington Post* media reporter Howard Kurtz complained that "the White House lied to the press. They put out a story saying the president will be spending Thanksgiving in Crawford with his family. . . . A lot of the journalists I've talked to today are upset that this kind of deception was engaged in, not for military secrecy—although clearly there was a security aspect, but to set up this grand turkey photo op for the president."[27] Kurtz and his colleagues are certainly free to debate Bush's motives, but the fourth estate is off its collective rocker if it expected the White House to disclose the truth and let the media, Saddam Hussein, and Osama bin Laden know exactly when he would be leaving from Washington and what time he would be arriving at Baghdad International Airport.

There are some things we can't know—and don't need to know now, not yet—while al Qaeda remains at large and at war with us. But barely three months after the September 11 attacks, the civil rights absolutists complained loudly about the government's decision to keep secret the names of individuals it detained immediately following the mass murders. An outfit called the Center for National Security Studies filed a Freedom of Information Act lawsuit demanding the "immediate disclosure of government documents concerning an estimated 1,000 individuals who have been arrested and detained in the wake of the September 11 attacks."[28] Supporters of the lawsuit included the Asian American Legal Defense and Education Fund, the Council on American Islamic Relations, the American Immigration Lawyers Association, Human Rights Watch, the American-Arab Anti-Discrimination Committee, *The Nation* magazine, the *New York Times*, and People for the American Way.

Among the kinds of information these groups sought were not only the names of the people detained and the lawyers representing them, but also the dates and circumstances of each arrest, any criminal charges filed, and the basis for keeping the records of each case under seal. Let's be clear: The plaintiffs in this case were asking the government in the name of the First Amendment not just to name names, but also to reveal its sources and methods of investigation in open court, to report on what evidence it had against members of particular terrorist cells, to reveal which plots the administration was aware of, and to disclose which cells the Justice Department was spending the most resources on. In August 2002, a federal district judge ruled in the civil liberties groups' favor; the ruling was overturned on appeal a year later. A complete list of the names "would give terrorist organizations a composite picture of the government investigation," a panel of the U.S. Court of Appeals for the District of Columbia Circuit concluded in siding with the Bush administration by a 2-to-1 margin. "The judiciary owes some measure of deference to the executive in cases implicating national security."

In January 2004, the U.S. Supreme Court refused to hear the civil liberties brigade's challenge to the secret detentions. Earlier, the high court had also declined to hear a challenge to secret deportation hearings of many of the detainees, which the government defended on similar grounds.[29] As the clear-eyed editorial board of the *New York Sun* observed,

> This is likely to be met with a good bit of hand-wringing in anti-war quarters. But we take it as an encouraging sign that the Supreme Court is not going to permit America, or its representatives, to be easily pushed around by the courts during the course of this war. We live in an extraordinary time, when America is once again, as it was in the Cold War, under attack in a vast, twilight struggle. There is absolutely no reason that this should be permitted to result in an unraveling of the civil liberties and the checks and balances that are such bedrock to our Constitution. But neither is there a constitutional reason to stretch the First Amendment and the subsidiary laws in ways that were not intended.[30]

In these cases, the courts stood firm, but the modern demand for public release of every last bit of sensitive and strategic information during wartime is recklessly unrelenting. The ultimatum by former New Jersey governor

Thomas Kean, chairman of the federal commission created to investigate the September 11 attacks (and the man who lobbied President Reagan to sign the 1988 wartime reparations bill), is a good example. He told the *New York Times* in October 2003: "Anything that has to do with 9/11, we have to see it—anything."[31] Even if it means jeopardizing counterterrorism efforts? Apparently so. "There are a lot of theories about 9/11, and as long as there is any document out there that bears on any of those theories, we're going to leave questions unanswered," Kean complained. "And we cannot leave questions unanswered."[32] What is needed is a "Loose Lips Sink Ships" education campaign updated for the twenty-first century, emphasizing the potential national security risks of demanding to know too much too soon.

CIVIL LIBERTIES OR SURVIVAL

After World War II and before September 11, civil rights absolutism flourished virtually unchallenged. The exclusionary rule, Miranda rights, and other measures designed to protect the rights of the accused made it harder to convict murderers, rapists, and child molesters, but it was a price American society was willing to pay. Prohibitions on racial profiling by law enforcement may have made it harder to apprehend drug dealers and other criminals, but that too was considered an acceptable cost. Indeed, seven months before the September 11 attacks, President Bush had declared, "Racial profiling is wrong, and we will end it in America."[33]

In the post-September 11 world, the belief that civil liberties must never be compromised has become a dangerous bugaboo. But in times of crisis, civil rights often yield to security in order to ensure the nation's survival. What is legal and what is necessary to preserve the Republic sometimes diverge.[34] During the Civil War, Abraham Lincoln suspended habeas corpus, which enabled him to detain thousands of rebels and suspected subversives without access to judges. In defying a Supreme Court order to restore habeas corpus, Lincoln refused to let "the government itself go to pieces" for the sake a single law.[35] As for civil liberties, Lincoln noted that the Constitution "is not in [its] application in all respects to be the same, in

cases of Rebellion or invasion, involving the public safety, as it is in times
of profound peace and public security.[36] Indeed, the Third Amendment for-
bids soldiers from being quartered in private homes without the consent of
the owner during peacetime—but allows it in wartime. The Fourth Amendment bans "unreasonable" searches, but the parameters vary in times of
tranquility and turmoil. During World War II, Roosevelt possessed an outlook similar to that of Lincoln, prompting his attorney general Francis Biddle, to write, "The Constitution has not greatly bothered any wartime
president."[37]

To modern civil rights absolutists, such talk (even from their New Deal
icons in the Roosevelt administration) is sacrilegious and in violation of
"acceptable debate." But providing for the common defense is the government's paramount function—not guaranteeing the right of Muslims to board
planes without hassles.

There are those who understand that we are engaged in a war unlike any
other and that we need to fight it in unprecedented ways. Then there are
those who, in *Chicago Sun-Times* columnist Mark Steyn's incomparable
words, "think 9/11 is like the 1998 ice storm or a Florida hurricane—just
one of those things."[38] We are not in the middle of freakish bad weather. We
are at war with stateless enemies abroad and Islamist infiltrators at home
who will not stop plotting to kill us unless we kill them first overseas and
nab them preemptively on our own soil.

The difference between past wars and the current war, as many critics such
as former *New York Times* columnist Anthony Lewis decry, is that the one we
are fighting now is seemingly eternal.[39] The argument from this quivering
quarter of the punditocracy posits that since no conclusion is in immediate
sight, any loss of liberty is unacceptable, since such loss would be inter-
minable. "Civil liberties have often been overridden in times of crisis and
war—as in the removal of Japanese Americans from the West Coast in World
War II," Lewis acknowledges. "Those occasions were followed by regrets and
apologies. But how will we protect civil liberties in a war without end?"

One answer is that civil liberties, however important, are not sacrosanct.
If we insist that the unparalleled personal freedoms we enjoyed prior to

September 11 never be abridged, not by one iota, then our ability to thwart future terrorist attacks will be severely compromised. The result may be tens of thousands of unnecessary deaths. In an age of unyielding terror coupled with weapons of mass destruction, we must steel ourselves for the possibility of a long-lasting reduction in the overall level of individual liberty we have heretofore possessed.

Those who have sought to cut off vital debate over these matters invoke the internment card and shriek that "the terrorists have won" if we curtail civil liberties. Wartime presidents can't afford to indulge such nonsense. Their first duty is the nation's preservation, not self-flagellation. As commander in chief, Roosevelt resolutely understood what Bush knows now: A nation can't stand for anything unless it is still standing. For defending this unalterable truth, America need never apologize.

Appendix A

Richard Kotoshirodo

CON~~FIDEN~~TIAL

Q Was he a principal?
A Hes, his first name was Seiichiro.

Q Did they supply the Consulate with information?
A I do not know. I have not seen one letter from anyone. Once or twice I
saw mysterious letters stating that somebody is in the United States illegally and that person should be deported.

Q Well, they probably came to the Secretary's desk.
A Yes, I think so.

Q MR. KOTOSHIRODO, I would like to ask some questions as to your background.
You do not have to answer them if you do not want to. How did you happen
to become associated with the Consul?
A I did not know anything about the Consul. I heard people mention the Consulate, but I did not know anything about it until I actually started working there. I was working for Otani, the contractors, and my former teacher
at the Japanese high school—the Hongwanji Mission on Fort Street—the Reve-
rend Miyagi 'phoned me one day and told me to come to his house, and I did,
and he explained that they needed a clerk at the Consulate. He said it was
very short hours and so he recommended me, I think, I imagine that he had known
somebody at the Consulate.

Q Did you get to interview them, or did they give you the job before you went
there?
A He took me to the Consulate.

Q What salary did they start you at?
A Sixty dollars ($60) a month.

Q And when you left how much salary were you getting?
A Seventy-five dollars ($75).

Q With room and board?
A No.

Q Any extra expense money?
A Yes, they used to give me bonus.

Q What was your gross income for 1939—roughly what was the gross income you
received from the Consul?
A Well, I did not figure it out. My wife was working, too.

Q Where did your wife work?
A She used to operate a dressmaking shop.

CON~~FIDEN~~TIAL

- 27 -

65-41886-18-27

Honolulu spy ring aide Richard Kotoshirodo, a *Nisei*, testifies about his loyalty
to Japan before an Internee Hearing Board. October 17, 1942.

CONFIDENTIAL

Q Has she still go that shop?
A No, she quit last year in August.

Q Have you any idea what your income was in 1940 and 1941? Did they pay you extra for outside work?
A No, just for the car expense.

Q They never gave you an extra one hundred dollars ($100) for any month's work?
A No.

Q When they started taking you on these outside trips did they come out and
tell you that it was for the purpose of finding out what America was doing,
or did they try to keep from you what they were doing?
A Well, they did not tell me anything about war. They just said they wanted
to know.

Q Well, what was your attitude as an American citizen in doing this sor of
thing? I realize that it was your job, but how did you feel about getting
this information against the country in which you were born?
A Well, I do not know exactly how I felt about that.

Q Was it easy to be doing something for the Imperial Japanese Government, or
were you doing it because you wanted to help Japan and not this country?
A Well, I did not have any particular hate for the United States or particular favor for the Japanese Government. I, myself, felt—and they told me
from the start—at first I heard about their plan of going out and counting
the ships, I knew it was espionage activity but Okuda said that all of the
world had Consular Agents with two businesses, and as long as your action
does not go beyond — well, what I mean to say is that as long as you remain legally outside from any place where people cannot get in, just see
what you can see from the outside, there is not anything that anyone can
do. It is a natural thing that every country is doing. Okuda said that in
Japan the American Consulate is gathering information.

Q Well, what I am trying to get at is this: your feeling toward Japan, was
it rather that you wanted to get that information for Japan—did you feel
that you were a Japanese subject because you were a dual citizen? Were
your loyalties to Japan or were your loyalties to the country in which you
were born.
A Well, I was employed at the Consulate and they looked upon us as Japanese
citizens and they expected us to be Japanese. For instance, on New Year's
Day we celebrated and on the Emperor's birthday we celebrated, or on the
Emperor Meiji's birthday we used to have ceremonies at the Consulate, and
I am sure we were the only citizens of the United States who used to attend
the ceremonies.

CONFIDENTIAL

CONFIDENTIAL

Q Was it a Buddhist or Shinto ceremony?
A It was not a religious ceremony at all. We used to hang the Emperor's picture in the Consul's residence, and we used to bow to it.

Q Well, what I am trying to get at is this: how did you feel in your own mind up to the war? Did you class yourself as being 100% for Japan, or did you class yourself as being an American.
A As I recall, I was 100% Japanese.

Q That is what I wanted to find out. At the times that you had your New Year's ceremony you went out and paid your respects to the Emperor and Empress at that time, and did those of you who were born here take an oath of allegiance to Japan? Do you know what an oath of allegiance to Japan is?
A Yes.

Q In Japan did you taken an oath of allegiance?
A No.

Q Were you on the outside enough to know what was going on up there, to know what the Consul and Vice-Consul were doing regarding preparations for war? Did you know what was going on about war coming in December?
A No, I did not suspect that there would be a war. I did not know what the relations between the United States and Japan were. The Vice-Consul used to tell me that there cannot be a war. The worst that could come would be to break diplomatic relations. There might be a day when the Consulate would close, but that there would not be a war.

Q Would you have left the Consul if you had thought there was going to be a war, or would you have stayed there?
A I do not know. I really do not know. I really did not know what the real meaning of war was.

Q Were you present when Nomura and Kurusu came through to go to Washington? Were you there when they were at the Consulate? Did you listen in on anything they said?
A They did not go to the Consul; they were at the Consul's residence. They were in the car driving; they did not enter the Consul office building. Mr. Kurusu I did not see at the Consulate—I just saw him in the newspaper.

Q Another question on this Pearl Harbor business? At any time, when you were at the Consul, did you see or hear of any maps—did you have access to the diplomatic pouches that went to Japan? Did you clerks know what was in those pouches?
A The Secretaries handled that type of business.

- 28 -   **CONFIDENTIAL**

65-41886-18-28

CONFIDENTIAL

Q Have you any reason for not voting?
A No, sir.

Q Is it due to the fact that your past view has been that you did not care to associate yourself with the political life of the Territory of Hawaii?
A I always missed my chance to register.

Q Did you take any active part in formulating a policy of backing any particular candidate running for office?
A No, sir.

Q Did anyone ever tell you not to register?
A No, sir."

On November 4, 1942 the Board, after reviewing the testimony in instant case, made the following findings and recommendations:

"1. That the detainee, RICHARD MASAYUKI (M.) KOTOSHIRODO, is a citizen of the United States of Japanese parentage, who has never expatriated himself from his Japanese citizenship, hence is a so-called dual citizen.

"2. That he is loyal to Japan and is not loyal to the United States.

"3. That he is not engaged in any specific subversive activities.

"The detainee was born in 1916, went to Japan early in 1923, and remained there until the end of 1930; he had seven and a half years of schooling in Japan and one year of student military training.

"While in Japan the detainee lived as a Japanese citizen. He has never been expatriated and has applied for deferment from the Japanese military service up until 1940.

"He became a clerk in the office of the Japanese Consul-General in Honolulu in 1935, and was employed as such up to and including December 7th, 1941. In 1940 Tadasi Morimura came to the Consulate as one of the Secretaries. Prior to his arrival he was not known by any of the other Secretaries, and the detainee did not know whether he was an officer of the Naval or Military Reserve, or in the Military service of Japan.

"In general, the testimony given by the detainee is in line with the testimony of the Government and it is believed that this Government testimony is so concisely stated as to need no repetition.

"He told in detail about his trips to the various Islands. He stated that while on the Island of Maui he delivered a package to a man by the name of Sone, a teacher or a principal at Sprecklesville, for a Miss Yamasaki. What

65-41886-18-54   - 54 -   CONFIDENTIAL

Hearing board concludes that Kotoshirodo "willingly assisted" and "conspired to commit the crime of espionage."

CONFIDENTIAL

was in the package he stated he did not know.

"He made the trip to Kauai with his wife, as stated in the Government's case, and stated that he tried to get information relative to the airport and also went up and looked at the power plant in the vicinity of Kapaa. He stated that he knew what they were doing — that they were collecting information for the Japanese Government. He stated that he was told that that was the customary thing, and he admits freely that he aided Morimura and Okuda in every way possible.

"On Hawaii he stated that they visited the photo studios of one Miyahara. He also stated that he helped burn pamphlets and letters that were burned in August of 1941.

"He also stated that he saw a large map of the Islands in the office of one of the Consular officials in which a cable line had been drawn to show its location.

"He stated that on the morning of the 7th of December he didn't know that there was going to be a war, and was not sure; but when he heard so much of the firing and the talking about it, he went down to the Consulate, and there found the officials — the Consul, Vice-Consul and Secretaries — gathered there and very much disturbed. He asked one of the Secretaries if it was actually war, and the answer in substance was 'no, that would be impossible.' He claims that he didn't know that war had actually broken out. A great deal of the time while there he was talking with Mr. Seki, a Secretary, who stated that he didn't even then understand that war had actually broken out. He states that he got no instructions while there and left there in ten or twenty minutes, and did not return again.

"As these findings have been decided upon some days subsequent to the hearing of the detainee, it is to be noted that he denied emphatically that they were ever asked, or told, anything about the possibility of war. This case should be read in connection with the testimony of SAHARA, to the effect that the Vice-Consul called each one in and asked him if war broke out whether or not he would go back to Japan or stay here.

"The Board finds that the detainee willingly assisted in whatever way he was told in collecting information, as stated in the Government's case; that he also conspired with Tadasi Morimura, Okuda, Seki, and others, exactly what others being unknown to the Board, to commit the crime of espionage by observing and reporting upon disposition of our troops, air fields, military movements, with a view of imparting it to the Japanese at a time when the feeling between the United States and Japan was very intense. This conspiracy continued up to and including December 7th, 1941, after they had knowledge that war had

      CONFIDENTIAL

CON~~FI~~DENTIAL

broken out, and as far as is known to this Board the conspiracy still may be in existence, there being no breaking off by any member of that conspiracy by any direct, affirmative action.

"It is believed, by the Board, that the conspiracy existing at the time after war was actually in existence, although not yet declared, that this man should be subject to trial by military commission."

P E N D I N G

- 56 -

41886-18-56   CON~~FI~~DENTIAL

Appendix B

MAGIC Cables

More than any other source of intelligence, it was the so-called "MAGIC" cables—Japan's diplomatic communications that were intercepted and decoded by American signal intelligence officers—which revealed in message after message the alarming extent of Japan's ongoing espionage operations on the West Coast, in Hawaii, and along America's southern border.

All MAGIC messages in this section were scanned from the 1977 Department of Defense publication, *The "MAGIC" Background of Pearl Harbor.* Each message contains two dates and two message numbers. The date and number on the upper right-hand corner of each message were assigned by the Japanese sender. The number in the upper left-hand corner, and the translation date on the bottom right-hand corner, were assigned by U.S. code breakers. The occasional appearance of blank spaces in the messages, marked by a series of dashes, indicates that portions of the original encrypted text were garbled, not intercepted, or could not be decrypted.

Section 1 highlights messages from January 1941 through May 1941 outlining Japan's intensive efforts to organize its intelligence network in the U.S. and abroad.

Section 2 highlights messages from June 1941 leading up to the Pearl Harbor attack detailing Japan's copious intelligence activities.

These messages represent only a small portion of the diplomatic traffic intercepted by the "Magicians" and read by the president and his top advisors before, during, and after the decision to evacuate the West Coast.

Section 1: Japan Organizes Its Espionage Network

No. 118

FROM: Tokyo (Matsuoka)
TO: Washington (Koshi)

January 30, 1941
043.

Foreign Office secret.

Heretofore, we have placed emphasis on publicity and propaganda work in the United States. In view of the critical situation in the recent relations between the two countries, and for the purpose of being prepared for the worst, we have decided to alter this policy. Taking into consideration the small amount of funds we have at our disposal, we have decided to de-emphasize propaganda for the time being, and instead, to strengthen our intelligence work.

Though we must give the matter of intelligence work our further study—in this connection we are at present conferring with the intelligence bureau—we have mapped out a fundamental program, the outline of which is contained in my supplementary cable No. 44ª.

Please, therefore, reorganize your intelligence set-up and put this new program into effect as soon as possible.

Cable copies of this message, as "Minister's orders" to Canada, Mexico, (a copy to be relayed from Mexico to Mexicali), San Francisco, (copies from San Francisco to Honolulu, Los Angeles, Portland, Seattle, and Vancouver), New York, New Orleans, and Chicago.

ªSee I, 119.

Trans. 2-7-41

No. 119

FROM: Tokyo (Matsuoka)   January 30, 1941
TO: Washington (Koshi)   # 44.

(In two parts—complete).

(Foreign Office secret).

(1) Establish an intelligence organ in the Embassy which will maintain liaison with private and semi-official intelligence organs (see my message to Washington #591[a] and #732[b] from New York to Tokyo, both of last year's series).
   With regard to this, we are holding discussions with the various circles involved at the present time.

(2) The focal point of our investigations shall be the determination of the total strength of the U.S. Our investigations shall be divided into three general classifications: political, economic, and military, and definite course of action shall be mapped out.

(3) Make a survey of all persons or organizations which either openly or secretly oppose participation in the war.

(4) Make investigations of all anti-Semitism, communism, movements of Negroes, and labor movements.

(5) Utilization of U.S. citizens of foreign extraction (other than Japanese), aliens (other than Japanese), communists, Negroes, labor union members, and anti-Semites, in carrying out the investigations described in the preceding paragraph would undoubtedly bear the best results.
   These men, moreover, should have access to governmental establishments, (laboratories?), governmental organizations of various characters, factories, and transportation facilities.

(6) Utilization of our "Second Generations" and our resident nationals. (In view of the fact that if there is any slip in this phase, our people in the U.S. will be subjected to considerable persecution, and the utmost caution must be exercised).

(7) In the event of U.S. participation in the war, our intelligence set-up will be moved to Mexico, making that country the nerve center of our intelligence net. Therefore, will you bear this in mind and in anticipation of such an eventuality, set up facilities for a U.S.-Mexico international intelligence route. This net which will cover Brazil, Argentina, Chile, and Peru will also be centered in Mexico.

(8) We shall cooperate with the German and Italian intelligence organs in the U.S. This phase has been discussed with the Germans and Italians in Tokyo, and it has been approved.
   Please get the details from Secretary Terasaki upon his assuming his duties there.
   Please send copies to those offices which were on the distribution list of No. 43[c].

---

[a] See I, 112.
[b] Has no bearing on this subject. #732 probably an error.
[c] (See No. 4)—See I, 118.

Trans. 2-7-41

No. 129

FROM: Tokyo (Matsuoka)
TO: Mexico City (Koshi)

February 5, 1941
239.

(Circular) (In 2 parts—complete).

In view of the critical times we wish to revise our information policy of our offices in South and Central America, along the following lines:

(1) Investigate the general national strength of the United States.

(2) Investigate the United States policy towards South and Central America.

(3) Investigate the extent of South and Central America's participation in the policy of the United States.

(4) Investigate the extent of competition between Germany, Italy and the United States in South and Central America.

1. Appoint persons to direct these investigations and report their names.

2. Consider plans to use South and Central America for obtaining information regarding the United States in the event that that country is drawn into war, and have an information gathering machinery ready for operation when that situation occurs.

3. Keep a close contact with the German and Italian organs (of information).

4. To organize Japanese residents, including newspaper men and business firms for the purpose of gathering information. Care should be taken not to give cause for suspicion of espionage activities.

5. To formulate a suitable plan for dispatching information obtained under any condition. Relay to Chile, Peru, Panama, Argentina (?), Venezuela (?), and Brazil and retransmit by code to Santos and Ribeiro Preto.

Trans. 2-14-41

No. 131

FROM: Tokyo (Matsuoka)   February 15, 1941
TO: Washington (Koshi)   #073.

(2 parts—complete)

Re my #43ª.

The information we particularly desire with regard to intelligence involving U.S. and Canada, are the following:

1. Strengthening or supplementing of military preparations on the Pacific Coast and the Hawaii area; amount and type of stores and supplies; alterations to air ports (also carefully note the clipper traffic).

2. Ship and plane movements (particularly of the large bombers and sea planes).

3. Whether or not merchant vessels are being requisitioned by the government (also note any deviations from regular schedules), and whether any remodelling is being done to them.

4. Calling up of army and navy personnel, their training, (outlook on maneuvers) and movements.

5. Words and acts of minor army and navy personnel.

6. Outlook of drafting men from the view-point of race. Particularly, whether Negroes are being drafted, and if so, under what conditions.

7. Personnel being graduated and enrolled in the army and navy and aviation service schools.

8. Whether or not any troops are being dispatched to the South Pacific by transports; if there are such instances, give description.

9. Outlook of the developments in the expansion of arms and the production set-up; the capacity of airplane production; increase in the ranks of labor.

10. General outlooks on Alaska and the Aleutian Islands, with particular stress on items involving plane movements and shipment of military supplies to those localities.

11. Outlook on U.S. defense set-ups.

12. Contacts (including plane connections) with Central and South America and the South Pacific area. Also outlook on shipment of military supplies to those areas.

Please forward copies of this message as a "Minister's Instruction" to New York, San Francisco, Los Angeles, Seattle, Portland, (Chicago or New Orleans ?) Vancouver, Ottawa, and Honolulu. Also to Mexico City and Panama as reference material.

ª"We have decided to de-emphasize our propaganda work and strengthen out intelligence work in the U.S." See I, 118.

Trans. 2-20-41

No. 132

FROM: Tokyo (Matsuoka)   February 15, 1941
TO: San Francisco (Riyoji)   # 020.

  Secret.

Re my # 73 to Washington°.

Will your office please pay particular attention to gathering intelligence material which will fall under the classifications outlined in paragraphs 1, 2, 3, 4, 5, 8, and 12.

     °Outlines details of intelligence information desired. See I, 131.

                                 Trans. 2-20-41

No. 133

FROM: Tokyo (Matsuoka)   February 15, 1941
TO: Los Angeles (Riyoji)   # 013.

  Secret.

Re my # 73 to Washington.

In connection with collecting intelligence material, your office will pay particular attention to contents of paragraphs 1, 2, 8, 9 and 11.

                                  Trans. 2-20-41

No. 134

FROM: Tokyo (Matsuoka)   February 15, 1941
TO: New York (Riyoji)   # 018.

Re my # 73 to Washington.

In gathering intelligence material, your office will pay particular attention to contents of paragraphs 4, 6, 7, and 9.

                                  Trans. 2-20-41

No. 135

FROM: Tokyo (Japanese Foreign Minister)   February 15, 1941
TO: Vancouver (Japanese Consul)   # 008.

  Secret.

Re my # 73 to Washington.

In gathering intelligence material, your office will lay particular stress on paragraph 10.

                                  Trans. 2-20-41

No. 136

FROM: Tokyo (Matsuoka)   February 15, 1941
TO: Honolulu (Riyoji)   # 008.

Re my # 73 to Washington.

In gathering intelligence material, your office will pay particular attention to paragraphs 1 and 2.

                                  Trans. 2-20-41

No. 143

FROM: Tokyo
TO: Washington

Regarding my # 43[a].

(1) Please put Secretary Terazaki[b] in full charge of directing information and propaganda in the United States.

(2) Please have him maintain close contact with all our offices for the purpose of coordinating information gathered through these channels.

Also please have him convene or visit officials concerned whenever he deems it necessary.

(3) Please allow him to travel to South and Central America, whenever he feels it necessary to contact our information officials in these countries.

(4) Bearing in mind that sufficient funds have been provided to give him a reasonable amount of freedom of action in pursuing his work, please offer him every assistance at your disposal.

March 17, 1941
126.

[a]"We have decided to de-emphasize our propaganda work and strengthen our intelligence work in the U.S. See I, 118.

See I, 119. Outline of major points of investigation in connection with setting up of intelligence operations in the U.S.

Cooperation of Jap bank and business officials in U.S. will be sought in connection with propaganda and intelligence work in U.S. See I, 112.

[b]Terazaki was formerly a secretary at the Legation in Peking; was ordered to Washington on 20 December, 1940.

Trans. 3–18–41

No. 174

FROM: Los Angeles (Nakauchi)   May 9, 1941
TO: Tokyo (Gaimudaijin)   # 067.

(In 2 parts—complete).

Strictly Secret.

Re your message # 180 to Washington.*

We are doing everything in our power to establish outside contacts in connection with our efforts to gather intelligence material. In this regard, we have decided to make use of white
persons and Negroes, through Japanese persons whom we can't trust completely. (It not only
would be very difficult to hire U.S. (military ?) experts for this work at the present time, but
the expenses would be exceedingly high.) We shall, furthermore, maintain close connections
with the Japanese Association, the Chamber of Commerce, and the newspapers.

With regard to airplane manufacturing plants and other military establishments in other
parts, we plan to establish very close relations with various organizations and in strict secrecy
have them keep these military establishments under close surveillance. Through such means,
we hope to be able to obtain accurate and detailed intelligence reports. We have already
established contacts with absolutely reliable Japanese in the San Pedro and San Diego area,
who will keep a close watch on all shipments of airplanes and other war materials, and report
the amounts and destinations of such shipments. The same steps have been taken with regard to traffic across the U.S.-Mexico border.

We shall maintain connection with our second generations who are at present in the (U.S.)
Army, to keep us informed of various developments in the Army. We also have connections
with our second generations working in airplane plants for intelligence purposes.

With regard to the Navy, we are cooperating with our Naval Attaché's office, and are sub-
mitting reports as accurately and as speedily as possible.

We are having Nakazawa investigate and summarize information gathered through first
hand and newspaper reports, with regard to military movements, labor disputes, communistic activities and other similar matters. With regard to anti-Jewish movements, we are having
investigations made by both prominent Americans and Japanese who are connected with
the movie industry which is centered in this area. We have already established connections
with very influential Negroes to keep us informed with regard to the Negro movement.

---

*See I, 165. It is routed as Foreign Minister's instructions to: Ottawa, Mexico, San Francisco, New York, New
Orleans. San Francisco to relay to Honolulu, Los Angeles, Seattle, Portland, Vancouver.

Trans. 5-19-41

No. 175

FROM: Seattle (Sato)   May 11, 1941
TO: Tokyo   # 45.

(3 parts—complete).

Re your # 180 to Washington.

1. *Political Contacts.*
We are collecting intelligences revolving around political questions, and also the question of American participation in the war which has to do with the whole country and this local area.
2. *Economic Contacts.*
We are using foreign company employees, as well as employees in our own companies here, for the collection of intelligences having to do with economics along the lines of the construction of ships, the number of airplanes produced and their various types, the production of copper, zinc and aluminum, the yield of tin for cans, and lumber. We are now exerting our best efforts toward the acquisition of such intelligences through competent Americans. From an American, whom we contacted recently, we have received a private report on machinists of German origin who are Communists and members of the labor organizations in the Bremerton Naval Yard and Boeing airplane factory. Second generation Japanese ----- ----- -----.
3. *Military Contacts.*
We are securing intelligences concerning the concentration of warships within the Bremerton Naval Yard, information with regard to mercantile shipping and airplane manufacturer, movements of military forces, as well as that which concerns troop maneuvers.
With this as a basis, men are sent out into the field who will contact Lt. Comdr. OKADA, and such intelligences will be wired to you in accordance with past practice. KANEKO is in charge of this. Recently we have on two occasions made investigations on the spot of various military establishments and concentration points in various areas. For the future we have made arrangements to collect intelligences from second generation Japanese draftees on matters dealing with the troops, as well as troop speech and behavior. ----- ----- -----.
4. *Contacts With Labor Unions.*
The local labor unions A.F. of L. and C.I.O. have considerable influence. The (Socialist ?) Party maintains an office here (its political sphere of influence extends over twelve zones.) The C.I.O., especially, has been very active here. We have had a first generation Japanese, who is a member of the labor movement and a committee chairman, contact the organizer, and we have received a report, though it is but a resume, on the use of American members of the (Socialist ?) Party. ----- OKAMARU is in charge of this.
5. In order to contact Americans of foreign extraction and foreigners, in addition to third parties, for the collection of intelligences with regard to anti-participation organizations and the anti-Jewish movement, we are making use of a second generation Japanese lawyer.
This intelligence ----- ----- -----.

Trans. 6-9-41

Section 2: Japan's Intelligence Activities

No. 221

FROM: Washington   June 10, 1941
TO: Tokyo   # 386.

(To San Francisco, Los Angeles, & Seattle, Cir. # 121)

Secret.

Because of the suppression exercised against our Naval representatives (Language Officers) by the United States authorities in a series of recent incidents, our Navy has, for the time being, stopped stationing these officials by limiting the personnel. Inasmuch as in the light of the relations at present prevailing between Japan and the United States, observation of the movements of the American Navy is one of the most important matters, will you observe the movements of ships and gather other information that may be of interest to our Navy and wire us the required information as it comes to you?

                                                              Trans. 6–25–41

No. 222

FROM: Seattle (Sato)   June 23, 1941
TO: Tokyo (Gaimudaijin)   # 056.

(1) Ships at anchor on the 22nd/23rd (?):
(Observations having been made from a distance, ship types could not be determined in most cases.)
    1. Port of Bremerton:
        1 battleship (Maryland type)
        2 aircraft tenders (one ship completed and has letter "E" on its funnel).
    2. Port of ------:
        1 destroyer
        11 coast guard cutters
        (Ships under repair):
        1 destroyer
        11 (appear to be) minesweepers
    3. Sand Point:
        2 newly constructed hangars
    4. Boeing:
        New construction work on newly built factory building # 2. Expansion work on all factory buildings.

                                                              Trans. 7–14–41

No. 224

FROM: Hollywood (Los Angeles)   June 2, 1941
TO: Washington   # 7.

(Circular)

Message to Tokyo # 83.

On the 20th, the Saratoga, and on the 24th, the Chester (?), Louisville, the 12th Destroyer Squadron and Destroyers # 364, 405, 411, 412, and 413 entered San Diego, and all of them left on the 31st.

                                                              Trans. 6–20–41

No. 289

FROM: Hollywood (Nakauchi)   June 10, 1941
TO: Washington   # 36.

Secret.

To the Naval Attaché from TERAI.

1. Our lawyer is of the opinion that KONO* should be (kept in the country for thirty days ?) in view of the danger that he might give evidence unsatisfactory to TACHIBANA*. It would be wise to subsidize him. Furthermore, as KONO has no funds, the lawyer has suggested that the Navy be responsible for paying this man a subsidy of $25,000 and all court costs. In order that the Navy be kept out of the picture, some of KONO's friends should be selected to appear to be supporting him. We are in the process of making these arrangements. Should you have any objection to this manner of procedure, please advise us.

Furthermore, in view of the fact that ----- is a good friend of the Intelligence Chief and in cahoots with the investigating authorities, it would be wise for the Navy to have little to do with the matter.

2. Though our lawyer would not predict the outcome of this incident, as the hearings will be complicated, at the very earliest it will be tomorrow, the 11th, before counter-schemes can be developed.

It is going to be necessary for TACHIBANA to have frequent communication with the lawyer; therefore, we believe that it would be ill-advised for TACHIBANA to go to Washington at the present time.

---

*TACHIBANA's chauffeur.
*Japanese Naval Language Official who has been held on charges of espionage.

Trans. 6-25-41

No. 354

FROM: Tokyo (Matsuoka)   June 11, 1941
TO: Washington   # 287.

With reference to propaganda among Negroes as a scheme against the United States, your immediate reply in regard to the following points is requested:

1. Training of Negroes as (fifth columnists ?).
2. The way to utilize them in order to begin the movement ?).
3. The method of contacting the agitators and leaders among the Negroes, as well as both right and left wings. Also, the amount of expenses involved.

The Minister requests that the above message be forwarded to New York, New Orleans, San Francisco and Los Angeles.

Trans. 5-27-42

No. 369

FROM: Tokyo   July 7, 1941
TO: Washington   # 335.

As a means of sending our communications from here, if worse comes to worse, we have plans for making use of the intelligence dispatches that are being sent out each night; but as a means of making contact from your end, we have been thinking of the possibility of having a wireless set with an operator of exceptional ability in your office, and at the time of the day that is most favorable for dispatches, sending them in relay via South America and Yaruto* in the South Seas. However, I would like to know your opinion as to the feasibility of the plan as regards the following three points.

(1) Could a transmitter of about 100 or 200 watts, or its parts, be assembled in your city under the guise of "amateur" use?

(2) Could this be set up and trial communications carried out as an "amateur" with the relay stations? Then after having it set up secretly in your office, would there be any chance of trying it out, if need be, in a very short trial transmission?

(3) It is expected that if the situation takes a turn for the worst, that extreme limitations, if not prohibitions, will be placed upon the use of the radio in general. In such an event is there any likelihood that the above-mentioned equipment could be used to good advantage?

_____
*Yaruto, principal island of Jaluit (Bonham) Atoll. (6° 00′ N., 169° 35′ E.)

Trans. 7-8-41

No. 384

FROM: Tokyo (Matsuoka)   June 2, 1941
TO: Mexico   # 93.

We have appropriated 100,000 yen for your intelligence and enlightenment expenses during the current fiscal year, and I am hereby sending you the first installment of 25,000 yen. This money is to be used as follows:

1. If worse comes to worst, we consider Mexico City, along with Rio de Janeiro, Buenos Aires, and Santiago as most important bases for intelligence concerning the United States. From a geographical standpoint it is most natural that we should endeavor to set up in Mexico City an establishment where we can carry on routine business in the matter of collecting intelligence concerning the United States. This point I stressed particularly in the outline in the first paragraph of my secret _____ # 62* with reference to propaganda activities.

2. Though the funds are in the main to be used in intelligence concerning the United States, what is left should be used in gathering intelligence in Mexico. Bear in mind that in putting this policy into effect our principal aim is to collect every possible bit of intelligence concerning the United States and, with this in view, I want you to contact and work out a cooperative policy with our officials in Los Angeles, Houston, New Orleans and New York. Furthermore, in this connection, Mexicali might well be used.

3. Please also plan to use RAFAEL MUNAS for purposes of interception.

4. Concerning propaganda and enlightment, in case the United States joins the war, we will endeavor to use our nationals there to our best possible advantage and we will do our very best to use Rightist and Leftist Labor organizations and promote their anti-American revolutionary influence. Please use your best efforts to achieve this.

Secret outside the Department.

_____
*Not available.

Trans. 7-1-41

No. 411

FROM: Tokyo   July 10, 1941
TO: Washington   # 349.

Secret outside the Department.

(To be handled in Government Code.)

Re # 18ª from New Orleans and # 244 (?)ᵇ from Mexico to this Foreign Minister.

We wish Consul ITO to go to Mexico City. Lately the offices housing the German and Italian Consulates were closed and their intelligence net broken. Intelligence activities in the Americas and suitable liaison are now essential, so we wish Secretary TERAZAKI also to go to Mexico to confer with our Minister there, in order to realize our plans in a concrete fashion based on the policy described in previous messages. We want Secretary TERAZAKI, and him only, to stop off at Quito, Los Angeles, San Francisco, etc. In this connection the points which we would like to bring to your attention are as follows:

1. We will have three routes to Mexico from the United States, consisting of Laredo, Ciudad Juarez and Mexicali. Mexicali in particular is a convenient point for us on the west coast. In case we need more personnel, we can get them from our Ministry in Mexico.

2. We will establish a Chile route from Mexico to Manzanillo and a Brazil route by way of Vera Cruz.

3. Various officials in the United States and Mexico will work out all the details of their own espionage nets, correlate them, and develop a concrete plan for making contacts and exchanges on the border.

4. In order to succeed in the objective, ways and means for keeping in contact through telegraphy, telephones, memoranda, and word of mouth will be decided upon and put into effect.

5. These routes are to be established against the day of evil and, while all is calm, nothing must be done which would jeopardize their security; therefore, at present investigate only the feasibility of circulating over them.

6. The expenses are to be paid by the several offices.

Because of its geographical position, Mexico is the main point for intelligence work in Brazil, Argentina and Chile, as well as in the United States. Therefore, before we think of relying too much upon Brazil, Argentina and Chile, let us concentrate on Mexico. However, the other three bases are different. In case the United States joins the war, they would inevitably come under her control, but so long as Mexico does not officially join the war, we can continue our intelligence schemes there. Paralleling these plans of ours, if you can also work out a plan for establishing a liaison net with Brazil, Argentina and Chile, it would be excellent groundwork for the establishment presently of an intelligence net. Please transmit this to Mexico City and take with you to New Orleans.

ªNot available.
ᵇNot available.

Trans. 7-25-41

No. 285

FROM: Hollywood (Nakuchi)   August 16, 1941
TO: Tokyo   # 156.

Re my message # 151°.

1. The St. Claire took on a cargo of 95,000 barrels of aviation gasoline and left port for Vladivostok on the afternoon of (date). The Fitzsimmons is in the process of taking on a similar cargo of 75,000 barrles at Erusegundo[b]. Aside from these two, three other ships are scheduled to leave port carrying similar cargoes. All of them, it is understood, are under charter with the Maritime Commission.

2. All of the above mentioned ships are to rendezvous at some point in the Pacific. It is understood that a number of United States destroyers are on maneuvers at the present time. Rumor has it that they are bound for Vladivostok.

3. The crew of the St. Claire, mentioned above, ----- ----- -----.

Relayed to Washington and San Francisco.

°Not available.
[b]Kana spelling.

Trans. 8-22-41

No. 286

FROM: Seattle (Sato)   August 16, 1941
TO: Tokyo   # 91.

(Secret outside the office)

According to a spy report, the English warship *Warspite* entered Bremerton two or three days ago.

Trans. 10-4-41

No. 287

FROM: Seattle (Sato)   August 21, 1941
TO: Tokyo   # 93.

The Russian ship *Vladimar Mayskovsky* arrived one or two days ago and entered dry dock for repairs which will require a week or more. The present movements of the ship are ----- -----, but as soon as it is repaired, it is going to California to load on freight for Vladivostok. The *Minsk* has left harbor as previously stated. The *Patrovsuky* is still in dry dock.

Trans. 8-25-41

No. 289

FROM: San Francisco (Muto)   August 26, 1941
TO: Tokyo   # 183.

The Russian freighter Yakut (1500 tons) which had been undergoing repairs here left on the 24th[a] for Vladivostok loaded with gasoline, shoes, socks and small arms. On the 20th[b] the Russian freighter Minsk arrived here from (?) and on the 23rd[c] the Russian tanker *Dombas(?)* arrived here from Los Angeles.

Relayed to Washington, Los Angeles, Seattle, & ———.

---
[a] Approximate dates.

Trans. 9–4–41

No. 294

FROM: San Francisco (Muto)   August 30, 1941
TO: Tokyo   # 191.

1. The Donbasu[a] took on a load of 80,000 barrels of aviation gasoline September 8[b] and left immediately for Vladivostok.

2. According to various newspaper reports in addition to the four American tankers bound for Vladivostok, tankers of the General Petroleum Company too are to be dispatched on the direct shipping route to Vladivostok.

Relayed to Washington, ———, ———, ——— New York.

---
[a] Kana spelling.
[b] Apparently an error in the date of loading, made either by the Japanese encoding the dispatch, or by operators in transmitting it.

Trans. 9–19–41

No. 298

FROM: Seattle (Sato)   September 4, 1941
TO: Tokyo   # 105.

(Part 2 of 2)

3. The 39th Bombardment Group (44 planes), the 89th Observation Squadron (15 planes), and the 310th Signal Company, all of Spokane, left August *23 (?)* to take part in the September maneuvers in Louisiana.

4. The planes (number unknown) which the 54th Bombardment Group at *(?)* near Everett are to get are *Republics (?)* or twin-motored *Lockheeds (?)*.

5. The Naval Air Base at Dutch Harbor was opened on the 2nd. W. N. Updegraff has been named Commandant *as has been previously reported (?)*. The Naval supply base at Port *Andrews* (?) was opened on the 4th, according to reports.

6. The *steering apparatus (?) (diameter 8 inches, double cylinders (?), gear ratio 410 to 1 (?)* for the 312 10,000 ton freighters to be leased to England are to be manufactured in two factories, one in Everett and one in *New York (?)*.

Trans. 9–10–41

No. 304

FROM: San Francisco (Muto)   September 8, 1941
TO: Tokyo   # 198.

The Minsk, having completed its repairs, left here on the 6th loaded with 8,000 drums of aviation oil, airplane engines, machine guns, ammunition, snow plows, etc.

Trans. 9–13–41

No. 307

FROM: San Francisco (Muto)   September 18, 1941
TO: Tokyo   # 217.

The Russian freighter Mejinski entered port here from Vladivostok on the 17th (?). The American tanker L. P. St. Clair, which is en route returning from Vladivostok, is expected to arrive on the 19th (?), according to reports.
Relayed to Washington, Los Angeles, and Seattle.

Trans. 9–25–41

No. 308

FROM: San Francisco (Muto)   September 18, 1941
TO: Tokyo   # 218.

According to a spy report, the English warship *Warspite* arrived here from Bremerton on the ----- and is at present moored near the (naval arsenal at Mare Island?). It has been determined that it requires two more months for repairs at Liverpool (my message # 187ª).
Relayed to -----, Los Angeles and Seattle.

ªSee II, 771.

Trans. 9–25–41

No. 309

FROM: Seattle (Sato)   September 20, 1941
TO: Tokyo   # 123.

1. The following warships are now at Bremerton:

The Warspite (repair work continuing. The upper part of the bridge and the port side of the bow spotted here and there with red paint).

Maryland class—one ship (the bridge, turrets and other main armaments have been painted red. Also, they seem to be constructing mountings on the foreward main deck for ten anti-aircraft guns).

Saratoga class air-craft carrier, 1 ship (tied up alongside the pier).

One ship which appears to be a cruiser (it has two smoke stacks but we were unable to distinguish anything else).

One other ship just arrived for repair.

2. The New Mexico class ship mentioned in message # 101ᵃ has departed.

ᵃ See II, 855.

                                                       Trans. 9–27–41

No. 310

FROM: San Francisco (Muto)   October 2, 1941
TO: Washington   # 222.

Message to Tokyo as # 230.

1. One Oklahoma class battleship has arrived in port and is moored in front of the Bethlehem ship-building yard. No reconstruction work is going on on the outside but a great deal of repair work appears to be in progress within the ship.

2. It has been announced by the local headquarters of Naval District # (?) that the Hunters Point shipyard, which was bought last year and which has been undergoing repairs, will be taken over formally in the near future in advance of expectations. (Refer to confidential letter # 216ᵃ of last year.)

Relayed to Washington, Los Angeles, Seattle and Honolulu.

ᵃ See II, 745.

                                                       Trans. 10–17–41

No. 311

FROM: San Francisco   October 16, 1941
TO: Tokyo   # 243.

Re my # 217ᵃ.

The Russian freighter, MEJINSKI, is now in the process of docking. The IGARKA is three days out of New York, the NANTES 7 days from Vladivostok, and the MICHULIN 10 or 12 days from Vladivostok.

The NANTES is loaded with a large quantity of wheat, 20,000 barrels of fuel oil, and also some machine guns, tanks, etc.

Relayed to Washington, Los Angeles, Seattle, Portland.

ᵃ See II, 29.

                                                       Trans. 10–23–41

No. 312

FROM: Hollywood (Nakauchi)   October 12, 1941
TO: Washington   # 48.

Message to Tokyo # 202.

Re my # 185ᵃ.

The Russian ship, Kiev, now in port here, will take on its load of war materials as soon as repairs are completed and proceed to Vladivostok when orders are received. For this purpose, it is equipped with a 500 watt radio for the reception of orders and war news from Moscow.
Relayed to ------, Seattle.

ᵃ Not available.

                                                                      Trans. 10-22-41

No. 313

FROM: Tokyo (Toyoda)   October 16, 1941
TO: Seattle   # 2187 (Circular).

Henceforth, I would like to have you refer in your reports to the movement of warships as follows.
1. As long as there are no great changes in the movement and basing of warships, report on them at least once every ten days. In the event of priority intelligence, report such on each occasion.
a. The arrival or departure of American flagships of the fleet or scouting force.
b. Should more than ten vessels of any type arrive or depart from port at one time.
c. The arrival or departure of warships of countries other than the United States (give as detailed a report as possible on the class of ------).
2. Should patrolling be inaugurated by naval planes, report it at once.

                                                                      Trans. 10-29-41

No. 356

FROM: Tokyo (Toyoda)   September 24, 1941
TO: Honolulu   # 83.

Strictly Secret.

Henceforth, we would like to have you make reports concerning vessels along the following lines insofar as possible:
1. The waters (of Pearl Harbor) are to be divided roughly into five sub-areas. (We have no objections to your abbreviating as much as you like.)
Area A. Waters between Ford Island and the Arsenal.
Area B. Waters adjacent to the Island south and west of Ford Island. (This area is on the opposite side of the Island from Area A.)
Area C. East Loch.
Area D. Middle Loch.
Area E. West Loch and the communicating water routes.
2. With regard to warships and aircraft carriers, we would like to have you report on those at anchor, (these are not so important) tied up at wharves, bouys and in docks. (Designate types and classes briefly. If possible we would like to have you make mention of the fact when there are two or more vessels along side the same wharf.)

                                                                      Trans. 10-9-41

No. 357

FROM: Honolulu (Kita)   September 29, 1941
TO: Washington   Circular # 041.

Honolulu to Tokyo # 178.

Re your Tokyo's # 083ᵃ.

(Strictly secret)

The following codes will be used hereafter to designate the location of vessels:
1. Repair dock in Navy Yard (the repair basin referred to in my message to Washington # 48ᵇ); KS.
2. Navy dock in the Navy Yard (the Ten Ten Pier); KT.
3. Moorings in the vicinity of Ford Island: FV.
4. Alongside in Ford Island: FG (East and west sides will be differentiated by A and B respectively).
Relayed to Washington, San Francisco.

ᵃSee III, 356.
ᵇNot available.

                                                          Trans. 10-10-41

No. 253

FROM: Seattle (Sato)   October 22, 1941
TO: Tokyo   # 147.

(Priority.)

The following warships entered Bremerton Naval Yard on the 21st: The Warspite (repairs are to be made to her bridge), the Maryland and a vessel which seems to be a cruiser.
Relayed to ——— and Los Angeles.

                                                          Trans. 11-4-41

No. 254

FROM: Seattle (Sato)   October 28, 1941
TO: Tokyo   # 150.

(Priority.)

In commemoration of Navy Day, the 27th, fifteen Coast Guard vessels sailed through the harbor here in single file. Their names were as follows: The *Kane, Giruma*ᵃ, the *Brooks*, the *Fox* (the above listed vessels have had their four-inch guns replaced by five-inch guns; all of these were brand-new ones), the Frigate *Bird,* the *Crow,* the *Pintail,* the *Eagle 57, Batukei*ᵃ, the *Butternut*, the *Amber*, the *YP 83, 87, 89,* and *90.*

ᵃKana spelling.

                                                          Trans. 11-19-41

No. 256

FROM: Seattle (Sato)   November 10, 1941
TO: Tokyo   # 165.

(Priority.)

(Message to Washington Circular # 80.)

Vessels anchored in Bremerton on the 9th: Saratogo, Warspite, Colorado, (I have confirmed that the latter ship is the one which I have reported on successive occasions as the Maryland) and the Charleston.
Relayed to —— and Los Angeles.

Trans. 11–19–41

No. 257

FROM: Washington (Nomura)   November 25, 1941
TO: Seattle   # 026.

Regarding Warspite, a British war ship now under repair at Bremerton.

Please investigate progress of repair, also when repair is completed report day and time of its departure and if possible find out its destination and report.

Trans. 12–4–41

No. 258

FROM: Tokyo   November 29, 1941
TO: San Francisco   Circular # 2431.

Make full report beginning December 1st on the following.
Ship's nationality, ship's name, port from which it departed, (or at which it arrived), and port of destination, (or from where it started), date of departure, etc., in detail, of all foreign commercial and war ships now in the Pacific, Indian Ocean, and South China Sea.

Trans. 12–4–41

No. 259

FROM: Seattle   December 6, 1941
TO: Tokyo   # 184.

Urgent intelligence.

1. The ships at anchor in Bremerton on the 5th were the Warspite (came out of the dock and at present is tied up at a pier) and the Colorado.
2. The Saratoga sailed the same day.

Trans. 12–8–41

No. 279

FROM: Tokyo (Togo)   November 15, 1941
TO: Honolulu (Riyoji)   # 111.

As relations between Japan and the United States are most critical, make your "ships in harbor report" irregular, but at a rate of twice a week. Although you already are no doubt aware, please take extra care to maintain secrecy.

Trans. 12–3–41

No. 280

FROM: Honolulu (Kita)   November 18, 1941
TO: Tokyo   # 222.

1. The warships at anchor in the Harbor on the 15th were as I told you in my # 219[a] on that day.
Area A[b]—A battleship of the Oklahoma class entered and one tanker left port.
Area C[c]—3 warships of the heavy cruiser class were at anchor.
2. On the 17th, the Saratoga was not in the harbor. The carrier, Enterprise, or some other vessel was in Area C. Two heavy cruisers of the Chicago class, one of the Pensacola class were tied up at docks "KS". 4 merchant vessels were at anchor in area D[d].
3. At 10:00 a.m. on the morning of the 17th, 8 destroyers were observed entering the Harbor. Their course was as follows: In a single file at a distance of 1,000 meters apart at a speed of 3 knots per hour, they moved into Pearl Harbor. From the entrance of the Harbor through Area B to the buoys in Area C, to which they were moored, they changed course 5 times each time roughly 30 degrees. The elapsed time was one hour, however, one of these destroyers entered Area A after passing the water reservoir on the Eastern side.
Relayed to –––––.

---

[a] Not deciphered. Dated 14 November 1941.
[b] Waters between Ford Island and the Arsenal.
[c] East Loch.
[d] Middle Loch.

Trans. 12–6–41

No. 282

FROM: Tokyo (Togo)   November 18, 1941
TO: Honolulu   # 113.

   Please report on the following areas as to vessels anchored therein; Area "N" Pearl Harbor, Manila Bay, and the areas adjacent thereto. (Make your investigation with great secrecy.)

                                                    Trans. 12–5–41

No. 283

FROM: Tokyo (Togo)   November 20, 1941
TO: Honolulu   # 111.

   Strictly secret.

   Please investigate comprehensively the fleet ----- bases in the neighborhood of the Hawaiian military reservation.

                                                    Trans. 12–4–41

No. 284

FROM: Honolulu (Kita)   November 24, 1941
TO: Tokyo   # 234.

   Part 1 of 2. Strictly secret.

   Re your # 114ᵃ.

   1. According to normal practice, the fleet leaves Pearl Harbor, conducts maneuvers and forthwith returns.
   2. Recently, the fleet has not remained for a long period of time nor conducted maneuvers in the neighborhood of Lahaina Roads. Destroyers and submarines are the only vessels who ride at anchor there.
   3. Battleships seldom, if ever, enter the ports of Hilo, Hanalei, or Kaneohe. Virtually no one has observed battleships in maneuver areas
   4. The manner in which the fleet moves:
   Battleships exercise in groups of three or five, accompanied by lighter craft. They conduct maneuvers for roughly one week at sea, either to the south of Maui or to the southwest. Aircraft carriers maneuver by themselves, whereas sea plane tenders operate in concert with another vessel of the same class. Airplane firing and bombing practice is conducted in the neighborhood of the southern extremity of the island of Kahoolawe.

   ᵃ Not available.

                                                    Trans. 12–16–41

No. 285

FROM: Honolulu   November 24, 1941
TO: Tokyo   # 234.

Part 2 of 2.

The heavy cruisers in groups of six carry on their operations over a period of two to three weeks, doubtless going to Samoa. The length of time that they remain at anchor in Pearl Harbor or tied up at docks is roughly four or five days at a stretch.

The light cruisers in groups of five spend one to two weeks in operations. It would seem that they carry on their maneuvers in the vicinity of Panama.

The submarines go out on 24-hour trips Monday, Wednesdays, and Fridays.

The destroyers, in addition to accompanying the principal units of the fleet, carry on personnel training activities in the waters adjacent to Hawaii.

Mine layers (old-style destroyers) in groups of -----, have been known to spend more than three weeks in operations in the Manila area.

Furthermore, on the night of the 23rd, five mine layers conducted mine laying operations outside Manila harbor.

Trans. 12–16–41

No. 286

FROM: Honolulu   November 28, 1941
TO: Tokyo   # 238.

Military report:

(1) There are eight "B–17" planes at Midway and the altitude range of their anti-aircraft guns is (5,000 feet?).

(2) Our observations at the Sand Island maneuvers are: number of shots—12; interval of flight—13 seconds; interval between shots—2 minutes; direct hits—none.

(3) 12,000 men (mostly marines) are expected to reinforce the troops in Honolulu during December or January.

(4) There has usually been one cruiser in the waters about (15,000 feet?) south of Pearl Harbor and one or two destroyers at the entrance to the harbor.

Trans. 12–8–41

No. 287

FROM: Tokyo (Togo)   November 28, 1941
TO: Honolulu   # 119.

Re your message # 243ᵃ.

Secret outside the Department.

Intelligences of this kind which are of major importance, please transmit to us in the following manner:

1. When battleships move out of the harbor if we report such movement but once a week the vessels, in that interval, could not only be in the vicinity of the Hawaiian Islands, but could also have traveled far. Use your own judgment in deciding on reports covering such movements.

2. Report upon the entrance or departure of capital ships and the length of time they remain at anchor, from the time of entry into the port until the departure.

ᵃ Not available.

Trans. 12–8–41

No. 288

FROM: Tokyo   November 29, 1941
TO: Honolulu   # 122.

We have been receiving reports from you on ship movements, but in future will you also report even when there are no movements.

Trans. 12–5–41

No. 289

FROM: Tokyo (Togo)   November 28, 1941
TO: Honolulu   # 118.

(Priority.)

Re your # 232ᵃ.

To be handled in government code.

Anticipating the possibility of ordinary telegraphic communication being severed when we are about to face the worst of situations, these broadcasts are intended to serve as a means of informing the diplomats in the country concerned of that situation without the use of the usual telegraphic channels. Do not destroy the codes without regard to the actual situation in your locality, but retain them as long as the situation there permits and until the final stage is entered into.

ᵃ Not available.

Trans. 12–7–41

No. 290

FROM: Honolulu (Kita)   December 1, 1941
TO: Tokyo   # 241.

(In 2 parts complete.)

Re your # 119[a].

Report on ship maneuvers in Pearl Harbor:
1. The place where practice maneuvers are held is about 500 nautical miles southeast of here.
Direction based on:
(1) The direction taken when the ships start out is usually southeast by south and ships disappear beyond the horizon in that direction.
(2) Have never seen the fleet go westward or head for the "KAIUI" straits northwards.
(3) The west sea of the Hawaiian Islands has many reefs and islands and is not suitable as an ocean maneuver practice sea.
(4) Direction of practice will avoid all merchant ship routes and official travel routes.
Distance based on:
(1) Fuel is plentiful and long distance high speed is possible.
(2) Guns cannot be heard here.
(3) In one week's time, (actually the maneuvers mentioned in my message # 231[b] were for the duration of four full days of 144 hours), a round trip to a distance of 864 nautical miles could be reached (if speed is 12 knots), or 1152 miles (if speed is 16 knots), or 1440 nautical miles (if speed is 20 knots) is possible, however, figuring on 50% of the time being used for maneuver technicalities, a guess that the point at which the maneuvers are held would be a point of about 500 miles from Pearl Harbor.
2. The usual schedule for departure and return of the battleship is: leaving on Tuesday and returning on Friday, or leaving on Friday and returning on Saturday of the following week. All ships stay in port about a period of one week.

---

[a] See IV, 287.
[b] Not available.

Trans. 12-10-41

No. 291

FROM: Tokyo (Togo)   December 2, 1941
TO: Honolulu   # 123.

(Secret outside the department.)

In view of the present situation, the presence in port of warships, airplane carriers, and cruisers is of utmost importance. Hereafter, to the utmost of your ability, let me know day by day. Wire me in each case whether or not there are any observation balloons above Pearl Harbor or if there are any indications that they will be sent up. Also advise me whether or not the warships are provided with anti-mine nets.

Trans. 12-30-41

No. 292

FROM: Honolulu (Kita)   December 3, 1941
TO: Tokyo   # 245.

(In 2 parts complete.)

Military secret.

From Ichiro Fujii to the Chief of # 3 Section of Military Staff Headquarters.

1. I wish to change my method of communicating by signals to the following:
a. Arrange the eight signals in three columns as follows:

Meaning		*Signal*
Battleship divisions including scouts and screen units	Preparing to sortie	1
A number of carriers	Preparing to sortie	2
Battleship divisions	All departed between 1st and 3rd.	3
Carriers	Several departed between 1st and 3rd.	4
Carriers	All departed between 1st and 3rd.	5
Battleship divisions	All departed between 4th and 6th.	6
Carriers	Several departed between 4th and 6th.	7
Carriers	All departed between 4th and 6th.	8

2. Signals.
a. Lanikaiª Beach. House will show lights during the night as follows:

	Signal
One light between 8 and 9 p.m.	1
One light between 9 and 10 p.m.	2
One light between 10 and 11 p.m.	3
One light between 11 and 12 p.m.	4
b.	
Two lights between 12 and 1 a.m.	5
Two lights between 1 and 2 a.m.	6
Two lights between 2 and 3 a.m.	7
Two lights between 3 and 4 a.m.	8

Part 2.

c. Lanikai[a] Bay, during daylight.

If there is a "star" on the head of the sail of the Star Boat it indicates signals 1, 2, 3, or 4.

If there is a "star" and a Roman numeral III it indicates signal 5, 6, 7, or 8.

d. Lights in the attic window of Kalama House[b] will indicate the following:

Times	Signal
1900 – 2000	3
2000 – 2100	4
2100 – 2200	5
2200 – 23--	6
2300 – 2400	7
0000 – 0100	8

e. K.G.M.B.[c] Want Ads.

A. Chinese rug etc. for sale, apply P.O. box 1476 indicates signal 3 or 6.

B. CHICH..GO farm etc. apply P.O. box 1476 indicates signal 4 or 7.

C. Beauty operator wanted etc. apply P.O. box 1476 indicates signal 5 or 8.

3. If the above listed signals and wireless messages cannot be made from Oahu, then on Maui Island, 6 miles to the northward of Kula Sanatorium[d] at a point halfway between Lower Kula Road and Haleakala Road (latitude 20° 40′N, longitude 156° 19′W., visible from seaward to the southeast and southwest of Maui Island) the following signal bonfire will be made daily until your EXEX signal is received:

Time	Signal
From 7 – 8	3 or 6
From 8 – 9	4 of 7
From 9 – 10	5 or 8

---

[a] Between Waimanalo and Kailua Beaches on east coast of Oahu.

[b] A beach village on east coast of Oahu, 1 mile northwest of Lanikai.

[c] A radio broadcast station in Honolulu.

[d] At latitude 20–42–45 N., longitude 156–20–20 W.

Trans. 12–11–41

No. 293

FROM: Honolulu (Kita)   December 3, 1941
TO: Tokyo   # 247.

   Ship report.

   2nd. Military transport (name unknown) sailed out toward mainland.
   3rd. RARIN came into port from San Francisco.

                                                      Trans. 12–10–41

No. 294

FROM: Honolulu (Kita)   December 3, 1941
TO: Tokyo   # 248.

   Ship report.

   December 3rd. Wyoming and 2 seaplane tenders left port. No other movement.

                                                      Trans. 12–10–41

No. 295

FROM: Honolulu (Kita)   December 4, 1941
TO: Tokyo   # 249.

   On the afternoon of the 3rd, one British gunboat entered Honolulu Harbor. She left port
early on the morning of the 4th. She was roughly of the 1,100 tons class. She had but one funnel
and carried one 4 inch gun fore and aft. ----- -----.
   Furthermore, immediately after the vessel entered port, a sailor took some mail to the
British Consular Office and received some mail in return.

                                                      Trans. 12–12–41

No. 296

FROM: Honolulu (Kita)   December 5, 1941
TO: Tokyo   # 252.

   (1) During Friday morning, the 5th, the three battleships mentioned in my message # 239[a]
arrived here. They had been at sea for eight days.
   (2) The Lexington and five heavy cruisers left port on the same day.
   (3) The following ships were in port on the afternoon of the 5th:
   8 battleships
   3 light cruisers
   16 destroyers
Four ships of the Honolulu class and ----- were in dock.

   ---
   [a] Not available.

                                                      Trans. 12–10–41

No. 297

FROM: Honolulu   December 6, 1941
TO: Tokyo   # 253.

Re the last part of your # 123[a].

1. On the American continent in October the Army began training barrage balloon troops at Camp Davis, North Carolina. Not only have they ordered four or five hundred ballons, but it is understood that they are considering the use of these balloons in the defense of Hawaii and Panama. Insofar as Hawaii is concerned, though investigations have been made in the neighborhood of Pearl Harbor, they have not set up mooring equipment, nor have they selected the troops to man them. Furthermore, there is no indication that any training for the maintenance of balloons is being undertaken. At the present time there are no signs of barrage balloon equipment. In addition, it is difficult to imagine that they have actually any. However, even though they have actually made preparations, because they must control the air over the water and land runways of the airports in the vicinity of Pearl Harbor, Hickam, Ford and Ewa[b], there are limits to the balloon defense of Pearl Harbor. I imagine that in all probability there is considerable opportunity left to take advantage for a surprise attack against these places.

2. In my opinion, the battleships do not have torpedo nets. The details are not known. I will report the results of my investigation.

[a] See IV, 291.
[b] Kana spelling.

Trans. 12–8–41

No. 298

FROM: Honolulu   December 6, 1941
TO: Tokyo   # 254.

1. On the evening of the 5th, among the battleships which entered port were ----- and one submarine tender. The following ships were observed at anchor on the 6th:

9 battleships, 3 light cruisers, 3 submarine tenders, 17 destroyers, and in addition, there were 4 light cruisers, 2 destroyers lying at docks (the heavy cruisers and airplane carriers have all left).

2. It appears that no air reconnaissance is being conducted by the fleet air arm.

Trans. 12–8–41

No. 457

FROM: Tokyo   December 5, 1941
TO: Washington   # 896.

Re your # 1245[a].

Will you please have Terasaki, Takagi, Ando, Yamamoto and others leave by plane within the next couple of days.

[a] See IV, 442.

Trans. 12–6–41

APPENDIX C

Intelligence Memos

These memos—written and distributed both before and after the Pearl Harbor attack—reveal the rigorous attention that military intelligence and FBI officials were paying to Japan's espionage operations and activities in the United States and elsewhere. Many of the memos are clearly derived, sometimes verbatim, from MAGIC. To protect the code-breaking operation, recipients were told that the information came from "highly confidential and reliable sources."

The following documents vividly illustrate historian David Kahn's conclusion about MAGIC: "It had become a regular and vital factor in the formation of American policy. . . . The chief of army intelligence regarded MAGIC as the most reliable and authentic information that the War Department was receiving on Japanese intentions and activities. The navy war plans chief thought that MAGIC . . . affected his estimates by about 15 percent. The high officials not only read MAGIC avidly and discussed it at their conferences, *they acted upon it* (emphasis added)."

DECLASSIFIED -277-
By ____ NARS. Date 5/1/65

CONFID

WAR DEPARTMENT
WAR DEPARTMENT GENERAL STAFF
MILITARY INTELLIGENCE DIVISION G-2
WASHINGTON

G-2
RSB

WAR DEP/

February 12, 1941

MEMORANDUM FOR THE CHIEF, COUNTER INTELLIGENCE BRANCH:

Subject: Reorganization of Japanese Intelligence
Service in the United States.

1.   This Branch has information from a highly reliable source
to the effect that the Japanese intelligence service in the United
States is being reorganized and enlarged and is cooperating with
German and Italian services.

2.   The salient points of the directive sent to the Embassy
in Washington are as follows:

"1. Establish an intelligence organ in the
Embassy which will maintain liaison with private and
semi-official intelligence organs.

"2. The objective of investigations is to determine the total strength of the United States. Investigations will cover the political, economic and
military fields.

"3. Surveys to be prepared of all persons or
organizations which either openly or secretly oppose
participation in the war.

"4. Investigation to be made of all anti-
Semitism, communism, Negro movements, and labor movements.

"5. Utilization to be made of citizens of
foreign extraction (other than Japanese), aliens (other
than Japanese), communists, Negroes, labor union
members, and anti-Semites, in carrying out investigations, to get best results. These agents should have
access to governmental establishments, laboratories,
governmental organizations of various sorts, factories,
transportation facilities, etc.

CONFIDENTIAL

The memos on the reorganization of Japan's intelligence network, sent by army
MID, ONI, and FBI respectively, were all based on MAGIC message No. 119
(#44). The MAGIC message was translated February 7, 1941. The MID and
ONI memos were distributed five days later.

CONFIDENTIAL

"6. Utilization of second generation Japanese to be made with utmost caution as a slip in this phase would subject Japanese in America to considerable persecution.

"7. Plans to be made to move the Japanese intelligence net to Mexico in the event the United States enters the war.

"8. The net covering Brazil, Argentina, Chile, and Peru to be centered in Mexico.

"9. Close cooperation to be had with German and Italian intelligence organs in the United States."

C. H. MASON,
Colonel of Infantry, G.S.C.,
Chief, Intelligence Branch.

fk

NAVY DEPARTMENT
Office of the Chief of Naval Operations
OFFICE OF NAVAL INTELLIGENCE
WASHINGTON

In reply refer to No.

Op-16-B

February 12, 1941

CONFIDENTIAL

MEMORANDUM for the Chief of Naval Operations

Subject: Japanese Espionage Organization in the United States

1.   It is recommended that the following be brought to
the attention of the President and the Secretary of the Navy.
This information has been compiled from highly confidential and
reliable sources by the Domestic Intelligence Branch of the
Office of Naval Intelligence from documentary evidence in its
possession.

"In view of the critical situation existing between the United
States and Japan, the latter has decided to strengthen its
intelligence network in the United States upon the arrival of
Admiral Kichisaburo NOMURA, the new Japanese Ambassador.

"Japanese Diplomatic and Consular representatives have been
instructed to reorganize and strengthen their intelligence nets
in this country. A fairly accurate portrayal of Japan's espionage
organization is as follows:

1. Hidenari TERASAKI, Secretary of the Japanese Embassy, Washington,
will be the guiding influence. He will establish an intelligence
unit which will maintain liaison with private and semi-official
intelligence organizations.
2. Focal point of all Japanese investigations shall be the
determination of the total strength of the U.S.   Investigations
will be divided into political, economic and military classifications,
and a definite course of action shall be mapped out.
3. Intelligence net will make a survey of all persons and organization
which either openly or secretly oppose U.S. participation in the
present war.
4. The net will make a survey of all anti-Jewish, Communistic,
Negro and labor movements.
5. Citizens of foreign extraction except Japanese, aliens except
Japanese, Communists, Negroes, labor union members and/anti-Semites
and men having access to government departments, experimental
laboratories, factories, transportation facilities and governmental
organizations of various characters will be utilized.

DECLASSIFICATION ON 5/14/85

- 2 -

6. Nisei Japanese and Japanese resident nationals are
to be employed but if there is any 'slip' in this phase,
the Japanese Government thinks these nationals in the
United States will be subject to considerable persecution;
therefore, extreme caution should be exercised.
7. Japanese representatives in this country are cautioned
to bear in mind that war between Japan and the United States
is an eventuality. In such a case, the Japanese intelligence
setup will be moved to Mexico, making that country the nerve
center of the intelligence net in the western hemisphere.
In further anticipation of such an eventuality, the United
States - Mexico international intelligence route will be
established. The Japanese intelligence net covering Argentina,
Brazil, Chile and Peru will be centered in Mexico.

"The Japanese shall cooperate with the German and Italian
intelligence organizations. This phase has been discussed
in Tokyo with German and Italian representatives and has been
approved.

Los Angeles, San Francisco, Seattle, New Orleans, Chicago,
New York and Washington will be the espionage centers in the
United States, all instructions emanating from Washington.
Mexicali, Sonora and Vancouver, B. C. will also be centers
along our boundary."

    2.   This information has been transmitted to the
Military Intelligence Division of the Army and the Federal
Bureau of Investigation.

                            Jules James
                            Captain, U.S. Navy
                            Acting Director of Naval Intelligence

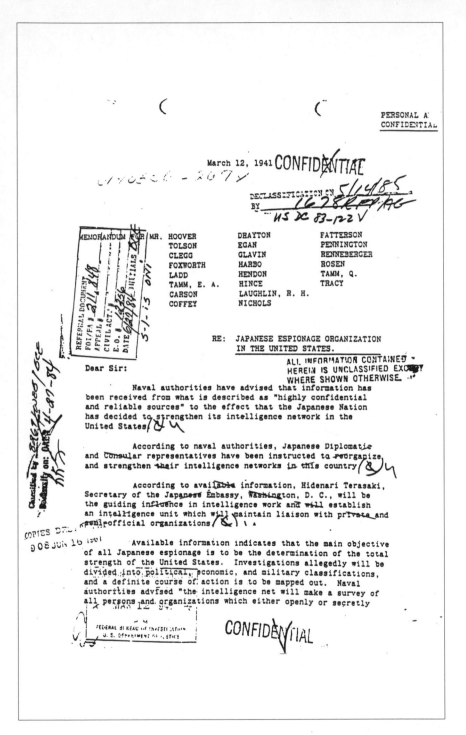

PERSONAL A
CONFIDENTIAL

March 12, 1941 CONFIDENTIAL

DECLASSIFICATION ON 5/1/85
BY 1628REF/AG
US DC 83-122

MEMORANDUM FOR MR. HOOVER   DRAYTON   FATTERSON
                    TOLSON   EGAN   PENNINGTON
                    CLEGG   GLAVIN   RENNEBERGER
                    FOXWORTH   HARBO   ROSEN
                    LADD   HENDON   TAMM, Q.
                    TAMM, E. A.   HINCE   TRACY
                    CARSON   LAUGHLIN, R. H.
                    COFFEY   NICHOLS

                    RE: JAPANESE ESPIONAGE ORGANIZATION
                          IN THE UNITED STATES.

                                          ALL INFORMATION CONTAINED
    Dear Sir: HEREIN IS UNCLASSIFIED EXCEPT
                                          WHERE SHOWN OTHERWISE.
         Naval authorities have advised that information has
    been received from what is described as "highly confidential
    and reliable sources" to the effect that the Japanese Nation
    has decided to strengthen its intelligence network in the
    United States.

         According to naval authorities, Japanese Diplomatic
    and Consular representatives have been instructed to reorganize
    and strengthen their intelligence networks in this country.

         According to available information, Hidenari Terasaki,
    Secretary of the Japanese Embassy, Washington, D. C., will be
    the guiding influence in intelligence work and will establish
    an intelligence unit which will maintain liaison with private and
    semiofficial organizations.

         Available information indicates that the main objective
    of all Japanese espionage is to be the determination of the total
    strength of the United States. Investigations allegedly will be
    divided into political, economic, and military classifications,
    and a definite course of action is to be mapped out. Naval
    authorities advised "the intelligence net will make a survey of
    all persons and organizations which either openly or secretly

                                          CONFIDENTIAL

    FEDERAL BUREAU OF INVESTIGATION
    U. S. DEPARTMENT OF JUSTICE

- 2 -

oppose the United States participation in the present war, and
will make a survey of all anti-Jewish, Communistic, Negro, and
labor movements. (R.)..

It is reported that citizens of foreign extraction,
Communists, Negroes, labor union members, anti-Semites, and
men having access to government departments, experimental
laboratories, factories, transportation facilities, and governmental
organizations of various characters will be utilized. While
second generation Japanese and Japanese resident nationals are
also to be employed, the Japanese authorities have allegedly indicated
that any Japanese individual who might be caught will be subject
to considerable persecution/R

Naval authorities report that Japanese representatives
in this country have been cautioned to bear in mind that war
between Japan and the United States is an eventuality, in which
case the Japanese intelligence setup will be moved to Mexico,
making that country the nerve center of the intelligence net in
the western hemisphere. In further anticipation of such an
eventuality, the United States - Mexico international intelligence
route will be established. It is stated that the Japanese
intelligence net covering Argentina, Brazil, Chile, and Peru
will be centered in Mexico. Japanese representatives allegedly
have been instructed to cooperate with German and Italian organizations
which move has reportedly been approved in Tokyo by representatives
of the Axis Alliance/R \ ..

It has been stated by Naval authorities that Los
Angeles, San Francisco, Seattle, New Orleans, Chicago, New York,
and Washington will be the espionage centers in the United States,
with all instructions emanating from Washington, whereas Mexicali,
Sonora, and Vancouver, B. C. will also be centers in proximity
to the United States boundary/R \ \

Very truly yours,

J. E. Hoover

John Edgar Hoover
Director

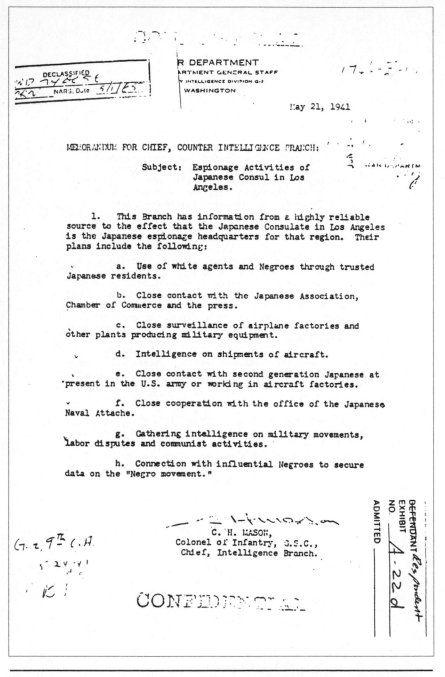

CONFIDENTIAL

R DEPARTMENT
ARTMENT GENERAL STAFF
Y INTELLIGENCE DIVISION G-2
WASHINGTON

DECLASSIFIED
NND 74028
NARS, Date 5/1/65

May 21, 1941

MEMORANDUM FOR CHIEF, COUNTER INTELLIGENCE BRANCH:

Subject: Espionage Activities of
           Japanese Consul in Los
           Angeles.

1.   This Branch has information from a highly reliable
source to the effect that the Japanese Consulate in Los Angeles
is the Japanese espionage headquarters for that region.   Their
plans include the following:

a.   Use of white agents and Negroes through trusted
Japanese residents.

b.   Close contact with the Japanese Association,
Chamber of Commerce and the press.

c.   Close surveillance of airplane factories and
other plants producing military equipment.

d.   Intelligence on shipments of aircraft.

e.   Close contact with second generation Japanese at
present in the U.S. army or working in aircraft factories.

f.   Close cooperation with the office of the Japanese
Naval Attache.

g.   Gathering intelligence on military movements,
labor disputes and communist activities.

h.   Connection with influential Negroes to secure
data on the "Negro movement."

C. H. MASON,
Colonel of Infantry, G.S.C.,
Chief, Intelligence Branch.

CONFIDENTIAL

DEFENDANT Respondent
EXHIBIT NO. A-22 d
ADMITTED

These two memos from the MID and FBI respectively, were based on MAGIC
message No. 174 (#67), which was translated May 19, 1941.

May 22, 1941

THP:AB

MEMORANDUM FOR THE ATTORNEY GENERAL

The Office of Naval Intelligence, Washington, D. C., has advised this Bureau that a considerable amount of general information concerning Japanese Intelligence activities in the United States has been received from a source which is described as "thoroughly reliable and highly confidential."

With reference to their intelligence activities in Southern California, it is stated that Japanese authorities are making every effort to establish useful contacts and in this connection they are endeavoring to make use of white persons and negroes, as well as Japanese associations, Japanese chambers of commerce and Japanese newspapers. It is stated that they have already established contacts with reliable Japanese in the San Pedro and San Diego areas who will observe closely all shipments of airplanes and other war materials and who will report the amounts and destinations of such shipments. It is indicated that they have also taken steps to have the traffic of war materials across the Mexican border closely watched.

It is further stated that Japanese authorities plan to establish close relations with appropriate individuals and organizations in order to keep airplane manufacturing plants, as well as military and naval establishments under close surveillance. In this connection, it is stated that a number of second-generation Japanese have been placed in airplane plants for intelligence purposes and it is stated that Japanese authorities maintain contact with the second-generation Japanese who are now in the United States Army, in order that the Japanese authorities may be currently informed of developments in that branch of the service.

It appears that Japanese authorities are interested in negro movements and anti-Semitic movements in this country. It is stated that they have established contacts with influential negroes for the purpose of being informed with reference to negro movements. They are reported to have employed prominent Americans and Japanese connected with the motion picture industry to investigate anti-Semitic movements, particularly on the West Coast.

Respectfully,

John Edgar Hoover
Director

USE _____
PLAINTIFF _Respondent_
HIBIT A-23a
) _____
MITTED _____

CONFIDENTIAL

June 9, 1941

MEMORANDUM FOR THE CHIEF, COUNTER INTELLIGENCE BRANCH:

Subject: Japanese Espionage.

This branch has information from a highly reliable
source to the effect that the Japanese intelligence and
espionage unit centering in the Seattle Consulate has
made the following "contacts":

   a.   Political.

John Sylvester, Speaker of the State Lower House.
Ralph Horr, Chairman local committee, Republican
Party,
Daniel Trefethen, local Republican Party official.

From these men the Japanese collect information on political
questions and on the degree of America's participation in the
war.

   b.   Economic.

Employees in American and Japanese companies.

These men furnish information as to our war effort, construction of ships, number of planes produced, copper, zinc and
aluminum production, the yield of tin for cans, lumber, etc.
One such person (name unknown) recently gave the Japanese a
report on machinists of German origin who are communists and
members of the labor organizations in the Bremerton Naval Yard
and the Boeing Aircraft Factory.

   c.   Military.

One Kaneko is in charge of men sent out into the
field to get information concerning movement of naval craft,
mercantile shipping, airplane manufacture, troop movements

1628 KED/AE 5/14/85

MID memo dated June 9, 1941 based mostly on MAGIC message No. 175
(#45), which was translated the same day. Note reference to the *Nisei* lawyer
identified as Ito—which is presumed to be Seattle lawyer Kenji Ito.

CONFIDENTIAL

and maneuvers. These men contact a Major/Okada (not listed in The Diplomatic List) who wires his reports to Tokyo.

Second generation Japanese selectees report on the military service, morale, discipline, etc.

d. **Labor Unions.**

One/Okamura, a first-generation Japanese and a member of the C.I.O. reports on labor disorders, etc.

A second-generation Japanese lawyer named Ito collects information on anti-war-participation organizations.

C. H. MASON,
Colonel of Infantry, G.S.C.,
Chief, Intelligence Branch.

CONFIDENTIAL

-2-

M I D

NAVY DEPARTMENT
Office of Naval Intelligence
Washington, D. C.

~~CONFIDENTIAL~~

December 4, 1941

Subject: JAPANESE INTELLIGENCE AND PROPAGANDA IN THE UNITED STATES
DURING 1941.

Note : Prepared by the Counter Subversion Section, Office of Naval
Intelligence, from information received from various sources.

INTRODUCTION

The Kurusu mission to Washington represents the culmination of a
year of intense activity which has streamlined Japanese espionage pat-
terns, conditioned programs of sabotage and determined the character
and extent of their propaganda launched throughout this hemisphere.

As Ambassador to Berlin, Kurusu signed the Tripartite Pact of September 1940, but it is said that he did so with no great enthusiasm. A
top-flight diplomat, he has also been Japanese Consul in New York,
Chicago, and Honolulu, as well as Consul General in Manila. In 1929 he
was Minister to Chile and for seven years thereafter served in Tokyo as
a director of the Commercial Bureau of the Foreign Office.

Methods of Operation and Points of Attack

With tension growing between the United States and Japan, the Japanese Government decided its system for securing information was inadequate to meet a situation involving war. As early as February, 1941 and
coincident with the arrival of the new ambassador Admiral Kichisaburo
Nomura, diplomatic and consular representatives were instructed to reorganize and strengthen the intelligence network in this country and to
relax the former policy of "cultural propaganda and enlightenment".

Designed to continue in operation, even in the event diplomatic
and commercial relations between the two countries were severed, an
intelligence machine geared for war was put into operation. As a pre-
liminary measure, Japanese representatives in the United States were
instructed to maintain constant watch over American politics, as well
as over the economic and social activities of representatives of the
U.S.S.R. in this country, particularly as they affect Latin America.
For this work, the Japanese planned not only to hire Americans but also
to send competent "researchers" from Japan. A decision was also made

~~CONFIDENTIAL~~

DECLASSIFIED 755004

ONI memo written three days before the Pearl Harbor attack provides good
overview of the Japanese espionage network.

to spread as much political propaganda as possible throughout the United States by means of personal contacts with members of the press and persons influential in American politics and business.

The focal point of the Japanese Espionage effort is the determination of the total strength of the United States. In anticipation of possible open conflict with this country, Japan is vigorously utilizing every available agency to secure military, naval and commercial information, paying particular attention to the West Coast, the Panama Canal and the Territory of Hawaii. To this end, surveys are being made of persons and organizations opposing U. S. intervention in the present European War, and close attention is being paid to all anti-Jewish, Communist, Negro and Labor Movements.

Although not yet fully developed, this new Espionage organization is characterized by a high degree of decentralization. The activity of the Military and Naval section, which is divided into a number of different groups, is supplemented by the work of independent agents, and the general pattern includes individuals, small groups and commercial organizations functioning separately and energetically. In the background lies the Imperial Japanese Government exercising direct control over individuals and organizations through the Embassy and the Consulates.

The new program envisages the use of citizens of foreign extraction, aliens, communists, negroes, labor union members, anti-semites, and individuals having access to Government departments, experimental laboratories, factories, transportation facilities, and governmental organizations of various kinds. Nisei (second generation) Japanese and alien Japanese residents have not been overlooked. Realizing, however, that its nationals in this country would be subject to prosecution "in the event of a slip," the Japanese Government has advised extreme caution in their employment.

In the event of open hostilities, Mexico will probably be the Japanese Intelligence nerve center in the Western Hemisphere, and in anticipation of war, U. S. - Mexican Intelligence routes are being established. This network, covering Argentina, Brazil, Chile, Peru and the Central American countries, will come together in Mexico City, and Japanese co-operation with the German and Italian Intelligence organizations is expected. Such co-operation has been discussed in Tokyo with representatives of the Axis powers and the plan is said to have been approved by them.

At the present time, the District of Columbia, New York City, New Orleans, Los Angeles, San Francisco and Seattle are the espionage centers in the United States with Mexicali, Baja California and Vancouver, British Columbia important boundary outposts.

-2-

GERMAN-JAPANESE COLLABORATION

As an incident of the treaty with the Axis powers, all possible
avenues by which mutual benefit could be achieved began to be explored.
Instructions were sent to all diplomatic and consular missions to maintain close contact with officials of Germany and Italy for purposes of
exchanging information and to encourage friendships between citizens of
the three nations who were living abroad.

A recent investigation conducted in New York City disclosed that
Takeo Ezima and Kanegoro Koike, Japanese Naval Officers attached to the
Naval Inspector's Office, were co-operating with German espionage agents
by accepting confidential data for transmittal to Germany by way of Japan.

On October 19, 1940, instructions were issued from Germany by shortwave radio for a German agent in the United States to contact E. Sato at
the NIPPON CLUB in New York City. He made unsuccessful attempts to comply
with these instructions until October 31, 1940 when another radio message
was received from Germany directing that these efforts be discontinued.

Germany radioed again on May 18, 1941 asking whether its agent in
the United States was prepared to turn over material, inscribed "Sato
from Staemer", on May 22, 1941, to E. Sato in the Miyako Restaurant, 20
East 56th Street, New York City. The message also indicated that further
meetings should be agreed upon and that this method of transmitting material was safe.

Shortly thereafter, two German agents in the United States complied
with these instructions and established contact with an individual who
gave his name as Kato. After identifying themselves, they were taken
by him to a Japanese restaurant at 41 East 19th Street, New York City,
where they occupied a private room. Kato there identified himself as
Lt. Commander Takeo Ezima, I.J.N. and took from them a number of items
for transmittal to Germany by way of Japan. These items consisted of
information developed through the activities of the German Espionage
system in the United States, some of which had been microfilmed. However,
the original physical articles such as ammunition, a drawing of a hydrau-
lic unit with pressure switch A-5 of the Sperry Gyroscope and an original
drawing from the Lawrence Engineering and Research Corporation of a
soundproofing installation were also turned over to Ezima on this occasion.

Immediately following a meeting on June 24, 1941, when Ezima received a number of microphotographs of material obtained by German espionage agents, he contacted Kanegoro Koike, Paymaster Commander of the Japanese Imperial Navy, assigned to the Office of the Japanese Naval Inspector in New York City. At the request of the State Department, Ezima was
not prosecuted. However, he sailed for Japan on July 5, 1941, and
Kanegoro Koike followed on August 14, 1941.

-3-

CONFIDENTIAL

Reports from the middle west indicate that German and Japanese nationals are carrying on espionage activities through their control of re-insurance companies who underwrite insurance carried by National Defense industries. Although they appear to be owned and operated by Americans, the largest re-insurance companies in the world are German owned.

In the summer of this year, the German Consul Fritz Wiedemann was said to have been considerably perturbed because Japanese steamship lines were not co-operating with him in evacuating German nationals from the United States. He was particularly incensed over the refusal of the NYK Steamship Company to grant accommodations to Karl Anton Bayer and claimed that the failure of the Japanese Consul General to override the Captain of the boat gave the Germans grounds for suspicion that the Japanese were working against them. Additional reports of friction were received from Shanghai where it was stated that the Japanese were generally hated by the Germans. However, German war vessels are known to have been overhauled in the ports of Nagasaki and Kobe and there has been a certain amount of trade in metals between the Germans living in Mexico and Japan.

German-Japanese conferences were scheduled to take place in Havana early in September, and it was reported that they would be attended by such important Germans as Wiedemann, Vonspiegel and Arthur Dietrich.

RELATIONS WITH THE NEGROES

As early as May 1941, the Office of Naval Intelligence became aware that the Japanese Government was establishing connections with influential Negroes in this country for the purpose of studying the negro movement. A short time later it became apparent that representatives of the Japanese Government in the United States were attempting to organize the Negroes for the purpose of retarding National Defense efforts and to commit sabotage. In furtherance of this project, the Japanese expect to take advantage of the political strength of such organizations as the NEGRO CONGRESS, THE NEGRO ALLIANCE, and the NATIONAL ASSOCIATION FOR THE ADVANCEMENT OF COLORED PEOPLE.

The Japanese decision to utilize this minority group for their own advantage was first manifest in the latter part of 1940 when the government in Tokyo financed the opening of a news service for negro newspapers by a negro literary critic named Utley. According to reliable reports, Utley has had relatively good results in stimulating subversive activities among the negroes.

A Japanese by the name of Hikida (probably K. Hikida of 257 W. 85th Street, New York City) is the most intimate contact with negro groups and their leaders. Reported to be a well-to-do research worker and writer, he led a round-table discussion on the Negro problem in the office of the

-4-

CONFIDENTIAL

Japanese Naval Inspector in New York City in December 1938. Since then, he is reported to have received grants of money from the Consul General in New York City to carry on propaganda among the Negroes in an effort to organize them.

The District of Columbia is the focal point of this particular branch of the Japanese Espionage system because nearly all Negro organizations have their headquarters in this city. However, Hikida's organization in New York will receive strong support for the purpose of encouraging its rapid expansion, and when organizations in both cities are working satisfactorily, attention will be turned to Chicago, Los Angeles, and New Orleans.

Japanese authorities are watching closely the Negroes who are employed in defense production plants, naval stations, and other military establishments, particularly in the naval bases at Norfolk, Va., Philadelphia, Pa., and Brooklyn, N.Y. They plan to organize skilled and unskilled workmen in these cities to secure military and naval information for the Japanese Government.

In the summer of 1941, a closer association between young Japanese and young Negroes in the San Francisco Bay area was observed. Meetings have been held at the Mikado Grill, 1699 Post Street, San Francisco, Calif. but no definite connections between these mixed groups and Japanese Government representatives have been established. Such mixed parties are known to have gone to Oakland, Calif., to attend meetings of the Nisei Young Democratic Club.

In propagandizing the Negroes, the Japanese are utilizing the services of J. H. Smythe and Walker Matteson. Because of his success in arousing negro opinion, Smythe has been put in charge of the column "Behind the Headlines" for negro publications and both men will be used for editorializing.

FALANGE

Suppression of Axis organizations has caused a shift of totalitarian support to nationalist Latin American groups and these are employed to create unrest with the ultimate object of destroying Pan-American solidarity.

For years it has been a well established fact that Nazi, Fascist, and Falange agents are co-operating extensively in their espionage activities, and it now appears that the Japanese as well as the Germans and Italians are making increasing use of members of Falange organizations because of the limitations on their own connections and activities throughout the Americas.

-5-

The present organization of the Falange Party dates from April 18,
1937 when General Franco was chosen as its leader. One day later, he
announced that the Falange would be the one and only official party in
Spain. In direct opposition to Pan-Americanism and the Monroe Doctrine,
the basic aim of this group is the restoration of the Spanish Empire of
the days before the defeat of the Spanish Armada. This group, together
with Nazi and Fascist organizations, is believed to subsidize financially
the Union Nacional de Sinarquistas, generally known as "Sinarquistas",
which was organized in Mexico in 1936. Drawing its membership and support from the Peons and lower middle-class Mexicans, it is opposed by the
Mexican Federal Authorities as well as by labor unions in that country.

According to the terms of an agreement signed by Berlin, Madrid, and
Tokyo, the Philippine Falange is coupled with that in Japan and instead
of being a German, its chief is Japanese. The Spanish Board for the
Philippines is subordinate to the Spanish Embassy at Tokyo and also has
a Japanese Councillor.

SILVER SHIRTS MOVEMENT

In the summer of 1941, it became apparent that the Japanese Government was interested in the Silver Shirts Movement in the United States.
Kazuyoshi Inagaki, attached to the office of the Japanese Consul General
in San Francisco has been mentioned as a Government contact man in the
west coast area, and Totaro Iwasaki, an alien Japanese, is also reported
as having made inquiries about the status of this group. The Japanese
Government appears to be interested in acquiring detailed information
about the movement with particular emphasis on its world views and the
personal and intellectual capacities of its members.

It appears that Tokyo wishes to use this political group as a means
of establishing "Justice" in the United States. If, after a thorough investigation, it is found that Iwasaki has the proper background and training, he will be sent to Japan at Government expense in connection with the
movement.

LABOR UNIONS

In the spring of 1941, the Japanese Government indicated that in the
event of war with the U.S., labor unions would become a major political
factor in obstructing the unification of this country. With that in mind,
Japanese officials here were instructed to contact leaders of labor unions,
the Communist party, Socialist groups and other anti-Roosevelt movements.
In this connection, the Japanese are studying the possibility of using a
self-exiled Japanese socialist now living at Northwestern University in
Evanston, Illinois. His name is believed to be Oyama (O. Oyama or Iku
Oyama).

-6-

CONFIDENTIAL

ESPIONAGE AND PROPAGANDA

For many years, the Japanese have maintained an extensive organization in the United States to gather intelligence information and to disseminate propaganda. Information of a commercial and political nature
has normally been collected by the various consulates which also carry on
propaganda under the direction of the Embassy in Washington. Numerous
agents have been employed at various times to supplement this work and
military and naval information has been gathered by groups of Army and Navy
officers and technical experts attached to the Office of the Japanese Army
Ordnance Inspector and the Japanese Naval Inspector's Office in New York
City. Regular military and naval attaches have also contributed to the
pool of information, as have the personnel of Japanese business organizations located throughout the United States. In general, although much
information of a military and naval character has been obtained, the system
as a whole has been effective only in producing data of a general nature
and in disseminating propaganda favorable to the Japanese point of view.

Organization

The military and naval espionage system is organized into more than
one independent de-centralized machine. Information sought may b : classified as professional, commercial, domestic, and political, and while the
duty of each section is practically the same, the detection and destruction of one group will in no way lead to the destruction of the remaining
ones!

In addition to the organized machines operating under their respective chiefs, there are many individual agents whose trail will never be
picked up. If they are apprehended, they can never be proved to be anything but irresponsible individuals operating without pay, authority, or
direction. It is also well to remember that every Japanese commercial
organization is an actively functioning information unit for the Japanese
Government. Their normal business activities are nationwide, as are their
contacts, and the Japanese Government exercises direct control over these
groups through its Embassy in Washington as well as through its many
consulates.

The Second Secretary of the Japanese Embassy, Hidenari Terasaki,
was reportedly charged with the responsibility of co-ordinating and directing Intelligence operations in the United States. Morita Morishima,
Japanese Consul General at New York City, is the directing head of the
New York unit, and there is a possibility that the Washington and New
York units may be combined into one agency with the latter as the "nerve
center".

New Policies

In March, 1941 a meeting was held at the Japanese Embassy to formulate new policies concerning intelligence activities. A decision was

CONFIDENTIAL   -7-

made to carry out a most vigorous and comprehensive program and the
Embassy requested an allotment of $500,000 for its development during
the year.

　　In reorganizing the Espionage Network and pursuing a new Propaganda
policy, Japanese officials decided to dismiss immediately all persons of
little value; to divert the most capable persons currently being used for
the dissemination of propaganda into intelligence collecting and espionage
activity; and to transfer to the JAPAN INSTITUTE the most effective groups
and persons in their employ. Because of "freezing legislation" which
brought about a shortage of funds available for distribution to civilian
personnel, salaries and expense funds were also streamlined.

　　Pursuant to this program, the "Culture on Wheels" Library was transferred to the JAPAN INSTITUTE which was also made responsible for the
distribution of propaganda films. Operated for several years by Helmut
Ripperger, an American citizen who registered with the Department of State
as a propaganda agent for the Japanese Government, this reference library
carried propaganda by truck to various parts of the U. S., concentrating
particularly on American colleges and universities. Until recently,
Ripperger received approximately $1,300 a month from the Consulate General
in New York City. The JAPAN INSTITUTE is an affiliate of the KOKUSAI
BUNKA SHINKOKAI (Society for Promotion of International Cultural Relations) in Tokyo, a powerful quasi-official propaganda organization, international in scope.

　　Early in July, it was disclosed that the Japanese were financing the
"Living Age" Magazine. At that time its backers decided to sell it and
ceased publication in September. If a purchaser is not found soon, the
organization will probably go into bankruptcy.

　　Publication of the "Foreign Observer" was discontinued during the
summer; the distribution of films through the Y.M.C.A. and other agencies
is to be discontinued as soon as present contracts have expired; plans
for publishing propaganda booklets in connection with the World-Over Year
Book have been scrapped; the English edition of the Japanese American
newspaper has been temporarily suspended; the Japanese subsidy of the
Globe Wireless Company has been withdrawn. In addition, in accordance
with the policy of utilizing to better advantage the services of its
propagandists, two lecturers for the JAPAN INSTITUTE, Arthur Clifford Reed
and Arthur Donald Bate, are in reality being used as espionage agents.

　　Approximately one year ago, Japanese Consulates on the West Coast
began to collect information about the movement of British, French and
American naval and air forces, stressing the importance of having eye
witnesses make reports. At the same time, it was suggested in Tokyo
that a naval officer be assigned to each consulate in the United States
as a "clerk" to secure information for the Naval Ministry.

CONFIDENTIAL

The officer in charge of intelligence at the Embassy in Washington, was designated "Press Attache". His duties include investigation and the gathering of secret information on the division of American public opinion about Japanese-American relations.

In accordance with instructions to pay particular attention to German and Italian fifth column activities, the Japanese studied the reactions of German and Italian Americans in the recent Presidential Election and the attitude of the Communist party at that time.

Latin America

In accordance with its new Espionage policy, the Japanese have established an organization in Latin America to evaluate U.S. public opinion as well as our military and diplomatic situation. Its function is to collect and evaluate information obtained from the offices and personnel of American ministries in Latin America; to study the effectiveness of American and Latin American printed matter and radio broadcasts; and to secure information from offices of third powers in Latin America as well as from individuals in government offices in those countries.

In this connection, it is interesting to note that the Foreign Office in Tokyo has announced the reassignment of Hidenari Terasaki to the Legation in Brazil.

Close attention is being paid to the selection of spies by all Japanese representatives in the Americas. They are particularly anxious to obtain the services of any informants who have been seamen, in order to place them in the employ of steamship companies, and are prepared to spend large sums of money for this purpose. They have advised extreme caution in making selections since they believe FBI makes a practice of trying to get its men into confidential positions in the offices of the Axis Powers. The importance of broadcasts is also stressed and a modified radio monitoring system is envisaged. Leading U.S. newspapers and magazines are carefully scrutinized and efforts are made to obtain detailed information about Panama. To this end, telegraphic sections of all offices concerned are being expanded, sources of information open to Domei News Agencies and other special correspondents tapped and indirect use of Spanish and Portugese language correspondents is being made. The Japanese plan to keep abreast of current U.S. economic conditions through their merchants.

In the event German and Italian diplomatic officers are ordered out of the country before the Japanese, Tokyo plans to take over confidential informants used by Axis representatives. These informants are not limited to Latin Americans but include those living in Spain and Portugal.

-9-

CONFIDENTIAL

Continental United States

In June 1941, after the Tachibana Espionage Case was exposed to the public, the Japanese consulates at Los Angeles, San Francisco, and Seattle were instructed to observe the movements of American warships, to gather other information of interest to the Japanese Navy, and to cable it to Tokyo without delay. This action was taken because the activities of Japanese Naval Representatives (Language Officers) in the United States had been suppressed by the U.S. authorities in a series of "incidents", and there was a shortage of naval personnel to do this work.

In reporting progress in the U.S. shipbuilding industry to the Foreign Minister in Tokyo, an espionage agent in this country stated that "America is moving heaven and earth in her Defense Program."

West Coast

In an effort to establish an integrated intelligence organization in the Southern California area, Japanese authorities are intensifying their efforts to establish contacts. Dr. Ken Nakazawa, who is Professor of Japanese Culture and Oriental Studies at the University of Southern California at Los Angeles, is actively engaged in this work. An attache of the Los Angeles Japanese Consulate, as well as an Aide for Japanese propaganda, he is investigating and summarizing first hand information as well as newspaper reports about military movements, labor disputes, communist activities, and other matters of interest to the Government in Tokyo.

Working through white persons as well as Negroes and maintaining close relationships with Japanese Associations, Chambers of Commerce, and newspapers, this group is attempting to keep aeroplane manufacturing plants, military and naval establishments under close surveillance. Its members have already added to the ranks of this group reliable Japanese in the San Pedro and San Diego areas who will keep a close watch on all shipments of aeroplanes and other war materials, and will report the amounts and destinations of such shipments. In addition, observers have been stationed to watch traffic in war materials across the U.S. - Mexican border.

Reports of activities within the United States Army are sought from second generation Japanese in that branch of the armed services, and although the information has not yet been confirmed, there are reports which indicate second generation Japanese are working in west coast aeroplane plants for intelligence purposes.

Prominent Americans and Japanese connected with the motion picture industry have been employed by the Consular Intelligence Network to investigate anti-Jewish movements in this country, particularly on the West Coast, and influential Negroes have kept this group currently informed about the negro movement.

-10-

California-Mexican Border

Yoshiaki Miura, Japanese Minister in Mexico City, has been the head of the Japanese Intelligence Network in Mexico and Central America. In June, 1941, Kiyoshi Yamagata, travelling Japanese Ambassador, conferred with Miura about plans for organizing the Mexico City office on a wartime basis. During the same month, Yamagata held a conference with Fujio Kato, Japanese Consul at Mexicali. Kato told Yamagata that due to the predominance of American influence in that area and the fact that its many Japanese inhabitants were uneducated, personnel and funds should be supplied/ to operate Mexicali only as a branch intelligence center. They both agreed that in spite of the difficulty in carrying on their work in a border city with a population of only 15,000 persons, work there would prove useful providing the intelligence network in Los Angeles and vicinity was well organized and particularly if the Japanese Government found it necessary to withdraw its officials from the United States. As a result, Yamagata recommended that connections be established at once between Los Angeles and Mexicali.

Pacific Northwest

In this region also, there is considerable evidence that Japanese agents have put into operation their new policies of espionage.

Kanji Kaneko, Chancellor of the Japanese Consulate at Seattle, is in charge of Intelligence and has been collecting information from second generation Japanese draftees on matters dealing with troops and morale in the United States Army.

Labor unions and political organizations in this area appear to have been intensely utilized by the Japanese. The legal representative of the Cannery Workers and Farm Laborers Union (C.I.O. Local #7 in Seattle) is a second generation lawyer whose name is Kenji Ito. Legal Adviser to the Japanese Consulate in Seattle, he has been active in the collection of information about anti-government organizations and the anti-Jewish movement. It is worth noting that this particular union is composed of about 70% Filipinos and 30% Japanese.

Shoji ("Welly") Okamaru, an American born Japanese with dual citizenship, is head of a unit which contacts labor unions in search of Communist Party members. For the past six or seven years, he has acted as a Secretary of the Japanese Consulate at Seattle, but was promoted to Consular Assistant in June, 1940. He has as an associate an alien Japanese who is active in the labor movement as a committee chairman and organizer.

Before war broke out between Germany and Russia, communist machinists of German origin who are members of labor organizations at the Bremerton Navy Yard and Boeing Aeroplane factories, were supplying information to Japanese authorities. This is but another example of the

-11-

effort Tokyo is making to obtain information on military efforts, construction of ships, aeroplane production, production of copper, zinc, aluminum, yield of tin from cans and labor resources through competent Americans.

Such efforts were supplemented until July, 1941 by the activities of Lieutenant Commander Sadatomo Okada of the Imperial Japanese Navy. He, like Commander Itaru Tachibana, who operated from Los Angeles, was requested by the State Department to leave the country because of his espionage activities in the Pacific Northwest.

Information on political questions is sought by the Japanese in this area, from John Sylvester, speaker of the lower house in the state of Washington, Ralph Horr, chairman of the Republican Party's local committee, and Daniel Trefethen, who is a strong Catholic layman.

Alaska.

Although their reliability has not been ascertained, reports have been received which indicate that the Japanese Consulate in Vancouver, B. C., is endeavoring to employ Canadians to visit Alaska to obtain information on land and sea-plane bases in the Yukon, the strength of military supplies and personnel in that area, the distribution, location, and quantity of heavy oil, and progress of base construction in Fairbanks, Seward, Anchorage, and Kodiak. Tokyo is also said to be interested in having a description of dry-docks, data on troops and arsenals in the vicinity of Kodiak and the number of war craft visiting Alaska during the past year. Further, they would like to have a confirmation or denial of the fact of U.S. troops crossing Canada from Fort Haynes to Alaska and their construction of a military road. The Japanese are particularly anxious to determine whether roads are being built to carry heavy oil from Fort Nelson to Alaska.

TERRITORY OF HAWAII

Out of a total population of 423,330 in the Hawaiian Islands, there are 157,905 Japanese, approximately one third of which are aliens. Japanese are known to organize for every conceivable purpose, and social, civic, educational and religious societies have existed in the Hawaiian Islands from the time of the earliest Japanese migrations. It is believed that every Japanese resident in Hawaii belongs to one or more purely Japanese organizations. However, only the more important groups are of interest, since they are in a position to engage in espionage, sabotage and other acts inimical to the best interests of the U. S.

A study of these organizations discloses interesting inter-relations through duplication of activity and plurality of position held by many

-12-

individuals. For example, a Buddhist priest may be the principal of a Japanese language school as well as a consular agent or an officer or member of an organization appearing in another category.

Each of these groups is at least strongly influenced if not directly controlled by similar ones in Japan. The consular organization is obviously controlled by the Japanese Foreign Ministry, and religious sects are supervised from headquarters in Japan, which in turn are under governmental domination.

Consular Agents

The center of the consular organization, as well as of alien Japanese activity, is the Japanese Consulate General at Honolulu under the direction of Consul General Nagao Kita. For purposes of disseminating instructions or news, it is said to utilize the services of such prominent organizations as the United Japanese Society of Honolulu, the Honolulu Japanese Chamber of Commerce, the Hilo Japanese Chamber of Commerce as well as the Hilo Japanese Society and the Japanese Language Press.

By far the largest and most diversified group under the direction of the Consulate General is that of the "Consular Agents" or "Toritsuginin". Two hundred and nineteen of these agents are located geographically so as to form a comprehensive information system for the Consulate General throughout the Hawaiian Islands. These men are well educated American born and alien Japanese above average in intelligence. Many of them are non-quota aliens operating as Buddhist priests and principals or teachers in Japanese language schools. Scattered throughout the Island, these agents have denied being under the control of the Consul General, and there are none located in the City of Honolulu.

Propaganda

The Buddhist and Shinto sects, the Japanese language schools and civic and commercial societies are powerful propaganda agencies because of the nature of their work with the Japanese community and the fact that their business is carried on usually in the Japanese language.

Each community in the Hawaiian Islands where there are Japanese residents has one or more Buddhist temples or preaching places (Fukkyojo). Because of respect which the Japanese have for priests, they are readily influenced by these men who hold services in accordance with Japanese custom. In this connection, many Buddhist and Shinto priests are non-quota aliens who have lived in the Islands a comparatively short time.

-13-

Schools

The Japanese educational system in the Territory of Hawaii centers around the Hawaiian Japanese Language School Association. This is an organization composed of representatives or directors from each of fourteen districts. These districts or sub-groups all carry distinct titles and in turn are composed of teachers from the individual schools and school boards under their jurisdiction. In this connection, it should be noted that while the majority of male teachers are alien, many of the citizen teachers were also educated in Japan. Almost invariably, school principals are aliens and frequently they are Buddhist priests.

At the present time, more than 39,000 pupils attend Japanese schools in Hawaii.

Newspapers

Of nineteen newspapers and magazines printed in the Japanese language, the NIPPU JIJI and the HAWAII HOCHI, published daily at Honolulu, are of principal importance. All of the news organs, however, carry pro-Japanese editorials and news items from time to time.

THE TACHIBANA CASE

Head of the Japanese Espionage Network on the West Coast during 1940 was Commander Itaru Tachibana, IJN, who came to the United States as a language officer. Following his arrest in 1941 for violation of the espionage statutes, he was released on $50,000 bond and finally left the country in June, 1941 at the request of the State Department.

Other Japanese Naval Officers involved in this subversive group were Lieutenant Commander Sadatomo Okada, Commander Iwao Arisaka, Lieutenant Commander Sadayoshi Nakayama and Engineer Lieutenant Wataru Yamada. Okada and Yamada, like Tachibana, were requested to leave the U. S. because their activities were considered to be inimical to the safety of this country, and Commander Arisaka and Lieutenant Commander Nakayama sailed suddenly from New York for Brazil in July, 1941.

Prominent among the organizations which were apparently furnishing information to the Japanese Government through Tachibana were the NIPPON KAIGUN KYOKAI (Japanese Navy Association), the SAKURA KAI (Cherry Association) and the SUIKO SHA (Reserve Officers Club).

The many ramifications of Tachibana's activities were disclosed by translating into English numerous Japanese papers, documents, and reports which were seized by the F.B.I. at the time of his arrest at the Olympic Hotel in Los Angeles.

Part of the material seized consisted of the records of the North
American branch of the JAPANESE NAVY ASSOCIATION (Nippon Kaigun Kyokai).
With headquarters in Tokyo, this organization has as its chief objectives
the dissemination of information about navies of other countries and
the development of Japanese Naval strength. To this end, it has
established investigating agencies to study domestic and foreign navies,
maritime transportation and other maritime matters. Investigation disclosed that members of the Japanese Navy Association had been working
in collaboration with rank officers of the Imperial Japanese Navy
stationed in Los Angeles, and it appears that Tachibana, who was collecting
intelligence for the benefit of the Japanese Navy, was assisted by the
investigating branch of that association.

Among Tachibana's effects was found considerable correspondence from
Dr. Takishi Furusawa, director of the Los Angeles Suiko Sha, which is
an organization composed of officers and reserve officers of the Imperial
Japanese Navy. He and his wife, Mrs. Sachiko Furusawa, appear to be
the directive force behind this organization. Both of them are exceedingly
prominent in Japanese affairs.

The names of Dr. Kijima Amano, secretary of the Sakura Kai, Shunten
Kumamoto, president of the Los Angeles Japanese Association and Gongoro
Nakamura, president of the Central Japanese Association of California,
also appear among Tachibana's papers and it is interesting to note that
all of them, including the Furusawas, are on the research committee of
the Sakura Kai.

During the course of investigation of the activities of Dr. Furusawa
and the Japanese Navy Association, a large amount of evidentiary material
was uncovered indicating a probable violation of federal statutes. As
a result, the FBI is conducting a vigorous investigation of this association at the present time.

Tachibana's correspondence also included the names of representatives
of a few of the important Japanese language newspapers such as the RAFU
SHIMPO (Los Angeles News), KASHU MAINICHI (California Daily), and the
NANKA SANGYO NIPPO (Southern California Industrial Daily News).

EXPATRIATION

Reports from Hawaii indicate that the Japanese are resorting to
subterfuge to convince Americans that expatriation is reducing the number
of dual citizens in that territory. Recently, the acting Japanese Consul
General announced that he had asked the Foreign Office for additional
employees to handle the increasing number of expatriation applications
received by the Consulate in Honolulu. He stated that more than four
hundred such applications are submitted each month and that a marked

-15-

increase has been noted during the past eight months. It is worth noting,
however, that the total number of expatriations in 1940 was only slightly
higher than the figure for 1933.

Formal expatriation of Japanese citizenship, heretofore required of
public school teachers as a condition precedent to their continued employment in the Territory of Hawaii, was recently relaxed in the case of
American citizens of Japanese ancestry who are not registered with the
Japanese Government. This action was reported to be the result of inter-
cession on the part of the Hawaiian-Japanese Civic Association of Honolulu.

Out of a total Japanese population of 320,000 in the United States
and its possessions, it is estimated that more than 127,000 have dual
citizenship. This estimate is based on the fact that more than 52% of
American born Japanese fall into this category. In the Territory of Hawaii
alone, dual citizens constitute approximately 35% of the total Japanese
population.

Recently, a petition carrying over 30,000 signatures was submitted
to the Secretary of State requesting this government to negotiate a more
simplified expatriation procedure with the Japanese Government. Many
people who signed this petition were already expatriated and it appears
that the emphasis of the campaign was on obtaining an imposing number of
signatures to the petition rather than to represent the real desires of
dual citizens.

Expatriation is almost universally opposed by the parents of dual
citizens who claim that for the names of their children to be struck from
the family register is an affront to their ancestors and an act of disloyalty to Japan.

The present Japanese Nationality Law of 1924, which liberalized the
process of expatriation, was announced as a result of representations
made by a group of Hawaiian Japanese who went to Japan especially for that
purpose. It would seem that if the Japanese were sincere in their desire
to facilitate expatriation at this time, they would follow the method
previously so successfully employed. The fact that they now call upon
the State Department to intervene with the Japanese Government on their
behalf and surround the campaign with a fanfare of publicity, gives rise
to the belief that those behind the present movement are deliberately
trying to portray the dual citizens of Hawaii as the unwilling possessors
of Japanese citizenship.

It is worth noting that the various expatriation campaigns have
coincided with junctures in American-Japanese relations or with the
development of local issues which tend to bring the Japanese racial situation sharply into focus. This recent campaign in the Territory of Hawaii

is believed to have arisen from the questioning of Japanese candidates about their citizenship status during the recent Territorial elections.

Residents in the United States and Hawaii have had 18 years in which to renounce their Japanese allegiance. The fact that comparatively few have done so negates the supposition that they now desire to cast off their Japanese citizenship as an expression of their Americanism.

Recently it was brought to the attention of the Office of Naval Intelligence that out of a total of 198 postal employees in Honolulu, 51 have dual citizenship and that the foreman in the registry section, Ernest Hirokawa, is an alien Japanese. As a result of this discovery the registered mail for the fleet stationed in Hawaiian waters is now routed directly to the Pearl Harbor Navy Yard as a security measure.

MILITARY CONSCRIPTION

Japanese residents in the United States, especially dual citizens, have been urged to return to Japan to do military service with the armed forces of that country. In some cases even expatriated citizens of Japanese ancestry have been encouraged to do this while visiting Japan. All male Japanese citizens are eligible for military duty during the so-called "military age" (Tekirei Nendo) which is the year following that in which they reach their twentieth birthday.

Considerable evidence exists of such pressure being brought to bear on dual citizens and even expatriated citizens of Japanese ancestry who are in Japan as students or workers. In this connection, a certain Kazuichi Hashimoto of Terminal Island, California is reported to have taken a group of forty young Japanese to Japan, ostensibly for the purpose of teaching them fencing. However, it is suspected that these young people were taken to Japan for military duty.

Once each year, local Japanese consulates publish announcements in Japanese language newspapers concerning registration and deferment applications. Japanese males living abroad who have retained their Japanese citizenship, but who have already been excused from military duty, must nevertheless submit reports of residence. Those who wish to be deferred, upon reaching military age, must execute a "Deferment Application for Residents Abroad".

It is important to note that the categories of those eligible for military service in Japan include males with dual citizenship (Japanese born in the United States after 1924 whose birth was registered with the Japanese Consulate within fourteen days). Under Japanese law, these persons are just as liable to answer to the military authorities as are full Japanese citizens.

-17-

Toward the end of 1940, the Government in Tokyo conducted a national and international census. All persons of Japanese ancestry were required to fill out questionnaires, even those United States citizens of Japanese ancestry who had expatriated themselves.

JAPANESE NAVAL COMMUNICATION AND COURIER SERVICE

A heavy traffic of telegrams, radios, and cables has been noted between the Japanese Ministry of Marine in Tokyo, and the various Naval Attaches and Inspectors in the United States, Canada, Mexico, and Europe.

There is strong evidence that the Naval Attache's Office in Washington operates a short wave sending and receiving set disguised as an "Amateur Station", and that it is linked to the numerous "Ham" stations known to be operated by Japanese on the West Coast and in Hawaii. This fact has yet to be proved, but the interest shown by the Naval Inspector for Radio in New York City seems to be a bit out of the ordinary. In addition, leads from a radio transmitting antenna enter the building of the Japanese Embassy in Washington, and one of the Embassy clerks recently made an unsuccessful attempt to secure an amateur radio operator's license.

In addition to radio and cable, the Naval Attache has at his disposal the service of the diplomatic mail pouch. However, it is evident that the Naval Attache relies on his own couriers to transmit items between this country and Japan. It is believed that the greater part of this service is concerned with sending to Japan samples, charts, models, reports and other documents which are not entrusted to the usual mail and express service.

An analysis of the itineraries of visiting officials and certain language officers indicates a systematic and periodic movement between strategic points throughout this country. Language officers are used for transcontinental officer-messenger service only when there is no "visiting officer" available. Their primary function is to collect and distribute information to agents located in various key cities throughout the country. If no naval personnel are aboard incoming or outgoing Japanese ships, a language officer will contact the Captain (who is a Naval Reserve Officer) to receive and send Naval Attache mail.

Confidential mail service between the Japanese Embassy and the Naval Attache in Ottawa, Canada appears to be indicated by the regularity of officer travel between Washington and Buffalo. Likewise, at frequent intervals, officers are sent from Washington to Miami, New Orleans, Houston and return.

-18-

While in Miami, they invariably fly to Havana and return the same day. On the West Coast, a language officer from Los Angeles or Seattle. frequently travels up and down the Coast from Vancouver, B.C. to Tiajuana, Mexico for no apparent reason unless it is to contact agents to collect and distribute information. On occasion, the West Coast language officer will travel from Los Angeles to Chicago and return via Seattle, Portland, and San Francisco. On the East Coast, an officer frequently goes from Washington to Chicago via New York and Cleveland. It would appear therefore, that Chicago is the meeting place for officers stationed on the East and West Coasts.

EXPENDITURES

Secret funds in cash are maintained by the Japanese Embassy and Consulates for the purchase of intelligence information from civilian agents who report directly to consular agents and representatives.

While the Naval Inspector's Office was in operation, it was primarily interested in obtaining detailed technical information which could be used to advantage by the Japanese Navy. Disbursements of this office in New York City alone amounted to approximately $500,000 a month, but aside from fuel oil, the purchases were all nominal and varied. They covered aircraft parts, radio, electric equipment, tools and accessories which were apparently obtained for purposes of examination only.

Archer Seki Huntington reported that Fukichi Fukumoto, former New York representative of the OSAKA MAINICHI and TOKYO NICHI NICHI newspapers, paid him $2300 to obtain the drawings of an exhaust super-charger used in aeroplane engines.

Prior to the Executive Order freezing the assets of all Japanese and Chinese nationals in the United States, the Yokohama Specie Bank, Ltd. withdrew $150,000 in cash from the Guaranty Trust Company in New York City and $50,000 in cash from its account at the Chase National Bank.

In the summer of 1941 the Yokohama Specie Bank of San Francisco prepared to pack and ship a large number of Japanese bonds to Japan aboard the NYK Liner "Tatuta Maru". As a result of Federal action, Japanese bonds of various descriptions having a par value of $9,621,100 were recovered.

Through confidential sources it was learned that on July 25, 1941, cash funds amounting to $180,000 were allotted by the management of the Yokohama Specie Bank in San Francisco to its officers and employees, most of whom are Japanese nationals. These funds were distributed in

-19-

proportion to the yearly salary received by the individuals and this
move appears to have been made in order to prevent total loss of funds
through seizure by the U.S. Government in time of war.

Funds of Japanese nationals and corporations located in the District
of Columbia, New York City, San Diego, Los Angeles, San Francisco,
Seattle, Honolulu, and New Orleans are being monitored at the present
time to determine the source of income and the nature of withdrawals
made from accounts in various banks in these localities. Any deposits
of unusual size, and likewise any withdrawals, made by individuals,
Japanese owned corporations and organizations are brought to the
attention of the proper Federal authorities, and serial numbers of bills
in denominations of $500 and $1,000 are recorded in order to permit
investigation of subsequent negotiation of such bills. In this way,
it is possible to determine whether funds are being used for activities
inimical to the welfare of this country.

JAPANESE LANGUAGE NEWSPAPERS

Since November, 1940 there has been a definite effort on the part
of certain agencies and ministries of the Japanese Government to establish
control over the Japanese language press throughout the world. Following
the organization of the powerful OVERSEAS JAPANESE CENTRAL SOCIETY late
in 1940, officials of the Japanese Ministries of Commerce and Industry,
Foreign Affairs, Navy, War, Overseas Affairs, and other lesser agencies
determined to ensure further control over Japanese living abroad through
the medium of the press. They scheduled a convention to be held in Tokyo
in November, 1941 and invited the most pro-Japanese publishers and
editors to attend. At the conclusion of the convention, half the delegates
toured China, while the others traveled through Japan Proper at government
expense.

A similar tendency is revealed in a report of a meeting held in
Japan during the summer of 1941 by the WORLD ECONOMIC FEDERATION (formerly
the JAPANESE ECONOMIC FEDERATION) at which representatives of overseas
Japanese newspapers were requested to act as an investigative unit in a
study of world economic movements. Efforts of this sort on the part of
Tokyo are entirely in keeping with that Government's comprehensive reorganization of intelligence and propaganda policies. Close contact
between Japanese newspaper correspondents and officials of the Embassy
and Consulates has been observed during 1941, and many Japanese newspapers in the U.S. are being pressed into service by the Embassy, the
consulates and officials in Tokyo to assume intelligence duties previously carried on by regular military and naval agents. At the same time,
they are expected to function as instruments of propaganda.

-20-

As an example of this arrangement, when Fukuichi Fukumoto, the former New York representative of the Osaka Mainichi and Tokyo Nichi Nichi newspapers was ordered to return to Japan by his employers, the Embassy procured a recision of his orders and he was designated Washington representative of the Tokyo Nichi Nichi.

Most Japanese language newspapers in the U. S. appear to be conventional news organs with no more pro-Japanese bias than one would expect in view of their affiliations. Others, however, such as the NEW WORLD SUN DAILY NEWS and the JAPANESE AMERICAN NEWS, both of San Francisco, are strongly pro-Japanese, and their editorials, from time to time, severely criticize American domestic and foreign policy vis-a-vis the Japanese. Representatives of these two papers were particularly active in the Tokyo meetings mentioned above.

There is also a small category of radical Japanese newspapers published in this country, perhaps the most interesting of which is the DOHO, a communist organ in Los Angeles. The TAISHU weekly of Seattle, Washington, a one man proposition with no consistent editorial policy, would also be included in this category.

In conclusion it should be mentioned that in several instances where there have been both English and Japanese sections within a paper, two diametrically opposed points of view are expressed, that in English being either neutral or pro-American, whereas the Japanese language section is definitely pro-Japanese. The UTAH NIPPON of Salt Lake City, Utah, and the ROCKY NIPPON of Denver, Colorado, are perhaps the best examples of this dual editorial policy.

ORGANIZATIONS

Although many Japanese residents of the United States are leaving the country in anticipation of war, and many representatives and officials of Japanese commercial interests have been recalled or transferred South, the span of Japanese organizations across the United States continues to be useful in collecting intelligence and disseminating propaganda for Tokyo.

Commercial Interests

Normal business activities of Japanese commercial firms in this country are nation wide and until the advent of the National Defense Program, contacts of their employees were practically unlimited. Both the firms themselves and their directive heads are under the immediate control of the Embassy and the various consulates.

-21-

Until recent legislation forced their retrenchment or withdrawal there were sixty Japanese companies in New York City alone available for the collection of technical information as well as for the dissemination of propaganda. Chief among these were:

                    Bank of Chosen (Korea)
                    Bank of Taiwan (Formosa)
                    Domei News Agency
                    Japanese Army Ordnance Inspector's Office
                    Japanese Chamber of Commerce
                    Japanese Financial Commission
                    Japanese Naval Inspector's Office
                    Japanese Raw Silk Intelligence Bureau
                    Mitsui and Co.
                    Mitsubishi Shoji Kaisha, Ltd.
                    Nippon Yusen Kaisha
                    Okura and Co.
                    Osaka Shosen Kaisha
                    South Manchuria Railway Co.
                    Sumitomo Bank, Ltd.
                    Tokyo Commercial and Industrial Museum

Most of them, as well as other important ones not listed, maintain well staffed branch offices in other cities.

Such gigantic organizations as the Mitsui, Mitsubishi, Okura, and Sumitomo interests may be said without exaggeration to control the financial and economic life of Japan. They are all directly or indirectly subsidized by the Japanese Government and may be considered quasi-official in nature.

In connection with the intensification of Japanese Intelligence efforts in the Americas, it is worth noting that the Mitsubishi interests have been extremely active in the shipment of various metals, fuel and lubricating oils, concentrating particularly on scrap iron, heavy machinery, and machine tools. In addition, they are known to have collaborated with German interests in an attempt to corner the market on mercury at the expense of the United States.

Mitsubishi is one of the fourteen semi-official organizations specifically designated to collect and report intelligence information formerly sought by Tokyo through regular Military and Naval agents. Reports of ship and troop movements, arrangements of inspection trips for visiting Japanese officials to important American plants and military establishments and the collection of all available information about the National Defense effort are illustrations of the "extra curricula activities" carried on by this organization. The same general pattern holds true with respect to other Japanese business houses.

-22-

Since the freezing of funds in July of this year, all Japanese business houses in the United States are closing or continuing operations with a skeleton force.

Civic

By far the most important Japanese civic organization in the United States is the JAPANESE-AMERICAN CITIZENS' LEAGUE which is an outgrowth of the AMERICAN LOYALTY LEAGUE. It has a total membership of approximately 10,000 persons distributed among 51 individual chapters and grouped geographically into four regional councils which cover the Pacific Coast and extending inland as far as Arizona, Idaho, and Utah. Its alleged objective is to encourage better citizenship among Americans of Japanese ancestry. It also supports all movements designed to improve the status of the Japanese in the United States.

One section of this organization which warrants particular attention is the so-called KIBEI group. Representing approximately 6% of the total membership, these members must be considered as pro-Japanese in their ideas and affiliations. Although American born, they have been educated in Japan and ordinarily have little or no background of American culture or appreciation of our form of government.

Recent reports indicate that the JAPANESE-AMERICAN CITIZENS' LEAGUE flatly rejected an offer of subsidy from the CENTRAL JAPANESE ASSOCIATION, apparently for fear of loss of independence if it accepted financial aid from this source.

Religious

Japanese religious organizations in the U. S. embrace Buddhist and Shinto temples and Christian churches as well as affiliated social or welfare clubs and schools. The Buddhist and Shinto priests in the U. S. and Territory of Hawaii number over 350. In addition to serving as principals or teachers of Japanese Language Schools, most of them are Japanese consular agents. Inasmuch as strict supervision of religion has for centuries been a characteristic of Japanese governmental policy, it follows that both priests and teachers are to a considerable extent subject to orders from Tokyo or, what amounts to the same thing, from their religious superiors in Japan.

To appreciate fully the potentialities of these organizations as media for subversive activity, it should be noted first, that there are well over 100,000 Buddhists in the continental U. S. alone, and secondly, that every Japanese, no matter what his professed faith, is a Shintoist. Shintoism is commonly though somewhat erroneously referred to as a religion. In reality, it is defined by the Japanese Government as a patriotic code founded upon the worship of the imperial line and the mythological gods accredited with the creation of Japan.

-23-

The work of these priests involves travel along the West Coast of the U.S., throughout Hawaii and to Japan. Investigations of Japanese organizations suspected of subversive activity disclose that these priests frequently hold office in such suspect groups as the HOKUBEI ZAIGO SHOKO DAN (North American Reserve Officers Association) and the NICHIBEI KOGYO KAISHA (Nichibei Kinema Co.).

Affiliated with Buddhist and Shinto temples are Japanese Language Schools, welfare societies, young people's Buddhist societies, and Buddhist women's associations. They provide excellent resources for intelligence operations, have proved to be very receptive to Japanese propaganda, and in many cases have contributed considerable sums to the Japanese war effort.

Japanese Christian Churches are much less closely affiliated with the Japanese Government, and there is considerable evidence to indicate that their major concern outside of religious matters centers on improving Japanese-American relations and the restoration of peace in Eastern Asia. At the same time, it is true that some individuals and groups among Japanese Christians are working against the interests of this country. In this connection, the JAPANESE STUDENTS' CHRISTIAN ASSOCIATION in New York City, is reported to disseminate pro-Japanese propaganda among the Nisei in addition to carrying on its regular functions as a religious association.

Military

Of the many and varied types of Japanese organizations in the United States, by far the most active and subversive to the interests of this c o u n t r y are such military organizations as the NANKA TEIKOKU GUNYUDAN (Southern California War Veterans), Los Angeles, NIPPON KAIGUN KYOKAI (Japanese Naval Association), Los Angeles, SAKURA KAI (Patriotic Society), Los Angeles, HOKUBEI BUTOKU KAI (Military Virtue Society of North America), Alvarado, California, and the HOKUBEI HEIFKI GIRUSHA KAI (Association of Japanese in North America Eligible for Military Duty), San Francisco.

These organizations are intensely nationalistic and until recently made heavy contributions to the Japanese War Chest. Members of the NANKA TEIKOKU GUNYUDAN, NIPPON KAIGUN KYOKAI, and SAKURA KAI are suspected of being either veterans of or reservists in the Japanese armed forces. They have co-operated closely with official Japanese Agencies in the United States and the arrest of Commander Tachibana disclosed that the last two organizations, together with the SUIKO SHA (Reserve Officers' Club) in Los Angeles, were supplying him with intelligence information to be sent to Tokyo.

-24-

Although their membership is drawn from a younger age group, such
organizations as the HOKUBEI BUTOKU KAI and HOKUBEI HEIKKI GINUSHA KAI
are none the less loyal to Japanese principles, particularly to the ex-
pansionist program of the present military regime in Tokyo. In both of
these organizations, internal friction has been noted and in those branches
where the conservative element is dominant, there has been a tendency to
de-emphasize military activities and in some cases to sever altogether
affiliations with headquarters in Japan. On the other hand, where extremists have retained control, a marked increase in attendance to military
sports, to local intelligence activities, and closer co-operation with the
home government have been noted.

Many local branches of these organizations have changed their names
during the last few months in order to avert suspicion. In the event of
war between the United States and Japan, Japanese organizations of this
general type are certain to be delegated important espionage and sabotage
functions in the area where they now operate.

Cultural

Two of the most influential of the Japanese cultural organizations
in the U. S. coming under the direct control of the Government in Tokyo
are the JAPAN INSTITUTE in New York City, and the JAPANESE CULTURAL CENTER
OF SOUTHERN CALIFORNIA at Los Angeles. Operating on extremely generous
budgets they distribute propaganda of all kinds, sponsor lectures and
demonstrations, and subsidize American and Japanese scholarship in
Oriental studies. Many individuals associated with both organizations
are known dangerous propagandists and espionage agents.

It is interesting to note that the JAPAN INSTITUTE is preparing to
cease operations and early in December of this year began to destroy its
records.

Of minor importance are such cultural groups as the FAR EASTERN
INSTITUTES held every summer at different American colleges and universities, THE STUDENT INSTITUTE OF PACIFIC RELATIONS and the ZAIBEI NIPPON-
JIN JISEKI HOZON KAI. The latter is a small group carrying on American
historical research.

In March of 1941 the NICHIBEI KOGYO KAISHA of Los Angeles which is
one of the most active propaganda - espionage organizations in the United
States was reorganized under the name of the NICHIBEI KINEMA COMPANY, INC.
Incorporated in December, 1937, it was originally designed as a front for
the LITTLE TOKYO GAMBLING CLUB owned by Hideichi Yamatoda. At the present
time, however, most of the control rests with officials of the CENTRAL
JAPANESE ASSOCIATION of San Francisco, California, and the LOS ANGELES
JAPANESE CHAMBER OF COMMERCE. Most of its officers are suspects and
have wide affiliations with suspect organizations and firms. This organ-

ization acts as a distribution center for foreign and domestic motion
pictures and gramophone records. It also co-operates closely with Tokyo
in arranging engagements for lecturers, theatrical troupes and musicians
along the West Coast and in Hawaii. As an indication of the importance
of its function, this organization's capital stock was increased from
,25,000 to ,250,000 in March, 1940.

CONCLUSION

During the first week in December, large scale shifts in key diplomatic personnel from Canada and the United States to Mexico and Latin
America have taken place, and a mass exodus of Japanese residents is
under way. On December 1, 1941, the Consulate General on the West Coast
began to destroy its records, as did the Consulate General, the Japanese
Chamber of Commerce and the Japan Institute in New York City. Secret
codes and ciphers at the Japanese Embassy were burned on the night of
December 5, 1941.

Such organizations as the Japanese Raw Silk Intelligence Bureau,
the Silk Department of Mitsui & Co., Gunze Corporation, Asahi Corporation,
Japanese Cotton & Silk Trading Co., Hara & Co., Katakura & Co., Morimura
& Co., Arai & Co., and Shinyei & Co. closed on Saturday December 6, 1941,
and personnel of these commercial houses plan to leave this country
December 16 aboard the Tatuta Maru. The Japan Institute has announced
its closing date as December 9, 1941.

Although incomplete, the foregoing picture of Japanese intelligence
and propaganda activities during 1941 illustrates the extent of Tokyo's
effort to penetrate this Hemisphere. Current U.S.-Japanese relations
are not clearly defined. However, in anticipation of a possible crisis,
the FBI is prepared to take into custody and detain all persons whose
activities are inimical to the best interests of the United States.

To: All Naval Districts, FBI, MID, COI, State Dept.   B-7-J

NAVY DEPARTMENT
Office of Naval Intelligence
Washington, D. C.

CONFIDENTIAL

DECLASSIFIED BY *1678 RFP/AHR*   December 24, 1941
   5/14/95

Subject: JAPANESE TOKYO CLUB SYNDICATE, WITH INTERLOCKING AFFILIATIONS.

Note: Prepared by the Counter-Subversion Section, Office of Naval
          Intelligence, from information received from various sources.

INTRODUCTION

Custodial Detention

          With the sudden outbreak of hostilities between Japan and the
United States on December 7, 1941, a comprehensive program for the detention of enemy aliens was put into operation. Hundreds of known dangerous suspects were rounded up, official representatives of the Axis
Powers were put under surveillance or taken into custody, and Alien Enemy
Hearing Boards were appointed to inquire into the activities and loyalty
of the individuals concerned. Aided by their recommendations , the U. S.
Attorney General will decide whether an alien should be released uncon-
ditionally, paroled, or interned for the duration of the war.

Recent Japanese Activities in Latin America

          Although handicapped by the detention of many of its key indi-
viduals, the Japanese Intelligence Network in this hemisphere continues
in operation. Recent reports have been received of suspicious movements
of Japanese in various parts of Latin America, particularly in Mexico.
On December 13th, one vessel of the Japanese fishing fleet, the ALERT,
which was captured off Costa Rica by a Navy Air Patrol, was found to be
carrying some 10,000 gallons of Diesel fuel oil. The ALERT, of American
registry, is partly owned and manned by Japanese. At the time of her
capture, it is believed she was headed for a rendezvous with an enemy
submarine or surface raider.

          From Mexico have come numerous rumors that approximately five
thousand Japanese are congregating at some undetermined point in strategic
Baja California. In this connection, one hundred of a Japanese population
of six hundred in and around Ensenada, recently left the region in a ship
which had been anchored off the coast. Moreover, during the night of

CONFIDENTIAL

COPIES DESTROYED

8   JAN 1 6 1974

The first page of this post—Pearl Harbor memo from ONI, dated December 24,
1941, reports that the Japanese spy network "continues in operation" despite
detention of key leaders under the Alien Enemy Control Program. The full
memo is online at www.michellemalkin.com.

~~CONFIDENTIAL~~

WI 12/24/41
Jap. Tokyo Club)

WAR DEPARTMENT
M. I. D.

G2/GI
JTP

DECLASSIFIED
E. O. 11652, Sec. ?3
755004
E. **FPLN** : Date **2/27/65**

January 3, 1942.
(Date)

Subject: Japanese Activities and Intelligence Machine in the
Western Hemisphere.

Summary of Information:

  a. <u>Recent Japanese Activities in Latin America</u>. Recent
reports have been received of suspicious movements of Japanese in
various parts of Latin America, particularly Mexico. Approximately
5,000 Japanese are congregating at some undetermined point in strategic Baja California. In this connection,100 of a Japanese population of 600 in and around Ensenada, recently left the region in
a ship anchored off the coast.

  The Japanese practice of cloaking subversive operations
with "legitimate business fronts" exists in Mexico as well as in
the United States. The Japanese have placed Colonel Tadafumi Waki,
I.J.A., in an important position within their Intelligence Network
in Mexico. Reports believed reliable indicate that Colonel Waki
has in his possession maps of strategic areas in the Hawaiian Islands.

  In Peru it is reported that the 30,000 or more Japanese
living there are highly organized and that, following anti-Japanese
riots, they distributed rifles to all their establishments. In the
United States there is a possible infiltration of Japanese espionage
agents through Cuban and Florida ports. A similar danger exists on
the Pacific Coast and Mexican border.

  Since the outbreak of hostilities, Spanish Consuls in the
United States have taken over all official business for the Japanese
Consulates. Japanese and Spanish Fascist collaboration is carried
on extensively in Mexico and the Philippines through the following
organizations: Las Misiones Jesuite del Japon, Sociedad Hipo-
Espanola, Falange Exterior Espanola, and Liga Anti-Comintern Espanola.

  b. <u>Japanese Intelligence Machine in Western Hemisphere</u>. In
December, 1940, it became apparent that the Japanese were going to
effect a reorganization of their Intelligence Network in this hemisphe.

Previous Distribution:
FBI   State Dept.
MID   Sp.Def.Unit D.J.

Distribution:
1st C.A.   2nd C.A.
3rd C.A.   4th C.A.
5th C.A.   6th C.A.
7th C.A.   8th C.A.

~~CONFIDENTIAL~~

Evaluation
of source _____ of informa
_____ Reliable
_____ Candid
_____ Questionable
_____ Undetermined

10—17097-1

Post–Pearl Harbor memo from MID, dated January 3, 1942, warns that there
"can be no doubt that most of the leaders" of Japan's intelligence network "still
continue to function as key operatives for the Japanese government along the
West Coast."

~~CONFIDENTIAL~~

by intensifying the espionage activities of non-political agencies here.

In streamlining their Intelligence Machine the Japanese have been guided by two major considerations—that of a system of "total intelligence" such as the Germans have developed; and establishment of a completely integrated intelligence organization which in time of war and the breaking off of official relations would be able to take over intelligence operations on a major scale.

The focal point of the Japanese espionage effort has been the determination of the total strength of the United States. In anticipation of possible open conflict with this country, Japan vigorously utilized every available agency to secure military, naval, and commercial information, paying particular attention to West Coast, Panama Canal, and Hawaii. Surveys were made of persons and organizations opposing United States' intervention in the European War, and close attention was paid to all anti-Jewish, Communist, Negro, and Labor Movements.

Although never fully developed, this new espionage organization was characterized by a high degree of decentralization. The general pattern included individuals, small groups, and commercial organizations functioning separately yet directly controlled by Imperial Japanese Government through Embassy and Consulate.

The new program provided for the utilization of citizens of foreign extraction, aliens, Communists, Negroes, Labor union members, anti-Semites, and individuals having access to Government Departments, experimental laboratories, factories, transportation facilities and governmental organizations of various kinds. Nisei and Japanese aliens were not overlooked.

In event of open hostilities, Mexico was to be the Japanese intelligence nerve center in the Western Hemisphere, and in anticipation of war, U.S.-Latin American intelligence routes were established, involving extensive cooperation among Japanese, German and Italian intelligence organizations.

In this connection there should be kept in mind the proximity of San Diego to Tiajuana and of El Centro to Mexicali. Along with Yuma, Nogales, El Paso, Laredo, and Brownsville, are well known Japanese "post offices" and espionage centers.

Outstanding among the Japanese espionage projects was their comprehensive surveys of the entire western coast of North America.

Japanese Propaganda in the United States has for the most.

- 2 -

CONFIDENTIAL

part been under direction of a special division of the Japanese Foreign
Office in Tokyo. Local control was administered through the Embassy in
Washington, as well as the Consulates in key cities and Consular Agents
in Japanese communities.

g. The Tokyo Club Syndicate. This is an excellent illustra-
tion of the extremely complicated interlockings which characterize
Japanese groups.

Until recently the Tokyo Club of Los Angeles, with chief
subsidiaries, the Nichibei Kogyo Kaisha of Los Angeles and the Tokyo
Club of Seattle, constituted the nucleus of a system of gambling clubs
from Alaska to Mexico. A widespread decentralized system of Japanese
"clubs," labor organizations, and legitimate business groups has been
converted into an important unit of the central Japanese Intelligence
Network. There can be no doubt that most of the leaders have been and
still continue to function as key operatives for the Japanese Government
along the West Coast.

It is reported that the Tokyo Club is no longer in existence
but it may be that the former leaders have retired behind new "fronts."

h. Japanese Canneries, Alaska and West Coast. Whether
floating or shore-based, American- or foreign-owned, the Alaskan canneries employ a considerable amount of Japanese capital and labor.
American leaders in the fishing-canning industry stress the fact that
the Japanese involved are scattered in definitely strategic places
throughout Alaska, and that there exists the possibility that some of
these Japanese may have military or naval connections.

mh

- 5 -

CONFIDENTIAL

b7c

January 16, 1942

62-40185-322

Honorable James Lawrence Fly
Chairman
Federal Communications Commission
Washington, D. C.

Dear Mr. Fly:

     In regard to present conditions in the Hawaiian Islands, it is apparent that illicit short-wave radio transmissions are being sent from clandestine stations operating in the islands themselves, in communication with mobile units of the Japanese Navy, through which intelligence information is being reported to the enemy. It is extremely important that these clandestine stations be located and eliminated from operation and that the individuals concerned with their operation be dealt with appropriately as rapidly as possible. It is also highly important that bearings be obtained on radio transmissions from Japanese naval craft which may be operating in the vicinity of the Hawaiian Islands in order that their location and direction of travel may be determined and appropriate action taken by our armed forces.

     The question of monitoring the transmissions of the illicit radio stations in the Hawaiian Islands and vicinity was discussed with Rear Admiral Wilkinson, Director of the Office of Naval Intelligence, and Colonel Bissell of the Military Intelligence Division on January 14, 1942, and it was agreed that the problem presented is most serious and is one which should be given early attention. We were all of the same opinion, that radio monitoring activities in Honolulu, Hawaii, and throughout the islands are the primary responsibility of the Federal Communications Commission. On the occasion of this conference Rear Admiral Wilkinson and Colonel Bissell expressed the desire that I call your attention to the situation by letter and impress upon you the vital importance and necessity for establishing immediately an exhaustive coverage on these radio activities.

     In order that this situation in the Hawaiian Islands may be clarified with the least possible delay, it is urged that monitoring activities on the part of the Federal Communications Commission in the islands be intensified to the highest possible degree and that information developed and problems arising in connection with these activities be promptly worked out in collaboration with the military and naval authorities and with the office of the Federal Bureau of Investigation at Honolulu.

                           Sincerely yours,

b7c

                           John Edgar Hoover
                              Director

Post–Pearl Harbor memo from FBI Director J. Edgar Hoover, January 16, 1942, warns of continued illegal shortwave radio transmissions sent from clandestine stations on Hawaii to the Japanese Navy. The problem is "most serious and is one which should be given early attention."

JCH:ESX

February 9, 1942

ALL INFORMATION CONTAINED
HEREIN IS UNCLASSIFIED
DATE 5/14/86 BY 16782CFFAW

RECORD: 62-65880-25X1

MEMORANDUM FOR THE ATTORNEY GENERAL

Re: ENEMY ALIEN PROGRAM IN THE
WESTERN DEFENSE COMMAND

With reference to the above-entitled program, I wish to
advise you of the results of a series of searches and apprehensions
made by the Portland, Seattle, and Los Angeles Field Divisions on
the afternoon and evening of February 7, 1942.

The Portland Field Division searched eighty-one premises
and interviewed the one hundred fifty-one aliens who were found to
be occupying these premises. Four arrests were made in connection
with the seizing of twenty-one sticks of dynamite, sixty-two dynamite
caps, and one hundred forty feet of fuse. These searches were conducted at Hood River, Oregon, in the vicinity of Bonneville Dam.
The vicinity in which these searches were conducted is considered
to be the most vital military area in the Portland Field Division.

The Seattle Field Division conducted searches of the premises
and residences occupied by twenty-eight German and Japanese aliens
who reside on Vashon Island, near Bainbridge Island, on which a
Naval radio station is located. Two Japanese aliens and one German
alien were found to be in possession of prohibited articles and are
being held for custodial detention. During these searches one revolver, two cameras, one shortwave radio set, approximately twenty
feet of fuse, approximately one hundred dynamite blasting caps, and
one-half box of dynamite were found.

On the same date the Los Angeles Field Division conducted
searches of forty-six homes which were occupied by enemy aliens and
as a result of interviews with the occupants and the location of
prohibited articles, seventeen enemy aliens were apprehended. In
connection with these arrests, the following material was seized:
seven radio sets capable of receiving shortwave, one radio oscillator,
four boxes of assorted radio equipment, two cameras, twenty-three
flashlights, four large searchlights, three telegraphers' keys,

Mr. Tolson
Mr. E. A. Tamm
Mr. Clegg
Mr. Glavin
Mr. Ladd
Dr. Nichols
Mr. Tracy
Mr. Rosen
Mr. Carson
Mr. Coffey
Mr. Hendon
Mr. Holloman
Mr. Quinn Tamm
Mr. Nease
Miss Gandy

one small radio transmitting set, one microphone, one .38
caliber revolver, fifty cartridges, one .22 caliber rifle,
four blasting caps, three pounds of black powder, three
feet of fuse, and two reels of 8 millimeter film containing
photographs of battleships and fortifications. Further
investigation is being conducted regarding the aforementioned
film. The searches by the Los Angeles Field Division were
conducted in the Palos Verdes Hills area which adjoins Fort
MacArthur.

Respectfully,

J. Edgar Hoover

John Edgar Hoover
Director

Post-Pearl Harbor memo from Hoover to Biddle, February 9, 1942, that
details illegal contraband confiscated from West Coast enemy aliens.

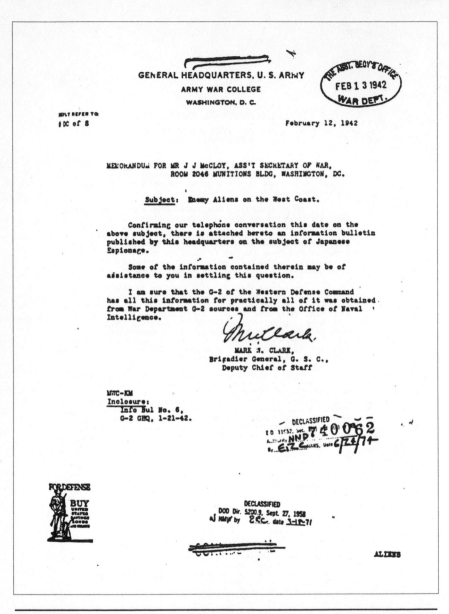

Cover letter from Army Deputy Chief of Staff Mark Clark to Assistant Secretary of War John McCloy and attached memo on continuing Japanese espionage on the West Coast. The memo concludes that the network containing *Issei* and *Nisei* "is now thoroughly organized and working underground." Sent February 12, 1942.

~~CONFIDENTIAL~~

INFORMATION BULLETIN)
                     :
NUMBER...........6)

G-2 SECTION
GENERAL HEADQUARTERS, U.S. ARMY,
Army War College,
Washington, D. C.,
January 21, 1942.

JAPANESE ESPIONAGE

1. _General_. - The alien Japanese organize for every conceivable purpose, a characteristic brought from Japan. Japanese societies existed in the Hawaiian Islands from the earliest migration. Every alien Japanese in Hawaii belongs to one or more organizations. These organizations exist in the United States, and are inimical to our best interests.

Japanese organization flows in specific and distinct channels, interlocked through the duplication of activity and the plurality of positions held by individual Japanese. Each of these channels is at least strongly influenced, if not directly controlled, by groups of similar type and purpose in Japan and under Japanese governmental supervision.

2. _Diplomatic and Consular Organization_. - _a_. Japanese espionage activities in the United States were participated in, directed and controlled by representatives of the Imperial Japanese Government through the officials of its Embassy and Consulates. The Secretary of the Embassy was charged with the responsibility of coordinating and directing Japanese Intelligence activities in this country. He was instructed to visit Japanese officials in North, South and Central American countries. During July, 1941, he traveled over 20,000 miles in Mexico, Central America, Peru, Ecuador and other South American countries. Further, his travels in the United States substantiated his position as the director of Japanese espionage in this country. The facilities of the Embassy and the Consulates were available to the Military and Naval Attaches for transmission of intelligence, and the Consulates maintained secret funds in cash for the purchase of information.

_b_. _Naval Attache_. - The Naval Attache, attached to the Japanese Embassy was particularly active. He was generally a Naval captain, with previous experience in the United States or England in the capacity of Assistant Attache or language officer, and was an experienced Intelligence officer. Working with the Attache were several assistants, one of whom was generally a Naval aviator with Intelligence experience. In addition, several experienced Navy men were employed as clerks. There were always a number of Naval officers in the United States on temporary visitors visas. The Office of Naval Intelligence pointed out that over one hundred Naval officers visited the United States last year.

_c_. _Naval Inspector_. - A counterpart of the Naval Attache's office was the Naval Inspector's Office at New York City, with a branch in Los Angeles, California. Aircraft parts, radio, electrical equipment, tools and accessories were purchased almost daily, apparently for examination. Japanese Naval officers connected with the Naval Inspector's Office cooperated with German agents by accepting confidential data for transmission to Germany via Japan.

- 1 -

~~CONFIDENTIAL~~

CONFIDENTIAL

    d. Military Attache. - The office of the Military Attache in Washington, D.C., was also active. During the early part of 1941, the Chief of the American Section of the Japanese Army made an extensive tour of the United States to ascertain the attitude of the people toward present conditions and to gather maps. During his brief visit to Cuba, he conferred with various Japanese colonists there.

    e. Ordnance Inspector. - A complement of the Military Attache's Office, the Japanese Ordnance Inspector's Office, was maintained in New York for some time, and was similar to the Naval Inspector's Office.

    3. Religious Organizations. - The Buddhist and Shinto sects acted as Japanese propaganda agencies with the Japanese communities, holding services in Japanese. The Priests, held in deep respect, are in an excellent position to disseminate propaganda. Many of the Buddhist and Shinto priests entered the Hawaiian Islands as non-quota aliens and resided there only a short time.

    4. Educational Organization. - Japanese espionage recognized the strategic position of the Japanese Language Schools in molding the beliefs and ideals of Japanese students and the effect on their behavior and loyalty to the United States.

    5. Commercial and Civic Organizations. - a. Commercial. - The value of representatives of Japanese business organizations, banks, and newspapers has not been overlooked. In Japan, several of the large business firms must be considered semi-official in nature.

    b. Civic. - The Overseas Japanese Central Society is a liaison agency for all Japanese residing in countries foreign to Japan. It is connected with all Japanese organizations in the United States, such as:

    (1) Japanese Association of America. - National headquarters at 1619 Laguna St., San Francisco, Calif. Estimated membership of 100,000, with 10,000 active members. The purpose of this organization is to protect the rights of alien Japanese residents residing in America and to assist them in coping with social and economic problems.

    (2) Japanese American Citizens League. - This organization of approximately 10,000 members is composed of persons of Japanese descent born in America. Headquarters are located at 1623 Webster St., San Francisco, Calif. In recent months, the league conducted a vigorous campaign to abolish dual citizenship and prove that the members are loyal to this country.

    (3) Sokoku Kai (Ancestral Country Society) Seattle, Wash. - Sokoku Kai is reported to have connection with the Silver Shirts in that state. It published a magazine devoting itself to building up pride in the superiority of the Japanese race.

    (4) Japanese Association of Utah. - This is comprised of native born Japanese with the purpose of building closer relations between Americans and Japanese. One function is to register births with the Japanese Consul at San Francisco to insure dual citizenship.

- 2 -

CONFIDENTIAL

(5) Intermountain Japanese Association. - This organization is a farmers cooperative concern, located at Ogden, Utah. It registers births with the Japanese Consul to insure dual citizenship and arranges passports and re-entry permits for its members. In August, 1941, it completed a survey of Japanese property holdings and a census of Japanese for the Consul. It received literature propagandizing Japanese justification in the Far East and directed the activities of the Japanese language schools in Utah.

6. Conclusions. - a. It may be expected that Japanese diplomatic and consular communications will be replaced now by using the diplomatic and consular organization of an allegedly neutral power identified with the Axis. They may also use officials of other neutral countries whom they have subverted.

b. Their espionage net containing Japanese aliens, first and second generation Japanese and other nationals is now thoroughly organized and working underground.

c. In addition to their communications net through neutral diplomats, they may be expected to have their own underground communication net.

d. Extensive use of Occidentals, such as Axis nationals, neutral nationals, and subverted Americans, is to be expected.

P. H. ROBINETT,
Lieut. Colonel, G.S.C.,
Ass't Chief of Staff, G-2.

Not to be disseminated
lower than division.

- 3 -

Op-16-B-7-J

NAVY DEPARTMENT
OFFICE OF THE CHIEF OF NAVAL OPERATIONS
WASHINGTON

February 14, 1942

MEMORANDUM for Mr. Tamm

SUBJECT: The Japanese Problem

There is transmitted herewith a copy of a report on the Japanese Question which was prepared by Lieutenant Commander K. D. Ringle, U.S.N.

This report was prepared at the request of the Office of Naval Intelligence following the statement by Mr. C. B. Munson, in his survey of the Japanese on the West Coast, that Lieutenant Commander Ringle was particularly well acquainted with the Japanese problem.

Although it does not represent the final and official opinion of the Office of Naval Intelligence on this subject, it is believed that this report will be of interest to the Federal Bureau of Investigation.

H. B. Kelsker,
Commander, U.S.N.R.

I ENCLO.

Mr. E. A. Tamm
Federal Bureau of Investigation
U. S. Department of Justice
Washington, D. C.

Copy to: Military Intelligence Division
Alien Enemy Control Unit, Department of Justice
Special Defense Unit, Department of Justice

ONI Lieutenant Commander K. D. Ringle's unofficial memo to the FBI on the "Japanese problem."

Branch Intelligence Office

BIO/ND11/EF37/A8-5   ELEVENTH NAVAL DISTRICT   26 JAN 1942

Serial LA/1055/re   Fifth Floor, Van Nuys Building
                          Seventh and Spring Streets
                          Los Angeles, California

CONFIDENTIAL

    From: Lieutenant Commander K. D. RINGLE, USN.
    To: The Chief of Naval Operations
    Via: The Commandant, Eleventh Naval District.

    Subject: Japanese Question, Report on.

    Reference: (a) OpNav ltr file (SC)A8-5/EF37 Op-16-B-7/RB A8-5/EF37
                    Serial No. 01742316 of 12/30/41.
                (b) Reports of Mr. C. B. Munson, Special Representative
                    of the State Department, on Japanese on the West
                    Coast, dated Nov. 7, 1941, and Dec. 20, 1941.
                (c) NNI 119 Report, file BIO/ND11/EF 37/A8-2, serial LA/861
                    of 3/27/41, subject-NISEI.
                (d) NNI 119 Report, file BIO/ND11/EF37/A8-2, serial LA/5223
                    of 11/4/41, subject-NISEI.
                (e) NNI 119 Report, file BIO-LA/ND11/FF37/P8-2, serial
                    LA/6524 of 12/12/41, subject-HEIMUSHA-KAI.
                (f) NNI 119 Report, file BIO-LA/ND11/FF37/P8-2, serial
                    LA/417 of 1/5/42, subject-KIBEI Organizations and
                    Activities.
                (g) Dept. of Commerce Bulletin, Series P-3, Number 23,
                    dated 12/9/41.

    Enclosures: (A) Transcripts of J. B. Hughes' broadcasts of Jan. 5, 6,
                    7, 9, 15, 19, and 20, 1942.
                (B) F.B.I.,L.A. Report re Japanese Activities, Los Angeles,
                    dated Jan. 20, 1942.

    1.   In accordance with paragraph 2 of reference (a), the follow-
ing views and opinions with supporting facts and statements are submitted.

        I OPINIONS.

                The following opinions, amplified in succeeding paragraphs,
are held by the writer:

                    DECLASSIFICATION ON 5/14/85
                    BY   678 LET 146

BIO/ND11/EF37/A8-5

Serial LA/1055/re

CONFIDENTIAL

Subject: Japanese Question, Report on.
- -

(a) That within the last eight or ten years the entire
"Japanese question" in the United States has reversed itself. The alien
menace is no longer paramount, and is becoming of less importance almost
daily, as the original alien immigrants grow older and die, and as more and
more of their American-born children reach maturity. The primary present
and future problem is that of dealing with these American-born United States
citizens of Japanese ancestry, of whom it is considered that least seventy-
five per cent are loyal to the United States. The ratio of these American
citizens of Japanese ancestry to alien-born Japanese in the United States is
at present almost 3 to 1, and rapidly increasing.

(b) That of the Japanese-born alien residents, the large
majority are at least passively loyal to the United States. That is, they
would knowingly do nothing whatever to the injury of the United States, but
at the same time would not do anything to the injury of Japan. Also, most
of the remainder would not engage in active sabotage or insurrection, but
might well do surreptitious observation work for Japanese interests if given
a convenient opportunity.

(c) That, however, there are among the Japanese both alien and
United States citizens, certain individuals, either deliberately placed by
the Japanese government or actuated by a fanatical loyalty to that country,
who would act as saboteurs or agents. This number is estimated to be less
than three per cent of the total, or about 3500 in the entire United States.

(d) That of the persons mentioned in (c) above, the most
dangerous are either already in custodial detention or are members of such
organizations as the Black Dragon Society, the Kaigun Kyokai (Navy League),
or the Heimusha Kai (Military Service Men's League), or affiliated groups,
The membership of these groups is already fairly well known to the Naval Intelligence service or the Federal Bureau of Investigation and should immediately be placed in custodial detention, irrespective of whether they are alien
or citizen. (See reference (e) and (f).

(e) That, as a basic policy tending toward the permanent solution of this problem, the American citizens of Japanese ancestry should be
officially encouraged in their efforts toward loyalty and acceptance as bona
fide citizens; that they be accorded a place in the national effort through
such agencies as the Red Cross, U.S.O., civilian defense, and even such
activities as ship and aircraft building or other defense production activities, even though subject to greater investigative checks as to background
and loyalty, etc., than Caucasian Americans.

-2-

BIO/MD11/EF37/A8-5

Serial LA/1055/re

CONFIDENTIAL

Subject: Japanese Question, Report on.
- -

(f) That in spite of paragraph (e) above, the most potentially dangerous element of all are those American citizens of Japanese ancestry who have spent the formative years of their lives, from 10 to 20, in Japan and have returned to the United States to claim their legal American citizenship within the last few years. These people are essentially and inherently Japanese and may have been deliberately sent back to the United States by the Japanese government to act as agents. In spite of their legal citizenship and the protection afforded them by the Bill of Rights, they should be looked upon as enemy aliens and many of them placed in custodial detention. This group numbers between 600 and 700 in the Los Angeles metropolitan area and at least that many in other parts of Southern California.

(g) That the writer heartily agrees with the reports submitted by Mr. Munson, (reference (b) of this report.)

(h) That, in short, the entire "Japanese Problem" has been magnified out of its true proportion, largely because of the physical characteristics of the people; that it is no more serious than the problems of the German, Italian, and Communistic portions of the United States population, and, finally that it should be handled on the basis of the individual, regardless of citizenship, and not on a racial basis.

(i) That the above opinions are and will continue to be true just so long as these people, Issei and Nisei, are given an opportunity to be self-supporting, but that if conditions continue in the trend they appear to be taking as of this date; i.e., loss of employment and income due to anti-Japanese agitation by and among Caucasian Americans, continued personal attacks by Filipinos and other racial groups, denial of relief funds to desperately needy cases, cancellation of licenses for markets, produce houses, stores, etc., by California State authorities, discharges from jobs by the wholesale, unnecessarily harsh restrictions on travel, including discriminatory regulations against all Nisei preventing them from engaging in commercial fishing—there will most certainly be outbreaks of sabotage, riots, and other civil strife in the not too distant future.

II   BACKGROUND.

(1) In order that the qualifications of the writer to express the above opinions may be clearly understood, his background of acquaintance with this problem is set forth.

-3-

BIO/ND11/EF37/A8-5

Serial LA/1055/re

CONFIDENTIAL

Subject: Japanese Question, Report on.
- -

        (a) Three years' study of the Japanese language and the Japanese people as a naval language student attached to the United States Embassy in Tokyo from 1928 to 1931.

        (b) One year's duty as Assistant District Intelligence Officer, Fourteenth Naval District (Hawaii) from July 1936 to July 1937.

        (c) Duty as Assistant District Intelligence Officer, Eleventh Naval District, in charge of Naval Intelligence matters in Los Angeles and vicinity from July 1940 to the present time.

        (2) As a result of the above, the writer has over the last several years developed a very great interest in the problem of the Japanese in America, particularly with regard to the future position of the United States citizen of Japanese ancestry, and has sought contact with certain of their leaders. He has likewise discussed the matter widely with many Caucasian Americans who have lived with the problem for years. As a result, the writer believes firmly that the only ultimate solution is as outlined in paragraphs I(e) and I(h) above; namely, to deliberately and officially encourage the American citizen of Japanese ancestry in his efforts to be a loyal citizen and to help him to be so accepted by the general public.

    III   ELABORATION OF OPINIONS EXPRESSED IN PARAGRAPH I.

        (1) For purposes of brevity and clearness, four Japanese words in common use by Americans as well as Japanese in referring to these people will be explained. Hereafter these words will be used where appropriate.

        ISSEI (pronounced ee-say) meaning "first Generation." Used to refer to those who were born in Japan; hence, alien Japanese in the United States.

        NISEI (pronounced nee-say) meaning "second generation." Used for those children of ISSEI born in the United States.

        SANSEI (pronounced san-say) meaning "third generation." Children of NISEI.

        KIBEI (pronounced kee-bay) meaning "returned to America." Refers to those NISEI who spent all or a large portion of their lives in Japan and who have now returned to the United States.

-4-

BIO/ND11/EF37/A8-5

Serial LA/1055/re

CONFIDENTIAL

Subject: Japanese Question, Report on.
- -

(2) The one statement in paragraph I(a) above which appears to need elaboration is that seventy-five per cent or more of the Nisei are loyal United States citizens. This point was explained at some length in references (c) and (d). The opinion was formed largely through personal contact with the Nisei themselves and their chief organization, the Japanese American Citizens League. It was also formed through interviews with many people in government circles, law-enforcement officers, businessmen, etc., who have dealt with them over a period of many years. There are several conclusive proofs of this statement which can be advanced. These are—

(a) The action taken by the Japanese American Citizens League in convention in Santa Ana, California, on January 11, 1942. This convention voted to require the following oath to be taken, signed, and notarized by every member of that organization as a prerequisite for membership for the year 1942, and for all members taken into the organization in the future:

> "I, _____, do solemnly swear that I will
> support and defend the Constitution of the
> United States against all enemies, foreign and
> domestic; that I will bear true faith and
> allegiance to the same; that I hereby renounce
> any other allegiances which I may have know-
> ingly or unknowingly held in the past; and that
> I take this obligation freely without any
> mental reservation or purpose of evasion. So
> help me God."

(b) Many of the Nisei leaders have voluntarily contributed valuable anti-subversive information to this and other governmental agencies. (See reference (d) and enclosure (3).

(c) That the Japanese Consular staff, leaders of the Central Japanese Association, and others who are known to have been sympathetic to the Japanese cause do not themselves trust the Nisei.

(d) That a very great many of the Nisei have taken legal steps through the Japanese Consulate and the Government of Japan to officially divest themselves of Japanese citizenship (dual citizenship), even though by so doing they become legally dead in the eyes of the Japanese law, and are no longer eligible to inherit any property which they or their family may have held in Japan. This opinion is further amplified in references (c) and (d).

-5-

BIO/ND11/CF37/A6-3

Serial LA/1055/re

CONFIDENTIAL

Subject: Japanese Question, Report on.
- -

            (3) The opinion expressed in paragraph I(b) above is based on
the following: The last Issei who legally entered the United States did so in
1924. Most of them arrived before that time; therefore, these people have been
in the United States at least eighteen years, or most of their adult life.
They have their businesses and livelihoods here. Most of them are aliens only
because the laws of the United States do not permit them to become naturalized.
They have raised their children, the Nisei mentioned in paragraph (1) above,
in the United States; many of them have sons in the United States army. Exact
figures are not available, but the local Military Intelligence office estimates
that approximately five thousand Nisei in the State of California have entered
the United States army as a result of the Selective Service Act. It does not
seem reasonable that these aliens under the above conditions would form an
organized group for armed insurrection or organized sabotage. Insofar as numbers go, there are only 40,697 alien Japanese in the eight western states.

            The following paragraph quoted from an Associated Press despatch
from Washington referring to the registration of enemy aliens is considered most
significant on this point: "The group which must register first comprises the
135,843 enemy aliens in the western command—Arizona, California, Idaho,
Montana, Nevada, Oregon, Utah, and Washington. The group includes 26,255
Germans, 60,905 Italians, and 40,697 Japanese." It is assumed that the foregoing figures are based either on the 1940 census or the alien registration
which was taken the latter part of 1940.

            There are two factors which must be considered in this group of
aliens: First, the group includes a sizeable number of "technical" aliens;
that is, those who, although Japanese born and therefore legally aliens, entered
the United States in infancy, grew up here, and are at heart American citizens.
Second, the parents of the Kibei, mentioned in paragraph I(f), should be considered as those who are most loyal to Japan, since they themselves are the ones
who sent their children to be educated and brought up entirely in the Japanese
manner.

            (4) Paragraph I)c) needs no further elaboration.

            (5) Paragraph I(d) has been elaborated at length in references
(e) and (f).

            (6) Elaboration of paragraph I(e). The United States recognizes
these American-born Orientals as citizens, extends the franchise to them,

                              -6-

BIO/MD11/EF37/A8-3

Serial LA/1055/re

CONFIDENTIAL

Subject: Japanese Question, Report on.
- -

drafts them for military service, forces them to pay taxes, perform jury duty, etc., and extends them to the complete protection afforded by the Constitution and Bill of Rights, and yet at the same time has viewed them with considerable suspicion and distrust, and so far as it is known to the writer, has made no particular effort to develop their loyalty to the United States, other than to permit them to attend public schools. They are segregated as to where they may live by zoning laws, discriminated against in employment and wages, and rebuffed in nearly all their efforts to prove their loyalty to the United States, yet at the same time those of them who grow to about the age of 16 years in the United States and then go to Japan for a few years of education find themselves viewed with more suspicion and distrust in that country than they ever were in the United States, and the majority of them return after a short time thoroughly disillusioned with Japan and more than ever loyal to the United States.

        It is submitted that the only practical permanent solution of this problem is to indoctrinate and absorb these people, accept them as an integral part of the United States population, even though they remain a racial minority, and officially extend to them the rights and privileges of citizenship, as well as demanding of them the duties and obligations.

        Furthermore, if some such steps are not taken, the field for proselyting and propaganda among them is left entirely to Japanese interest acting through Consulates, Consular agents, so-called "cultural societies", athletic clubs, Buddhist and Shinto priests—who through a quirk in the United States immigration laws may and have entered the country freely, regardless of exclusion laws or quota as "ministers of religion"—trade treaty aliens, steamship and travel agencies, "goodwill" missions, etc. It is well known to the writer that his acquaintance with and encouragement of Nisei leaders in their efforts towards Americanization was a matter of considerable concern to the former Japanese Consul at Los Angeles.

        It is submitted that the Nisei could be accorded a place in the national war effort without risk or danger, and that such a step would go farther than anything else towards cementing their loyalty to the United States. Because of their physical characteristics they would be most easily observed, far easier than doubtful citizens of the Caucasian race, such as naturalized Germans, Italians, or native-born Communists. They would, of course, be subject to the same or more stringent checks as to background than the Caucasians before they were employed.

BIO/ND11/EF37/A8-5

Serial LA/1055/re

CONFIDENTIAL

Subject: Japanese Question, Report on.

- -

           (7) No elaboration is considered necessary for paragraphs I(f), I(g), and I(h).

           (8) Elaboration of paragraph I(i). The opinion outlined in this paragraph is considered most serious and most urgent. There already exists a great deal of economic distress due to such war conditions as frozen credits and accounts, loss of employment, closing of businesses, restrictions on travel, etc. This condition is growing worse daily as the savings of most of the alien-dominated families are being used up. As an example, the following census, taken by missionary interest, of alien families in the fishing village on Terminal Island is submitted:

"How long can you maintain your family without work?"

Immediate attention	—	9 families
1 month	—	52 families
2 months	—	64 families
3 months	—	81 families
4 months	—	32 families
5 months	—	20 families
6 to 10 months	—	129 families
Over 10 months	—	90 families
Total		477 families.

           Large numbers of people, both Issei and Nisei, are idle now, and their number is growing. Children are beginning to be unable to attend school through lack of food and clothing. There have been already incipient riots brought about by unprovoked attacks by Filipinos on persons of the Japanese race, regardless of citizenship. There is a great deal of indiscriminate anti-Japanese agitation stirring the white population by such people as Lail Kane, former Naval Reserve Officer, James Young, Hearst correspondent, in his series of lectures, and Jonn B. Hughes, radio commentator, transcripts of whose broadcasts are submitted as enclosure (A).

           There are just enough half truths in these articles and statements to render them exceedingly dangerous and to arouse a tremendous amount of violent anti-Japanese feeling among Caucasians of all classes who are not thoroughly informed as to the situation. It is noted that in these broadcasts, lectures, etc., there are no distinctions made whatever between the actual members of the Japanese military forces in Japan and the second and third generation citizens of Japanese ancestry born and brought up in the

-8-

BIO/ND11/EF37/A8-5

Serial LA/1055/re

CONFIDENTIAL

Subject: Japanese Question, Report on.
- -

United States. It must also be remembered that many of the persons and groups
agitating anti-Japanese sentiment against the Issei and Nisei have done so for
some time from ulterior motives—notable is the anti-Japanese agitation by the
Jugo-Slav fishermen who frankly desire to eliminate competition in the fishing
industry. .

            It is further noted that according to the local press, Congress-
man Leland M. Ford has introduced a bill in Congress providing for the removal
and interment in concentration camps of all citizens and residents of Japanese
extraction, which according to the census figures would amount to about 127,000
people of all ages and sexes in the continental United States, plus an additional 158,000 in Hawaii and other territories and possessions, excluding the
Philippines, (see reference (g) for population breakdown). It is submitted
that such a proposition is not only unwarranted but very unwise, since it would
undoubtedly alienate the loyalty of many thousands of persons who would otherwise be entirely loyal to the United States, would add the extra burden of
supporting and guarding these people to the war effort, would disrupt many
essential businesses, notably that of the growing and supplying of foodstuffs,
and would probably cause a widespread outbreak of sabotage and riot.

      IV RECOMMENDATIONS.

            (1) Based on the above opinions, the following recommendations
for the handling of this situation are submitted:

            (a) Provide some means whereby potentially dangerous United
States citizens may be held in custodial detention as well as aliens. It is
submitted that in a military "theater of operations"—which at present includes
all the West coast—this might be done by review of individual cases by boards
composed of members of Military Intelligence, Naval Intelligence, and the
Department of Justice.

            (b) Under the provisions of (a) above, hold in custodial deten-
tion such United States citizens as dangerous Kibei or German, Italian, or
other subversive sympathizers and agitators as are deemed dangerous to the
internal security of the United States.

            (c) Similar procedure to be followed in cases of aliens—not
only Japanese, but other aliens of whatever nationality, whether so-called
"friendly" aliens or not. This suggestion is made since it is believed that

-9-

BIO/ND11/FF37/A8-5

Serial LA/1055/re

CONFIDENTIAL

Subject: Japanese Question, Report on.
- -

there exist other aliens--Spanish, Mexican, Portuguese, Slavonian, French, etc.,
who are active Axis sympathizers.

        (d) Other suggestions as listed in reference (a).

        (e) In the cases of persons held in custodial detention, whether
alien or citizen, see that some definite provision is made for the support of
their dependent families. This could be done by:

        (1) Releasing certain specified amounts from these people's
"frozen" funds monthly for the support of these dependents.

        (2) Making definite provisions through relief funds for the
support of such dependents, so that they will not become either public charges
or embittered against the United States, and themselves dangerous to the internal peace and security of the country.

        (f) In the interest of national unity and internal peace and
security some measures should be instituted to restrain agitators of both radio
and press who are attempting to arouse sentiment and bring about action--
private, local, state, and national, official and unofficial, against these
people on the basis of race alone, completely neglecting background, training,
and citizenship.

                                         K. D. RINGLE.

Copy to:
DIO(2)

Los Angeles, California
December 10, 1941

Director   PERSONAL AND ████████████
Federal Bureau of Investigation
Washington, D. C.

Dear Sir:

Reference is made to telephonic instructions from
Assistant Director E. A. TAMM on December 10, 1941, to the effect
that I was to communicate with MR. CURTIS MUNSON and inform him
that you have been advised by MR. J. F. CARTER of his statements
relative to the exhausted condition of Agents of this office due
to their overwork at this particular time.

Almost immediately after receiving this call from
MR. TAMM, MR. MUNSON called me and inquired if we would be able to
handle another situation such as we are now handling, and from our
previous conversations, I know that he was referring to the apprehension of Communists. I assured him that we are in a position to
do so in the same effective manner in which we are now operating
while apprehending alien enemies. He stated that the apprehension
of this new group was being considered in Washington, and that there
was a bottleneck in the Department, and he undoubtedly referred to
the Attorney General as he had in his conversations with MR. VINCENT
of this office on the occasion of his visit here on December 9, 1941.
I assured him that it would be a simple matter for the Bureau to coordinate its activities to the end that the individuals of any group
be apprehended. He inquired if this were extended to include the
persons in a "B" classification of this group, if it would be too big
a situation for us to handle, and I assured him it was not; that
there were many departments we had not called on at all in the present
situation, and there were many officers to assist us and it would be
easy from an administrative viewpoint in the office to handle this
situation. It was pointed out that the experience gained in this
present activity would enable us to handle a greater volume of it
in the future with the same force. I stated that it was necessary to
work hard, but that that was absolutely necessary at such a time as
this.

I advised MR. MUNSON that MR. HOOVER has informed me
of a telephone call from MR. J. F. CARTER in Washington, advising
that the Agents of this office were in a very exhausted condition and
were about to drop from overwork, and that I had informed MR. HOOVER
that such a statement was a lie. MUNSON immediately began to attempt

DECLASSIFIED BY 6080 [illegible]
ON 3-23-77

Businessman and interloper Curtis Munson, often cited as a champion of ethnic Japanese and heroic opponent of the West Coast evacuation, actually bad-
gered the FBI to lock up large numbers of *Nisei* on mere suspicion of
subversion. As long as roundup measures "were confined to aliens," Munson
warned the FBI, "the job would only be half done."

Director.　　　　　　　　　　- 2 -　　　　　　　　　December 10, 1941

to smooth things over and stated that he did not make that statement
at all; but his words to me were, "I said they were working very hard
day and night, and if any more work is placed on them now it might be
too much." He stated this was in order that the Bureau would be enabled
to obtain anything in Washington that it desired, and that he absolutely
did not mean it in a sense of criticism. He stated MR. CARTER is very
well known to MR. HOOVER and believes the Director would understand why
MR. CARTER would say that to him. He stated, however, if there were
any criticism it should be "pinned on him," but what he was actually
doing was trying to give us his help.

　　　　　I advised him that the Agents had worked hard, but
were not at all near the exhaustion point--in fact, almost to a man
they had volunteered to continue working when I had instructed them
to return to their quarters for some sleep. I could tell from his
reaction that MUNSON thought I was in exceedingly good spirits at the
time of our conversation. He was aware of the fact that I did not
appreciate receiving a complaint about this office from the Director
and he requested that I not be angry with him, as he had meant absolutely
no harm to this office.

　　　　　After my conversation with MR. HOOVER on December 10, I
called MR. MUNSON again at the Biltmore Hotel and informed him that you
had severely criticized me, for you had received a complaint that the
Los Angeles Office has picked up only half of the individuals who should
be apprehended, and if this is the case, I am at fault for not having
requested additional personnel from the Bureau. I informed MR. MUNSON
that this was not the situation at all, as I had sufficient personnel
and had not, therefore, made a request for additional Agents from the
Bureau, and those individuals whose names have been furnished us by
the Department as being satisfactory subjects for custodial detention
at this time have been and are being apprehended rapidly. There are
but a few outstanding at this time. I informed him very definitely
that we can apprehend only those persons whom the Department authorizes
be seized; and, therefore, we cannot take any action against any other
group at this time.

　　　　　MR. MUNSON stated that there must have been a misunder-
standing about this statement, as what he said was that only half of
the persons who should be picked up have to date been apprehended
because we have not gone into the citizens group; and it is his impression from what he has learned here on the Coast that the citizens who

Director   - 3 -   December 10, 1941

are disloyal constitute a large group of possible troublemakers in
the emergency. He feels that the apprehension of the aliens is only
half of the job, and the citizens constitute the other half of it.

He was very apologetic for having caused me any difficulties with the Bureau and stated that he was out here to give me
whatever assistance he possibly could. He did not want me to misunder-
stand his purpose and he hoped that I would feel free to communicate
with him at any time.

                                   Very truly yours,

                                   R. B. HOOD
                                   Special Agent in Charge

RBH:hlk
Air Mail Special Delivery

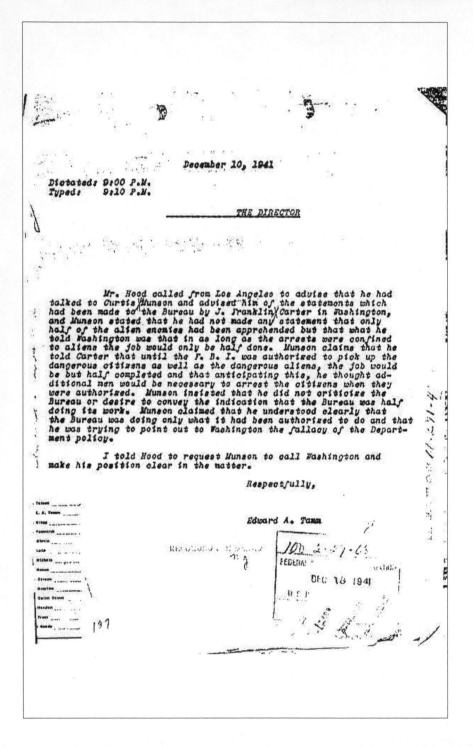

December 10, 1941

Dictated: 9:00 P.M.
Typed: 9:10 P.M.

THE DIRECTOR

Mr. Hood called from Los Angeles to advise that he had
talked to Curtis Munson and advised him of the statements which
had been made to the Bureau by J. Franklin Carter in Washington,
and Munson stated that he had not made any statement that only
half of the alien enemies had been apprehended but that what he
told Washington was that in as long as the arrests were confined
to aliens the job would only be half done. Munson claims that he
told Carter that until the F. B. I. was authorized to pick up the
dangerous citizens as well as the dangerous aliens, the job would
be but half completed and that anticipating this, he thought additional men would be necessary to arrest the citizens when they
were authorized. Munson insisted that he did not criticize the
Bureau or desire to convey the indication that the Bureau was half
doing its work. Munson claimed that he understood clearly that
the Bureau was doing only what it had been authorized to do and that
he was trying to point out to Washington the fallacy of the Department policy.

I told Hood to request Munson to call Washington and
make his position clear in the matter.

Respectfully,

Edward A. Tamm

Appendix D

The Kenji Ito Case

One day after Japan's attack on Pearl Harbor, federal prosecutors arrested Kenji Ito, a Seattle *Nisei*. Initially, Ito was charged with plotting to overthrow the U.S. government, according to the *Seattle Times*, but the charge was downgraded to twenty-five counts of failure to register as a foreign agent and one count for each pro-Japan speech Ito had made.[1]

On April 1, 1942, an all-white jury acquitted Ito on all counts. Later that year, Ito was sent to a relocation center.

The case against Ito faltered because prosecutors could not prove that Ito had engaged in his pro-Japan activities at the behest of the Japanese government.[2] What the jury did not know is that a May 11, 1941, top secret message sent from Japan's Seattle consulate to Tokyo said it was making use of a Seattle *Nisei* lawyer "for the collection of intelligences" on antiwar and anti-Jewish organizations.[3] Although the name of the lawyer was not stated, a MID memo written the same day the decrypt was translated indicated that the lawyer in question was Ito. This message—one of thousands of MAGIC messages surreptitiously intercepted and decrypted by American intelligence officials prior to Pearl Harbor—provides compelling evidence that Ito did in fact carry out his activities at Japan's urging. Had the jury members known about the message, they would have had a much stronger reason to find Ito guilty.

The federal prosecutors who tried the case against Ito did not have clearance for MAGIC. Even if they did, they could not have submitted the MAGIC message as evidence without allowing Ito to view it. For obvious reasons, this was not an option. Even if there were some way of keeping the evidence confidential—for example, a 1942 version of the Classified Information Protection Act—the court might have deemed the MAGIC message inadmissible on the ground that it was hearsay.

The May 11, 1941, MAGIC message explains why intelligence agencies regarded Ito with suspicion.[4] Allowing Ito and other suspected subversive citizens to remain at liberty on the West Coast posed a security threat that intelligence officers of the time considered a bona fide threat to national security.

In the debate over the War on Terror, it is sometimes argued that detaining an American citizen who has not been found guilty of a crime is never justified.[5] Johns Hopkins University law professor Ruth Wedgwood, commenting on the Jose Padilla case in the wake of the September 11 attacks, points out the implications of such reasoning:

Imagine if the intelligence dots had been replete and connected on September 10, 2001. What if we knew, from out-of-court sources, the names of [al] Qaeda operatives who were planning to hijack the jet-fueled airplanes for attacks on the World Trade Center and the Pentagon? Even then, we would likely have lacked admissible criminal proof. By the logic of [the December 2003 Court of Appeals decision requiring the release of Padilla], the president could not have held the hijackers as combatants— even after they had entered the United States, even with habeas corpus review of the president's decision, until the moment they appeared at Logan Airport with box cutters.[6]

Appendix E

The *Coram Nobis* Cases

I n the early 1980s, inextricably linked to the Japanese American reparations and redress movement, a legal team spearheaded by University of
California, San Diego, professor Peter Irons challenged the *Hirabayashi*,
Yasui, and *Korematsu* rulings of the World War II Supreme Court.[1] The
lawyers filed rarely-used petitions for writs of error or *coram nobis*, which
allow a person who has been tried, convicted, and served sentence to petition the courts when evidence can be presented that his or her conviction
was based on fundamental factual error.

Minoru Yasui, a *Nisei* graduate of the University of Oregon Law School
and a U.S. Army reserve officer, deliberately challenged the curfew order to
set up a test case for legality. Marching through the streets of Portland in
March 1942, he baited cops to arrest him. When no one did, he turned himself in at a police station. He was convicted of a curfew violation. Gordon
Hirabayashi, a *Nisei* college senior at the University of Washington, also
committed a conscious act of civil disobedience similar to Yasui's. He defied
a curfew order in Seattle in May 1942 and purposely failed to register at a
control center to prepare for departure to an assembly center. He was convicted on both counts. By contrast, Fred Korematsu was an Oakland-born
welder who surgically altered his appearance (he had eyelid surgery) and
changed his name to Clyde Sarah (which he used on a faked draft registra-

tion card) in an attempt to stay with his Caucasian girlfriend in the San Francisco Bay Area in violation of exclusion orders. He was convicted, sentenced to five years' probation, and sent to the Tanforan Assembly Center in San Bruno, California. The Supreme Court upheld all three convictions.

Irons *et al.* pinned their cases on dubious claims that the War Department had "altered and destroyed evidence and withheld knowledge of this evidence from the Department of Justice and the Supreme Court." Citing "smoking gun" documents discovered at the National Archives, the lawyers argued that "the military and the War and Justice Departments concealed and destroyed crucial evidence and deliberately misled the Supreme Court in 1944 when the *Korematsu* case was argued and the Court was assessing the military-necessity justification for the internment."[2]

In 1981, Commission on Wartime Relocation and Internment of Civilians researcher Aiko Herzig-Yoshinaga had discovered an initial draft of Western Defense Commander John DeWitt's final report on the West Coast evacuation at the National Archives. She passed it on to Irons, whose legal team seized on the report to argue that the decision to intern Japanese Americans was based on racial and cultural prejudice rather than military considerations. The first draft of DeWitt's final report did not reveal any facts that the government suppressed in the editing process. It did contain some overreaching, racially-based opinions that simply did not reflect the views of the United States. These were appropriately removed. The argument that the government committed "fraudulent concealment" when it edited (rather than released) the first draft of an official publication is ridiculous. During the *coram nobis* hearing for *Hirabayashi*, Hannah Zeidlik, chief of the historical records branch of the Army Center of Military History in Washington, testified that several versions of the early draft of the report had existed at one point and had been destroyed as standard operating procedure. Not all were destroyed, as Herzig-Yoshinaga discovered, which to Zeidlik demonstrated the opposite of concealment. If the War Department had meant to hide the fact that changes had been made to earlier versions, Zeidlik testified, why would it have retained an early copy— with corrections clearly marked on it? In fact, as the government noted, "dozens of documents memorializing the recall and amendment of the first printing [of the DeWitt report] were preserved. . . . Under the prevailing procedures during World War II, both the first and second printing draft and plates were destroyed and a certificate of destruction prepared. However, two copies of the first printing and two copies of the second printing were each carefully preserved and inventoried."[3]

Contrary to the Irons team's claims that allegedly exculpatory documents were intentionally destroyed, all the documents still exist. The draft document found by Herzig-Yoshinaga, melodramatically dubbed the "smoking gun of the redress issue," wasn't locked away in some government safe. It was, as Herzig-Yoshinaga herself recounted, lying around "on an archivist's desk."[4]

Irons's team attacked DeWitt's final report for disseminating factual errors, particularly with regard to illicit ship-to-shore signaling. The legal team further charged that the government knew the report contained false information. But remember this: At the time of the report's public release in 1944, while the war was still ongoing, DeWitt could not make reference to the most critical evidence in support of the West Coast evacuation, namely MAGIC intelligence. As former NSA official David Lowman noted, "DeWitt couldn't very well describe how we were reading Japanese government messages derived from broken Japanese codes and ciphers and what those messages had revealed about espionage by resident Japanese on the West Coast."[5] Neither could DeWitt reveal other supporting intelligence gathered by conventional means that was also highly classified.

Those who attack the final DeWitt report assume it was a smokescreen for racism, rather than the government's best effort to provide a plausible cover story for the West Coast evacuation without jeopardizing classified intelligence sources on which the decision rested. Critics, who diffidently dismiss the relevance of MAGIC to the West Coast evacuation decision, will undoubtedly dismiss such a possibility as absurd. But recall that there was precedent for the public release of an incomplete government report that omitted key information to protect vital U.S. code-breaking operations. As noted in Chapter 7, General George Marshall privately informed Republican presidential candidate Thomas Dewey that the Roberts report, released publicly after the Pearl Harbor attack, was necessarily incomplete because the inclusion of MAGIC would have compromised our greatest intelligence asset at the time.

Moreover, as the government pointed out in its closing argument in the *Hirabayashi coram nobis* case, the Justice Department had readily informed the Supreme Court in 1943 "that it was not declassifying all the confidential military information which went into the difficult policy decisions to issue" the West Coast regulations.[6]

Herzig-Yoshinaga, Irons, his legal team, and their academic acolytes make the fundamental error of overinflating DeWitt's role in the decision to evacuate the West Coast (see Chapter 7). Doing so allows them to bolster their claims that the policy was based on racism, rather than on the voluminous record of intelligence at the Roosevelt administration's disposal. Rather than acknowledge this extensive record, Irons's legal team further claimed that the government had "suppressed evidence relative to the loyalty of Japanese Americans and to the alleged commission by them of acts of espionage."[7] This charge focused primarily on the supposed attempt to conceal naval district-level ONI officer Ken Ringle's January 26, 1942, report on the "Japanese question" (see Appendix C) from the Court.

Some background: In preparation for the *Hirabayashi* case in the spring of 1943, the solicitor general of the Justice Department had dismissed a recommendation by Justice Department lawyer Edward Ennis (who had served as head of the Alien Enemy Control Unit) arguing that the Ringle document be included in the government's briefs defending the military necessity of the West Coast evacuation. Ennis had written in an April 1943 memo that Ringle's work "represent[ed] the view of the Office of the Naval Intelligence." This, however, was patently untrue. The cover memo accompanying Ringle's evaluation stated plainly that it did "not represent the final and official opinion" of ONI.[8] Ringle was very knowledgeable about ethnic Japanese, but he was a peripheral figure—one assistant district intelligence officer in one naval district among fifteen—who did not have access to MAGIC. Ennis likewise had no access to MAGIC and did not play a primary role in the decision to evacuate the West Coast.

In his memo to the solicitor general, Ennis insisted that the Ringle report had been concealed for fourteen months. Yet the cover memo for the report listed the Department of Justice Special Defense Unit, the FBI, MID, and Ennis's own Alien Enemy Control Unit as recipients of the report fourteen months earlier, before the evacuation decision was made.[9] As the government noted in its reply brief to the *Hirabayashi coram nobis* petition, the Ringle report "apparently made little or no impression upon [Ennis] or his office at the time."[10] (Interestingly, the Ennis memo to the solicitor general embraced by the modern opponents of evacuation actually endorsed as "reasonable" the detention of some 10,000 people, including *Kibei*, their parents, and "a known group of aliens and citizens who were active members of pro-Japanese societies such as the Japanese Navy League, the Military Virtue Society, etc."[11])

After leaving the government to work for JACL and the American Civil Liberties Union in 1946, Ennis never bothered to publicly protest or otherwise publicize the supposed suppression of the Ringle report and the alleged gross misconduct of the government until nearly four decades later. He had at least one high-profile opportunity immediately after the war to make the supposed injustice known. In 1949, University of Chicago professor Morton Grodzins published a seminal anti-evacuation account titled *Americans Betrayed: Politics and the Japanese Evacuation*.[12] Ennis was interviewed extensively for the book, and is singled out for thanks in Grodzins's preface. The book provides a detailed account of the political and legal wrangling over the West Coast evacuation and ends with a discussion of the Supreme Court cases, including *Hirabayashi*. There is no mention of Ennis's memo or the Justice Department's alleged "misconduct." In fact, during one of the *coram nobis* hearings in 1985, Ennis testified that "the whole matter had entirely left [his] memory" until it was brought to his attention by legal activists in 1981 or 1982.[13]

GETTING THEIR DAY IN COURT

Luckily for the petitioners, they drew the most sympathetic judges and venues for the *coram nobis* cases. (The government didn't help matters by capitulating at the *Korematsu* hearing and bungling on procedural matters at the *Hirabayashi* hearing.) Federal judge Marilyn Hall Patel heard the *Korematsu* petition in San Francisco. "We exploded with whoops of joy and hand-slapping," Peter Irons recounted when the case was assigned to Patel by random drawing. Patel, Irons exulted, was "one of the most liberal judges in the district.... [She] had been appointed by President Jimmy Carter in 1980. She had a background in immigration law and worked with the National Organization for Women and other progressive groups. If the choice had been ours, we would have picked Judge Patel."[14] She did not disappoint. In 1984, Judge Patel promptly granted *Korematsu's* petition for a writ of error and reversed his conviction.

The *Yasui* case was assigned to Judge Robert Belloni in Portland; the *Hirabayashi* case was assigned to liberal judge Donald Voorhees in Seattle; Yasui died in 1986; his conviction was vacated and the petition rendered moot by the Supreme Court. Voorhees ruled that Hirabayashi's conviction for violating the West Coast exclusion order should be vacated, but not his conviction for violating the temporary curfew. While he allowed some testimony on MAGIC and intelligence reports related to the decision, Voorhees refused much of the information that bolstered the military necessity arguments for evacuation because government lawyers had not laid the proper groundwork for its introduction.[15] An appeals court which made clear its sympathy for Hirabayashi during questioning vacated his curfew conviction in 1987 on the belief that the case record "constituted objective and irrefutable proof of the racial bias that was the cornerstone of the internment [*sic*] orders."[16]

While many have embraced the outcome of these cases as proof that the West Coast evacuation of ethnic Japanese was "illegal" and "unconstitutional," the *coram nobis* rulings did not affect the underlying constitutionality of President Roosevelt's executive order or the curfew and exclusion orders issued under its authority. More important, the lawsuits offer no convincing refutation of the real and substantial national security threat posed by ethnic Japanese on the West Coast, before and after the Pearl Harbor attack, as underscored by MAGIC and related intelligence, and amply documented in this book. Judges can judge history. But the slams of their gavels, welcomed with "whoops of joy" by score-settling plaintiffs, cannot remake the truth.

Appendix F

The Camps And Centers

ASSEMBLY CENTERS

Camp	State	Jurisdiction
Mayer	Arizona	Military
Fresno	California	Military
Marysville	California	Military
Merced	California	Military
Pinedale	California	Military
Pomona	California	Military
Sacramento	California	Military
Salinas	California	Military
Santa Anita	California	Military
Stockton	California	Military
Tanforan	California	Military
Tulare	California	Military
Turlock	California	Military
Portland	Oregon	Military
Puyallup	Washington	Military

RELOCATION CENTERS

Camp	State	Jurisdiction
Gila River	Arizona	Wartime Relocation Authority (WRA)
Poston	Arizona	WRA
Jerome	Arkansas	WRA
Rohwer	Arkansas	WRA
Manzanar	California	WRA
Tule Lake	California	WRA
Granada	Colorado	WRA
Minidoka	Idaho	WRA
Topaz	Utah	WRA
Heart Mountain	Wyoming	WRA

CITIZEN ISOLATION CAMPS

Camp	State	Jurisdiction
Leupp	Arizona	WRA
Moab	Utah	WRA

INTERNMENT/DETENTION CAMPS[1]

Camp	State/Territory/Country	Jurisdiction
Angel Island	California	Military
Sharp Park	California	Dept. of Justice
Tuna	California	Dept. of Justice
Tujunga	California	Dept. of Justice
Fort Logan	Colorado	Military
Pine Island	Cuba	Dept. of Justice
Fort Barrancas	Florida	Military

Camp	State/Territory/Country	Jurisdiction
Miami	Florida	Dept. of Justice
Fort Ogelthorpe	Georgia	Military
Fort Screven	Georgia	Military
Fort McPherson	Georgia	Military
Hawaii	Hawaii	Military
Honouliuli	Hawaii	Military
Kauai	Hawaii	Military
Lanai	Hawaii	Military
Maui	Hawaii	Military
Molokai	Hawaii	Military
Sand Island	Hawaii	Military
Kooskia	Idaho	Dept. of Justice
4800 Ellis Avenue	Illinois	Dept. of Justice
Home of Good Shepherd, Chicago	Illinois	Dept. of Justice
Jung Hotel, New Orleans	Louisiana	Dept. of Justice
East Boston	Massachusetts	Dept. of Justice
Fort Howard	Maryland	Military
Fort Meade	Maryland	Military
Detroit	Michigan	Dept. of Justice
Kansas City	Missouri	Dept. of Justice
Fort Missoula	Montana	Military
Grove Park Inn, Ashville	North Carolina	Dept. of Justice
Fort Lincoln, Bismarck	North Dakota	Military
Good Shepherd Convent, Omaha	Nebraska	Military
Gloucester City	New Jersey	Dept. of Justice
Fort Stanton	New Mexico	Military
Lordsburg	New Mexico	Dept. of Justice

Camp	State/Territory/Country	Jurisdiction
Santa Fe	New Mexico	Dept. of Justice
Camp Upton	New York	Military
Home of Good Shepherd, Buffalo	New York	Dept. of Justice
Ellis Island	New York	Dept. of Justice
Niagra Falls	New York	Dept. of Justice
Home of Good Shepherd, Cleveland	Ohio	Dept. of Justice
Hotel Gibson, Cincinnati	Ohio	Dept. of Justice
McAlester	Oklahoma	Military
Fort Sill	Oklahoma	Military
Stringtown	Oklahoma	Military
Portland	Oregon	Dept. of Justice
Home of Good Shepherd, Philadelphia	Pennsylvania	Dept. of Justice
San Juan	Puerto Rico	Military
Camp Forrest, Tullahoma	Tennessee	Military
Fort Sam Houston	Texas	Military
Fort Bliss	Texas	Military
Seagoville	Texas	Dept. of Justice
Kenedy	Texas	Dept. of Justice
Crystal City	Texas	Dept. of Justice
Laredo	Texas	Dept. of Justice
Salt Lake City	Utah	Dept. of Justice
Sullivan Lake, Metaline Falls	Washington	Military
Seattle	Washington	Dept. of Justice
Spokane County Jail	Washington	Dept. of Justice
Camp McCoy	Wisconsin	Military

Camp	State/Territory/Country	Jurisdiction
Home of Good Shepherd, Milwaukee	Wisconsin	Dept. of Justice
Milwaukee Barracks (County Jail)	Wisconsin	Dept. of Justice

STATE DEPARTMENT "INTERNMENT HOTELS"[2]

Hotel	State	Jurisdiction
Cascade Inn, Hot Springs	Virginia	Dept. of State
Greenbrier Hotel, White Sulpher Springs	West Virginia	Dept. of State
Ingleside Hotel, Staunton	Virginia	Dept. of State
Shenvalee Hotel, New Market	Virginia	Dept. of State
Bedford Springs Hotel, Bedford	Pennsylvania	Dept. of State
Grove Park Inn, Asheville	North Carolina	Dept. of State
Assembly Inn, Montreat	North Carolina	Dept. of State
Bel Air, Augusta	Georgia	Dept. of State
Belleview Biltmore, Clearwater	Georgia	Dept. of State

The Niihau Incident

Burl Burlingame AirChive/Allan Beekman Collection

Japanese Naval Airman 1st Class Shigenori Nishikaichi. After his plane was hit during the Pearl Harbor raid, the fighter pilot crash-landed on Niihau Island, where he received assistance from several ethnic Japanese. Naval intelligence officer C.B. Baldwin wrote that the facts of the case "indicate a strong possibility that other Japanese residents of the Territory of Hawaii, and Americans of Japanese descent...may give valuable aid to Japanese invaders in cases where the tide of battle is in favor of Japan and where it appears to residents that control of the district may shift from the United States to Japan."

Yoshio Harada, an American citizen, was one of three ethnic Japanese Niihau residents (the island's entire adult ethnic Japanese population) who sided with Nishikaichi.

Ishimatsu Shintani, a permanent resident alien *(Issei)*, tried to persuade Hawila "Howard" Kaleohano to return Nishikaichi's papers. Several postwar historians have stated that most Hawaiian *Issei* remained loyal to Japan even after Pearl Harbor.

Nishikaichi's Zero fighter plane. Before this picture was taken, Nishikaichi and Harada set the plane's cockpit on fire.

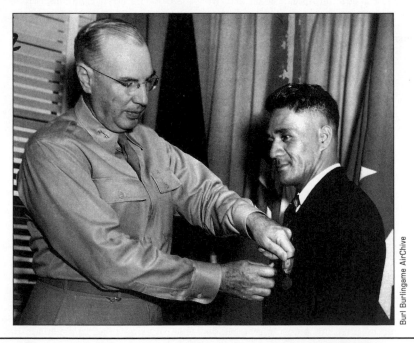

Hawila "Howard" Kaleohano, the first to reach Nishikaichi's crashed plane, seized Nishikaichi's papers and refused to return them. For his actions, Kaleohano received the Medal of Freedom and $800 from the army.

Burl Burlingame AirChive

Ben Kanahele, who disarmed Nishikaichi and killed him, received the Purple Heart and Medal of Merit.

The Honolulu Spy Ring

Ensign Takeo Yoshikawa of the Imperial Japanese Navy led the Honolulu espionage team that provided Japan with intelligence on the U.S. fleet. This information was instrumental in the design of the Pearl Harbor attack.

Federal Bureau of Investigation

Richard Kotoshirodo, a *Nisei*, assisted Yoshikawa in gathering intelligence. Despite the conclusion of a hearing board in Hawaii that Kotoshirodo was a willing collaborator, he was not charged with a crime. Instead, he and his wife were interned in Hawaii, then sent to relocation centers in Topaz, Utah, and Tule Lake, California.

Key U.S. Decisionmakers

President Franklin D. Roosevelt, an avid reader of MAGIC cables and summaries, signed Executive Order 9066, which led to the evacuation and relocation of ethnic Japanese from the West Coast.

Republican Henry L. Stimson,
Roosevelt's eminent Secretary of War, worried about
Japanese raids on the West
Coast and the possibility of
cooperation by ethnic Japanese. The president vigor-
ously instructed Stimson
"to go ahead on the line that
[he] thought the best."

Republican John McCloy, Assistant Secretary of War, was a pivotal figure in the decision to evacuate. He read MAGIC messages every day and night, and later told Congress that MAGIC was a "very important" factor in the development of the evacuation policy.

Lieut. Gen. John DeWitt, U.S. Army, was commander of the Western Defense
Command. Most historians portray DeWitt as the primary instigator of the
West Coast evacuation. In truth, the push came from the top—where knowledge
of the MAGIC intelligence rested.

National Archives

Attorney General Francis Biddle was the highest-ranking opponent of evacuation. He was not privy to MAGIC, although he sometimes received "sanitized" summaries that attributed the information to a "highly reliable source."

National Archives

FBI Director J. Edgar Hoover opposed evacuation of ethnic Japanese from the entire West Coast, but several of his field offices supported large-scale evacuation from major cities. Hoover wanted the authority to detain suspected subversives without having to prove guilt of a crime. Like Biddle, he was not privy to MAGIC.

U.S. Intelligence

Some of the U.S. Army Signal Intelligence Service team members who broke the PURPLE code and built the first PURPLE analog machine. Left to right: Frank Bearce, Dr. Solomon Kullback, Capt. Harrod Miller, Louise Nelson, William Friedman, Dr. Abraham Sinkov, Lt. L.D. Jones, Frank Rowlett.

The Army's first PURPLE analog machine, used to decrypt secret Japanese diplomatic messages, on display at the National Cryptologic Museum in Ft. Meade, Maryland. The code-breaking operation, dubbed MAGIC, is believed by many to be the greatest feat in cryptologic history.

Capt. Kenneth D. Ringle. Ringle was knowledgeable about ethnic Japanese, but he was not a high-ranking official and did not have access to MAGIC. His opposition to mass evacuation of ethnic Japanese is often cited, but his support for military tribunals and racial profiling has been ignored.

Life in the Camps

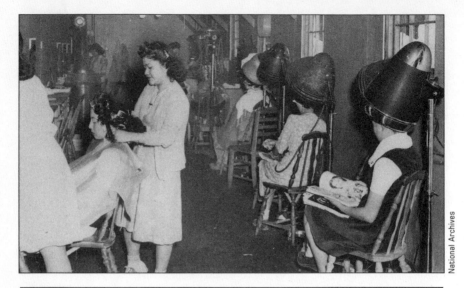

A beauty parlor at the Tule Lake camp.

Two Gila River camp residents carrying the JACL banner in a Thanksgiving Day parade. At the time, JACL vigorously supported the evacuation policy.

Gila River kindergarten class.

Landscaping done by camp residents at Poston.

National Archives

High school senior party at Tule Lake. The man to the left is the high school principal.

Arthur Jacobs/www.foitimes.com

The Crystal City internment camp band included both Japanese and German internees. The Civil Liberties Act of 1988 provided reparations to Japanese internees but not Germans.

January 26, 1945: Members of the Hokoku Seinen Dan gather at Tule Lake
Segregation Center to give *banzai* send-off to 171 members of their pro-
Japan group being sent to a Department of Justice interment camp in Santa
Fe, New Mexico.

February 11, 1945: Members of the Hokoku at Tule Lake give a *banzai* send-
off to 650 members of their group being sent to a Department of Justice
interment camp in Bismarck, South Dakota.

March 4, 1945: The Bugle Corps of the Hokoku at Tule Lake gives a send-off to 125 of their members being sent to a DOJ interment camp in Santa Fe, New Mexico.

Contraband concealed weapons at Tule Lake.

A Note on Research
and Sources

Most of the primary documents cited herein were located at the National Archives in College Park, Maryland. Others were obtained from the National Archives Records Administration in Seattle; the Bancroft Library at the University of California at Berkeley; and the Library of Congress in Washington, D.C. I refer to documents included in the Numerical File Archive of the Commission on Wartime Relocation and Internment of Civilians ("CWRIC papers") by their Numerical File Number, when available. I refer to MAGIC cables using both the number that appeared in the original message sent by Japanese diplomats as well as the number later assigned by the Department of Defense.

A treasure trove of government and military documents, transcripts of oral histories, and legal documents are readily available to the lay researcher on the Internet. Citations herein include website addresses for primary and secondary documents whenever possible. Among the many valuable sites that I utilized were the U.S. Army Center of Military History's online bookshelves at www.army.mil/cmh-pg/online/Bookshelves/WW2-AT.htm, which contain the full, annotated report on the U.S. Army in World War II by Army historian Stetson Conn; the Pearl Harbor archive maintained by www.ibiblio.org, which includes documents and intelligence reports from the congressional hearings investigating the attack; and the National Park Service's online book section, www.cr.nps.gov/history/online_books/anthropology74/index.htm, which includes the out-of-print report, "Confinement and Ethnicity: An Overview of World War II Japanese American Relocation Sites."

In addition, the Internet allowed me to obtain with great efficiency many rare and out-of-print books—including the memoirs of Francis Biddle, Henry Stimson, Milton Eisenhower, Edward Layton, Dillon Myer, and Frank Rowlett—through a variety of online booksellers. I purchased the complete eight-volume set of The "Magic" Background of Pearl Harbor from a seller on Amazon.com's Marketplace.

A selected bibliography with Internet links will be available on my website, www.michellemalkin.com. Finally, in any undertaking of this nature, factual errors are inevitable. I take full responsibility for any and all errors, and will be maintaining an errata list on my website as well.

Note to the Reader

1.　50 USC 21-24.
2.　Mitchel Yockelson, "The War Department: Keeper of Our Nation's Enemy Aliens During World War I," presentation to the Society for Military History Annual Meeting, April 1998, http://www.lib.byu.edu/~rdh/wwi/comment/yockel.htm (accessed March 21, 2004).
3.　See Chapter 6.

Introduction: A Time to Discriminate

1.　Recently published titles focusing on the "debate" over civil liberties and national security include: The War on Our Freedoms: Civil Liberties in an Age of Terrorism; The War on the Bill of Rights and the Gathering Resistance; Terrorism and Tyranny: Trampling Freedom, Justice and Peace to Rid the World of Evil; Enemy Aliens: Double Standards and Constitutional Freedoms in the War on Terrorism; Lost Liberties: Ashcroft and the Assault on Personal Freedom; Terrorism and the Constitution: Sacrificing Civil Liberties in the Name of National Security. As you can see, there's not really much of a debate.
2.　Arnold Krammer, Undue Process: The Untold Story of America's German Alien Internees (London: Rowman & Littlefield Publishers Inc., 1997); John Christgau,

Enemies: World War II Alien Internment (San Jose, CA: Authors Choice Press, 1985); Lawrence DiStasi, ed., *Una Storia Segreta: The Secret History of Italian American Evacuation and Internment during World War II* (Berkeley, CA: Heydey Books, 2001).

3. Ibid.

4. Krammer, *Undue Process,* 68; Lawrence DiStasi, "A Tale of Two Citizens," in DiStasi, ed., *Una Storia Segreta,* 139.

5. William H. Rehnquist, *All the Laws But One: Civil Liberties in Wartime* (NY: Vintage Books, 1998).

6. Lowell Ponte, "FDR and Manzanar," Frontpagemagazine.com, Jan. 4, 2002, http://www.frontpagemag.com/Articles/ReadArticle.asp?ID=4030 (accessed Jan. 31, 2004).

7. Japanese American Citizens League Bulletin #142, April 7, 1942, http://www.pbs.org/itvs/conscience/compliance/better_americans/08_bulletin01_i.html (accessed Feb. 1, 2004). In testimony before Congress in 1984, Masaoka, who became an advocate for reparations and redress for West Coast evacuees, disavowed this position.

8. A relatively small number of third-generation Japanese Americans, called *Sansei*, were also evacuated.

9. Dorothy Swaine Thomas and Richard S. Nishimoto, *The Spoilage* (Berkeley, CA: University of California Press, 1946).

10. The Commission on Wartime Relocation and Internment of Civilians (CWRIC), *Personal Justice Denied* (Washington, DC: The Civil Liberties Public Education Fund and the University of Washington Press, 1997), xiii. The same report states, "The promulgation of Executive Order 9066 was not justified by military necessity, and the decisions which followed from it—detention, ending detention and ending exclusion—were not driven by analysis of military conditions. The broad historical causes which shaped these decisions were race prejudice, war hysteria and a failure of political leadership." See ibid.,18.

11. Japanese American Citizens League, "A Lesson in American History: The Japanese American Experience," Curriculum and Resource Guide, (4th ed. San Francisco: JACL, 2002), 5.

12. U.S. House of Representatives, *Congressional Record*, Vol. 150, No. 26 (March 3, 2003), H778-H784. The resolution, H.R. 56, passed unanimously by a vote of 404–0 on March 4, 2004.

13. Jasmine Kripalani, "Reno criticizes White House over Muslim policies," *Miami Herald*, sec. B1, Sept. 14, 2003.

14. See, generally, Herbert Romerstein and Eric Breindel, *The Venona Secrets: Exposing Soviet Espionage and America's Traitors* (Washington, DC: Regnery, 2001).

15. See Chapter 4 and Appendix C.

16. Burl Burlingame, *Advance Force-Pearl Harbor* (Annapolis, MD: United States Naval Institute, 2002). For more details, see Chapter 2.

17. William. H. Rehnquist, *All the Laws but One*, 208–9.

18. David D. Lowman, *MAGIC: The Untold Story of U.S. Intelligence and the Evacuation of Japanese Residents From the West Coast During WW II* (Provo, UT: Athena Press Inc., 2000), 3.

19. Associated Press, "N.C. Congressman says internment of Japanese-Americans during World War II was appropriate," Feb. 5, 2003.

20. Associated Press, "Democratic chairman calls for Coble to resign chairmanship," Feb. 28, 2003.

21. In testimony before the House Select Committee Investigating National Defense Migration on February 23, 1942, http://www.javoice.com/masaoka.html (accessed March 17, 2004). Masaoka had the following exchange with Rep. John J. Sparkman (R-Ala.):

> REP. SPARKMAN: But in the event the evacuation is deemed necessary by those having charge of the defenses, as loyal Americans you are willing to prove your loyalty by cooperating?
>
> MR. MASAOKA: Yes. I think it should be...
>
> REP. SPARKMAN (interposing): Even at a sacrifice?
>
> MR. MASAOKA: Oh, yes; definitely. I think that all of us are called upon to make sacrifices. I think that we will be called upon to make greater sacrifices than any others. But I think sincerely, if the military say "Move Out," we will be glad to move, because we recognize that even behind evacuation there is not just national security but also a thought as to our own welfare and security because we may be subject to mob violence and otherwise if we are permitted to remain.

22. Associated Press, "N.C. Rep.: WWII Internment Camps Were Meant to Help," Feb. 5, 2003, http://www.foxnews.com/story/0,2933,77677,00.html (accessed March 17, 2004).

23. B.J. Reyes, "House committee approves resolution on congressman's remarks," Associated Press, Feb. 20, 2003.

24. Ben Pershing, "Asian-American Members Unhappy With Coble Letter," *Roll Call*, Feb. 13, 2003.

25. Matt Continetti, "Commission Inquisition," *National Review Online*, July 25, 2002, http://www.nationalreview.com/comment/comment-continetti072502.asp (accessed March 17, 2004).

26. Ibid.

27. See, for example, David Cole, *Enemy Aliens: Double Standards and Constitutional Freedoms in the War on Terrorism* (NY: The New Press, 2003), for a contrary take.

28. Andrew Chow, "Lawyers Decry Reference to Korematsu Case; Landmark APA Legal Team Demands Commissioner's Ouster," *Asian Week*, Aug. 9, 2002, http://www.asianweek.com/2002_08_09/news_korematsu.html (accessed March 14, 2004).

29 Devon Alisa Abdallah, "Arab Community Pack Your Bags: Civil Rights Commissioner Doesn't Believe in Civil Rights," *International Examiner*, Aug. 20, 2002, 4.

30. Letter to President Bush from the Leadership Conference on Civil Rights, July 22, 2002, http://www.civilrights.org/issues/enforcement/details.cfm?id=9682 (accessed March 14, 2004).

31. Lynette Clemetson, "Traces of Terror: Arab-Americans; Civil Rights Commissioner Under fire for Comments on Arabs," *New York Times*, sec. A14, July 23, 2002.

32. "Bush Nominee Refuses to Condemn Japanese Internment: Daniel Pipes Says He Does Not 'Know Enough' About Subject to Comment," Council on American-Islamic Relations, April 21, 2003 press release, http://www.commondreams.org/news2003/ 0421-06.htm (accessed Jan. 31, 2004).

33. William Glaberson, "War on Terrorism Stirs Memory of Internment," *New York Times*, sec. A18, Sept. 24, 2001.

34. Phuong Ly and Petula Dvorak, "Travels and Travails: Japanese Americans Recall '40s Bias, Understand Arab Counterparts' Fear," *Washington Post*, sec. B1, Sept. 20, 2001.

35. Florangela Davila, "Japanese Americans know how it feels to be 'the enemy,'" *Seattle Times*, sec. A1, Oct. 3, 2001.

36. Martha Groves and Erika Hayasaki, "Reaction Reopens Wounds of WWII for Japanese Americans; Prejudice: Citing internment camps, civil rights groups plan a candlelight vigil in support of Muslims and Arab Americans," *Los Angeles Times*, Part II, 6, Sept. 26, 2001.

37. Irene Hirano, Statement from the Japanese American National Museum, Sept. 27, 2001.

38. Rita M. Gerona-Admins, "Asian Pacific Americans Display Support for Arab, Sikh Americans: Praise Bush, Others for Denouncing Profiling, Hate Crimes," *Asian Fortune*, Oct. 2001.

39. CNN, *Mornings with Paula Zahn*, Nov. 16, 2001, Transcript #111609CN.V74.

40. Jeet Thayil, "Discrimination suit against Continental Airlines approved ," *India Abroad*, Nov. 1, 2002, 8.

41. MSNBC News, "Questions and Answers: The Legacy of Internment Camps," Oct. 17, 2001, http://www.msnbc.com/news/644274.asp?cp1=1 (accessed Jan. 31, 2004).

42. Steve Croft, "That dirty little word 'profiling'; Pros and cons of profiling Arab-American men at airports after the September 11th attacks," *60 Minutes*, CBS, Dec. 2, 2001.

43. Mohammed Atta reportedly was fluent in English, but fellow hijacker Hani Hanjour had poor English skills, as did Ziad Jarrah, the hijacker who reportedly took the controls of Flight 93. All four of the Flight 93 hijackers reportedly spoke with accents.

44. *Capital Gang*, CNN, Sept. 15, 2001,Transcript #091500CN.V40.

45. Page Smith, *Democracy on Trial* (NY: Simon & Schuster, 1995), 15.

46. Deborah Ramirez, a leading scholar on racial profiling and a consultant to the U.S. Department of Justice, defines racial profiling broadly as "the inappropriate use of race, ethnicity, or national origin, rather than behavior or individualized suspicion, to focus on an individual for additional investigation. This quote is from Margaret Chon and Eric K. Yamamoto, "Resurrecting Korematsu: Post-September 11th National Security Curtailment of Civil Liberties," in *Race, Rights, and Reparation*, Eric Yamamoto et al., eds. (NY: Aspen Publishers, 2001), http://www1.law.ucla.edu/~kang/racerightsreparation/Update__Ch__8/chon_yamamoto_race_rights_ch8.pdf (accessed Feb. 2, 2004).

47. David Reinhard, "Far more to fear than hurt feelings," *Oregonian*, sec. B9, Oct. 4, 2001.

48. Katherine Stapp, "Muslims still being deported despite rules change," Inter Press Service, Dec. 17, 2003.

49. Mark Engler and Saurav Sarkar, "Ashcroft's roundup," *The Progressive*, March 2003, 24.

50. Annie Nakao, "Haunting echoes of Japanese internment," *San Francisco Chronicle*, sec. D8, Feb. 18, 2003.

51. Ibid.

52. U.S. Department of Justice Office of the Inspector General, "The September 11 Detainees: A Review of the Treatment of Aliens Held on Immigration Charges in Connection with the Investigation of the September 11 Attacks," June 2003, http://www.usdoj.gov/oig/special/03-06/index.htm (accessed Feb. 2, 2004).

53. USA Patriot Act, Public Law 107-56, Sec. 412.

54. Aldrin Brown, "Deportation plan causes an outcry: O.C. activists say racial profiling is at the heart of an attempt to round up Mideast and Islamic immigrants," *Orange County Register,* Feb. 9, 2002.

55. Sandra Marquez, "FBI interrogations of Iraqi immigrants stirs unease," Associated Press, March 22, 2003.

56. Susan M. Akram and Kevin R. Johnson., "Race, Civil Rights, and Immigration Law After September 11, 2001: The Targeting of Arabs and Muslims," 58 *New York University Annual Survey of American Law* 295, 2002.

57. David Cole, "Enemy Aliens," 54 *Stanford Law Review* 953, 2002.

58. Palm Beach Post, "End Ashcroft's Excesses," sec, A18, June 5, 2003.

59. Michelle Malkin, *Invasion: How America Still Welcomes Terrorists Criminals & Other Foreign Menaces to Our Shores* (Washington, DC: Regnery, 2002).

60. And, for what it's worth, perfectly legal. In 1979, the U.S. Court of Appeals for the District of Columbia in *Narenji v. Civiletti* upheld against constitutional challenge a Federal regulation imposing special registration requirements solely on Iranian students in the U.S. in the wake of the hostage crisis in Iran. The U.S. Supreme Court declined to hear an appeal.

61. *The O'Reilly Factor*, FOX News Channel, Sept. 30, 2003, Transcript # 093005cb.256.

62. Mary Beth Sheridan and Douglas Farah, "Jailed Muslim Had Made a Name in Washington: Alamoudi Won Respect as a Moderate Advocate," *Washington Post*, sec. A1, Dec. 1, 2003.

63. Kate O'Beirne, "The Chaplain Problem: What gives with imams (and others) in the military?" *National Review* (Oct. 27, 2003).

64. Daniel Pipes, "Counting Mosques," *New York Post,* Feb. 4, 2003, http://www.danielpipes.org/article/1018 (accessed Feb. 4, 2004).

65. U.S. Newswire, "CAIR: FBI Urged to Rescind Mosque Tally Policy; Counting Mosques to Set Goals for Investigations Called 'Profiling,'" Jan. 27, 2003.

66. Heather Mac Donald, "The Hunt for Terrorists Runs Up Against Political Correctness," *New York Sun*, Nov. 5, 2002, http://www.manhattan-institute.org/html/_nysun-the_hunt.htm. See also, generally, http://www.manhattan-institute.org/html/ mac_donald.htm (accessed March 25, 2004).

67. Federal News Service, "Panel One of a Hearing of The Senate Judiciary Committee: Oversight on Counterterrorism," June 6, 2002.

68. Eric Lichtblau and Josh Meyer, "Response to Terror; Missed Memo Stirs More Trouble at FBI," *Los Angeles Times*, sec. A1, May 25, 2002.

69. Ibid.

70. David Johnston and Don Van Natta Jr., "Wary of Risk, Slow to Adapt, F.B.I. Stumbles in Terror War," *New York Times*, sec. A1, June 2, 2002.

71. Maureen Dowd, "Dump Dem Bums," *New York Times*, sec. A19, June 2, 2002.

72. Nicholas D. Kristof, "Liberal Reality Check," *New York Times*, sec. A23, May 31, 2002.

73. Richard Posner, *Breaking the Deadlock: The 2000 Election, the Constitution, and the Courts* (Princeton, NJ: Princeton University Press, 2001).

74. Interestingly, liberal Supreme Court Justice William O. Douglas defended the wartime *Korematsu* and *Hirabayashi* rulings (which upheld the constitutionality of curfew and relocation measures) in a case challenging race-based affirmative action policies at the University of Washington Law School. In *DeFunis v. Odegaard*, Douglas contrasted the questionable use of systematic racial preferences in college admissions with the wartime classifications upheld in *Korematsu* and *Hirabayashi*:

> "Those cases involved an exercise of the war power, a great leveler of other rights. Our Navy was sunk at Pearl Harbor and no one knew where the Japanese fleet was. We were advised on oral argument that if the Japanese landed troops on our west coast nothing could stop them west of the Rockies. The military judgment was that, to aid in the prospective defense of the west coast, the enclaves of Americans of Japanese ancestry should be moved inland, lest the invaders by donning civilian clothes would wreak even more serious havoc on our western ports. The decisions were extreme and went to the verge of wartime power; and they have been severely criticized. It is, however, easy in retrospect to denounce what was done, as there actually was no attempted Japanese invasion of our country. While our Joint Chiefs of Staff were worrying about Japanese soldiers landing on the west coast, they actually were landing in Burma and at Kota Bharu in Malaya. But those making plans for defense of the Nation had no such knowledge and were planning for the worst." See footnote 20 in *DeFunis v. Odegaard*, 416 US 312, 343 (1974).

75. Peter S. Canellos, "Japanese internees see modern parallels," *Boston Globe*, sec. A1, Nov. 2, 2003.

76. Jonathan Turley, "60 Years On, Again Battling an Abomination of Power," *Los Angeles Times,* Part II, 11, Nov. 17, 2003.

77. Nikkei for Civil Rights and Redress, "An NCRR Statement: Remembering August 10, 1988," http://www.ncrr-la.org/news/9_7_02/8.html (accessed March 14, 2004).

78. Steve Lash, "Supreme Court takes on first anti-terrorism case," Cox News Service, Nov. 10, 2003.

79. Following is a partial listing of Muslims convicted of terrorism-related crimes in the U.S. since September 11, 2001: shoe bomber Richard Reid; Taliban soldier John Walker Lindh; Abdel-Ilah Elmardoudi; Karim Koubriti; Enaam Arnaout; James Ujaama; Yahya Goba, Shafal Mosed, Yasein Taher, Taysal Galab, Mukhtar al-Bakri and Sahim Alwan of Lackawanna, New York; Jeffrey Battle, Patrice Ford, Ahmed Bilal, Muhammad Bilal, and October Lewis of Portland, Oregon; and Masoud Ahmad Khan, Seifullah Chapman, and Hammad Abdur-Raheem from the Washington, DC metropolitan area.

80. In addition to Hamdi and Padilla, suspected al Qaeda operative Ali Saleh Kahlah al-Marri, a Qatar native, was designated an enemy combatant in June 2003.

81. See Government's Post-Hearing Brief, U.S. District Court for the Western District of Washington, *Hirabayashi v. United States,* Sept. 5, 1985, cited in Peter Irons, ed., *Justice Delayed: The Record of the Japanese Internment Cases* (Middletown, CT: Wesleyan University Press, 1989), 326.

82. T. B. Maucaulay, *Critical, Historical, and Miscellaneous Essays and Poems* (Boston: Estes and Lauriat, 1880).

83. Japanese American Citizens League National Education Committee, "A Lesson in History: The Japanese American Experience," 2002, 74.

84. "Transformation and Learning; Gayleen Fujimura's The United States & WWII in the Pacific Resource Page," http://www.k12.hi.us/~gfujimur/gft3/curriculum_res/ us&ww2.htm (accessed March 12, 2004).

85. "World War II Experience In Hawai'i," http://www.nuuanu.k12.hi.us/nuuanuweb/ harbors/litolpt.html (accessed March 12, 2004).

86. Judy Woo and Jolynn Asato, "Citizenship Denied: An Integrated Unit on the Japanese American Internment," http://www.csupomona.edu/~tassi/intern.htm (accessed March 12, 2004).

87. Memorandum prepared by Messrs. Cohen, Cox and Rauh, "The Japanese Situation on the West Coast," Feb. 10, 1942, DOJ 146-13-7-2-0 (in CWRIC papers, 12682–89).

CHAPTER 1: THE TURNCOATS ON NIIHAU ISLAND

1. Unless otherwise noted, all material in this chapter is derived from Allan Beekman, *The Niihau Incident* (Honolulu: Heritage Press of Pacific, 1982); Lt. Jack Mizuha, "Report of Events Since Sunday, December 7, 1941 on Niihau," and C.B. Baldwin, "Crash of Enemy Plane on Niihau," Dec. 16, 1941. The reports by Mizuha and Baldwin were published in the U.S. Congressional Joint Committee on Pearl Harbor Attack Hearings: Pt. 24, Proceedings of the Roberts Commission, pp. 1448–53. For another account, see Burl Burlingame, "The One-Week War of Niihau Island," *Honolulu Star-Bulletin & Advertiser*, four-part series Dec. 7–10, 1986.

2. Herbert A. Holbrook, "The Niihau Island Incident," July 2001, http://www.pac-shiprev.com/PacificArchivesSubDirectory/page21.html (accessed Jan. 8, 2004). This article was first published in the Pacific Ship and Shore Historical Society Newsletter of March 1996.

3. Burlingame, "The Final Confrontation on Niihau," *Honolulu Star-Bulletin & Advertiser*, sec. C7, Dec. 10, 1986.

4. U.S. Naval Intelligence Service, Source File No: 14 ND, ONI File No #1798. Jan. 26, 1942.

5. Ibid.

6. John J. Stephan, *Hawaii Under the Rising Sun: Japan's Plans for Conquest After Pearl Harbor* (Honolulu: University of Hawaii Press, 1984), 85.

CHAPTER 2: THE THREAT OF THE RISING SUN

1. Address of President Franklin Roosevelt on the Conduct of the War, Feb. 23, 1942, http://www.multied.com/documents/FDRSTwenteenthFireside.html (accessed Jan. 8, 2004).

2. Ibid.

3. James Anderson, "Japanese Fired on California," *Tulsa World Newspaper*, Feb. 23, 1992.

4. James Anderson, "1942 Shelling of California Coastline Stirred Conspiracy Fears," *Los Angeles Times*, sec. B5, March 1, 1992.

5. Sally Cappon, "If These Timbers Could Speak . . ." *South Coast Beacon,* undated, http://scbeacon.com/beacon_issues/03_02_20/timber_tale.html (accessed Jan. 8, 2004).

6. Justin M. Ruhge, "50th Anniversary of the Shelling of the Ellwood Oil Fields,"
    Goleta Historical Notes (Goleta, CA: Goleta Valley Historical Society, Fall 1992),
    15.

7. Burl Burlingame, *Advance Force-Pearl Harbor* (Annapolis, MD: United States
    Naval Institute, 2002).

8. Stephan, *Hawaii Under the Rising Sun,* 125.

9. Gordon William Prange with Donald M. Goldstein and Katherine V. Dillon, *At
    Dawn We Slept: The Untold Story of Pearl Harbor* (NY: Penguin Books, 2001), 561.

10. It is believed that the "enemy planes" were actually anti-aircraft shell bursts or
    meteorological balloons. See California State Military Museum, "The Battle of Los
    Angeles," http://www.militarymuseum.org/BattleofLA.html (accessed Jan. 8,
    2004).

11. Burlingame, *Advance Force – Pearl Harbor*, 175-177.

12. Ibid., 293–303.

13. Ibid., 328–329.

14. Ibid., 329–330.

15. Burlingame, *Advance Force – Pearl Harbor.* See also The California State Military
    Museum, "California and the Second World War," http://www.militarymu-
    seum.org/ HistoryWWII.html (accessed Jan. 8, 2004).

16. Ibid.

17. Ibid.

18. Ibid.

19. Popular movies about German U-boats include *Das Boot* (1981) and *U-571*
    (2000).

20. Milton Eisenhower wrote in his autobiography that the historian Stetson Conn
    "reports that there had been no Japanese submarine attacks or surface vessels any-
    where near the West Coast during the preceding months"(p. 103), referring to
    the time period prior to January 1941. In fact, Conn said there had been no Japan-
    ese submarine attacks during the preceding *month,* meaning the month between
    late December and late January. See Milton Eisenhower, *The President Is Calling*
    (Garden City, NY: Doubleday, 1974) and Stetson Conn, "The Decision to Evacu-
    ate the Japanese from the Pacific Coast" in *Guarding the United States and Its Out-
    posts* (Washington, DC: U.S. Army Center of History), http://www.army.mil/
    cmh/books/wwii/guard-us/ch5.htm (accessed March 12, 2004).

21. Thurston Clarke, *Pearl Harbor Ghosts: The Legacy of December 7, 1941* (NY: Bal-
    lantine Books, 2001), 65-67.

22. Ibid., 109.

23. Henry L. Stimson and McGeorge Bundy, *On Active Service in Peace and War* (NY: Harper & Brothers, 1947), 406. These words were written by Bundy, who attempted to capture Stimson's views as accurately as possible.

24. Stephan, *Hawaii Under the Rising Sun,* 104-5. Stephan states that other Japanese officers were unenthusiastic about Yamaguchi's plan.

25. Ibid., 128.

26. Ladislas Farago, *The Broken Seal: The Story of "Operation Magic" and the Pearl Harbor Disaster* (NY: Random House, 1962), 93.

27. Walter Lippmann, "The Fifth Column on the Coast," Feb. 13, 1942, http://www.cr.nps.gov/nr/twhp/wwwlps/lessons/89manzanar/89facts1.htm (accessed Jan. 8, 2004).

28. Arnold Krammer, *Undue Process,* 3.

29. Ibid.

30. Philip Snow, *The Fall of Hong Kong: Britain, China, and the Japanese Occupation* (Hartford, CT: Yale University Press, 2003), 36.

31. Ibid.

32. Ibid., 37.

33. Carlos Romulo, *I Saw the Fall of the Philippines* (Garden City, NY: Doubleday, Doran, 1943), 34.

34. Ibid.

35. Tony Matthews, *Shadows Dancing: Japanese Espionage Against the West, 1939–1945* (NY: St. Martin's Press, 1993), 28.

36. Matthews, *Shadows Dancing,* 46–47.

37. Stephan, *Hawaii Under the Rising Sun,* 151.

38. Eric Robertson, *The Japanese File: Pre-war Japanese Penetration in Southeast Asia* (Hong Kong: Heineman Asia, 1979), 68. According to Robertson, "The bulk of the Japanese estates were grouped astride strategic roads in Johore, on the landward approaches to Singapore. There was a group of big estates located in an arc round Batu Pahat, a west coast port at which the Japanese army made one of its most important and successful outflanking attacks in the invasion of Malaya. These plantations bordered the coast road between Malacca and Singapore and the roads connecting this road with the main road further east, running down the centre of the developed part of Johore. Three other big estates commanded the important inland route in the region of Kulai, only twenty miles from the Straits of Johore between the Malay mainland and Singapore. There were other large estates in the Kota Tinggi district, covering the eastern sea approaches to Singa-

pore and the naval base as well as a few smaller estates bordered important roads and railways in Negri Sembilan." Furthermore, "survey work essential on any well-managed rubber estate provided extremely detailed maps of localities which eventually became the scene of major military operations. There is reason to believe that the survey work undertaken by the technical staff of these estates was not carried out only within their boundaries." Japanese government officials routinely visited the plantations, and such visits "provided a perfect channel for safe hand delivery of maps and reports."

39. Ibid.

40. Stephan, *Hawaii Under the Rising Sun,* 150.

41. Frances B. Cogan, *Captured: The Japanese Internment of American Civilians in the Philippines, 1941–1945* (Athens, GA: University of Georgia Press, 2000), 23

42. See, e.g., MID, "Tentative Lessons from the Recent Active Campaign in Europe," Bulletin No. 6, June 29, 1940.

CHAPTER 3: SYMPATHIZERS AND SUBVERSIVES

1. Quoted in "Patton Formulated Plan to Take Japanese Hostages in Hawaii," Associated Press, Feb. 28, 1984.

2. Page Smith, *Democracy on Trial: The Japanese American Evacuation and Relocation in World War II* (NY: Simon & Schuster, 1995), 78.

3. MID, "Japanese Ex-Servicemen's Organization," Oct. 14, 1941. This memo is reproduced in Lowman, *MAGIC,* 337.

4. Page Smith, *Democracy on Trial,* 78-9.

5. Federal Bureau of Investigation Files 51287 and 51288. The reference letters are contained in the Los Angeles Field Division's File #100-8075.

6. Ibid.

7. Ibid.

8. ONI, "Japanese Intelligence and Propaganda in the United States During 1941," Dec. 4, 1941. See Appendix C.

9. Page Smith, *Democracy on Trial,* 79.

10. ONI, "Japanese Intelligence and Propaganda in the United States During 1941."

11. Ibid.

12. Stephan, *Hawaii under the Rising Sun*, 30.

13. Ibid., 34.

14. Ibid., 52.

15. Ibid., 33.

16. ONI, "Japanese Intelligence and Propaganda in the United States in 1941," Dec. 4, 1941.

17. Smith, *Democracy on Trial*, 80.

18. ONI, "Japanese Intelligence and Propaganda in the United States in 1941," Dec. 4, 1941.

19. Stephan, *Hawaii Under the Rising Sun*, 26–7.

20. Ibid., 34.

21. Ibid.

22. Ibid., 27.

23. Ibid., 31.

24. Greg Robinson, *By Order of the President: FDR and the Internment of Japanese Americans* (Cambridge, MA: Harvard University Press, 2001), 56.

25. Burlingame, *Advance Force-Pearl Harbor*, 19.

26. Gary Y. Okihiro, *Cane Fires: The Anti-Japanese Movement in Hawaii* (Philadelphia: Temple University Press, 1991), 173.

27. Stanley High, "Japanese Saboteurs in Our Midst," *Reader's Digest*, Jan. 1942, 14.

28. ONI, "Japanese Intelligence and Propaganda in the United States in 1941," Dec. 4, 1941, 23–4.

29. Ibid., 14.

30. Smith, *Democracy on Trial*, 77.

31. Ibid.

32. Daniel K. Inouye with Lawrence Elliot, Journey to Washington (Englewood Cliffs, NJ: Prentice-Hall, 1967), 36–7.

33. ONI, "Japanese Intelligence and Propaganda in the United States in 1941," Dec. 4, 1941, 14.

34. Smith, *Democracy on Trial*, 78.

35. Swaine Thomas and Nishimoto, *The Spoilage,* 3.

36. See Kenneth Ringle's Jan. 26, 1942, memo in Appendix C.

37. Stephan, Hawaii Under the Rising Sun, 171.

38. Ibid., 172.

39. ONI, "Japanese Intelligence and Propaganda in the United States in 1941," Dec. 4, 1941, 17.

40. High, "Japanese Saboteurs in Our Midst," 14.

41. ONI, "Japanese Intelligence and Propaganda in the United States in 1941," Dec. 4, 1941, 17.

42. Stephan, *Hawaii Under the Rising Sun,* 36. See also John J. Stephan, "Hijacked by Utopia: American Nikkei in Manchuria," *Amerasia Journal* vol. 23, no. 3, winter 1997–98, 40, 168.

43. David Rosenzweig, "POW Camp Atrocities Led to Treason Trial; Tomoya Kawakita claimed dual citizenship, abusing captured GIs in Japan in World War II, then moving to the U.S.." *Los Angeles Times*, Sept. 20, 2002, Metro section, 2.
44. *Kawakita v. U.S.*, 343 U.S. 717 (1952).

CHAPTER 4: SPIES LIKE US

1. CWRIC, *Personal Justice Denied*, 457. Similar assessments have been made with respect to Hawaii. See, e.g., Mike Masaoka congressional testimony, 155, where he states there was not "a single instance" of espionage or sabotage by ethnic Japanese in Hawaii.
2. Edwin T. Layton with Roger Pineau and John Costello, *"And I Was There:" Pearl Harbor and Midway—Breaking the Secrets* (NY: Quill William Morrrow, 1985), 146, 148. Layton notes that the prosecution of forty suspected agents working as assistant consuls was blocked in July 1941 for fear, as General Walter Short put it, that the prosecution would "unduly alarm the entire population and jeopardize the success [of] our current campaign to secure [the] loyalty of the Japanese population."
3. Farago, *The Broken Seal*, 150.
4. Layton, *"And I Was There,"* 104.
5. "Bay Area's Bob Anderson Retires: Documentarian's Last Look at Pearl Harbor," *San Francisco Chronicle*, Nov. 24, 1991, 52.
6. "A Sunday in December; Chapter 2; A Spy in the Cold," *Los Angeles Times*, Dec. 3, 1991, 4.
7. Prange, *Miracle at Midway*, 72, 75.
8. Ibid.
9. Stephan, *Hawaii Under the Rising Sun*, 84.
10. Clarke, *Pearl Harbor Ghosts*, 15.
11. Ibid.
12. FBI file 65-41886-32, 5.
13. FBI file 65-41886-18, 27A.
14. Ibid., 28.
15. Ibid.
16. After the war Kotoshirodo returned to Hawaii, where he continues to live today, according to a 2004 telephone directory. He did not respond to my request for an interview.
17. FBI file 65-51886-3x-6, 6.

18. Fourteenth Naval District, U.S. Navy, District Intelligence Office, Honolulu, Territory of Hawaii. Report of origin dated February 15, 1943, 23–24. Route slip 1303. Source: National Archives, San Bruno, California, Record Group 181, Confidential Files, Commandant.

19. Lowman, *MAGIC*, 192.

20. Cited in James Gannon, *Stealing Secrets, Telling Lies: How Spies and Codebreakers Helped Shape the Twentieth Century* (Washington, DC: Brasseys, 2001).

21. Layton, *"And I Was There,"* 106.

22. Ibid., 105.

23. Pedro Loureiro, "The Imperial Japanese Navy and Espionage: The Itaru Tachibana Case," *Intelligence and Counterintelligence*, Spring 1989), 111.

24. Ibid., 108.

25. Ibid., 113.

26. Irons, like many opponents of internment and evacuation, uses the term "Japanese Americans" to refer to both *Nisei*, who were U.S. citizens, and *Issei*, who were not.

27. Peter Irons, *Justice at War: The Story of the Japanese-American Internment Cases* (NY: Oxford University Press, 1983), 23.

28. ONI, "Japanese Intelligence and Propaganda in the United States in 1941," Dec. 4, 1941, 14–5.

29. Ibid., 24.

30. MAGIC message No. 289 (#36), June 10, 1941, in *The "MAGIC" Background of Pearl Harbor,* Vol. II Appendix (Washington, DC: Department of Defense, 1977), A-153.

31. See Bob Kumamoto, "The Search for Spies: American Counterintelligence and the Japanese American Community 1931-1942," *Amerasia Journal*, Fall 1979, 55 and Loureiro, 111.

32. Paul Dean, "Speed ahead: Shhhh! Spy wrap-up is under this cover," *Los Angeles Times*, sec. E5, Jan. 29, 1998.

33. Loureiro, "The Imperial Japanese Navy and Espionage," 114.

34. ONI, "Japanese Tokyo Club Syndicate, With Interlocking Affiliations," Dec. 24, 1941. This memo is reproduced in full in Lowman, *MAGIC*, 277-311.

35. Ibid.

36. Ibid.

37. Layton, *"And I Was There,"* 104.

Chapter 5: The MAGIC Revelations

1.   Costello, The *Pacific War*, 211.

2.   Layton, *"And I Was There,"* 81.

3.   Roberta Wohlstetter, *Pearl Harbor: Warning and Decision* (Stanford, CA: Stanford University Press, 1962), 170.

4.   Carl Boyd, *Hitler's Japanese Confidant: General Oshima Hiroshi and Magic Intelligence, 1941-1945* (Lawrence, KS: University of Kansas Press, 1993), 2.

5.   Wohlstetter, *Pearl Harbor: Warning and Decision,* 176.

6.   David Kahn, *The Codebreakers: The Story of Secret Writing* (NY: Scribner, 1967), 24.

7.   Ibid.

8.   Joseph E. Persico, *Roosevelt's Secret War: FDR and World War II Espionage* (NY: Random House, 2001), 162.

9.   Kahn, *Codebreakers,* 28,140.

10. The delivery system to the president and the State Department was hampered briefly in mid-1941 by an old army-navy rivalry. To appease egos in both camps, military and naval aides had taken turns every other month delivering MAGIC (including summaries, briefs, paraphrases, and/or the full messages) to Roosevelt and Secretary of State Cordell Hull. After its turn was over at the end of May, the army discontinued its service to the White House as part of a security lockdown and also in the belief that the White House should receive diplomatic information through State. Despite the glitch, the navy continued its MAGIC deliveries through the spring and summer and MAGIC information continued to be sent to Roosevelt from State. Annoyed at the army's failure to deliver MAGIC in September, even though he was receiving MAGIC from State, Roosevelt demanded a new system. The Navy formally took over delivery of all original MAGIC intercepts to the White House in November. (See memo from Captain A. D. Kramer, "Dissemination to White House," Nov. 7, 1941, extracted from "Congressional Investigation Pearl Harbor Attack," p. 5476. See also Proceedings of Hewitt Inquiry, Exhibit No. 2, Chapter XII., 413, http://www.ibiblio.org/pha/pha/narrative/12.html (accessed March 28, 2004) and Kahn, *Codebreakers*, 30-31).

11. MAGIC messages No. 118 (#043) and No. 119 (#44), Jan. 30, 1941,Volume I of U.S. Department of Defense, *The "Magic" Background of Pearl Harbor* (Washington, DC: Government Printing Office, 1977), A-76 and A-77.

12. C.H. Mason, Chief, Intelligence Branch, MID, "Memorandum for the Chief, Counter Intelligence Branch; Subject: Reorganization of Japanese Intelligence Service in the United States," Feb. 12, 1941; Jules James, Acting Director of Naval

Intelligence, "Memorandum for the Chief of Naval Operations," Feb. 12, 1941.
Both memos are reproduced in full in Appendix C.

13. See Government's Post-Hearing Brief, Sept. 5, 1985, in Peter Irons, *Justice Delayed: The Record of the Japanese American Internment Cases*, Peter Irons, ed. (Middletown, CT: Wesleyan University Press, 1989), 319.

14. J. Edgar Hoover, "Japanese Espionage Organization in the United States," March 12, 1941. The memo is reproduced in full in Appendix C.

15. MAGIC message No. 129 (#239), Feb. 5, 1941, p. A-81 of Vol. I of *The "Magic" Background of Pearl Harbor.*

16. Ibid., MAGIC message No. 131 (#073), Feb. 15, 1941, A-82.

17. Ibid., MAGIC message No. 143 (#126), March 17, 1941, A-86.

18. Ibid., MAGIC messages No. 167 (#40), No. 168 (#162), No. 169 (#8), No. 170 (#044), No. 171 (#12), A-95 to A-97.

19. Ibid., MAGIC message No. 168 (#162), A-96.

20. Ibid., MAGIC message No. 174 (#067), May 9, 1941, A-99.

21. C. H. Mason, Chief Intelligence Branch, MID, "Memorandum for Chief, Counter Intelligence Branch; Subject: Espionage Activities of Japanese Consul in Los Angeles," May 21, 1941. See Appendix C.

22. J. Edgar Hoover, "Memorandum for the Attorney General," May 22, 1941. See Appendix C.

23. Government's Post-Hearing Brief, Sept. 5, 1985, in Peter Irons, *Justice Delayed*, 319.

24. J. Edgar Hoover letter for Major General Edwin Watson, Secretary to the President, June 27, 1941. This letter is reproduced in full in Lowman, *MAGIC*, 217.

25. MAGIC message No. 175 (#45), May 11, 1941, A-99 to A-100 of Vol. I of *The "Magic" Background of Pearl Harbor.*

26. *Ibid.*, MAGIC message No. 175 (#45), May 11, 1941, A-100.

27. Ibid.

28. Ibid.

29. See ONI, "Japanese Tokyo Club Syndicate," op. cit., 23. This memo states: "OKA-MARU, Welley or Welly Shoji – American-educated *Nisei* (with *Kibei* classification) Class A espionage suspect. Reported (July 1941) to have repudiated his American citizenship....OKAMARU is reported to head a unit which contacts labor unions, particularly members of the Communist Party in the A.F. of L. and C.I.O."

30. MAGIC message No. 175 (#45), May 11, 1941, A-100 of Vol. I of *The "Magic" Background of Pearl Harbor.*

31. C.H. Mason, Chief Intelligence Branch, MID, "Memorandum for Chief, Counter Intelligence Branch; Subject: Japanese Espionage," June 9, 1941. See Appendix C.

32. See ONI, "Japanese Tokyo Club Syndicate," op. cit., 22.

33. MAGIC message No. 222 (#056), June 23, 1941, A-126 of Vol. II Appendix of *The "Magic" Background of Pearl Harbor.*

34. MAGIC message No. 286 (#91), Aug. 16, 1941, A-164 of Vol. III Appendix of *The "Magic" Background of Pearl Harbor.*

35. Ibid., MAGIC message No. 290 (#92), Aug. 18, 1941, A-165 to A-166.

36. Ibid., MAGIC message No. 298 (#105), Sept. 4, 1941, A-169.

37. Ibid.

38. Ibid., MAGIC message No. 309 (#123), Sept. 20, 1941, A-172.

39. MAGIC message No. 224 (#7), June 2, 1941, A-127 of Vol. II Appendix of U.S. Department of Defense, *The "Magic" Background of Pearl Harbor.*

40. MAGIC message No. 308 (#218), Sept. 8, 1941, A-172 of Vol. III Appendix of *The "Magic" Background of Pearl Harbor.*

41. Ibid., MAGIC messages No. 310 (#222), Oct. 2, 1941, and No. 311 (#243) Oct. 16, 1941, A-172 to A-173.

42. See, e.g., MAGIC message No. 385 (#487), Aug. 20, 1941, A-204 Vol. III Appendix of *The "Magic" Background of Pearl Harbor.*

43. Ibid., MAGIC message No. 285 (#156), Aug. 16, 1941, A-164.

44. Ibid.

45. Ibid., MAGIC message No. 287 (#93), Aug. 21, 1941, A-164.

46. Ibid.

47. Ibid., MAGIC message No. 289 (#183), Aug. 26, 1941, A-165.

48. Ibid., MAGIC message No. 304 (#198), Sept. 8, 1941, A-171.

49. Ibid., MAGIC message No. 307 (#217), Sept. 18, 1941, A-171.

50. Ibid., MAGIC message No. 312 (#48), Oct. 12, 1941, A-173.

51. Ibid., MAGIC message No. 301 (#263), Sept. 4, 1941, A-170.

52. Ibid., MAGIC message No. 300 (#170), Sept. 6, 1941, A-169.

53. Ibid., MAGIC message No. 302 (#121), Sept. 20, 1941, A-170.

54. Ibid., MAGIC message No. 303 (#124), Sept. 24, 1941, A-170.

55. Ibid., MAGIC message No. 288 (#749), Aug. 21, 1941, p. A-165.

56. Ibid., MAGIC message No. 297 (#105), Sept. 4, 1941, A-168.

57. Ibid.

58. Ibid., MAGIC message No. 428 (#184), Sept. 16, 1941, A-223.

59. See, e.g., MAGIC messages No. 279 (#111), Nov. 15, 1941, A-147; No. 282

(#113), Nov. 18, 1941, A-148; No. 283 (#111), Nov. 20, 1941, A-148; No. 287 (#119), Nov. 28, 1941, A-148 to A-149; No. 288 (#122), Nov. 29, 1941, A-150; No. 291 (#123), Dec. 2, 1941, A-151 of the Vol. IV Appendix of *The "Magic" Background of Pearl Harbor.*

60. MAGIC message No. 356 (#83), Sept. 24, 1941, A-189 to A-190 of Vol. III Appendix of *The "Magic" Background of Pearl Harbor.*

61. MAGIC message No. 279 (#111), Nov. 15, 1941, A-147 of Vol. IV Appendix of *The "Magic" Background of Pearl Harbor.*

62. See, e.g., Ibid., MAGIC messages No. 280 (#222), Nov. 18, 1941, A-147; No. 284 (#234), Nov. 24, 1941, A-148; No. 285 (#234), Nov. 24, 1941, A-149; No. 286 (#238), Nov. 28, 1941, A-148; No. 290 (#241), Dec. 1, 1941, A-150 to A-151.

63. Chief SIS cryptanalyst Frank Rowlett wrote in the early 1980s that "as I look back at all the messages and other information available to us at that time [late 1941] regarding the Japanese intentions, it becomes crystal clear to me that this message ordering the destruction of certain of Washington's codes provided the necessary evidence that the Japanese unquestionably intended to take some action which would make war between the United States and Japan a certainty. Unfortunately, Pearl Harbor was never identified in either the Japanese intercepted messages or collateral information as the point of attack." Boyd, *Hitler's Japanese Confidant,* 38.

64. Gannon, *Stealing Secrets, Telling Lies,* 187-188. The literature debating who and what are to blame for the failure to anticipate Pearl Harbor is, of course, vast. For differing takes, see Wohlstetter, *Pearl Harbor: Warning and Decision,* and Robert B. Stinnett, *Day of Deceit: The Truth About FDR and Pearl Harbor* (NY: Simon & Schuster, 2000).

CHAPTER 6: THE INTERNMENT OF ENEMY ALIENS

1. W. F. Kelly, Immigration and Naturalization Service, Aug. 9, 1948, letter to A. Vulliet, World Alliance of Young Men's Christian Associations, New York City. Cited by Don Heinrich Tolzmann, ed., *German-Americans in the World Wars,* Vol. 4, sec. 1, pt. 1, (1995), 1513. This figure is an undercount because it excludes German and Italian Latin Americans, as well as four Japanese captured on Pacific islands other than Hawaii.

2. D. J. Carter, *Behind Canadian Barbed Wire: Alien, Refugee and Prisoner of War Camps in Canada 1914-1916* (Calgary, Canada: Tumbleweed Press, 1980); L.Y. Luciuk, *A Time for Atonement: Canada's First National Internment Operations and*

the Ukrainian Canadians 1914-1920 (Kingston: The Limestone Press, 1988), http://www.infoukes.com/history/internment/booklet02 (accessed Jan. 29, 2004).

3. National Archives of Australia, Fact Sheet 171, http://www.naa.gov.au/Publications/fact_sheets/FS171.html, (accessed Jan. 29, 2004).

4. Isle of Man Government, Manx National Heritage Library, "Internment during World Wars I and II," Sept. 2003, http://www.gov.im/mnh/internment.asp (accessed Jan. 29, 2004).

5. "Somes Prisoners," http://www.geocities.com/somesprisonersnz (accessed Jan. 29, 2004).

6. Section 21 of Title 50 of the United States Code, http://www4.law.cornell.edu/uscode/50/21.html (accessed Jan. 24, 2004).

7   Mitchel Yockelson , "The War Department: Keeper of Our Nation's Enemy Aliens During World War I," Presented to the Society for Military History Annual Meeting, April 1998, http://www.lib.byu.edu/~rdh/wwi/comment/yockel.htm (accessed Jan. 24, 2004).

8. Arnold Krammer, *Undue Process,* 14-15.

9. Ibid., 11.

10. Tetsuden Kashima, *Judgment Without Trial: Japanese American Imprisonment During World War II* (Seattle, WA: University of Washington Press, 2003), 22.

11. Joint Agreement of the Secretary of War and the Attorney General Respecting Internment of Alien Enemies, July 18, 1941, National Archives RG-338-2-7, 014.31 Enemy Aliens file, CWRIC papers, unnumbered.

12. J. Edgar Hoover, Memorandum to Tolson, Tamm, and Ladd, December 9, 1941, CWRIC papers, 5782.

13. "Japanese in U.S.," *Newsweek,* Oct. 14, 1940, pp. 12, 14. Cited by Robinson, *By Order of the President,* 87-88.

14. Loureiro, "The Imperial Japanese Navy and Espionage," 113.

15. MAGIC message No. 369 (#335), July 7, 1941, A-185. Vol. II Appendix of *The "Magic" Background of Pearl Harbor.*

16. Ibid., MAGIC message No. 370 (#558), July 23, 1941, A-186.

17. ONI, "Japanese Tokyo Club Syndicate."

18. Letter from J. Edgar Hoover to James Lawrence Fly, Jan. 16, 1942. See Appendix C.

19. J. Edgar Hoover, Memorandum for the Attorney General, Feb. 1, 1942, CWRIC papers, 10447-56.

20. J. Edgar Hoover, Memorandum for the Attorney General, Feb. 9, 1942. This memo is reproduced in full in Lowman, *MAGIC,* 227-8.

21. Ibid.

22. Krammer, *Undue Process,* 184.

23. Ibid.

24. John Christgau, *Enemies: World War II Alien Internment* (San Jose, CA: Authors Choice Press, 2001), 88.

25. Frances B. Cogan, *Captured,* 111-2.

26. For more, see George Hicks, *The Comfort Women: Japan's Brutal Regime of Enforced Prostitution in the Second World War* (NY: Norton, 1994).

27. Gloria Ricci Lothrop, "Unwelcome in Freedom's Land: The Impact of World War II on Italian Aliens in Southern California," in *Una Storia Segreta.*.

28. Stephen Fox, *The Unknown Internment: An Oral History of the Relocation of Italian Americans during World War II* (Boston: Twayne Publishers, 1990), 152.

29. Lothrop, "Unwelcome in Freedom's Land," 170.

30. Tetsuden Kashima, *Judgment Without Trial,* 17.

31. Michi Nishiura Weglyn, *Years of Infamy: The Untold Story of America's Concentration Camps,* updated edition (Seattle: University of Washington Press, 1996).

32. Stephen Fox, "Latin American Deportations," http://members.cox.net/steve.fox/plan9pdf.pdf (accessed Jan. 29, 2004).

33. Krammer, *Undue Process,* 89.

34. Max Paul Friedman, "Private Memory, Public Records, and Contested Terrain: Weighing Oral Testimony in the Deportation of Germans from Latin America During World War II," *Oral History Review,* Jan. 1, 2000.

35. Matthews, *Shadows Dancing,* 15-17.

36. MAGIC message No. 384 (#93), June 2, 1941, A-192 of Vol. II Appendix of *The "Magic" Background of Pearl Harbor.*

37. Tragically, German Jews were among those repatriated to Germany.

38. Robertson, *The Japanese File.*

39. Smith, *Democracy on Trial,* 107.

40. MAGIC message No. 174 (#067), May 9, 1941, p-A-99 of Vol. I of *The "Magic" Background of Pearl Harbor.*

41 *Ludecke v. Watkins,* 335 US 160 (1948); *Johnson v. Eisentrager,* 339 US 763 (1950).

42. *Johnson v. Eisentrager,* 339 US 763 (1950).

43. David Cole, *Enemy Aliens,* 94-95.

CHAPTER 7: THE RATIONALE FOR EVACUATION

1. Stetson Conn, "Guarding the United States and Its Outposts," 83.

2. Curtis B. Munson, "Japanese on the West Coast," Nov. 7, 1941, Commission on Wartime Relocation and Internment of Civilians, RG 220, CWIRC papers, 23683.

3. Munson, "Japanese on the West Coast," CWRIC papers, 3672.

4. Ibid., 3689.

5. Memorandum for the Secretary of War from President Roosevelt, Nov. 8, 1941, CWRIC papers, 3671.

6. Munson, "Report on Hawaiian Islands," attached to memorandum from John Franklin Carter, Dec. 8, 1941, CWRIC papers, 19501.

7. Weglyn, *Years of Infamy*, 35, 225.

8. Bob Kumamoto, "The Search for Spies: American Counterintelligence and the Japanese American Community 1931-1942," *Amerasia Journal*, Fall 1979, 68.

9. Government's Post-Hearing Brief, Sept. 5, 1985, in Peter Irons, *Justice Delayed*, 322-323.

10. Robinson, *By Order of the President*, 78.

11. Memo from R.B. Hood to J. Edgar Hoover, Dec. 10, 1941. See Appendix C.

12. Robinson, *By Order of the President*, 79.

13. ONI, "Japanese Tokyo Club Syndicate."

14. Government's Post-Hearing Brief, Sept. 5, 1985, in Peter Irons, *Justice Delayed*, 319.

15. MID, "Japanese Activities and Intelligence Machine in the Western Hemisphere," Jan. 3, 1942. See Appendix C.

16. Memo, Adm John W. Greenslade, Commandant Twelfth Naval District, for CG Northern California Sector, 8 Jan 42 ; Ltr, CG IX Army Corps to CG WDC, 8 Jan 42. Both documents are in WDC-CAD 014.31 Aliens. Tel Conv, Gen DeWitt with Maj Gen Kenyon A. Joyce, 8 Jan 42, WDC-CAD 311.3 Tel Convs (DeWitt, 42-43). Cited in Stetson Conn, *Guarding the United States and Its Outposts*, p. 119, available online at http://www.army.mil/cmh/books/wwii/guard-us/ch5.htm (accessed March 12, 2004).

17. D.M. Ladd, "Memorandum for Mr. E.A. Tamm, F.B.I., Dec. 17, 1941, CWRIC papers, 5816.

18. CWRIC, *Personal Justice Denied*, 51.

19. Weglyn, *Years of Infamy*, 56.

20. Francis Biddle, *In Brief Authority* (Garden City, NY: Doubleday, 1962), 217.

21. Tom Sando with J.P. Desgagne, *Wild Daisies in the Sand: Life in a Canadian Internment Camp* (Edmonton, Alberta: Newest Press, 2002), 3-5.

22. MAGIC message No. 131 (#073), Feb. 15, 1941, and No. 135 (#008), Feb. 15, 1941, A-82 to A-83 of Vol. I of *The "Magic" Background of Pearl Harbor.*

23. Kashima, *Judgment Without Trial,* 95.

24. MAGIC message No. 400 (#245) July 4, 1941, A-200 of Vol. II Appendix of *The "Magic" Background of Pearl Harbor.*

25. Ibid., MAGIC message No. 422 (#278) July 19, 1941, A-211.

26. Robinson, *By Order of the President,* 93.

27. *Congressional Record,* Vol. 88, Part 8, p. A261. Cited in "*Korematsu v. United States:* Petition for Writ of Error *Coram Nobis,* U.S. District Court for the Northern District of California," in *Justice Delayed: The Record of the Japanese American Internment Cases,* Peter Irons, ed. (Middletown, CT: Wesleyan University Press, 1989), 178-9.

28. Robinson, *By Order of the President,* 95.

29. Marshall letter to Dewey. Extracted from "Congressional Investigation- Pearl Harbor Attack," Part 3, 1132-33.

30. Less than two weeks after the attack, Knox stated that "the most effective Fifth Column work of the entire war was done in Hawaii, with the possible exception of Norway." It is clear now that Knox was referring to the activities of Japan's Honolulu spy ring, which, technically speaking, engaged in espionage, not Fifth Column activities. In the course of excoriating Knox for this error, anti-evacuation activists have falsely implied that there was no espionage carried out by ethnic Japanese residents on Hawaii prior to Pearl Harbor. See , e.g., Weglyn, *Days of Infamy,* 29.

31. For the argument that the concentrations of ethnic Japanese around military installations was not coincidental, see Lt. Gen. John DeWitt, U.S. Army, Western Defense Command and Fourth Army, *Final Report; Japanese Evacuation from the West Coast 1942* (Washington DC: Govt. Printing Office, 1943).

32. Jacobus tenBroek, Edward N. Barnhart, and Floyd W. Matson, *Prejudice, War and the Constitution* (Berkeley, CA: University of California Press, 1954), 101. Cited in *Justice Delayed,* Irons, ed., 179.

33. Cited in Robinson, *By Order of the President,* 95. Interestingly, Roberts later voted against the constitutionality of Executive Order 9066, which authorized the evacuation and relocation of ethnic Japanese from the West Coast.

34. *Harper's,* Oct. 1942, 489-97.

35. Government's post-hearing brief, Sept. 5, 1985, in Peter Irons, *Justice Delayed,* 326.

36. K.D. Ringle, Branch Intelligence Office, Eleventh Naval District, "Japanese Question, Report on," Jan. 26, 1942, See Appendix C.

37. Government's post-hearing brief, Sept. 5, 1985, in Peter Irons, *Justice Delayed*, 326.

38. J. Edgar Hoover, Memorandum for Mr. Francis M. Shea, Assistant Attorney General, Dec. 17, 1941, CWRIC papers, 5777.

39. Hoover, Feb. 2, 1941, memo.

40. J. Edgar Hoover, Memorandum for Mr. Tolson, Mr. Tamm, and Mr. Ladd, dated Dec. 17, 1941, CWRIC papers, 5831.

41. Cited in Stetson Conn, "The Decision to Evacuate the Japanese from the Pacific Coast" in *Guarding the United States and Its Outposts*, 117.

42. The most famous quote attributed to DeWitt is: "A Jap's a Jap. It makes no difference whether the Jap is a citizen or not." (See, for example, JACL Curriculum and Resource Guide 2002, 6.) The same quote is featured in the Smithsonian Institution's exhibit, A More Perfect Union: Japanese Americans and the U.S. Constitution. (See http://americanhistory.si.edu/perfectunion/non-flash/ removal_process.html.) Neither the guide nor the exhibit offers a citation for the quote—because no such actual quotation exists. In a telephone conversation with Assistant Secretary of War John McCloy, transcribed on Feb. 3, 1942, DeWitt said: "Out here, Mr. Secretary, a Jap is a Jap *to these people now*" (emphasis added) (see CWRIC papers, 137). In this instance, DeWitt was characterizing Californians' sentiments, not necessarily his own—though he repeats the phrase "A Jap's a Jap" later on in the transcript while explaining to McCloy the security difficulties faced by troops. (CWRIC papers, 138.) More than a year later, in public testimony before the House Naval Affairs Committee, DeWitt stated that ethnic Japanese still posed a threat to the West Coast and vital installations. "The danger of the Japanese was, and is now—if they are permitted to come back—espionage and sabotage. It makes no difference whether he is an American citizen, he is still a Japanese. American citizenship does not necessarily determine loyalty." (CWRIC, *Personal Justice Denied*, 66.) When modern-day ethnic activists and historians cite the "A Jap's a Jap" quote, the heavy-handed implication is that DeWitt's use of the term "Jap"—offensive now, but common in his time—makes him an unreconstructed racist. There are numerous instances of Attorney General Francis Biddle, who opposed evacuation, using the term "Jap." See, for example, CWRIC papers, 3794, for Biddle's thoughts on when to "let the Japs go home" and whether ". . . it would be wiser for us to turn the Japs back now as the Army had

suggested." Curiously, none of these quotes have turned up in the predominant anti-evacuation literature.

43. Stetson Conn, *Guarding the United States and Its Outposts*, 136.

44. Ibid., 128-129.

45. Telephone conversation, Gen DeWitt and Col Bendetsen with Gen Gullion, II Feb 42, WDC-CAD 31 1.3 Tel Convs (DeWitt, 42-43). Cited in Stetson Conn, 129 n 49.

46. Ibid.

47. Conn, "Guarding the U.S. and Its Outposts," 132.

48. Ibid., 132-133.

49. McCloy congressional testimony, "Japanese-American and Aleutian Wartime Relocation," hearings before the Subcommittee on Administrative Law and Government Relations of the Committee on the Judiciary, U.S. House of Representatives, Sept. 12, 1984, 125.

50. For more, see Jules Witcover, *Sabotage at Black Tom: Imperial Germany's Secret War in America, 1914-1917*, (Chapel Hill, NC: Algonquin Books), 1989.

51. Stimson, *On Active Service in Peace and War*, 342.

52. Ibid., 343.

53. *Korematsu v. United States*, 320 U.S. 214 (1944). In a separate decision, *Ex parte Endo*, the Supreme Court struck down the detention of admittedly loyal U.S. citizens, absent evidence of a crime, but only on the narrow ground that such actions were not based on statutory authority. See *Ex parte Endo*, 323 U.S. 283 (1944). The *Korematsu* decision is reviled by most constitutional law experts today. Of course, legal arguments about what the Constitution does and does not permit are largely irrelevant to the main thesis of this book—namely, that the evacuation and relocation were motivated by legitimate military considerations and were not based primarily upon racism and wartime hysteria. For more on the wartime Supreme Court decisions, see Appendix E on the *coram nobis* cases— which led to the vacation of Korematsu's conviction and two others.

54. Memorandum from Allen Gullion to John McCloy, Feb. 5, 1942, CWRIC papers, pp. 119-120.

55. Memorandum from Gullion to McCloy, Feb. 6, 1942, CWRIC papers, no page number available.

56. Henry Stimson, diary, Feb. 10, 1942, CWRIC papers, 19649.

Chapter 8: Executive Order 9066

1. Henry Stimson, diary, Feb. 11, 1942, CWRIC papers, 19652.
2. Lowman, *MAGIC,* 79-80.
3. MID, "Japanese Activities and Intelligence Machine in the Western Hemisphere," Dec. 24, 1941. See Appendix C.
4. J. Edgar Hoover, Memorandum for the Attorney General, Feb. 1, 1942, CWRIC papers, 10447-10456.
5. J. Edgar Hoover, Memorandum for the Attorney General, Feb. 2, 1942, CWRIC papers, 5797.
6. Francis Biddle, Memorandum to James Rowe, Feb. 9, 1942, File A 7.01, Japanese Evacuation and Resettlement Study, Bancroft Library, University of California, Berkeley. Interestingly, the attachment from Hoover is missing from the file. See also Deborah Lim, *Research Report prepared for Presidential Select Committee on JACL Resolution #7,* "The Decision to Cooperate with Evacuation," http://www.javoice.com/limreport/LimPartICID.htm#ID1 (accessed March 20, 2004).
7. After the war, Rauh became a critic of the West Coast evacuation. He argued that a "temporary nighttime curfew" would have sufficed as an effective alternative to guarding against potential invasion, espionage, sabotage, fifth column activity, and spot raids. See Joseph L. Rauh, Jr., letter to Joan Z. Bernstein, May 21, 1982, CWRIC papers, 14435.
8. Memorandum prepared by Messrs. Cohen, Cox and Rauh, "The Japanese Situation on the West Coast," Feb. 1942, CWRIC papers, 12682-89.
9. Henry Stimson, diary, Feb. 17, 1942, CWRIC papers, 19684.
10. Stetson Conn, *Guarding the United States and Its Outposts,* 87.
11. Krammer, *Undue Process,* 68; DiStasi, "A Tale of Two Citizens," in DiStasi, ed., *Una Storia Segreta,* 139.
12. See, generally, *Una Storia Segreta.*
13. Testimony of Rep. Eliot Engel, http://www.house.gov/judiciary/enge1026.htm (accessed March 12, 2004).
14. Lowman, *MAGIC,* 20, n 16.
15. John Franklin Carter, Memorandum on summary of West Coast and Honolulu reports by Munson, etc.," Dec. 16, 1941, CWRIC papers, 12006.
16. The Joint U.S. Chiefs of Staff/Hawaiian Defense Forces warned on Feb. 12, 1942: "The Japanese might attempt air and naval raids on outlying islands, destructive air and naval raids on Oahu or combined air, naval and ground operations to seize

one of the large outlying islands as a base for an attack on the fortress of Oahu. Japan has the forces available to carry out any one or all of the above operations." From J.C.S. 11, Feb. 12, 1942, CWRIC papers, 3664-5.

17. Bernstein congressional testimony, "Japanese-American and Aleutian Wartime Relocation," hearings before the Subcommittee on Administrative Law and Governmental Relations of the Committee on the Judiciary, U.S. House of Representatives, June 20, 1984, p.30. See also Mike Masaoka's congressional testimony, 157: "I keep referring to this Hawaiian experience because I think we have no better example that we can contrast with what took place on the west coast. If I may repeat again, in Hawaii the military situation was considered so dangerous that they had to impose martial law. On the U.S. mainland it wasn't considered dangerous enough to have that kind of special emergency status. Our courts were functioning all the time. And yet, for some reason—and we attribute much of it to racism on the Pacific coast—we were incarcerated as no other people have been incarcerated in American history."

18. Franklin D. Roosevelt, Memorandum for the Secretary of the Navy, Feb. 26, 1942, CWRIC papers, 4399.

19. For more on the implementation of these measures, see "Martial Law in Hawaii: The Papers of Major General Thomas H. Green, Judge Advocate General's Corps, U.S. Army," from the holdings of the Library of the Judge Advocate General's School, Charlottesville, Virginia.

20. According to Katsuma, *Judgment Without Trial*, 79, 347 *Nisei*, 30 German Americans, and 2 Italian Americans were in custody in Hawaii by Dec. 1, 1942. Many of the *Nisei* were ultimately sent to relocation camps on the mainland.

21. Masaoka congressional testimony, 159.

22. Karl R. Bendetsen Oral History, conducted by Jerry N. Hess for the Harry S. Truman Library, Oct. 24, 1971, http://www.trumanlibrary.org/oralhist/bendet1.htm (accessed March 21, 2004).

23. Daniels, *Concentration Camps U.S.A.*, 84.

24. Smith, *Democracy on Trial*, 148.

25. See letter from JACL president Jiro Tsukamoto to Utah Gov. Herbert B. Maw, March 23, 1942, cited in Lowman, *MAGIC*, 342.

26. Kenneth D. Ringle, confidential memo on "Japanese Situation—Supplementary report on," Feb. 25, 1942, CWRIC papers, 19527-8.

27. Ringle, confidential memo on "Recent trip through Southern California in connection with Japanese situation-results of," March 3, 1942, CWRIC papers, 19530-4.

28. Telegram, W. L. Wheeler to Phillip C. Hamblet, Executive Officer, Office of Government Reports, March 5, 1942, ASW 014.311 EAWC, CWRIC papers, 82-3).

29. Quoted in Milton Eisenhower, *The President Is Calling: A Veteran Advisor for the Presidency Suggests Far-Reaching Changes* (Garden City, NY: Doubleday, 1974), 112.

30. Executive Order 9102, March 18, 1942, http://www.nps.gov/manz/hrs/hrsab.htm (accessed March 25, 2004).

31. Stetson Conn, 88.

32. See Layton, *"And I Was There"*; Persico, *Roosevelt's Secret War*; Prange, *Miracle at Midway.*

33. Stetson Conn, 89.

34. Ibid.

35. Government's post-hearing brief, Sept. 5, 1985, in Peter Irons, *Justice Delayed*, 327.

36. Nicholas D. Kristof, "Nobuo Fujita, 85, Is Dead; Only Foe to Bomb America," *New York Times*, Oct. 3, 1997, D19.

37. K.D. Ringle, ONI, "Japanese Menace on Terminal Island, San Pedro, California," Feb. 7, 1942. This memo is reproduced in full in Lowman, *MAGIC*, 325-8.

38. Ibid.

39. MAGIC message No. 175 (#45), May 11, 1941, A-99 to A-100 of Vol. I of *The "Magic" Background of Pearl Harbor.*

40. *American concentration camps: a documentary history of the relocation and incarceration of Japanese Americans, 1942-1945* (NY: Garland, 1989), http://www.lib.washington.edu/exhibits/harmony/Documents/bain.html (accessed Jan. 30, 2004).

41. Ibid.

Chapter 9: The Myth of the American "Concentration Camp"

1. G. W. Miller III, "Refuge in South Jersey—After WWII, Japanese-Americans found a home in Seabrook," *Philadelphia Daily News*, Aug. 26, 2003.

2. Donald Teruo Hata and Nadine Ishitani Hata, *Japanese Americans and World War II: Exclusion, Internment, and Redress*, 2nd ed. (Wheeling, IL: Harlan Davidson, 1995), 12.

3. Thomas A. Bailey and David Kennedy, *The American Pageant: A History of the Republic*, 12th ed. (Boston: Houghton Mifflin, 2002), 828-9.

4. Roger Daniels, *Prisoners Without Trial* (NY: Hill and Wang, 1993), 46-47.

5. CWRIC, *Personal Justice Denied,* 27 footnote.

6. The situation in Hawaii, where martial law had been declared, differed from that on the mainland. Military rule gave authorities the power to lock up suspected subversives without proof of a crime, regardless of citizenship. A total of 2,392 Hawaiian residents of Japanese ancestry were kept in detention or internment facilities on the islands or sent to internment or relocation centers on the mainland. The great majority were *Issei* (Kashima, *Judgment Without Trial,* 86).

7. Krammer, *Undue Process,* 83. In addition, the War Relocation Authority established two citizen isolation camps for *Nisei* removed from the relocation camps for safety and security reasons. These camps were located in Moab, Utah, and Leupp, Arizona.

8. Daniels, *Concentration Camps USA,* 84.

9. Ibid.

10. *Korematsu v. United States*, 323 US 214 (1944).

11. Wendy Ng, *Japanese American Internment During World War II: A History and Reference Guide* (Westport, CT: Greenwood Press, 2002), xiv.

12. Tetsuden Kashima, Foreword to CWRIC, *Personal Justice Denied,* xv.

13. War Relocation Authority, *The Evacuated People: A Quantitative Description*, (Washington, DC: U.S. Government Printing Office, 1946), 23

14. Daniels, *Concentration Camps U.S.A.,* 100.

15. Weglyn, *Days of Infamy,* 352.

16. Kiyoaki Murata, *An Enemy Among Friends* (Tokyo: Kodansha International, 1991), 128-9.

17. War Relocation Authority, *The Evacuated People*, 13.

18. Jeanne Wakatsuki Houston and James D. Houston, *Farewell to Manzanar* (NY: Bantam Books, 1973), 22.

19. Weglyn, *Years of Infamy*, 21.

20. For more information on Ralph Lazo, see Mayerene Barker, "Japanese-Americans mourn an old friend," *Los Angeles Times*, Jan. 8, 1992, B1; Janice Harumi Yen, "Who was Ralph Lazo?" http://www.ncrr-la.org/news/7_6_03/2.html (accessed Feb. 5, 2004).

21. Smith, *Democracy on Trial,* 218.

22. Krammer, *Undue Process,* 85.

23. Ibid., 87.

24. Jerre Mangione, "Concentration Camps—American Style," in *Una Storia Segreta,* 120, 123, 125.

25. Thomas Chavez, "The forgotten history of internment camps," sec. F1, *Santa Fe New Mexican*, Dec. 14, 1997.

26. Gloria Ricci Lothrop, "Unwelcome in Freedom's Land," in *Una Storia Segreta,* 172-3.

27. Mangione, "Concentration Camps—American Style," in *Una Storia Segreta,* 126.

28. Memorandum from Spanish Embassy to U.S. Department of State, "Re: Japanese Interned in Ellis Island," Feb. 5, 1942.

29. Letter from Ryuchi Fujii, Japanese Spokesman, to James H. Keeley, U.S. Department of State, Oct. 18, 1943.

30. Mangione, "Concentration Camps—American Style," in *Una Storia Segreta,* 121-3.

31. Ibid.

32. Ibid., 129.

33. Jeffery F. Burton, Mary M. Farrell, Florence B. Lord, Richard W. Lord, National Park Service, "Confinement and Ethnicity: An Overview of World War II Japanese American Relocation Sites," *Publications in Anthropology* 1999 (rev. July 2000), http://www.cr.nps.gov/history/online_books/anthropology74/index.htm (accessed Feb. 6, 2004).

34. U.S. Army, Western Defense Command and Fourth Army, *Final Report; Japanese Evacuation from the West Coast 1942* (Washington DC: Government Printing Office, 1943), 227.

35. Smith, *Democracy on Trial,* 219.

36. Shay Glick, "All Bets Were Off: His early days at Santa Anita were spent as a GI, not a sportswriter," *Los Angeles Times,* sec 4, p. 1, Nov. 4, 2003.

37. Carey McWilliams, "Moving the West Coast Japanese," *Harper's,* Sept. 1942, 359.

38. American National Red Cross, "Report of the American Red Cross Survey of Assembly Centers in California, Oregon, and Washington," Aug. 1942, unpublished manuscript, 18-19. Quoted in CWRIC, *Personal Justice Denied,* 139.

39. Saburo Kido, "'Fair American Chance' Asked for *Nisei* by JACL President," *Pacific Citizen,* July 17, 1943, 4.

40. Bulletin #1, May 8, 1942, JACL Archives, cited in Lim, *Research Report prepared for Presidential Select Committee on JACL Resolution #7,* "The Decision to Cooperate with Evacuation," 43.

41. Swaine Thomas and Nishimoto, *The Spoilage,* 28.

42. War Relocation Authority, "Relocation of Japanese Americans," May 1943; http://www.sfmuseum.org/hist10/relocbook.html, (accessed Feb. 6, 2004).

43. War Relocation Authority, "Relocation of Japanese Americans."

44. Lowman, *MAGIC,* 319.

45. Kido, "Fair American Chance," 4.

46. Swaine Thomas and Nishimoto, *The Spoilage,* 61.

47. Weglyn, *Years of Infamy,* 136.

48. Charles Kikuchi, *The Kikuchi Diary,* John Modell, ed. (Urbana, IL: University of Illinois Press, 1993), 26-27.

49. Smith, Democracy on Trial, 215.

50. Murata, *An Enemy Among Friends,* 113.

51. Ng, *Japanese American Internment During World War II,* 45.

52. Weglyn, *Years of Infamy,* 122-24, 343.

53. Daniel S. Davis, *Behind Barbed Wire: The Imprisonment of Japanese Americans During World War II* (NY: Prentice-Hall Inc., 1967), 79.

54. Undated memorandum, District Intelligence Officer,11th Naval District, to Director of Naval Intelligence, File "War Relocation Authority," 1-2, cited in Lim, 57.

55. Swaine Thomas and Nishimoto, *The Spoilage,* 318-9.

56. See, for example, Eric Muller, *Free to Die For Their Country: The Story of the Japanese American Draft Resisters in World War II,* (Chicago: University of Chicago Press, 2001) and "Conscience and the Constitution," PBS, http://www.pbs.org/itvs/conscience/index.html. Among the vocal critics of the draft resistance movement in the camps was veteran journalist Bill Hosokawa, who wrote an April 1, 1944 column for the *Pacific Citizen* newspaper criticizing resisters' committees that had sprung up in several relocation centers: "Undoubtedly many of the individuals behind these committees are sincere, and their loyalty is beyond question. But there are others who can be identified as periodical patriots, individuals who protest their Americanism and demand their rights as citizens only when they are confronted with the task of fulfilling the responsibilities of that citizenship." Quoted in Lim, 66.

57. Lauren Kessler, "Fettered Freedoms: The Journalism of World War II Japanese Internment Camps," *Journalism History,* Summer/Autumn 1988, 73. In July 2000, the national JACL apologized to draft resisters for denouncing their protests. Two years later, Heart Mountain draft resistance leader Frank Emi demanded that the organization apologize "for the excesses committed by wartime JACL leaders, such as acting as informants for the government causing many innocent people to suffer." (http://www.resisters.com/study/jacl_apology.htm)

58. A few brave Japanese Americans volunteered even before the war to assist the government in combating subversives. They established "defense committees" or

"anti-Axis committees" in major West Coast cities that were "charged with gathering information on subversive activities; this information was to be turned over
directly to Naval Intelligence." According to Togo Tanaka of the JACL, all of its
national officers in 1940-41 had been in personal contact with the FBI, military
intelligence, and naval intelligence; several became government informants. See
Deborah Lim, *Research Report prepared for Presidential Select Committee on JACL
Resolution #7*, "The Decision to Cooperate with Evacuation," 11,
http://www.javoice.com/limreport/LimPartICID.htm#ID1 (accessed March 20,
2004).

59. Christgau, *Enemies*, 152.

60. Swaine Thomas and Nishimoto, *The Spoilage*, 322.

61. Ibid., 156.

62. Ibid., 319.

63. Minoru Kiyota, *Beyond Loyalty: The Story of a Kibei* (Honolulu: University of
Hawaii Press, 1997), 105.

64. For more information, see Burton et al., "Confinement and Ethnicity," and War
Relocation Authority, *The Evacuated People*, 181.

65. At the end of the war, thousands of renunciants who had remained in the U.S.
argued that they had been pressured to give up their citizenship under duress. As
the government noted, however, most renunciants expressed second thoughts
about giving up American citizenship only after the A-bomb was dropped and
Japan surrendered. A federal judge in San Francisco cancelled the renunciations
after determining they were made under duress and coercion, and told the government to come back with more proof that the plaintiffs acted freely. The same
judge, however, refused to consider factors such as membership in militant organizations, *Kibei* status, and voluntary deportee status to show that renunciation
was freely made. An appeals court ruled that minors who had renounced had
done so unconstitutionally, but that the remaining 3,300 adult plaintiffs
renounced based on "simply expediency and crass material considerations, not
duress." The court remanded their cases to the district court for individual assessment. After a protacted legal battle, in which the Justice Department relented to
public protests and litigious overload, all but 84 of the U.S.-based renunciants
regained citizenship.

66. Norihiko Shirouzu, "Decades on, a legacy of war still haunts Japanese-Americans," *Wall Street Journal*, sec. P1, June 25, 1999.

Chapter 10: Reparations, Revisionism, and the Race Card

1. Civil Liberties Act of 1988 (Public Law 100-383).

2. CWRIC, *Personal Justice Denied*, xi.

3. CWRIC, *Personal Justice Denied*, 51-60.

4. CWRIC, *Personal Justice Denied*, 459.

5. *Pacific Citizen*, "Mock hearing set for Seattle," May 15, 1981, 8.

6. Tanaka report cited in Deborah Lim, *Research Report prepared for Presidential Select Committee on JACL Resolution #7*, "The Decision to Cooperate with Evacuation," 34, http://www.javoice.com/limreport/LimPartICID.htm#ID1 (accessed March 20, 2004).

7. Ibid.

8. Center Staff Reports, p. 1, Correspondence, Manzanar, File 0 7.50, Japanese Evacuation and Resettlement Study, cited in Lim, *Research Report prepared for Presidential Select Committee on JACL Resolution #7*, 35.

9. Paul Huston, "Japanese-Americans Ask Reparations," *Los Angeles Times*, sec. A5, April 29, 1986.

10. Kashima, *Judgment Without Trial*, 288.

11. Weglyn, *Years of Infamy*, 277

12. Ibid.

13. For more information, see Mitchell T. Maki, Harry H. L. Kitano, and S. Megan Berthold, *Achieving the Impossible Dream: How Japanese Americans Obtained Redress* (Urbana, IL: University of Illinois Press, 1999); Robert Sadamu Shimabukuro, *Born in Seattle: The Campaign for Japanese American Redress* (Seattle: University of Washington Press, 2001); William Hohri, *Repairing America: An Account of the Movement for Japanese-American Redress* (Pullman, Wash.: Washington State University, 1988); Leslie Hatamiya, *Righting a Wrong: Japanese Americans and the Passage of the Civil Liberties Act of 1988* (Stanford, CA: Stanford University Press, 1993); and Yasuko I. Takezawa, *Breaking the Silence: Redress and Japanese American Ethnicity* (Ithaca, NY: Cornell University Press, 1995).

14. Alice Yang Murray, ed., *What Did the Internment of Japanese Americans Mean? (Historians at Work)*, (Bedford/St. Martin's Press, 2000), 25.

15. Tetsuden Kashima, "Redressing Wrongs; A Never-Ending Hurt for Japanese Americans," *Washington Post*, sec, C3, Aug. 16, 1998.

16. U.S. Congress, U.S. Senate Judiciary Committee, Subcommittee on Administrative Practice and Procedure "Japanese-American Evacuation Redress," 1st Session, July 27, 1983 (Washington DC: GPO), 422.

17. Cited in James J. Kilpatrick, "$1.2 billion worth of hindsight," *St. Petersburg Times*, sec. 19A, March 8, 1998,   http://bss.sfsu.edu/internment/Congressional%20Records/ 19880420b.html (accessed Feb. 7, 2004).

18. Ibid.

19. Letter from John R. Bolton, Assistant Attorney General, U.S. Department of Justice, to Rep. Peter Rodino, Chairman, Committee on the Judiciary, April 25, 1986.

20. Ibid.

21. "President Gerald R. Ford's Proclamation 4417, Confirming the Termination of the Executive Order Authorizing Japanese-American Internment During World War II," http://www.ford.utexas.edu/library/speeches/760111p.htm (accessed Feb. 6, 2004).

22. Bruce Stokes, "Learning the Game," *The National Journal*, Oct. 22, 1988, 2649.

23. Congressman Mike Honda, "Brief History and Background of the Japanese American Internment," http://www.house.gov/honda/InCongress/Coble/coble_ history_ internment.html, (accessed Feb. 7, 2004).

24. See Nikkei for Civil Rights and Redress, "Special recognition, Redress litigants and advocates," http://www.ncrr-la.org/news/dor1.html, (accessed March 28, 2004).

25. CWRIC, *Personal Justice Denied*, 464.

26. Carla Hall, "Japanese fired in WWII win redress," *Los Angeles Times*, sec. B1. Feb. 28, 1998.

27. *Jacobs v. Barr*, 959 F.2d 313 (D.C. Cir. 1992), *vacated*, 482 U.S. 64 (1987). See also Laurie Asseo, "Justices Reject Arizona Man's Claim to Payments for WWII Internment," *Washington Post*, Oct. 5, 1992, and for Jacobs' self-published autobiographical account, see Arthur D. Jacobs, *The Prison Called Hohenasperg: An American Boy Betrayed By His Government During World War II*, Upublish.com, May 1999.

28. Chizu Omori, *International Examiner*, Oct. 14, 1997, 11.

29. Hohri, *Repairing American*.

30. *The Epistolarian*, November 1990, http://ohp.fullerton.edu/Epistolarian/eplhtm/ EP9011.htm (accessed Feb. 7, 2004).

31. CWRIC, *Personal Justice Denied*, 459.

32. Stokes, "Learning the Game."

33. Elaine Povich, "Commission studies World War II internments," United Press International, July 11, 1981.

34. *Pacific Citizen*, "Washington Profile: Introducing the Redress Commission chair," May 1, 1981, 4.

35. Harry F. Rosenthal, "Inquiry begins on internment of 120,000 Japanese," Associated Press (July 14, 1981).

36. Ibid.

37. Peter Imamura, "Goldberg says Supreme Court erred on E.O. 9066," *Pacific Citizen*, May 15, 1981, 1.

38. CWRIC, *Personal Justice Denied*, 401, 403, 404.

39. Thomas Y. Fujita-Rony, *Frontiers: A Journal of Women Studies*, "Destructive Force: Aiko Herzig-Yoshinaga's Gendered Labor in the Japanese American Redress Movement," vol. 24, 2003, 38.

40. Four cases dealt with the West Coast mass exclusion, evacuation, and relocation of ethnic Japanese: *Hirabayashi v. U.S.* (320 U.S. 81 [1943]), *Yasui v. U.S.* (320 U.S. 115 [1943]), *Korematsu v. U.S.* (323 U.S. 214 [1944]), and *Ex parte Endo* (323 U.S. 273 [1944]). In *Hirabayashi* and *Yasui*, the Supreme Court upheld a temporary curfew for ethnic Japanese living in prescribed military areas on the West Coast. In *Korematsu*, the court upheld the West Coast exclusion of ethnic Japanese on the grounds of military necessity. In *Endo*, issued the same day as *Korematsu*, the court ruled that mass exclusion could not apply to "concededly loyal" citizens seeking to return to the West Coast from relocation camps. Volumes and volumes have been written about these cases. For basic history of the cases from the predominant perspective of a civil liberties activist, see *Justice At War* and *Justice Delayed* by Peter Irons. For a dissenting perspective sympathetic to national security concerns, see William Rehnquist, *All the Laws But One*.

41. Fujita-Rony, "Destructive Force."

42. Keith Robar, *Intelligence, Internment and Relocation*, (Seattle: Kikar Publications, 2000), 362-3.

43. Frank Chin, "Unfocused L.A. Hearings: 'A Circus of Freaks,'" *Rafu Shimpo*, Aug. 21, 1981, p. 1.

44. John McCloy, congressional testimony, "Japanese-American and Aleutian Wartime Relocation," hearings before the Subcommittee on Administrative Law and Governmental Relations of the Committee on the Judiciary, U.S. House of Representatives, June 21, 1984, 125.

45. Karl Bendetsen, congressional testimony, "Japanese-American and Aleutian Wartime Relocation," hearings before the Subcommittee on Administrative Law and Governmental Relations of the Committee on the Judiciary, U.S. House of Representatives, Sept. 12, 1984, 682-3.

46. Ibid., 683.

47. CWRIC, *Personal Justice Denied*, xii.

48. Ibid., xx.

49. Ibid., 253-260.

50. Ibid., 41.

51. ONI, "Japanese Intelligence and Propaganda in the United States," Dec. 4, 1941.

52. CWRIC, *Personal Justice Denied*, 8.

53. Ibid., 5.

54. See Chapter 3.

55. CWRIC, *Personal Justice Denied*, 9.

56. "The Cabinet, presumably at FDR's request, went on to discuss briefly the evacuation of Japanese Americans as a real possibility," Robinson, *By Order of the President*, 98.

57. CWRIC, Personal Justice Denied, 9.

58. Ibid., 8-9.

59. See, e.g., MID, "Japanese Espionage," (Jan. 21, 1942), 3.

60. The memo concluded that the "espionage net containing Japanese aliens, first- and second-generation Japanese, and other nationals is now thoroughly organized and working underground." See Ibid. This Army MID report, which the commission did not mention, was reproduced in full in Stetson Conn's 1964 study, which the commission cited as a reference.

61. McCloy congressional testimony, 120.

62. "I was cleared for MAGIC, and day after day and evening after evening I was reading from this thing. To say that wasn't a major factor, it was a very important factor in considering where we stood and what we had to do in order to avoid the consequences of this disastrous surprise attack which had so deeply damaged and maimed our first line of defense on the west coast," McCloy in Ibid. See also this exchange on p. 137 of McCloy's testimony:

    Mr. Hall: "Did the MAGIC cables help shape the decisions of those who ordered the evacuation of persons of Japanese ancestry persons from the west coast?"

    Mr. McCloy: "Oh, I haven't the slightest doubt about it."

63. The Commission's report was published in February 1983. Its recommendations were released on June 22, 1983. The MAGIC addendum was released on June 28, 1983. See Lowman, *MAGIC*, 106.

64. Charles Mohr, "1941 Cables boasted of Japanese-American spying ," sec. A18, *New York Times*, May 22, 1983.

Chapter 11: The "Puffery" Defense

1. Charles Mohr, "1941 Cables boasted of Japanese-American spying," sec. A18, *New York Times,* May 22, 1983.

2. CWRIC, *Personal Justice Denied,* 474.

3. U.S. Congress *"Hearings Before The Joint Committee On The Investigation Of The Pearl Harbor Attack,"* 79th Congress, 1st Session, 232, 253.

4. CWRIC, *Personal Justice Denied,* 473.

5. See Chapter 5 and Lowman, *MAGIC,* for more information.

6. CWRIC, *Personal Justice Denied,* 474.

7. McCloy congressional testimony, 120.

8. CWRIC, *Personal Justice Denied,* 472.

9. Ibid., 58.

10. Ibid., 59.

11. See Chapter 5.

12. Loueiro, "The Imperial Japanese Navy and Espionage," 113-4.

13. CWRIC, *Personal Justice Denied,* 477.

14. John A. Herzig, congressional testimony, "Japanese-American and Aleutian Wartime Relocation," hearings before the Subcommittee on Administrative Law and Governmental Relations of the Committee on the Judiciary, U.S. House of Representatives, Sept. 12, 1984, 815.

15. Ibid., 814.

16. U.S. Congress, House, Joint Committee on the Investigation of the Pearl Harbor Attack, 1936, *Pearl Harbor Attack: Hearings Before the Joint Committee on the Investigation of the Pearl Harbor* Attack, 79th Con., 1st sess., 1946, 39 vols., Government Printing Office, Washington DC, pt. 35, 556. Cited in Loureiro, "The Imperial Japanese Navy and Espionage," 115.

17. Ibid., 857.

18. Peter Irons, *Justice Delayed,* 35.

19. Forward to U.S. Department of Defense, *The "Magic" Background of Pearl Harbor.*

20. See Memorandum for the President, Sept. 22, 1945, Papers of Gen. Of the Army George C. Marshall, George C. Marshall Research Foundation, Lexington, VA., Box 42 and Hearings Before the Joint Committee on the Investigation of the Pearl Harbor Attack, Congress of the United States, 79th Congress of the United States, Washington DC 1946, Part 3, 1125, 1132-33, cited in Prange, *At Dawn We Slept,* 646.

21. Presumably, Robinson is referring to MAGIC intercepts, not "excerpts."

22. Robinson, *By Order of the President,* 63, 66, and 277.
23. U.S. Congress "Hearings Before The Joint Committee On The Investigation Of The Pearl Harbor Attack," 79th Congress, 1st Session, 514.
24. Kashima, *Judgment Without Trial,* 39.
25. Clarke, *Pearl Harbor Ghosts,* 20.
26. Hoover, Memorandum for the Attorney General, Feb. 2, 1942, CWRIC papers, 5801.
27. Ibid.
28. Ibid.

CHAPTER 12: DAMNING AMERICA

1. National Park Service, Manzanar Historic Research Study, Ch.16, http://www.nps.gov/manz/hrs/hrs16d.htm (accessed Feb. 7, 2004).
2. Junji and Katherine Kumamoto, "The Manzanar lesson," *Riverside Press Enterprise,* Sept. 30, 1996.
3. Richard Estrada, "Don't rewrite our World War II history," *Dallas Morning News,* sec. 25A, Sept. 20, 1996.
4. "Truth about Japanese internment eluded columnist," *Seattle Post-Intelligencer,* sec. A19, Oct. 18, 1996.
5. Chizu, Omori, "Year of Infamy: U.W. Press publication still unmatched," *Northwest Asian Weekly,* Nov. 22, 1996, 10.
6. Ralph Frammolino, "Ferguson fights labeling war internment as racist," *Los Angeles Times,* sec. A1, Aug. 25, 1989.
7. Robert B Gunnison, "Assembly Rejects Internment Measure: Japanese Americans lobbied against it." *San Francisco Chronicle,* sec. A6, Aug. 29, 1990.
8. Jack Cheevers, "Japanese-American leaders criticize Wright, La Follette," *Los Angeles Times,* sec. B3, Aug. 30, 1990.
9. *The American Pageant,* 12th ed., 828-9.
10. Andrew Cayton, Elisabeth Israels Perry, Linda Reed, & Allan M. Winkler, *America: Pathways to the Present* (Upper Saddle River, N.J.: Prentice Hall, 2000), 626.
11. Gary B. Nash, *American Odyssey: The United States in the 20th Century* (NY: Glencoe McGraw Hill, 1999), 547-9.
12. CWRIC, *Personal Justice Denied,* xiii.
13. Ken Masugi, congressional testimony, "Japanese-American and Aleutian Wartime Relocation," hearings before the Subcommittee on Administrative Law and Gov-

ernment Relations of the Committee on the Judiciary, U.S. House of Representatives, June 27, 1984, 570.

14. The biased grant process is aptly illustrated by the California Civil Liberties Public Education Fund's rejection of a proposal by Athena Press, Inc., the publisher of David D. Lowman's book, *MAGIC*, to distribute the book to public schools and libraries.

15. Memorial inscriptions are provided online at: http://www.njamf.com/quotes.htm (accessed Feb. 7, 2004).

16. Civil Liberties Public Education Fund projects, http://www.momomedia.com/CLPEF/proj/cproj.html (accessed Feb. 7, 2004).

17. "Smithsonian Response to Critique forwarded from Congressman Cannon's Office," http://www.athenapressinc.com/smithsonian/response.html (accessed Feb, 7, 2004).

18. Athena Press Inc. press release, "Japanese Americans Lose 5,000 Purple Hearts in Smithsonian Exhibit," http://www.athenapressinc.com/smithsonian/press_release.html (accessed Feb. 7, 2004).

19. Ibid.

CONCLUSION: 12/7, 9/11, AND BEYOND

1. See, e.g., Dan Rather, "My September 11," *Texas Monthly*, Nov. 2001, p. 40; Ron Dzwonkowski, "September 11: The Day Changed Everything," *St. Charles County Business Record*, sec. 2E, Aug. 11, 2002.

2. Though he comes to opposite conclusions from mine, University of North Carolina law professor Eric Muller published a thoughtful essay on this topic. See Eric Muller, "Inference or Impact? Racial Profiling and the Internment's True Legacy," *Ohio State Journal of Criminal Law*, Vol 1: 103-118.

3. Greg Robinson, *By Order of the President*, 58.

4. Edwin T. Layton, *"And I Was There,"* (NY: Quill William Morrow, 1985), 147.

5. John Mintz and Gregory L. Vistica, "Muslim Troops' Loyalty a Delicate Question: Military's Religious Tolerance May Have Aided Infiltrators, Led to Complacency," *Washington Post*, sec. A10, Nov. 2, 200), p. A10.

6. This despite being on a State Department terrorist watch list before securing his visa.

7. David Zucchino, "GI Held in Attack at Base Made Anti-U.S. Remarks," *Los Angeles Times*, sec. A1, March 24, 2003.

8. Evan Thomas, "Descent into Evil," *Newsweek*, Nov. 4, 2002, 20. Curiously, Muhammad was admitted to the Army despite service in the Louisiana National Guard that was marked by being court-martialed for willfully disobeying orders, striking another noncommissioned officer, wrongfully taking property, and being absent without leave. Although Muhammad was led away in handcuffs and transferred to another company pending charges for the grenade attack, an indictment never materialized. Muhammad was honorably discharged from the Army in 1994.

9. Zucchino, "GI Held in Attack at Base Made Anti-U.S. Remarks."

10. Paul Barrett, "How a Muslim Chaplain Spread Extremism to an Inmate Flock," *Wall Street Journal,* sec. A1, Feb. 5, 2003.

11. Ibid.

12. Ibid.

13. An April 2004 report by the Justice Department's Inspector General found that the Bureau of Prisons "typically does not examine the doctrinal beliefs of applicants for religious service positions to determine whether those beliefs are inconsistent with BOP security policies" and that the BOP and FBI "have not adequately exchanged information regarding the BOP's Muslim endorsing organizations." See *A Review of the Bureau of Prisons' Selection of Muslim Religious Service Providers,* Office of the Inspector General, U.S. Department of Justice, April 2004, http://www.usdoj.gov/oig/special/0404/index.htm (accessed May 1, 2004).

14. Yee, who ministered to terrorism suspects detained at Guantanamo Bay, was arrested in September 2003 on suspicion of participating in an espionage ring, but eventually was charged with only two counts of mishandling classified information. He was released after 76 days in a Navy brig and then charged with making a false statement, adultery and storing pornography on his computer at Guantanamo. All criminal charges were later dropped; the Army instead reprimanded Yee for violating the Uniform Code of Military Justice. See John Hendren, "Army Gives Muslim Chaplain Written Reprimand," *Los Angeles Times,* sec. A13, March 23, 2004.

15. Robert H. Bork, "Civil liberties after 9/11," *Commentary*, July 1, 2003, 29.

16. David A. Harris, "Let's Look at What Counts; Racial profiling doesn't stop common criminals. It won't stop terrorists, either," *Legal Times*, Sept. 22, 2003, 60.

17. Wade Henderson, "No justification for racial profiling," *San Diego Union-Tribune*, sec. B-11, March 21, 2003.

18. Harris, "Let's Look at What Counts."

19. Niraj Warikoo, "Poll shows more than 80 percent of Arab Americans approve of Bush," *Detroit Free Press*, Oct. 12, 2001.
20. Ann Scales, "Polls say blacks tend to favor checks," *Boston Globe*, sec. A16, Sept. 30, 2001.
21. Barry Steinhardt, "Profiling is poor technique," *USA Today*, sec. 23A, Nov. 27, 2002.
22. Ruth Wedgwood, "Justice will be done at Guantanamo," *Financial Times*, July 10, 2003, 19.
23. "A Military Commission for Moussaoui," *Wall Street Journal: Review and Outlook*, July 16, 2003, http://www.opinionjournal.com/editorial/feature.html?id= 110003752 (accessed March 21, 2004).
24. Ringle, Report on Japanese Question.
25. CWRIC, *Personal Justice Denied*, 200.
26. John Hendren, "Amid Secrecy, Bush Visits Troops in Iraq; only a small group of aides and journalists was told about the trip," *Los Angeles Times*, sec. A1, Nov. 28, 2003.
27. CNN, *Newsnight with Aaron Brown*, Nov. 27, 2003, Transcript # 112700CN.V84.
28. Center for National Security Studies, amended complaint for injunctive relief, Civil Action No. 01-2500, Dec. 10, 2001, http://www.cnss.org/. Of the nearly 1,000 people arrested, the government eventually released the names of 129 against whom it brought criminal charges.
29. Ironically, President Bush himself opposed the use of secret evidence in deportation hearings during the 2000 election season.
30. "Sentelle's Sense," *New York Sun*, Jan. 13, 2004, 8.
31. Philip Shenon, "9/11 Commission Could Subpoena Oval Office Files," *New York Times*, sec. A1, Oct. 26, 2003.
32. Ibid.
33. Jon Sawyer, "Ashcroft announces racial profiling initiative," *St. Louis Post-Dispatch*, sec. A1, March 2, 2001.
34. Masugi, "Necessity and Politics: War with Justice."
35. Lincoln, Message to Congress, July 4, 1861.
36. Letter to Erastus Corning, June 12, 1863, in *Words of Lincoln*, 6: 267, cited in Masugi, "Necessity and Politics: War with Justice," 214.
37. Biddle, *In Brief Authority,* 219.
38. Mark Steyn, "Iraqi spy case shows media at it again," *Chicago Sun-Times*, March 14, 2004.
39. Lewis, Anthony, "Taking Our Liberties," *New York Times*, sec. A15, March 9, 2002.

APPENDIX C

1. Kahn, *The Codebreakers*, 31.

APPENDIX D

1. Jonathan Martin, "Civic leader, lawyer acquitted in 1942 of U.S. spy charges: Kenji Ito, 1909 – 2003," *Seattle Times*, sec. B1, Aug. 16, 2003.
2. Court documents were obtained from National Archives Records Administration in Seattle.
3. MAGIC message No. 175 (#45), May 11, 1941, A-99 to A-100 of Vol. I of *The "Magic" Background of Pearl Harbor.*
4. A Dec. 24, 1941, ONI memo reveals that ONI categorized Ito as a "Class 'A' suspect." The memo is reproduced in full in Lowman, *MAGIC*, 277-311. The reference to Ito is on p. 304.
5. "Jose Padilla should either be tried or released. If he is a terrorist who was plotting to set off a radioactive bomb, he should rot in prison but only *after* he is convicted at a trial in which he is given the rights of an American." This simpleminded argument appeared in "Rules of engagement for civilians, too," *Seattle Times*, sec. B6, Dec. 22, 2003.
6. Ruth Wedgwood, "The Rule of Law and the War on Terror," *New York Times*, sec. A27, Dec. 23, 2003.

APPENDIX E

1. The legal and historical record of these cases can be found in Peter Irons, ed., *Justice Delayed: The Record of the Japanese Internment Cases* (Middletown, CT: Wesleyan University Press, 1989).
2. Eric K. Yamamoto, Susan K. Serrano, and Michelle Natividad Rodriguez, "American racial justice on trial - again: African American reparations, human rights, and the war on terror," *Michigan Law Review* 101(5), March 2003, 1269-1337.
3. Government's post-hearing brief, Sept. 5, 1985, in Peter Irons, *Justice Delayed*, 329.
4. Marjorie Williams, "The 40-Year War Of Aiko Yoshinaga," *Washington Post*, sec. C1, Aug. 4, 1988.
5. Lowman, *MAGIC*, 93.
6. Government's post-hearing brief, Sept. 5, 1985, in Peter Irons, *Justice Delayed*, 316.

7. Peter Irons, *Justice Delayed*, 144.

8. Government's post-hearing brief, Sept. 5, 1985, in Peter Irons, *Justice Delayed*, 325.

9. David Lowman, *MAGIC*, 98.

10. Government's post-hearing brief, Sept. 5, 1985, in Peter Irons, *Justice Delayed*, 331.

11. Edward J. Ennis, "Memorandum for the Solicitor General, Re: Japanese Brief," April 30, 1943, Exhibit Q, 2.

12. Grodzins, Martin, *Americans Betrayed: Politics and the Japanese Evacuation* (Chicago: University of Chicago, 1949).

13. Government's post-hearing brief, Sept. 5, 1985, in Peter Irons, *Justice Delayed*, 331.

14. Irons, *Justice at War,* 368.

15. Lowman, *MAGIC*, 88.

16. Ibid., 375-76.

APPENDIX F

1. Adapted from Krammer, *Undue Process,* op cit., 175-6, and Japanese-American National Museum web site: http://www.janm.org/nrc/internfs.html (accessed March 13, 2004). This list is not necessarily complete.

2. Adapted from http://uscis.gov/graphics/aboutus/history/eados.htm (accessed March 20, 2004).

Acknowledgments

This endeavor would not have been possible without the selfless contributions of a great American: Lieutenant Colonel Lee Allen. I cannot thank him enough for his astute insights and dedication to historical accuracy. Allen's son, Sam Allen, was also tremendously helpful. For those interested in further reading on the topic of this book, be sure to visit the Allens' website, www.internmentarchives.com, for a treasure trove of World War II evacuation- and relocation-related documents.

Though they may not agree with any or all of the conclusions of this book, I must extend a note of appreciation to Burl Burlingame of the *Honolulu Star-Bulletin*, Robert Stinnett of the Independent Institute, Arnold Krammer of Texas A&M University, John Stephan, emeritus professor of history at the University of Hawaii, and retired U.S. Air Force Major Arthur Jacobs for their cooperation. I recommend the books by these five gentlemen (listed in my online bibliography at www.michellemalkin.com), as well as Major Jacobs's fascinating website, www.foitimes.com, which provides extensive research on the World War II internment of German enemy aliens and their American-born families.

Heartfelt thanks to Thomas Culbert of Aviation Information Research Corporation, a true professional who went above and beyond the call of duty in locating documents, photographs, and other useful information.

Additionally, I am grateful to R. Lee Sims, Joo Lee Lim, and the staffs of the National Archives, National Security Agency, Library of Congress, Bancroft Library at the University of California at Berkeley, and Goleta Historical Society for their assistance.

For reading my manuscript in whole or parts, special thanks go to Mike Fumento, Ken Masugi, Sean-Patrick Lane, E. F., Kirby Wilbur, David Horowitz, Heather Mac Donald, and Colonel Gayle Gardner of the Hawaii Eagles.

For their courage, enthusiasm, and willingness to embrace this unorthodox project, my deepest thanks go to everyone at Regnery Publishing and Eagle Publishing—especially Marji Ross, Jeff Carneal, Harry Crocker, Rowena Itchon, and Kristina Phillips.

Finally, to Jesse: For your sacrifices, intellectual partnership, and stalwart emotional support, "thank you" will never be enough. You make my best better. I love you with all my heart.

Index

Italicized page numbers indicate photos.

A

ABC list, 55, 56
Abdallah, Devon Alisa, xx
ACLU, xxvi
Afghanistan, 153
AFL-CIO, xviii, 46
African embassy bombings, 152
Afrika Korps, 81
Ahmed, Fayez, xxii
Aikoku Fujin Kai, 19
air raids, 89–90, 92, 126. *See also* Pearl
  Harbor attack
airport security, xxi–xxii, 152, 155
Akbar, Asan, 153
Akram, Susan M., xxvi
al-Halabi, Ahmad I., 152
Al-Midhar, Khalid, xxii
al-Muhajir, Abdullah, xxxi
al Qaeda fighters, xxxi
al Qaeda members, xxii, 152, 157, 158,
  159
al Qaeda plans, 272
al Qaeda presences, xxv
al Qaeda training, xxviii
Al-Shehhi, Marwan, xxii
Al Suqami, Satam, xxii

Alamoudi, Abdurahman, xxvii
Alaska, 43, 70, 123
Aleutian Islands, 43, 70, 89, 120, 123
Alghamdi, Ahmed, xxii
Alghamdi, Hamza, xxii
Alghamdi, Saeed, xxii
Alhamzi, Nawaf, xxii
Alhamzi, Salem, xxii
Alhaznawi, Ahmed, xxii
alien enemies. *See* enemy aliens
Alien Enemies Act, xi, xv, 54–55, 63, 97
Alien Enemy Control Unit, 246, 276,
  277
Alien Registration Act, 55–56
All the Laws But One, xviii
allegiance, 6, 25, 63, 107
Allen, Lee, 148
Alnami, Ahmed, xxii
Alomari, Abdulaziz, xxii
Alshehri, Mohald, xxii
Alshehri, Wail, xxii
Alshehri, Waleed M., xxii
Amboina Island, 81
America: Pathways to the Present, 145
American-Arab Anti-Discrimination
  Committee, xviii, xix, xx, 161

American Civil Liberties Union, 123, 155, 277

American Concentration Camps: A Documentary History of the Relocation and Incarceration of Japanese Americans, 1941–1945, 122

American Immigration Lawyers Association, 161

American Jewish Committee, 123

American Muslim Council, xxviii

American Odyssey: The United States in the 20th Century, 145

American Pageant, The, 144–45

American POWs, 59

Americans Betrayed: Politics and the Japanese Evacuation, 277

And I Was There, 35

Anderson, Ryan G., 152–53

antiprofilers, xxvi–xxx, 150, 156

Arab Americans, xxi, 155

Arabic linguists, 152

Argentina, 61

Arizona, 57, 85

Army Signal Corps, 138

army volunteers, 106–7, 111, 151

Asahi newspaper, 90

Ashcroft, John, xxi, xxv, xxvii, xxxii, 73

Asia, 59

Asian American Legal Defense and Education Fund, 161

assembly centers, xv, 102–3, 281

Atta, Mohammed, xxii

Auslandsorganisation, 61

Awad, Nihad, xx, xxviii

Axis "underground railroad," 85

B

Baghdad, 160–61

Bainbridge Island, 92, 144

Bainbridge Island evacuation, 92–93

Baja California, 61

Baldwin, C. B., 5, 72

barbed wire, 95, 96, 100, 108–11

Bataan, 12

Bataan Death March, 59

Battle, Jeffrey Leon, 153

"Battle of Los Angeles," 9, 83

Battle of Midway, xxxiii, 89

Battle of the Java Sea, 12

Bauer, Gary L., 119

Bearce, Frank, *304*

Beekman, Allan, 2

Behind Barbed Wire, 95

Belloni, Robert, 278

Bellow Field, 1

Bendetsen, Karl

    background of, 75

    and commission claims, 121, 124, 136

    and evacuation order, 83

    and evacuation support, 76–77, 87

    and MAGIC messages, 131

    testimony of, 148

Bennett, William J., 119

Berentson, Kip, 153

Bergen-Belsen, 99

Berlin, 49

Bernstein, Joan, 85–86, 122, 134

Biddle, Francis

    and commission claims, 126–27

    and enemy aliens, 56–57

    and evacuation opposition, 80, 126–27

    and evacuation order, 83

    and internment camp, 101

    and MAGIC messages, 41

    memos from, 82–83

    memos to, 44, 72, 251

    photo of, *301*

    and Ringle memo, 72–73

    visit from, 101

    on wartime presidents, 164

bin Laden network, 157

bin Laden, Osama, 154, 161

Binalshibh, Ramzi, 158
Black Dragon Society, 109
Blake, Al, 31–33
Bly, Oregon, 152–53
Boeing activities, 47, 49–50
Bolivia, 61
Bolton, John R., 118
Bork, Robert H., 154
Born in Seattle, 123
Boston Globe, xxxi
Boston, Massachusetts, 152, 155
Brawley, California, 115
Brazil, 61
Bremerton Naval Shipyard, 45, 92
Bremerton Port, 47, 48
Bremerton, Washington, 57
Britain, 74, 81
British Columbia, 70
British Islands, 12
Broken Seal, The, 129
Brookings, Oregon, 90
Buddhist religion, 21–22
Buenos Aires, 61
Bush administration, xix, xx, xxi, xxxi,
    xxxii, 73, 150, 157–58, 162
Bush, George H. W., 119
Bush, George W.
    critics of, 150
    determination of, 149
    and racial profiling, 163
    and secrecy, 160–61
    and threat profiling, xxvii
    understanding of, 165
bushido, 19
*By Order of the President: FDR and the
    Internment of Japanese Americans*, 137

C
California coast attack, xxiv, 7–10
California exclusion zones, 85
camps, 280–85, 307–12. *See also* intern-
    ment camps

Canadian Army, 69
Canadian evacuations, 70–71, 79, 127
Cape Flattery, Washington, 89
Cape Mendocino, California, 10
Capone, Al, xxvii
Carter, Jimmy, 131, 278
Carter, John Franklin, 66
Center for National Security Studies,
    161
Central America, 43, 60, 61
Central Japanese Association of Califor-
    nia, 32
Chaplin, Charlie, 33, 139
chemical weapons, 89
Chicago, 41, 43, 44
Chicago Sun-Times, 164
Chin, Frank, 123
China, 13, 54, 59
Churchill, Joan, 8
citizen isolation camps, 282
citizenship, 23–24, 111
civil liberties, xiii–xiv, xviii, xix–xx,
    155, 159, 161–65
Civil Liberties Act, 113, 119
Civil Liberties Public Education Fund,
    146–47
civil rights, xix–xx, xxx
civil rights absolutists, xxxiv, 155, 159,
    161, 163, 164
civil strife, 87–88
Civil War, xxxii, 163
civilian informants, 66
Clark, Mark, 77, 82, 83, 252–55
Clark, Ramsey, 158
Clarke, Thurston, 11, 29
classified information, 38, 40–41, 50–51
Classified Information Protection Act,
    157, 272
Clinton administration, 120
Clinton, Bill, 160
Coble, Howard, xviii
Codebreakers, The, 40, 129

Cohen, Benjamin, 82
Cold War, xvii
Cole, David, xxvi, 63
Come See the Paradise, 143
"comfort women," 59
Commission on Wartime Relocation
    and Internment of Civilians, xvi, 27,
    85, 114, 117, 120, 121, 122, 129,
    146, 274
compensation, 115–21
"concentration camp" myth, xv–xvi, xx,
    xxv, xxxv, 95–111
Conn, Stetson, 65, 76, 77, 83, 88, 135
Connecticut, 84
"Contacts with Labor Unions," 46
contraband, 57–59
coram nobis cases, 273–79
Cosmopolitan Brotherhood Association,
    123
Costello, John, 37
Council on American-Islamic Relations
    (CAIR), xx, xxvi, xxviii, 161
counter-espionage investigations, 55
counter-terrorism efforts, xxviii, xxix
Cox, Oscar, 82
Crime, Terrorism and Homeland Secu-
    rity, xviii
Croft, Steve, xxii
Crouter, Natalie, 16
cryptanalysts, 38, *304*
Crystal City, Texas, camp, 60, 101, 120,
    310
cultural prejudice, 274
curfew orders, 278
curriculum material, xvi, 144–45, 147
Custodial Detention Index, 55, 56

D
Dachau, 99
Dallas Morning News, 143
Damashii, Yamato, 17
Daniels, Roger, 96, 122

Davidson, General, 11
Davis, Daniel S., 95, 109
Davis, Elmer, 106
Declaration of Independence, xiv
Defence Zone, 70
defense act rules, 86
defense installations, 80
Defense of the Realm Act, 74
Delaware, 84
Democratic National Committee, xviii
Department of Defense, 130, 135
deportation, xxv, 60
detention camps, 282–85. *See also*
    internment camps
detention challenges, 156–60
Detroit Free Press, 155
Dewey, Thomas, 71, 136–37, 275
DeWitt, John
    and commission claims, 126
    and enemy aliens, 56
    on exclusion zones, 84–85
    and Executive Order 9066, 83
    on internment, 74–77
    photo of, *300*
    report from, 88, 274–76
    view of, 104
diplomatic traffic, 38, 40–41, 50–51
discrimination, xvi. *See also* "racial prej-
    udice"
Distinguished Service Cross, 119
Douglas, William O., 25
Dowd, Maureen, xxix
Drinan, Robert, 122, 134
Drum, Hugh, 84
dual citizens, 23–24, 28, 44, 97, 107
Dutch East Indies, 12, 16, 81

E
Eastern Defense Commander, 84
"Economic Contacts," 45
education misinformation, 5, 24, 37–39,
    95–96, 125, 141, 144–45

Egypt, 54, 152
Eisenhower, Dwight D., 24
Ellis Island camp, 100, 101
Ellwood, California, 7, 9, 10
Eltantawi, Sarah, xxvii
Emergency Advisory Committee for
    Political Defense, 60
Emmons, Delos C., 106
Empress of Asia, 81
enemy aliens
    categories of, 55
    deporting to America, 60
    internment of, 53–63
    number of, 53–54
    presumptions on, 107
    restraining, xi–xiv
    rules governing, 55, 56, 57
    surveillance of, 74–75, 78, 82
Enemy Among Friends, An, 98
enemy combatants, xxv, xxxi–xxxiii, 79,
    158, 159
Ennis, Edward J., 53, 136, 276–77
Equal Protection clause, 120
espionage agents, 32
espionage fronts, 33
espionage investigations, 55
espionage network
    capabilities of, 84
    in Central America, 61
    disruption of, 79
    establishment of, 46–47
    in Honolulu, 27–31, 37, 71, 126,
        132, 146, *293–95*
    of Japanese, xvii, 16, 19, 27, 31, 66,
        124, 133–34, 146, 150, 160,
        177–85, 210–17, 220–49,
        252–55
    on mainland, 31, 41
    in South America, 61
    on Terminal Island, 90–92
    on West Coast, xvii, 31–37, 75,
        124–26, 132–34, 139, 141, 146,
        160

see also intelligence activities
espionage-related crimes, 139, 156
Estrada, Richard, 143–44
ethnic activists, 113, 114, 116–17, 124,
    134
ethnic profiling, xiii, xxii, xxx,
    xxxiv–xxxv, 155–56
evacuation. *See* West Coast evacuation
Evacuation Claims Act, 116, 118
exclusion orders, 278
exclusion zones, 85
exclusionary rule, 163
Executive Order 9012, 88
Executive Order 9066, xi, xv, 13, 35, 37,
    81–93, 114, 118, 119, 121, 122, 131

F
Farago, Ladislas, 28, 129
Faraj, Ra'id, xxvi
Farewell to Manzanar, 143
Federal Bureau of Investigation (FBI)
    counter-terrorism efforts, xxviii,
        xxix
    espionage investigations, 55
    memos from, 124, 214–15, 217,
        250–51
    memos to, 44–45, 256–70
    and Munson reports, 67–68
    surveillance measures, xxviii–xxix
Federal Communications Commission,
    58
Federation of Italian War Veterans, 55
Ferguson, Gil, 144
fifth column activities, 13–16, 67, 82,
    85, 90, 132
*Final Report: Japanese Evacuation from
    the West Coast, 1942*, 126
First Amendment, 162
first-generation resident aliens, xi, xv
Fitzsimmons, 48
Florida, 84
Fly, James L., 58
Ford, Gerald, 118

Foreign Organization, 61
foreign student tracking, xxii–xxiv,
    xxviii
Fort Douglas, Utah, camp, xii
Fort Lincoln, North Dakota, camp, 60,
    100, 101, 111, *311*
Fort MacArthur, California, 9, 58
Fort McPherson, Georgia, camp, xii
Fort Missoula, Montana, camp, 60,
    100–101
Fort Oglethorpe, Georgia, camp, xii
Fort Stanton, New Mexico, camp, 60,
    100
Fort Stevens, Oregon, 89
Fort Ward, Washington, 92
Franco, Francisco, 14, 61
Freedom of Information Act lawsuit,
    161
Fremon, David, 102
Frenzel, Bill, 117
Friedman, William, 38, *304*
Fuji, Tatsuki, 16
Fujita, Nobuo, 89
Fukuchi, Agent, 32, 57, 132
Furusawa, Sachiko, 33–34, 132
Furusawa, Takashi, 32–34, 132

G
Gannon, James, 50–51
Gardena Valley, California, 18–19, 33
Geneva Convention, 59, 97, 101
Georgia, 84
German Latin Americans, 60–61
German seamen, 60
German U-boats, 10
Germany, 14–15, 48, 54, 61
Ghungking, 13
Gianella, Lawrence, 9
Gila, Arizona, relocation center, 98,
    104, 108, 109, *308, 309*
Glick, Shav, 103
Gloucester City, New Jersey, camp, 100

Goebbels, Josef, 29
Goldberg, Arthur, 122
Goleta, California, 7, 9, 10, 83
Grodzins, Morton, 277
Gromoff, Ishmael Vincent, 122
Grotjan, Genevieve, 38
Ground Zero, xxiv
Guam, 12
Guantanamo Bay, xxxi, 152
Guatemala, 61
Gulf War, 153, 158
Gullion, Allen, 74, 76, 80, 83

H
Hagen, Bernard, 7–8
Halsey-Doolittle raid, 88, 89
Hamad, Imad, xx
Hamdi, Yaser Esam, xxxi
Hanjour, Hani, xxii
Harada, Irene, 2–6, 72
Harada, Yoshio, 2–6, 72, *289*
Harper's, 72, 103
Harris, David, 155
Harsch, Joseph C., 11
Hawaii
    and evacuation policy, 85–86
    martial law in, xiv, 86
    Niihau Island incident, 1–6
    spy ring in, 27–31, 37, 71, 126, 132,
        146, *293–95*
    surveillance of, 29, 50–51
Hayakawa, S. I., 117
Heart Mountain, Wyoming, relocation
    center, xxi, 104
Heimusha Kai, 18
Hendzel, Kevin, 152
Herzig, Jack, 122, 134–35, 138
Herzig-Yoshinaga, Aiko, 122–23,
    274–76
Hirabayashi, Gordon, 273
Hirabayashi ruling, 123, 274–78
Hirano, Irene, xxi

Hiroshi, Oshima, 49

history books, 5, 24, 37, 95–96, 125,
    141, 144–45

Hitler, Adolf, xxxiii, 14–15, 39, 49, 61,
    96, 136

HMS *Prince of Wales*, 12

HMS *Repulse*, 12

Hohri, William, 121

Hokoku Joshi Seinen-Dan, 111

Hokoku Seinen-Dan, 110, *311*, *312*

Hokubei Butoku Kai, 18–19

Holland, 54

Hollister, J. J., III, 7–8

Holocaust, xviii, 95, 143

homeland defense
    during Roosevelt administration,
        8–9
    and War on Terror, xvii, 155
    see also national security

Honda, Mike, xvi

Hong Kong, 12, 15

Honolulu
    messages from, 51
    messages to, 41, 43, 50–51
    spy ring in, 27–31, 37, 71, 126, 132,
        146, *293–95*

Honolulu Star Bulletin, 5, 11

Hood, R. B., 68

Hoover, J. Edgar
    and commission claims, 126
    and Custodial Detention Index, 55
    on espionage prosecutions, 30, 33
    evacuation opposition, xxxii, 73–74
    on intelligence sharing, 82
    and MAGIC messages, 41
    memos from, 41, 42, 44–45, 58, 82,
        139–40, 214–15, 217, 250–51
    memos to, 68
    photo of, *302*
    and Ringle memo, 72–73

Hoshi, Hiroshi "Paul," 34

Hull, Cordell, 40

human rights, 59, 144. *See also* civil lib-
    erties

Human Rights Watch, 161

Hussein, Saddam, 161

I

I-9 submarine, 9

I-17 submarine, 7–8, 10

I-19 submarine, 10

I-21 submarine, 10

I-23 submarine, 10

I-25 submarine, 89–90

I-76 submarine, 9

Idaho, 85, 92

Il Conte Biancamano, 60

illegal aliens, xv, xix, xxv–xxvii, 99,
    156–57

Immigration and Naturalization Service,
    156–57

immigration enforcement, xxvi–xxvii

immigration laws, xxvii

Imperial Army, 9, 12, 14–15, 20, 24

Imperial Army's Special Service Organi-
    zation, 15

Imperial Comradeship Society, 18

Imperial forces, xxiv, 6–16, 20–21, 24,
    31, 59–60

Imperial Japanese Army Ordinance, 34

Imperial Navy, 7–10, 12–13, 16, 21, 24,
    31

Imperial war bonds, 19

Inouye, Daniel, 22, 117, 122

intelligence activities
    by Japanese, 15, 20, 27–35, 43–44,
        47–51, 62, 68–70, 187–207
    memos on, 42–43, 209–70
    by United States, xvii–xviii, xxxiv,
        38, 44, 69, 71, 75–76, *303–5*
    see also espionage network; MAGIC
        messages

International Examiner, 121

International Red Cross, 100, 103

Internee Hearing Board, 29
internment camps
    conditions at, 99–101
    defense of, xi–xii
    distortions regarding, xi–xii, xv–xx
    explanation of, xi, xiii, xv–xvi
    and humane treatment, 59
    in Japan, 54, 59
    legal basis, 62–63
    life in, 99–101
    lists of, 280–85
    number of, 97
    photos of, *307–12*
    versus relocation centers, 96–99
    visits to, 100
    volunteers for, xvi, xxxiii
    see also West Coast evacuation
"internment hotels," 285–86
Invasion, xxvi
Iraqi illegal aliens, xxvi
Irons, Peter, 32, 122–23, 134–36,
    273–78
Isenberg, Phillip, 144
Ishihara, Koichiro, 16
Ishihara Sangyo Koshi (I.S.K.), 16
Islamic charities, 150
Islamic terrorism, xxviii
Islamic terrorist network, 150–53
Isobe, Takashi, 19
isolation camps, 282
Issei
    evacuation of, xv, xxiii
    explanation of, xi
    in Hawaii, 21, 23
    loyalty of, 66–67, 72
    network of, 252
    as spies, xvii
    taking advantage of, 115
    threat from, 72–73
    transfer of power from, 108
Italian enemy aliens, 84
Italian seamen, 60

Ito, Kenji, 46, 78, 140, 156, 218,
    271–72

J

Jacobs, Arthur D., 120
Japanese American Citizens League
    (JACL), xiv, xvi, xviii, xxv, 82,
    103–4, 107, 116–17, 277
Japanese American Human Rights Vio-
    lations Act, 117
"Japanese American internment," xi,
    xii, xv, xix. *See also* internment
    camps
Japanese American Memorial, 147
Japanese American National Museum,
    xxi
Japanese American News, 20
Japanese American residents, xi, 1–6
Japanese ancestry compensation,
    115–21
Japanese ancestry reparations, 113–21,
    147
Japanese attacks, 7–12, 83, 89–90. *See
    also* Pearl Harbor attack; West Coast
    attacks
Japanese carriers, 88–89
Japanese citizenship, 23–24
Japanese espionage network. *See* espi-
    onage network
Japanese fishermen, 16, 62
Japanese Foreign Office, 16
Japanese intelligence activities. *See* espi-
    onage network; intelligence activi-
    ties
Japanese Intelligence Network, 68
Japanese invasion, 1–10
Japanese-language schools, 22–24
Japanese Latin Americans, 60–61
Japanese Military Servicemen's League,
    18
Japanese Nationality Law, 23
Japanese Naval Association, 19, 31, 33

Japanese naval codes, 38
Japanese Naval Intelligence, 16
Japanese newspapers, 20, 44, 150
Japanese propaganda, 17–18, 44
Japanese resident aliens, xi
Japanese submarine attacks, 7–10
Japanese sympathizers, 17–18
Japanese threat, 7–16
Japanese Tokyo Club Syndicate, 132
Japan's Department of Education, 125
Jarrah, Ziad, xxii
Java, 59, 81
Java Sea Battle, 12
Jersey City, New Jersey, 77
jihadists, xxviii, xxxi
Jitsugyo no Hawaii, 20
Johnson, Kevin R., xxvi
Johnson, Lyndon, 131, 158
Johnson v. Eisentrager, 62–63
Joint Congressional Committee, 138
Jones, L. D., *304*
Judgment Without Trial: Japanese American Imprisonment During World War II, 123, 138
Justice Delayed: The Record of the Japanese Internment Cases, 134
Justice Department. *See* U.S. Department of Justice

K

Kadomatsu, Tsugunori, 16
Kahn, David, 40, 129, 209
kais, 17–19, 32, 55, 125
Kaleohano, Hawila "Howard," 2–5, *290*
Kanahele, Ben, 4–5, *291*
Kanehoe Bay, 1
Kaneko, 45
Kanjo Kai, 19
Kashima, Tetsuden, 116, 117, 123, 124, 138
Kauai, 2–5
Kawakita, Tomoya, 23–25

Kean, Thomas, 119, 162–63
Kenedy, Texas, camp, 60
Kenji Ito case, 271–72
Kennedy, John F., 24, 131
Kennedy, Robert F., xxvii
Khobar Towers bombings, 152
Kibei
    explanation of, 23, 28
    and leave clearance, 106
    loyalty of, 66–67
    threat from, 72–73, 109–10, 133
    training of, 74
Kido, Saburo, 103–4, 107
Kiev, 49
Kikuchi, Charles, 108
Kilpatrick, James J., 118
King, Mackenzie, 71
Kirsanow, Peter, xix–xx
Kita, Nagao, 28
Kiyota, Minoru, 111
Knox, Frank, 11, 40, 71, 85
Kono, Toraichi, 33, 132
Korematsu case, xix, 98, 123, 127, 273–74, 278
Korematsu, Fred, xxxi–xxxii, 273
Kota Bahru, 12
Kotoshirodo, Richard
    conclusions on, 140, 171–73
    photo of, *295*
    in relocation centers, 30
    as spy, 27–29, 78, 132
    testimony of, 168–71
Kramer, Alvin D., 40
Krammer, Arnold, 14, 100
Kristof, Nicholas, xxix
Kuehn, Bernard Julius Otto, 29
Kuehn, Ruth, 29
Kullback, Solomon, *304*
Kumamoto, Shunten, 32
Kurisaki, Lyle, 109–10, 115
Kurokawa, Agent, 32, 132
Kurtz, Howard, 161

Kuwait, 153
Kyl, Jon, xxviii

L

*Last Witnesses: Reflections on the
    Wartime Internment of Japanese Amer-
    icans*, 95
Latin American internees, 60–61, 97
Layton, Edward T., 27–28, 31–32, 34
Lazo, Ralph, 99
Leadership Conference on Civil Rights,
    xx
leave clearance, 92, 97–99, 105–7
Leupp, Arizona, isolation center, 111
Lewis, Anthony, 164
liberals, xx, xxix, xxx, xxxiv
Lincoln, Abraham, 163
Lindsay, California, 20
Lippmann, Walter, 14
Logan Airport, 152, 155
Long Beach, California, 61–62
Los Angeles
    defense of, 89
    hearings in, 123
    messages from, 46, 48, 49, 50
    messages to, 41, 43, 49
    ports of, 65
    and shortwave radios, 58
"Los Angeles Battle," 9, 83
Los Angeles Harbor, 61–62, 90–92
Los Angeles Japanese Association, 32
Los Angeles Times, xxi, xxix, 50, 103, 153
Loureiro, Pedro, 32
Lowman, David, 107, 128, 134, 135,
    275
Lowry, Mike, 117
loyalty
    and intelligence, 124–28
    to Japan, 18, 23, 28–30, 106–7
    views on, xxii–xxiii
LP *St. Clair*, 10
Lungren, Dan, 124, 133, 134

M

Macassar, 16
Macaulay, Lord, xxxiii
MacBeth, Angus, 129–35, 139
Mac Donald, Heather, xxviii
*"MAGIC" Background of Pearl Harbor,
    The*, 175
Magic Book, The, 40
MAGIC messages
    access to, 41
    and commission claims, 128–29,
        131, 134–35
    in court cases, 271–72, 275–76, 278
    decoding of, xvii–xviii, 37–51
    and evacuation policy, 77
    examples of, 175–207
    and Kenji Ito, 271–72
    revelations of, 41–51, 57, 62, 66, 70,
        75–76, 85, 92, 114, 126, 132–34,
        137, 151, 175–207, 209–17
    value of, 50–51
MAGIC publication, 129–30, 135
"magicians," 39
Maine, 84
Maki, Agent, 32, 132
Malaya, 12, 16, 62, 81
Malveaux, Julianne, xxi
Mangione, Jerre, 101
Manila, 9, 12, 15
Manzanar, California, relocation center,
    92, 99, 102, 109, 143
Marshall, George C., 11, 40, 65, 71, 88,
    136–37, 275
Marshall Islands, 10
martial law, xiv, xxxii, 79, 86
Martin, Joan, 8
Marutani, William, 122
Maryland, 84
Marysville, California, relocation center,
    102
Masaoka, Mike, xiv–xv, 86–87, 106, 121
Massachusetts, 84

Masugi, Ken, 146
Matsui, Robert, xxii–xxiv
Mauborgne, Joseph, 39
Mayer, Arizona, relocation center, 102
Mayfield, Irving, 5, 139
McCloy, John
    background of, xxxiv, 76–77, 131
    and commission claims, 121, 127,
        136
    credit for, 106
    drafting evacuation order, 83
    and evacuation support, 77, 80, 82
    and MAGIC messages, 41, 77,
        130–31
    memo from, 76–77
    memo to, 252
    photo of, 299
    testimony of, 124, 148
McNutt, Mr., 82
McWilliams, Carey, 103
Mehalba, Ahmed, 152
Melzer, Richard, 100
Mexican evacuations, 70–71, 79, 127
Mexico City, Mexico, 41, 42, 43, 61, 70
Middle Easterners, xv, xxvi, 150,
    155–57
Midway Battle, xxxiii, 89
Mikami, John Yoshige, 29, 30, 132
Military Area No. 1, 85, 88, 92
Military Area No. 2, 85
"Military Contacts," 45–46
Military Intelligence Division (MID)
    and espionage investigations, 55, 82
    memos from, 42, 44, 69, 82, 124,
        210–11, 216, 218–19, 247–49
military police, 108, 109
Military Virtue Society of North Amer-
    ica, 18–19
Miller, Harrod, 304
Minami, Dale, xix
Mindoka, Idaho, relocation center, 92,
    104, 144

Mineta, Norm, xxi–xxii
Minsk, 49
Miranda rights, 163
Mitsubishi Shoji Kaisha, 31
Miyatake, Henry, 117
Moab, Utah, isolation center, 111
Modell, John, 108
Mohamed, Ali A., 152
Montana camps, 60, 62, 100–101
Montana exclusion zones, 85
Monterey Bay, California, 10
Moqed, Majed, xxii
Moussaoui, Zacarias, xxix, 158, 159
Mueller, Robert, xxviii–xxix
Muhammad, John, 153
Munson, Curtis, 41, 66–68, 72, 124,
    267
Murao, Helen, 146
Murata, Kiyoaki, 98, 109
Muslim Americans, xxi, 153
Muslim civil rights groups, xxviii
Muslim clerics, 153–54
Muslim extremists, 152
Muslim Public Affairs Council, xxvii
Muslim soldiers, 153

N

NAACP, xviii
Nakamura, Gongoro, 32
Nakao, Annie, xxv
Nanking, China, 13
Nantes, 48
Narasaki, Karen, xxi
Nation, The, 161
National Asian Pacific American Legal
    Consortium (NAPALC), xxi
National Coalition for Redress and
    Reparations, 147
National Council for Japanese American
    Redress, 123
National Journal, 119, 121
National Origins Act, 146

national security
    and civil liberties, xiii–xiv, xviii,
        xix–xx, 82–83, 155, 159, 161–65
    impact on, xxxiv–xxxv
    importance of, xiv, xxiv, 164–65
    lessons on, xvi, xxxiii–xxxiv
    plan for, xxvi–xxvii
    and secrecy, 75–76, 160–63
    threat to, 278–79
    urgency of, xvii
    and War on Terror, xvii, xviii, xix,
        xx, xxii, xxiv–xxvii, 155
National Security Agency (NSA), 107
nationality profiling, xiii, xxii, xxv, xxx,
    xxxiv–xxxv, 155
Nazi death camps, xviii, 95, 99
Nazi Party, 61
Nelson, Louise, *304*
Nevada exclusion zones, 85
New Guinea, 12
New Hampshire, 84
New Jersey, 84, 162–63
New Orleans, 41, 43
New World Sun Daily News, 20
New York, 41, 43, 44, 84, 153–54
New York Sun, 162
New York Times, xxi, xxix, 128, 161,
    164
New Zealand, 54
newspapers for Japanese, 20, 44, 150
Newsweek, 153
Ng, Wendy, 109
Nihon Bunka Shinkokai, 19
Nihro, Katsumi, 15
Niihau Island incident
    and commission claims, 124, 146
    photos of, *287–91*
    report of, 1–6, 72
Nikkei for Civil Rights and Redress,
    xxxi
Nippon Kaigun Kyokai, 19, 31, 33
Nippon Yusen Kaisha, 31

Nisei
    and citizenship laws, 23
    confinement of, 86
    discharge of, 106
    evacuation of, xv, xxiii
    explanation of, xi
    in Hawaii, 21
    loyalty of, 66–67
    and relocation, 108
    as spies, xvii
    threats from, 72–73
    threats to, 110
    transfer of power to, 108
Nisei children, xxxi, 23
Nisei lawyer, 46, 218
Nisei network, 252
Nisei opportunists, 115
Nisei soldiers, xxxiii, 119, 125, 133,
    151–52
Nisei spies, 91
Nisei volunteers, 125
Nishikaichi, Shigenori, 1–6, *288*, *290*
Nishimoto, Richard, 104
Nishino, Kozo, 7–8
Nixon, Richard, 131
Nobori, Teruo, 111
North Africa, 81
North Carolina, 84
North Dakota camps, 60, 62, 100, 101,
    111, *311*
Norway, 15

O
Oahu
    evacuation from, 85–86
    raid on, xxiv, 1, 11
    spies on, 71
    surveillance of, 29
Office of Naval Intelligence (ONI)
    concerns of, xxxii, 21
    and *coram nobis* cases, 276

and espionage investigations, 55,
  138
memos from, 19, 24, 34, 42, 57–58,
  68–69, 124, 212–13, 220–46
memos to, 44
Office of Redress Administration, 113
Okada, Sadatomo, 32, 45
Okamaru, "Welley" Shoji, 46
Okuda, Otojiru, 28
Okuda, Shoji, 89
Omori, Chizu, 121
OP-20-G, 38
Operation Iraqi Freedom, xxvi
Oregon bombings, 10, 89–90
Oregon exclusion zones, 85
Oregonian, xxiv
Oshima, Baron, 136
Oshima, Hiroshi, 39
Osman, Semi, 152
Ottawa, Canada, 43
Owens Valley, 92, 102

P
Pacific Ocean, xvii, xxiv, 9, 13
Padilla, Jose, xxxi, xxxii, 159, 272
Palm Beach Post, xxvi
Panama Canal, 43, 60, 61, 100
Paradise of the Pacific, 11
Paraguay, 61
Patani, 12
Patel, Marilyn Hall, 278
Patriot Act, xxvi
Patriotic Society, 19
Patriotic Women's Society, 19
patriotism, xv, xxi, xxxii
Patrovsuky, 48
Patton, George S., Jr., 17
Pearl Harbor attack
  aftermath of, xiv, xv, xxiii, xxxiv, 11,
    53–54, 56, 58, 149–65
  and Niihau Island incident, 1–6
  surveillance of, 50–51

Pearl Harbor Ghosts, 11
Pearl Harbor: Warning and Decision, 39,
  129
Pennsylvania, 84
Pentagon attack, xxiv, 272. *See also* ter-
  rorist attacks
People for the American Way, 161
Perl, Lila, 95
Personal Justice Denied, 114, 117
Pettigrew, Moses, 106
Philippines, 12, 15, 16, 59
Pinedale, California, relocation center,
  102
Pipes, Daniel, xx
plane movements, 15, 43–44, 49, 51,
  62, 70
Point Reyes, California, 58
political correctness, xii, xiv, xx, xxviii,
  xxxv
Port of Bremerton, 47, 48
Portland, Oregon, 41, 43, 44, 58, 102,
  273, 278
Posner, Richard, xxx
Poston, Arizona, relocation center, 98,
  102, 104, 109, *309*
Prange, Gordon, 29
Presidential Proclamations, 56
prisoners of war, 59
*Prisoners Without Trial: Japanese Ameri-
  cans in World War II*, 122
prisons, 153–54
pro-Japanese militants, 109–11
pro-Japanese newspapers, 20, 42
pro-Japanese propaganda, 17–18
pro-Nazi Falangists, 61
pro-Nazi German-American Bund, 55
pro-Nazi militants, 101
propaganda, 17–18, 44, 143
prosecution challenges, 140–41, 156–60
Public Law 100-383, 113
Public Law 503, 84
Public Proclamation No. 3, 88

Public Proclamation No. 4, 88
"puffery" defense, 129–41
PURPLE analog decrypting machine, 38, 71, *304*
PURPLE code, 38, 44, 75–76
Pye, Admiral, 11

Q
Quisling, Vidkun, 15

R
race card, 113–28
"racial discrimination," xvi
"racial prejudice," 121, 132, 144, 274, 276, 278
"racial profiling"
    contemplating, xxxiv–xxxv
    defense of, xiii, xxii, xxiv, xxx
    and media, xxix
    opposition to, xxi, xxii, xxvi, xxviii–xxix, xxx, 73, 151, 154–57, 163
    support of, 68, 73
    and War on Terror, xiii
Rahman, Omar Abdul, 158
Rashid, Amir Abdul, 153
Rathbone, Tom, 93
Rauh, Joseph, 82
Reagan, Ronald, xxxiv, 113, 119, 131, 146, 162
RED code, 38
Red Cross, 100, 103
redress, 113, 123, 147
registration program, xxv, 55–57
Rehnquist, William, xvii–xviii
Reinhard, David, xxiv
religious centers, 150
religious extremists, xxviii
religious profiling, xiii, xxii, xxviii, xxx, 155
relocation centers
    barbed wire, 108–11

conditions at, 102–11
critics of, 113–28, 143–48
evacuation to, 92–93
explanation of, xv
versus internment camps, 96–99
life in, 102–11
lists of, 282
number of, 97, 104
policies on, xi, xii, xiii, xv
visits to, 100
and voluntary evacuation, 86–87
Reno, Janet, xvii
reparations, 113–21, 147
Reserve Officers' Club, 19, 33
resident aliens, xi, xv, xxiii
revisionism, 113–28
Rhode Island, 84
Ridge, Tom, xxvii
Ringle, Kenneth
    and commission claims, 126
    and *coram nobis* cases, 276–77
    evacuation opposition, xxxii
    and MAGIC messages, 41
    memos from, 72–73, 87, 90, 124, 256–66
    photo of, *305*
Rio de Janeiro, 60, 61
Roberts, Owen, 71
"Roberts Report," 71–72, 275–76
Robertson, Eric, 16
Robinson, Aylmer, 1–4
Robinson, Greg, 71, 137, 151
Rommel, Erwin, 81
Romulo, Carlos, 15
Roosevelt administration, xxxii, xxxiv, 5, 8–10, 69, 160
Roosevelt, Franklin D.
    and "Battle of Los Angeles," 7
    and civilian informants, 65–66
    and commission claims, 126–27
    critics of, xvi
    and decrypted messages, 40

defenders of, xviii
and espionage investigations, 55
and Executive Order 9066, xi, xv, 13, 37, 83, 278
and MAGIC messages, 41
memos to, 45
on Pearl Harbor attack, 149
photo of, *298*
Presidential Proclamations, 56
and Roberts Report, 71–72
and sabotage concerns, 67
understanding of, 165
and U.S. citizenship law, 111
and West Coast evacuation, 77
Rowe, James, 82
Rowlett, Franklin B., 38, 39, *304*
Russia, 48–49
Russian espionage network, xvii
Russian Military Commission, 49

S

sabotage investigations, 55, 67, 89
Sacramento, California, relocation center, 102
St. Claire, 48, 49
Sakura Kai, 19, 32–33
Saleh, Noel John, xix
samurai, 19
San Bruno, California, 274
San Diego, 18, 44, 62, 74
San Francisco, 18, 41, 43, 46, 48–49, 65, 89, 123, 274, 278
San Francisco Chronicle, xxv
San Jose, California, xxi
San Pedro, California, 44, 61–62, 66
Sand Point, Hawaii, 30, 47
Santa Ana, California, 119
Santa Anita, California, relocation center, 102–3
Santa Barbara, California, 7–8
Santa Fe, New Mexico, camp, 30, 100, 111, *311*, *312*

Santayana, George, 148
Santiago, 61
Seagoville, Texas, camp, 60, 100, 101
Seattle Times, xxi, 153, 271
Seattle, Washington, 41, 43, 45–50, 58, 65, 74, 273, 278
second-generation resident aliens, xi, xv
secrecy and national security, 75–76, 160–63
"segregation camp," 110
Seki, Kohichi, 28
September 11 attacks
aftermath of, xx–xxvii, 149–65, 272
horror of, xxiv, 164–65
and illegal aliens, xv
Shanksville, Pennsylvania, xxiv
Shea, Francis, 74
Shimabukuro, Robert Sadamu, 123
Shinozaki, Mamoru, 16
Shintani, Ishimatsu, 2–5, *289*
Shinto religion, xxxii, 21, 73
Shiozawa, Koichi, 21
ship movements, 15, 43–44, 47–51, 62, 70
shortwave radio transmissions, 57–58
Shuford, Reginald, xxi
Signal Intelligence Service (SIS), 38, *304*
Singapore, 12, 16, 81
Singapore Herald, 16
Singora, 12
Sinkov, Abraham, *304*
Sino-Japanese War, 18
Sixth Amendment, 157
Slackman, Michael, 17
Smith, Page, 22, 108
Smith, Walter Bedell, 40
Smithsonian Institution, 147–48
Snow Falling on Cedars, 143
Snow, Philip, 15
Society for Defending the Country by Swords, 19

Society for the Promotion of Japanese
    Culture, 19
Society of Educating the Second Gener-
    ation in America, 19
South America, 43, 60, 61
South Carolina, 84
South China Sea, 81
South Pacific, xxiv, 43
Southeast Asia, xxiv, 16
Soviet espionage network, xvii
Soviet Union, 48–49
Spain, 61
Spanish Civil War, 14
Special Defense Unit, 55
spies, xvii, 23, 27–35, 78, 132. *See also*
    espionage network
spiritual centers, 150
Spokane, Washington, 47
Srabaya, 81
Srikantiah, Jayashri, xxvi
SS *Absaroka*, 10
SS *Agwiworld*, 10
SS *Barbara Olson*, 10
SS *Connecticut*, 10
SS *Cynthia Olson*, 9
SS *Dorothy Philips*, 10
SS *Emidio*, 10
SS *H. M. Storey*, 10
SS *Larry Doheny*, 10
SS *Manini*, 9
SS *Montebello*, 10
SS *Prusa*, 9, 10
SS *Samoa*, 10
Steinhardt, Barry, 155
Stephan, John, 12, 16, 19, 21, 23
Stewart, Lynne, 158
Steyn, Mark, 164
Stimson, Henry
    and commission claims, 127
    and evacuation support, xxxiv,
        80–83, 88
    on John McCloy, 77
    and MAGIC messages, 41

on mainland invasion, 12
photo of, *298*
and Roberts Report, 71–72
and sabotage concerns, 67
submarine attacks, 7–10, 89–90
Suiko Sha, 19, 33
Sumitomo banks, 19
Supreme Court, xvii, 273, 276–78
surveillance
    of enemy aliens, 74–75, 78, 82
    by FBI, xxvii–xxix
    of Hawaii, 29, 50–51
    of mainland, 44
Suzuki, Suguru, 5
Swiss embassy representatives, 100
Sword Society, 19
Syria, 152

T
Tachibana, Itaru, 31–35, 57, 134–36
Tachibana spy ring, 31–35
Tacoma, Washington, 152
Takahashi, Charles Theodore (Takeo),
    34
Taliban fighters, xxxi
Tamaru, Tado, 20
Tanaka, Togo, 115
Tanforan, California, relocation center,
    102
Tateishi, John, xxv
Terasaki, Hidenari, 31, 44
Terminal Island internees, 61–62, 90–92
terrorism ties, xxvi, xxviii, 152–53, 157
terrorist attacks
    aftermath of, xx–xxvii, 149–65, 272
    horror of, xxiv, 164–65
    and illegal aliens, xv
    see also War on Terror
terrorist network, 150, 157–58
terrorist trials, 157
"terrorists have won" mentality, 165
Thai-Burma Death Railway, 59
Thailand, 12

"theater of war," 56

Third Amendment, 164

Third Reich, 49, 61

Thomas, Dorothy Swaine, 104

"threat of predatory incursion," 56

threat profiling, xxiv, xxvii, xxx, 54–60, 151–56. *See also* wartime profiling

Togo Kai, 19

Tokumu Kikan, 15

Tokyo

    communications from, 38, 42

    instructions from, 42–43

    messages from, 50–51, 61

    messages to, 15, 39, 45–48, 61–62, 70

    see also espionage network; intelligence activities

Topaz, Utah, relocation center, 30, 109

Torii, Takuya, 33

Tsukiyama, Ted, 106

Tule Lake, California, relocation center, xxii, 30, 104, 109, *308, 310, 311, 312*

Turley, Jonathan, xxxi

U

Ugaki, Matome, 5

Ujifusa, Grant, 119

"underground railroad," 85

United States decision makers, *297–302*

United States Employment Service, 105–6

U.S. Civil Rights Commission, xix

U.S. Department of Interior, xv

U.S. Department of Justice

    and enemy aliens, xxi, 55

    evacuation opposition, 80

    internment practices, xii, 274, 276, 277

    and mobsters, xxvii

U.S. Department of Transportation, xxi

U.S. Department of War, xii, xvii–xviii, 75–80, 209, 274

U.S. Institute of Peace, xx

U.S. intelligence, xvii–xviii, xxxiv, 44, 69, 71, 75–76, *303–5*. *See also* MAGIC messages

U.S. mainland attacks, 7–10, 68–69, 83, 89–90

U.S.-Soviet relations, 48–49

USS *Arizona*, 17

USS *Panay*, 13

Utah exclusion zones, 85

V

Vancouver, 41, 43, 44

Vancouver Island, 70, 89

VENONA decrypts, xvii

Vermont, 84

Virginia, 84

visa holders, xxv, 150, 155–56

Vladimar Mayskovsky, 48

voluntary evacuation, xvi, xxxiii, 86–87, 99

volunteer recruits, 106–7, 111, 151

Voorhees, Donald, 278

W

Wake Island, 12

Wall Street Journal, 153

War Department. *See* U.S. Department of War

War of 1812, 54–56

War on Terror

    and court system, 157–58

    and criminal proof, 272

    critics of, xxv

    and homeland security, xvii, xviii, xix, xx, xxii, xxiv–xxvii, 155

    impact on, xxxiv

    importance of, 164–65

    measures of, xvii

    and "racial profiling," xiii

    and religious profiling, xxviii

    and secrecy, 160–63

War on Terror (continued)
   and terrorism ties, xxvi
   and World War II, 150–51
War Relocation Authority (WRA),
   xv–xvi, 73, 97, 104–6, 115
Warren Commission, 131
Warspite, 47, 48
wartime atrocities, 13, 59–60
Wartime Civil Control Administration,
   83
wartime presidents, 164, 165
wartime profiling, 54–60. See also threat
   profiling
Washington, D.C., 49, 61, 84
Washington exclusion zones, 85
Washington Post, xxi, 152, 161
Watson, "Pa," 40
weapons of mass destruction, 165
Weckerling, John, 89
Wedgwood, Ruth, 157, 272
Weglyn, Michi, 98, 109, 116
West Coast attacks, xxiv, xxxiii, 7–10,
   83, 89–90
West Coast espionage network, xvii,
   31–37, 75, 124–26, 132–34, 139,
   141, 146, 160
West Coast evacuation
   assistance with, 92–93
   from Bainbridge Island, 92–93
   beginning of, 86–90
   and commission claims, 129–33
   constitutionality of, 82–83
   and coram nobis cases, 274–78
   critics of, xvi, xxi–xxiii, xxv, xxxii,
     8–10, 113–28, 143–48
   decision on, 41, 79
   defense of, xii, xiii
   explanation of, xi, xv
   myths about, 27
   rationale for, 65–80
   support for, xiv
   from Terminal Island, 90–92
West Coast evacuation order. See Executive Order 9066

West Coast exclusion zones, 85
West Coast military bases, 13–14
West Coast restricted areas, 57
West Coast ship attacks, 9–10
West Coast spy ring. See West Coast
   espionage network
Western Defense Command, 56, 57, 74,
   89, 126, 159
Williams, Kenneth, xxviii, xxix
Wilson, Woodrow, 55
Wohlstetter, Roberta, 39, 129
Women's Patriotic Society of Japan, 33
World Trade Center attacks, xxiv, 156,
   157, 272
World War I, xii, 54–56
World War II
   declaration of war, 55
   enemy aliens during, xii, xiv, 53–54
   lessons from, 149–51
   and War on Terror, 150–51
   see also Pearl Harbor attack; West
     Coast attacks
writ of habeas corpus, xxxii, 73, 86, 163

Y
Yakut, 48
Yamagata-Noji, Audrey, 144
Yamaguchi, Tamon, 12–13
Yamamoto, Isoroku, 5
Yasui, Minori, 273
Yasui ruling, 123, 273, 278
Years of Infamy: The Untold Story of
   America's Concentration Camps, 98
Yee, James, 154
Yokohama banks, 19, 31
Yokohama Specie Bank, 31
Yoshikawa, Takeo, 28, 30–31, 294

Z
Zaibei Ikuei Jai, 19
Zeidlik, Hannah, 274
Zogby, James, 155
Zogby, John, 155